Ruby on  oft Developers

Ruby on Rails®
for Microsoft Developers

Ruby on Rails®
for Microsoft Developers

Antonio Cangiano

02·78

LIMERICK
COUNTY LIBRARY
0059 36 78

WITHDRAWN FROM STOCK

Wiley Publishing, Inc.

Ruby on Rails® for Microsoft Developers

Published by
Wiley Publishing, Inc.
10475 Crosspoint Boulevard
Indianapolis, IN 46256
www.wiley.com

Copyright © 2009 by Wiley Publishing, Inc., Indianapolis, Indiana

Published simultaneously in Canada

ISBN: 978-0-470-37495-5

Manufactured in the United States of America

10 9 8 7 6 5 4 3 2 1

Library of Congress Cataloging-in-Publication Data is available from the publisher.

No part of this publication may be reproduced, stored in a retrieval system or transmitted in any form or by any means, electronic, mechanical, photocopying, recording, scanning or otherwise, except as permitted under Sections 107 or 108 of the 1976 United States Copyright Act, without either the prior written permission of the Publisher, or authorization through payment of the appropriate per-copy fee to the Copyright Clearance Center, 222 Rosewood Drive, Danvers, MA 01923, (978) 750-8400, fax (978) 646-8600. Requests to the Publisher for permission should be addressed to the Permissions Department, John Wiley & Sons, Inc., 111 River Street, Hoboken, NJ 07030, (201) 748-6011, fax (201) 748-6008, or online at http://www.wiley .com/go/permissions.

Limit of Liability/Disclaimer of Warranty: The publisher and the author make no representations or warranties with respect to the accuracy or completeness of the contents of this work and specifically disclaim all warranties, including without limitation warranties of fitness for a particular purpose. No warranty may be created or extended by sales or promotional materials. The advice and strategies contained herein may not be suitable for every situation. This work is sold with the understanding that the publisher is not engaged in rendering legal, accounting, or other professional services. If professional assistance is required, the services of a competent professional person should be sought. Neither the publisher nor the author shall be liable for damages arising herefrom. The fact that an organization or Web site is referred to in this work as a citation and/or a potential source of further information does not mean that the author or the publisher endorses the information the organization or Web site may provide or recommendations it may make. Further, readers should be aware that Internet Web sites listed in this work may have changed or disappeared between when this work was written and when it is read.

For general information on our other products and services please contact our Customer Care Department within the United States at (877) 762-2974, outside the United States at (317) 572-3993 or fax (317) 572-4002.

Trademarks: Wiley, the Wiley logo, Wrox, the Wrox logo, Wrox Programmer to Programmer, and related trade dress are trademarks or registered trademarks of John Wiley & Sons, Inc. and/or its affiliates, in the United States and other countries, and may not be used without written permission. Ruby on Rails is a registered trademark of David Heinemeier Hansson. All other trademarks are the property of their respective owners. Wiley Publishing, Inc., is not associated with any product or vendor mentioned in this book.

Wiley also publishes its books in a variety of electronic formats. Some content that appears in print may not be available in electronic books.

For Jessica, my guiding star.

To my parents, Carmela and Ciro.

About the Author

Antonio Cangiano is a Software Engineer and Technical Evangelist at the IBM Toronto Software Lab. He authored the initial ActiveRecord adapter for IBM DB2 and received an IBM Outstanding Technical Achievement Award for his work with Rails. As a long-standing programmer, he has developed with Microsoft .NET since its first public beta, while maintaining a keen interest in multiple programming languages and technologies as well. He discovered Ruby and Ruby on Rails in 2004, immediately recognizing their potential, and has adopted them as his favorite development tools ever since. Cangiano has contributed to books on the subject in both English and Italian, as well as to a few Open Source projects. You can find more of his writing on his blog, Zen and the Art of Programming (`http://antoniocangiano.com`).

Credits

Acquisitions Editor
Jenny Watson

Development Editors
Kelly Talbot
Gus A. Miklos
Sydney Jones

Technical Editor
Dr. Ian Piper

Production Editor
Kathleen Wisor

Copy Editor
Kim Cofer

Editorial Manager
Mary Beth Wakefield

Production Manager
Tim Tate

Vice President and Executive Group Publisher
Richard Swadley

Vice President and Executive Publisher
Barry Pruett

Associate Publisher
Jim Minatel

Project Coordinator, Cover
Lynsey Stanford

Compositor
Craig Woods, Happenstance Type-O-Rama

Proofreader
Jen Larsen, Word One
Nate Pritts, Word One

Indexer
J & J Indexing

Acknowledgments

Winston Churchill once said, "Writing a book is an adventure. To begin with, it is a toy and an amusement; then it becomes a mistress, and then it becomes a master, and then a tyrant. The last phase is that just as you are about to be reconciled to your servitude, you kill the monster, and fling him out to the public." There is a lot of truth to those sentiments and I feel compelled to briefly thank the people who helped me "kill that monster," as well as those who made the whole process enjoyable.

It has been my pleasure to work with the good folks at Wrox. In particular, I would like to thank Jenny Watson for giving me the opportunity to write this book, my two development editors Kelly Talbot and Sydney Jones for their advice and help with keeping me on track, and my technical editor Ian Piper, as well as Gus Miklos, for their invaluable suggestions. I also would like to thank my manager Leon Katsnelson, who first brought the possibility of writing this book to my attention, and for his continuous support.

I would like to express my gratitude to several people who helped me out in various ways; these friends and world class programmers are (in alphabetical order): Piergiuliano Bossi, Ninh Bui, Marco Ceresa, Paolo Corti, Giovanni Intini, Hongli Lai, Ludovico Magnocavallo, Carlo Miron, Lawrence Oluyede, Gregg Pollack, and Valentino Volonghi. I can't help but also thank Antani and Tarapia Tapioco. A huge thank you goes straight to Marco Beri who was writing a book at the same time as I was writing mine. I'd sometimes tease him by saying that he wasn't as lucky as me, since his book wasn't on Rails, but on Django, a framework for the Python language. Inside jokes aside, our interaction via instant messaging kept my spirits high and provided encouragement during the many long nights spent in front of a glowing monitor. My appreciation also goes out to several people who kindly offered their help with reviewing this book as it was being written. I'm sorry that time constraints and logistics didn't allow for this. As well, I can't forget to mention Andrea Peltrin, a great Web designer who helped me improve the look and feel of the sample blog application that was developed for Chapters 5 and 6. All the people mentioned here did an amazing job in helping me to write the book you are holding, but I want to highlight how any mistakes or shortcomings that may appear here are mine and mine alone, and are in no way representative of these fine people's work.

I feel it's also important to acknowledge three people who didn't work directly on this book, yet were hugely influential in its coming to be. These are Yukihiro Matsumoto (a.k.a Matz), David Heinemeier Hansson, and Dave Thomas. Matz invented the Ruby language, one of the most beautiful programming languages out there. David created the Ruby on Rails framework, whose value will be revealed throughout the book. And finally, Dave Thomas wrote some of the earliest available books on the subject of Ruby and Rails. His work helped to popularize both of these and gave a large part of the programming public the opportunity to learn about this pair of technologies. These three people affected my life more than they will ever know, and for this I deeply respect and thank them.

Acknowledgments

A sincere, heartfelt thank you goes to my unofficial editor, my wife Jessica, whose mastery of the English language and craft of writing may only be surpassed by her patience, dedication, and beauty. Though not a programmer, her help has been invaluable in improving the quality of this book. Writing a book while maintaining a full-time day job and a regularly updated blog is a challenging task and an effort that leaves little to no time for your family. So I must thank Jessica once again for being the undemanding, lovely companion who helped me maintain my sanity during these busy times.

In conclusion, I want to thank you, my readers. You are investing your time, money, and trust in this book. For this I thank you and I want to reassure you that a great deal of care was placed into the writing of this book, so as not to betray your trust.

Contents

Contents

Contents

Contents

Contents

Introduction

In July 2004 David Heinemeier Hansson released Ruby on Rails, a Web framework for the Ruby programming language. It quickly gained momentum and became notorious for being a highly productive Model-View-Controller (MVC) Web framework that was particularly well suited to Agile development.

Favoring sensible conventions over verbose configuration files, Rails (as it is often called for short) aimed to simplify and improve the lives of developers by allowing rapid prototyping of Web applications.

Fast-forward a few years, and Rails is now considered to be an established framework that has had a significant influence on the world of Web development. It inspired many other frameworks, helped boost the popularity of dynamic programming languages on the Web, and has been used to implement some of the largest sites that are out there today.

Despite Rails' wide success and adoption, its community still remains Unix-centric, favoring Mac OS X, GNU/Linux, or BSD variants over Microsoft Windows. Consequently the majority of books on the subject and most of the literature you'll find online assume that you are using Unix-like operating systems and tools. Though I personally use all of the operating systems I just mentioned, I believe that learning a new language and framework can be challenging in its own right, so there is no need to make the whole experience more difficult by adding a new operating system and its ecosystem of tools to the learning curve.

Until today, if you were to approach Rails as a "Microsoft developer" you would most likely be in for a culture shock. I felt compelled to change that by writing a book that helps bridge that cultural gap and make the experience of learning Rails, when you have a Microsoft background, much less traumatic. I attempt to be a friendly voice that can help you reach a better understanding of what Rails is and how you can use it for your own projects, while utilizing tools you are (already) comfortable with, leveraging your existing .NET or other Microsoft technologies skills, and understanding what caveats are associated with developing Ruby on Rails applications on Windows.

Who This Book Is For

This book is introductory in nature and as such is intended for beginner to intermediate programmers. Throughout the book I assume that you are somewhat familiar with object-oriented programming and Web application development, but not with Ruby or Rails in particular.

If you are an absolute beginner you may find some parts more challenging or obscure than others, but you should still be able to grasp the gist of things and get a glimpse of the bigger picture of what Rails can do for you. Conversely, if you are an experienced .NET developer, you'll probably appreciate a few in-depth considerations and the occasional comparison in the text, whenever similarities between the two worlds exist.

I also assume that you'll be using Windows, even though it is possible to follow along using any operating system, because the commands and examples are cross-platform.

To successfully keep up with this book, the following skills would be beneficial:

❑ A general understanding of how the Web works

❑ XHTML and JavaScript

❑ A basic understanding of object-oriented programming (OOP)

❑ Entry level knowledge of working with databases

Rails is extremely good at abstracting details. Therefore it provides you with one of the gentlest introductions to the world of Web development (if your current understanding of the Web is not overly advanced).

Several Ruby helpers and mechanisms are also provided by Rails, in order to minimize the amount of raw XHTML or JavaScript that you have to write. You don't have to be an expert in either of these languages, especially because this book is focused on Rails, not Ajax.

If you are in need of a refresher course for either XHTML or JavaScript, Appendix A provides links to excellent online material.

Ruby is important if you want to properly develop in Rails. Ruby is viewed as being multi-paradigm, but it's still fully object oriented. Understanding OOP will therefore help you become a better Rails programmer.

This book is general enough to be used by any developer, whether or not you're accustomed to Microsoft development models and tools. It is, however, particularly aimed at Microsoft developers. These days, when people talk about Microsoft programmers, they almost always inevitably think about .NET developers given that .NET has been the flagship development platform in the Microsoft world for several years. The book that you are holding in your hand now has been written with a clear understanding of this fact.

For example, in Chapter 2 you find a comparison overview of Rails and ASP.NET programming, whereas in Chapters 3 and 4, when I introduce you to the Ruby language, I refer to .NET languages (in particular C#) more than others.

The term "Microsoft developers" is rather broad and encompasses more than just .NET developers though. In this book I've (roughly) divided the spectrum of Microsoft developers into a few groups (not a complete list by any means). In your own specific case, different group descriptions could very easily overlap to describe the experiences, skills, and the roles that characterize your background.

Depending on which category (or categories, if more than one applies) you fall into, you'll have an easier or harder time meeting the preceding requirements and approaching the process of learning Ruby and RoR.

Microsoft Web Developers

I expect the majority of my readers to be Web developers. After all, this is a book about Web technologies; hence it wouldn't be surprising if the largest volume of interest came from Microsoft Web developers, who're planning on learning more about what all the fuss surrounding Rails is about.

If you're a Web developer, I have great news for you: the framework and the methods for creating applications may be different in Rails, but the Web is still the same. Your understanding of how the Web works, and of technologies like HTML, CSS, JavaScript, and Web Services, are a great starting point, which will help make you feel somewhat at home as you learn new Rails concepts.

If you are an ASP.NET developer, things get even better. Rails is much slimmer and simpler to learn than ASP.NET, and the fact that you have a solid understanding of object-oriented programming, through languages like C# and VB.NET, will ensure that you can quickly pick up Ruby, which happens to be much easier than the aforementioned languages, as well. Of course, the same can be said for C++ developers who may have old-school ISAPI programming experience.

ASP.NET developers will also benefit from being accustomed to a development environment where presentation and business logic are separated. The same thing can't always be said for ASP developers though, who also may not be as strong in terms of OOP skills, especially if VBScript is the sole language that they've worked with.

If you are an ASP classic developer, don't worry; essential Ruby knowledge is easy enough to grasp and, by following this book, you'll be able to learn Rails from scratch. In your case, your biggest asset is your knowledge of how the Web works.

Microsoft Windows Developers

Developers of MFC, Windows Forms, and WPF applications will find the MVC paradigm and the principle of separation of concerns rather intuitive, even when applied to the Web. And if you're well versed in programming languages like C++, C#, VB.NET, or Java, this will definitely play in your favor as you approach Ruby.

The biggest challenge for you will be switching to a relatively different platform. Programming in Rails is very different than producing desktop applications for Windows using Visual Studio.

On the bright side, if you've decided that it's time to give Web development a try, Rails will make your life much easier and will teach you a great new way of developing for the Web.

Microsoft Office Developers

If you are a Microsoft Office developer, you're in a somewhat similar scenario to that of a Windows developer (I'm assuming that you don't have any Web development experience yet). Your challenge is further increased, though, if you've only ever programmed in VBA and haven't switched to .NET yet. Again, in this book Ruby and Rails are taught from scratch, so you should be able to learn them both nevertheless.

Database Programmers

As a database programmer you have an invaluable asset when using Rails. Though ActiveRecord doesn't require advanced SQL skills from programmers, mastering SQL and database design will remove many limits from the set of possible applications that you can develop. Understanding the Active Record pattern will be much easier for you and you'll be able to truly take advantage of it.

Possessing a good knowledge of SQL will help you query the database, whenever the default abstractions provided by ActiveRecord are not enough for you or when a particularly efficient, custom query is needed. Conversely, when developing Rails projects you still decide what structure the database is going to have. A concrete understanding of normalization and its trade-offs, indexes, and advanced features such as stored procedures, will aid you when trying to decide if Rails conventions are sufficient, or when it's absolutely necessary to break the rules and do otherwise to satisfy your project's requirements.

Rails has an adapter for SQL Server, so if you decide to work with the database that you're most likely familiar with, you can do so.

> *Please note that, at this stage, there is little to no support for Microsoft Access databases. You can experiment with a rough draft of an adapter provided at* `http://blog.behindlogic.com/2007/07/msaccess-for-rails-heres-your-rough.html`, *but it's probably easier to just migrate your data to a different, fully supported database system.*

How This Book Is Structured

The book begins by setting up the development environment and introducing the framework in the first two chapters.

Chapters 3 and 4 provide you with a crash course in Ruby programming.

In Chapters 5 and 6, a step-by-step sample blog application is developed. References to this simple app are occasionally made elsewhere in the book.

Chapter 7, 8, and 9 carefully examine the three components of the MVC triad, which is covered in the order of model, controller, and view.

Chapter 10 discusses exposing and consuming Web Services through Rails. And last but not least, Chapter 11 wraps up the book by covering the topic of moving into production, by briefly introducing security, performance and optimization, and deployment considerations. This last chapter also features a few pointers regarding aspects that may concern Enterprise developers.

Though the best results are probably achieved by reading the book cover to cover, this book was organized to be fairly modular and as such it's almost always possible to read chapters independently from the others.

That said, and as tempting as it is to jump right in, don't skip the first two chapters. They'll help you get started, set up your machine, and provide you with the right perspective to start building your knowledge of Rails. Likewise, unless you are familiar with Ruby, you shouldn't skip Chapters 3 and 4 either. Rails is a framework that is written in Ruby for Ruby programmers; having a solid understanding of Ruby will make your life a lot easier down the road.

What You Need to Use This Book

Throughout the book I assume that you're using Ruby 1.8.x and Rails 2.2.2. Newer versions will probably work too, with little to no adjustments, but it is recommended that you follow along using the same version as the book. The main idea is that once you've learned the main concepts, you will be able to use any future version of Rails. That said, when differences between Rails 2.2.2 and Rails 2.3 (the next Rails version, which has not been released yet at the time of writing) exist, these are pointed out. Other software that has been employed includes SQLite, a lightweight file-based database, and Mongrel, which is a relatively fast HTTP Web server. Instructions for installing this development stack on Windows, Mac OS X, and GNU/Linux are provided in Chapter 1.

Conventions

To help you get the most from the text and keep track of what's happening, we've used a number of conventions throughout the book.

> **Boxes like this one hold important, not-to-be forgotten information that is directly relevant to the surrounding text.**

Notes, tips, hints, tricks, and asides to the current discussion are offset and placed in italics like this.

As for styles in the text:

❑ We *highlight* new terms and important words when we introduce them.

❑ We show keyboard strokes like this: Ctrl+A.

❑ We show file names, and code within the text like so: persistence.properties.

❑ We present code in two different ways:

```
We use a monofont type with no highlighting for most code examples.
We use gray highlighting to emphasize code that's particularly important in the
present context.
```

Source Code

As you work through the examples in this book, you may choose to either type in all the code manually or to use the source code files that accompany the book. All of the source code used in this book is available for download at http://www.wrox.com. Once at that site, simply locate the book's title (either by using the Search box or by using one of the title lists) and click the Download Code link on the book's detail page to obtain all the source code for the book.

Because many books have similar titles, you may find it easier to search by ISBN; this book's ISBN is 978-0-470-37495-5.

Once you've download the code, just decompress it with your favorite compression tool. Alternatively, you can go to the main Wrox code download page at http://www.wrox.com/dynamic/books/download .aspx to see the code available for this book and all other Wrox books.

Errata

We make every effort to ensure that there are no errors in the text or in the code. However, no one is perfect, and mistakes do occur. If you find an error in one of our books, like a spelling mistake or faulty piece of code, we would be very grateful for your feedback. By sending in errata you may save another reader hours of frustration and at the same time you will be helping us provide even higher quality information.

To find the errata page for this book, go to `http://www.wrox.com` and locate the title using the Search box or one of the title lists. Then, on the book details page, click the Book Errata link. On this page you can view all errata that has been submitted for this book and posted by Wrox editors. A complete book list including links to each book's errata is also available at `www.wrox.com/misc-pages/booklist.shtml`.

If you don't spot "your" error on the Book Errata page, go to `www.wrox.com/contact/techsupport.shtml` and complete the form there to send us the error you have found. We'll check the information and, if appropriate, post a message to the book's errata page and fix the problem in subsequent editions of the book.

p2p.wrox.com

For author and peer discussion, join the P2P forums at `p2p.wrox.com`. The forums are a Web-based system for you to post messages relating to Wrox books and related technologies and interact with other readers and technology users. The forums offer a subscription feature to e-mail you topics of interest of your choosing when new posts are made to the forums. Wrox authors, editors, other industry experts, and your fellow readers are present on these forums.

At `http://p2p.wrox.com` you will find a number of different forums that will help you not only as you read this book, but also as you develop your own applications. To join the forums, just follow these steps:

1. Go to `p2p.wrox.com` and click the Register link.
2. Read the terms of use and click Agree.
3. Complete the required information to join as well as any optional information you wish to provide and click Submit.
4. You will receive an e-mail with information describing how to verify your account and complete the joining process.

   You can read messages in the forums without joining P2P but in order to post your own messages, you must join.

Once you join, you can post new messages and respond to messages other users post. You can read messages at any time on the Web. If you would like to have new messages from a particular forum e-mailed to you, click the Subscribe to this Forum icon by the forum name in the forum listing.

For more information about how to use the Wrox P2P, be sure to read the P2P FAQs for answers to questions about how the forum software works as well as many common questions specific to P2P and Wrox books. To read the FAQs, click the FAQ link on any P2P page.

Ruby on Rails®
for Microsoft Developers

1

Getting Started with Rails

First they ignore you,
then they laugh at you,
then they fight you,
then you win.

— *Mahatma Gandhi*

Ruby on Rails is a highly productive Web application framework for the Ruby language. It will change the way you think about Web development and simplify the process of creating, deploying, and maintaining your Web applications. It could be argued that Ruby on Rails will ultimately make you a better developer.

These statements may seem like bold claims now, but over the course of the next few chapters, sufficient evidence is presented that will help to convince you otherwise.

The aim of this chapter is to provide you with an introduction to the Rails framework, and help you set up your favorite operating system so that it's ready to work with Rails.

What's in a Name?

The name Ruby on Rails is often shortened to Rails. Another common abbreviation is the acronym RoR (pronounced like a lion's "roar"). I feel it is important to clarify something that is often a source of confusion for newcomers: Ruby is a modern, object-oriented programming language, which predates Rails by about a decade. Ruby on Rails is simply the "full name" of a great Web framework written in Ruby, for Ruby developers. This name is also used for the URL of the official project website, available at http://rubyonrails.org.

The Rise and Challenges of Web Development

Over the past few years the development world has experienced a radical paradigm shift from desktop to Web applications. It may be premature to call traditional desktop programs obsolete, but the rapid rise of Web-based software is a clear sign of the ever-increasing popularity and significance of Web development.

Web applications provide developers and users alike with a wealth of advantages. In particular, programmers can leverage a more immediate development, deployment, and maintenance cycle, while end users are able to utilize applications with desktop-like features and interfaces (often referred to as Rich Internet Applications or RIAs) directly from their browser. This enables users to access data in a platform-independent manner, on the operating system and device of their choice, and from anywhere an Internet connection is available. A significant part of the success of Web applications resides in this ability to respond well to the needs of a world that is continually more and more connected. Web development is therefore a stimulating and worthwhile endeavor.

The new Web — commonly dubbed Web 2.0 (a term that's attracted its fair share of critics) — poses a few challenges for developers, especially for beginners. The Web as a development platform is exciting, but far from perfect.

The main problem in this regard arises from the Web's origins. The HTTP protocol was created as a means to store and retrieve documents. HTML, on the other hand, is a markup language that was created to represent interlinked documents (hypertext). Traditionally, the Web's entire architecture was document-based.

Yet, its worldwide success and the growing reliance upon it by more than a billion people has forced the Web to rapidly evolve over the past 15 years to the point where multimedia and very complex applications are possible. In moving from an era of documents to one of rich applications and interfaces, a series of new technologies were introduced. It isn't far-fetched to say that we're pushing the Web far beyond the limits for which it was initially created.

It is very challenging to approach the new Web with general-purpose languages and tools. For example, though it is possible to write CGI scripts today, far better-suited tools exist, which make a developer's job much easier and more enjoyable, while delivering solid applications that are simple to maintain. These tools — and Rails is an excellent poster child for this — are specifically tailored for the new challenges of the modern Web and for this reason are often considered to be an example of Domain Specific Languages (DSLs). Rails and similar frameworks incarnate and adhere to the best practices assimilated by the industry, and attempt to hide the tedious, repetitive, low-level work required by Web applications from the developer.

Web applications are often developed by a small team and tend to change at a rather fast pace. This is in stark contrast to development scenarios that are present within the Enterprise world, where extensive planning and long release cycles are not uncommon. It is therefore necessary to use development methodologies and tools that allow the developer to be productive and embrace change.

It is also important to understand that a user typically interacts with a Web application through a browser, hence its limits will inevitably affect the user's experience on the Web.

One of the toughest quirks to work around is the issue of cross-browser compatibility. The contents of non-trivial Web pages are displayed and behave differently based on the browser that's being used. In some cases, a Web application may not work at all in certain browsers.

Dozens of Web browsers exist, even limiting the playing field to the most popular and widely adopted choices (multi-browser compatibility); at the very least, attentive developers must test their applications with common browsers such as Internet Explorer, Mozilla Firefox, Safari, and Opera. Plus, one has to keep in mind that different versions of the same browser will typically render the content in a different manner (for example, IE 6 and IE 7). Sadly, this aspect is often overlooked, and it isn't uncommon for many companies and developers to verify their Web apps with Internet Explorer alone.

Browser vendors are making a conscious effort to improve their browsers in order to achieve better compliance with major Web standards and specifications, but it would be naïve to expect complete compatibility anytime soon. Coping with this flock of browsers adds to the complexity and can be detrimental to the fun of programming.

If you are already a Web developer or a Web designer, you're probably aware of the importance of adopting the W3C recommendations (for example, XHTML, CSS, and DOM), and international standards (for example, ECMAScript, aka JavaScript), as well as testing your application in multiple browsers.

Mentioning the names of a few commonly adopted languages brings up another issue: the modern Web is rather complex and, in order to work well, requires a set of server- and client-side technologies that you should be familiar with. The skills required encompass (depending on your role): a solid understanding of the HTTP protocol, XHTML, CSS, JavaScript, Ajax (or Flex, or Microsoft Silverlight), server-side programming, database design, SQL, Web Services, security, Web servers, and so on, with a list that could continue on for a good long while. Contrary to popular belief — that is perhaps a remnant of the early days of simple HTML homepages — Web development is a complex balance between art and engineering.

As the number of Internet users grows, so too does the demand for a higher degree of interaction, useful features, and — thanks to fast connections and technologies like Ajax — responsive and advanced Web UIs. A few examples of such Web applications are Gmail, Google Docs (an online Office suite), Google Maps, YouTube, Flickr, and more recently, Adobe Photoshop Express (Photoshop on the Web). In other words, the bar for what constitutes a good Web application has been raised considerably over the past few years.

Luckily for you, Ruby on Rails is the ideal tool when it comes time to approach these challenges.

What Is Rails?

Rails is an open source, cross-platform, full-stack, Model-View-Controller (MVC) framework for the Agile development of database-driven Web applications that use the Ruby language. This dense definition incorporates quite a few concepts that you may not be familiar with. Let's break things down so as to get a better overview of the framework.

Open Source

Rails is an open source project. It's released under a very liberal license (MIT) that enables you to freely modify, contribute, and distribute the framework. In the vernacular of the Free Software world, Rails is free as in beer and as in speech. As a Microsoft developer, you're probably used to proprietary software, where several of the components that you employ in your applications are closed source.

The fact that Rails is open source implies that, whenever you encounter a bug in the framework itself, you'll have full access to the source code of the libraries that constitute the framework. You will be able to identify where the problem lies, report it with accuracy, and even correct it yourself and submit a patch to the project. In other words, stepping through and reviewing the source code helps you to better understand how the framework operates and in turn enables you to build better applications.

Cross-Platform

Unlike ASP.NET (with an exception made for its alternative implementation through the Mono project), Rails runs on a number of platforms. The most popular choices within the community are operating system members of the *nix family (like GNU/Linux, Mac OS X, and *BSD), but Rails can be used on Windows as well.

Full-Stack

The term *full-stack* means that the framework provides you with a supportive, integrated environment in which it's possible to develop complete Web applications from start to finish. To borrow an expression from the Python world, Rails "comes with batteries included." Aside from handling the request-response cycle and providing you with the necessary libraries for easier database, server-side, and Web Service programming, on the client side, Rails also includes a JavaScript framework (Prototype) and a library (script.aculo.us) for creating Ajax-powered applications.

Support for testing, a very important topic for Rails developers, is baked-in as well. To top it all off, Rails provides you with a handy HTTP server known as WEBrick which, albeit meant for development purposes only, enables you to get started right away without having to worry about configuring more complicated Web servers.

If you're accustomed to developing with large frameworks such as ASP.NET or J2EE, Rails' full-stack nature may seem "not full enough." This is intentionally so, in order to avoid complexity and bloat in the framework and leave a core that's reasonably slim and extendable through free, third-party plugins. Rails' plugin architecture encourages code reuse and enables the developer to extend Rails' core behavior and out-of-the-box features in reusable plugins that are often shared with the whole world. As a Rails beginner, you can learn a lot by simply studying the code of high-quality Rails plugins, and you can take advantage of a wealth of functionalities by simply installing them within your own Rails projects on an as-needed basis. Plugins are, in my opinion, one of Rails' best features.

The MVC Pattern

MVC is an architectural pattern designed to satisfy the principle of separation of concerns. When successfully applied to the design of a software project, it promotes the isolation of the user interface from the business logic. This separation is extremely important in order to create maintainable applications, and it's especially true on the Web, where the distinction between business logic (server side) and presentation layer (client side) is almost intrinsic to the medium.

Models represent the data, views the user interface, and controllers act as coordinators, controlling the flow of the application. Controllers are the glue of the application; they allow modification and retrieval of model data, and preparation of the content so it can be rendered in the view. Changes performed to the view by, your designer, for example, shouldn't affect the team of developers working on the backend.

If you have done ASP (classic) or PHP development, where access to the database, business logic, and presentation layer are often intermingled, you'll find RoR's approach rather refreshing, tidy, and even elegant.

Rails generates the skeleton of an application and, in effect, forces you to adopt an MVC-style of programming. Every Rails application applies separation between the model, the view, and the controller, storing the files for each of these components in different folders. You'd have to go out of your way to be able to intentionally break the enforcement of this pattern in Rails. But don't let this apparent strictness toward MVC get you down. In most cases ASP.NET developers who switch to Rails find themselves liberated by the rigidity of the language (be it C# or VB.NET) and the framework they were used to.

In Chapter 2, the MVC pattern is described in further detail, with particular emphasis on the way Rails implements each entity and their interaction with each other.

Agile Development

Agile development is a perfect match for the Rails developer. It can be argued that Rails is an attempt to bring Agile methodologies to the Web, where development has often been led by opposite principles. If you are not familiar with the Agile movement, I invite you to read the following Manifesto for Agile Software Development (http://agilemanifesto.org). The Agile Manifesto was the brainchild of 17 pioneers who decided to start a movement to improve the practice of software development. Among these folks, three individuals (Martin Fowler, Dave Thomas, and Andy Hunt) are deeply involved with the Ruby and Rails communities.

Manifesto for Agile Software Development

We are uncovering better ways of developing software by doing it and helping others do it. Through this work we have come to value:

- ❏   Individuals and interactions over processes and tools
- ❏   Working software over comprehensive documentation
- ❏   Customer collaboration over contract negotiation
- ❏   Responding to change over following a plan

That is, while there is value in the items on the right, we value the items on the left more.

— *Kent Beck, Mike Beedle, Arie van Bennekum, Alistair Cockburn, Ward Cunningham, Martin Fowler, James Grenning, Jim Highsmith, Andrew Hunt, Ron Jeffries, Jon Kern, Brian Marick, Robert C. Martin, Steve Mellor, Ken Schwaber, Jeff Sutherland, Dave Thomas.*

Rails absolutely embraces each of these four principles, and the so-called "Rails Way" of programming faithfully adheres to the Agile methodologies. Rails' main philosophies are often condensed into mnemonic mantras that originated and are well-known in the Extreme Programming (XP) and Agile communities. The three canonical ones are: Don't Repeat Yourself (DRY), Convention over Configuration, and You Ain't Gonna Need It (YAGNI).

"Convention over Configuration" expresses Rails' philosophy of adopting a series of sensible assumptions, which frees programmers from defining and configuring every single detail of their application. Most Web applications share common elements and Rails requires configuration only when the conventions adopted by the framework are not endorsed and, therefore, need to be overwritten. For example, Rails assumes that the class `Order` will correspond to the pluralized `orders` table in the database. Unless you're required to overwrite this convention, the mapping between the Ruby class and the database table is automatic and no explicit configuration is required.

Even if you intend to overwrite a given convention, unlike with other frameworks, Rails' configuration is performed in simple readable text files, rather than using verbose XML files. A medium-sized application in a traditional framework can end up having hundreds, if not thousands, of lines of XML just to define a correspondence between the objects within the code and the relational structure in the database. This is intentionally not the case with Rails, even if it provides programmers with the ability to configure and overwrite conventions in order to meet their needs.

The "Don't Repeat Yourself" mantra implies that writing less redundant code and reducing duplication ends up producing maintainable and less bug-prone applications, which can easily evolve and change. A change in a given point of an application should not affect unrelated elements and should be properly reflected in related ones, without requiring multiple changes. Localizing change is a principle that is fundamental to Rails development, and the framework structure promotes and enforces this.

Finally, the "You Ain't Gonna Need It" principle is a reminder about the importance of implementing features that are actually needed now, and fighting the urge to write code for features that may only be necessary in the future. This approach to software engineering has been embraced by Rails' creators as well as being common among developers using Rails. Following the YAGNI principle offers a greater focus on the required core functionalities, keeps software lean, and helps in retaining the application's flexibility to change as needed. 37signals endorses this principle and extends it into the principle of "less software," which is aimed at outsmarting the competition with focused software that has fewer features than their competitors. So far, it has worked wonders for them.

Understanding the Rails philosophy of Web development is essential to successfully employing the framework and becoming an effective programmer.

These principles are closer to the Unix philosophy, rather than the one that's common within the Microsoft development world. This by no means implies that, as a Microsoft developer, you may not have already adopted and sought out these development practices, but it was essential to explain them further and state their importance throughout the book.

Database Driven

Rails assumes that each Web application is going to store data within a database. It is a reasonable assumption for all but the most trivial of applications. More importantly, Rails uses an Object Relational Mapper (ORM) Ruby library called ActiveRecord, that follows the Active Record design pattern as defined by Martin Fowler in his popular book, *Patterns of Enterprise Application Architecture* (Addison-Wesley 2002).

ActiveRecord greatly simplifies CRUD, the four basic functions of persistent storage — create, read, update, and delete — enabling you to favor Ruby code over SQL queries (most of the time). It's the abstraction that allows domain models to wrap database objects and handle their underlying relationships. Thanks to a series of adapters, ActiveRecord, and therefore Rails, can be used with all of the most popular databases, from the file-based SQLite (Rails' current default) to more "enterprisey" choices such as Microsoft SQL Server, IBM DB2, or Oracle. The Rails community has a clear preference toward open source databases such as MySQL and PostgreSQL, but you are more than welcome to adopt whatever RDBMS you have at hand or are more comfortable with.

This book uses the default database (SQLite) and recommends that you do the same to follow along, but don't be too concerned if you're using a different one. That's the beauty of ActiveRecord's abstraction: the Ruby code will be (virtually) the same no matter what database is being used. That said, there are special considerations for SQL Server, DB2, and Oracle, and pointers for these are provided in Chapter 11.

Ruby: Rails' Secret Sauce

Ruby is an open source, modern, object-oriented programming language — and a fantastic one at that. It synthesizes the best lessons learned from other programming languages like Smalltalk, Perl, and Lisp, combining the elegance of the object-oriented paradigm (in Ruby everything is an object; there are no primitive types) with the immediacy of a scripting language, further combined with functional programming. If you are not familiar with this last programming style, but have had a chance to try out the language extensions to C# 3.0 and Visual Basic 9 — provided by LINQ in the .NET 3.5 Framework — you've already had your first contact with the functional world.

If you're used to programming languages like C#, VB.NET, C++, or Java, you'll be blown away by how Ruby is concise yet readable, expressive, powerful, and easy-to-learn. Its dynamic, interpreted nature makes it much less tedious to work with, when compared to the aforementioned compiled programming languages.

Ruby is a very high-level language and it's truly Rails' secret sauce. Its flexibility and reflective nature make it an ideal language with which to implement a framework/DSL like Rails.

A good part of the fun of writing Rails applications lies in the fact that you get to code in Ruby, a language that was invented by Yukihiro Matsumoto (commonly known as Matz), with the specific intention of being programmer-friendly, productive, and maintainable.

Rails takes Ruby to the next level, by expanding its out-of-the-box capabilities through utility classes and extension to the Standard Library; on the other hand, Ruby's openness and flexibility enable you, the developer, to extend Rails to suit your needs.

Rails is written in Ruby for Ruby programmers, so it is essential to be well versed in Ruby before attempting to create interesting Rails applications. This is a common mistake by people who are trying to learn Rails. They skip Ruby and dive right into the framework, tempted by Rails' approachability. The end result is not pretty, with a lot of confused newcomers and very basic Ruby questions popping up in the Rails mailing lists and forums.

> *In this book Ruby is not an afterthought. I deemed it crucial to include two whole chapters dedicated to the language, as opposed to a simple appendix as often happens in other Rails books. I've also tried to emphasize and clarify aspects of the language throughout this book, whenever required.*

Greater Than the Sum of Its Parts

Reading about Rails features and design choices may lead you to realize that Rails didn't invent anything particularly new. The powerful MVC pattern was first described back in 1979 and was already adopted by other MVC frameworks. Conversely, the Active Record pattern was well known, too. Over the past few years, all sorts of Ajax libraries and frameworks have been released into the wild; and Test Driven Development (TDD) and the Agile methodologies were also not invented by Rails.

What Rails did was to put each component in the right place, in a coherent manner, while attempting to keep everything as simple as possible for the programmer. The end result is a powerful and fun toolkit that lets you concentrate on the actual application, rather than on small technical details that are repeated over and over in each project. Does the programmer really need to specify the whole connection string in order to access the data within the database? Rails doesn't think so. Rails favors "Convention over Configuration" because when these conventions are sensible, they truly free the developer from having to take care of minutiae in configuration files.

This homogeneous set of features, conveniences for the developers, "best practices," and guiding philosophies make Rails invaluable when it comes to producing solid Web applications in very short time frames, when compared to other existing solutions. The Rails community has done a good job of conveying the framework's strengths, and understandably many developers are excited about the chance to use Ruby on Rails in their projects.

A Brief History of Rails

To fully understand the reasons behind Rails' design choices, it is beneficial to very briefly learn about its history.

Understanding Rails' Origins

Rails was released to the world back in July 2004. The framework was extracted from a Web-based management and collaboration application project called Basecamp. Rails was created by David Heinemeier Hansson (often referred to simply as "DHH"), a Danish programmer and partner with 37signals, the firm that produces Basecamp and other similar Web applications. This brief piece of information offers us some important preemptive insight.

Rails was not designed by a committee. It was extracted from a real-world application. Even after Rails' incredible success, David has insisted that there won't be a Rails, Inc. because he firmly believes in the importance of working on real applications and only then applying the most useful lessons learned (and possible missing features) back into the framework.

This approach guarantees that Rails doesn't end up becoming a bloated framework that includes all sorts of features, to satisfy the requirements of any possible company or scenario out there. Rails is intentionally general enough to be used for a wide range of applications, but its focus has always been the needs of 37signals and other companies/developers who take up similar principles. That's where Rails really shines. To paraphrase what David said during a keynote at Startup School (http://startupschool.org): 37signals targets Fortune 5,000,000 companies.

37signals' team has strong opinions about how software development should be done. They embrace Agile development, simplicity, and software that focuses on a relatively small number of features (the previously mentioned YAGNI principle). Rails is opinionated software because it was tailored for the needs of 37signals, their products, and their way of developing. The good news is that, not only are they very successful, but the practices that they promote are well proven within the industry, and make a great deal of sense from a business and engineering standpoint.

Born into this kind of context, Rails makes assumptions about your applications. It assumes that you are going to use a database and that you'll be dividing your work into three environments: development, test, and production. It assumes that you'll be starting from scratch, rather than working with legacy databases. Ruby is not the fastest language out there, but that's acceptable because from 37signals' viewpoint, a need for extra hardware implies a greater number of paying customers. Developer time is much more expensive than hardware. Having to make a choice while creating Rails, they opted in favor of programmer productivity, code maintainability, scalability, and speed of development, as opposed to the raw speed of the framework and the chosen language.

> ### 37signals
> If you'd like to learn more about 37signals, I invite you to read their popular design and usability blog, "Signal vs. Noise" (`http://www.37signals.com/svn/`) and their book on how to build successful Web-based applications, called "Getting Real" (`https://gettingreal.37signals.com`).

Rails' origins help you better comprehend what its sweet spot is. Rails is particularly well suited to applications that have the following characteristics:

- ❑ Applications and sites that aren't trivial. Employing a whole framework for a page or two is still probably overkill and there are more straightforward solutions.

- ❑ Applications built from scratch, following Rails conventions. Working against Rails conventions is possible, but if your project heavily requires going against the stream, working with Rails won't be as easy. An example of this situation is when you are trying to deal with legacy databases and corporate environments.

- ❑ Applications hosted on VPS (Virtual Private Servers), dedicated servers, or elastic/cloud computing services. Shared hosting is an acceptable solution for non-critical applications and low volume websites, but it is neither ideal nor within Rails' sweet spot. You can read more on deployment options and considerations in Chapter 11.

Rails doesn't usually prevent you from building any type of applications, but it is opinionated and you'll be able to get the best out of it when you take advantage of "the Rails Way" of development or, in other words, when your opinions match those of Rails.

If the core Rails functionalities don't quite cut it for your project, you can still decide to use other open source plugins (or write them yourself) in order to allow Rails to behave in manner that's closer to one of your specific needs. For example, you may require support for composite primary keys, which by default are not supported by Rails. There is a homonym plugin that extends ActiveRecord to add this functionality.

It isn't uncommon for the Rails core team (a group of a few open source developers captained by David) to reply to requests of the "wouldn't it be cool if Rails was able to…" sort with the acronym PDI, which stands for Please Do Investigate. Theirs is not a flippant answer, but rather a pragmatic one. It's an open source project after all and anyone can contribute or pay someone else to do it for them in order to get the kind of features that they may require for their own purposes, which don't quite fit into the Rails core.

If your development style, environment, and practices are entirely opposite to the Agile ones promoted by Rails, chances are that you have a bigger problem than deciding whether or not Rails is a good tool for you. In this case, the answer is clear: Rails may not be the best tool in this kind of context, and a .NET or J2EE solution might end up being less problematic.

Powering the Web 2.0

Since its release in the summer of 2004, Rails has managed to become one of the most used and appreciated frameworks on the Web. By 2006, Rails had arguably already achieved its tipping point, and nowadays most developers have heard about Ruby on Rails. It quickly became the tool of choice for most of the (so-called) Web 2.0 startups, and today is widely adopted by some of the largest sites on the Web.

Scribd.com, YellowPages.com, Hulu.com, Twitter.com, RevolutionHealth.com, 43things.com, Helium.com, and Funnyordie.com are but a few examples of popular sites that are currently written in Rails, which you may have visited or heard of.

And the list of Rails users doesn't end with startups and popular websites. Companies of all sizes are employing Rails talent and starting new projects, embracing Ruby and a more Agile style of programming in pursuit of productivity. While typically very popular with smaller and medium companies, Rails has also been used within the borders of giants like IBM (which I work for), Amazon, Yahoo!, NASA, Oracle, EA, BBC, Cisco, and a long list of other successful Fortune 500 members.

Endorsements

"Ruby on Rails is a breakthrough in lowering the barriers of entry to programming. Powerful Web applications that formerly might have taken weeks or months to develop can be produced in a matter of days."– *Tim O'Reilly*

This enthusiastic quote from the founder of O'Reilly Media is just one of many great comments that Rails has received, from all sorts of experienced developers and IT veterans. You can read more at `http://rubyonrails.org/quotes`.

Ruby on Rails took the Web by storm and, along with Ajax, it became one of the greatest "revolutions" in modern Web development history. In fact, Rails' influence isn't limited to the Ruby community. It helped popularize the concept of MVC for many beginners, and inspired other developers to start similar projects (or clones) using Ruby and other programming languages, including but not limited to C#, PHP, Python, Java, and even JavaScript.

You may be familiar with the fact that the .NET community created its own open source version, called MonoRail, through the Castle Project (`http://castleproject.org`) before Microsoft made the wise move to respond to Rails' success with its ASP.NET MVC framework.

The Rise of Ruby

Despite its tagline of being a "programmer's best friend," and its ever growing popularity in its homeland (Japan), Ruby's worldwide adoption was initially limited by its lack of English documentation. In 2000, with the appearance of the first English literature on Ruby, and the involvement of "The Pragmatic Programmers" within the community, Ruby started to become more widely used. But the advocacy and promotion from early adopters was not enough to bring it directly into the spotlight because, at this stage, relatively few programmers had even heard of this thing called Ruby.

When Rails became such a smash hit, developers started using Ruby and began to appreciate it for its own merits. Today, most people still use Ruby to develop with RoR, but it has become quite a common choice outside of the Web or in conjunction with alternative Web frameworks, too. Ruby made Rails great, and Rails made Ruby much more common and accepted within the development world.

This works well for Rails developers, who can benefit from a larger Ruby community that's ready to improve the existing implementation of the language and share libraries for all sorts of development purposes.

Installing Rails

This section takes a break from discussing theory in order to get your environment set up. It provides you with step-by-step instructions for installing Ruby, Rails, and all the other necessary components of a development stack on Microsoft Windows, GNU/Linux, and Mac OS X.

For the Windows installation, two different methods are illustrated: the first leverages an installer and the second uses a learning environment known as Instant Rails.

Can You Use Rails on Windows?

Macs are very popular within the Rails community. If you ever get the chance to attend a Rails conference, you'll see a very high percentage of Apple laptops. The entire Rails core team uses Macs. The community seems to be keen on GNU/Linux as well, which is another common option for Rails development, and the most popular deployment one. In fact, most Rails hackers that I know develop on a Mac and deploy on GNU/Linux or *BSD, a combination that I adopt and enjoy myself.

You probably won't see many Windows systems. Generally speaking, the community prefers Unix-like environments and few people would admit in public to consciously choosing Windows at any Ruby or Rails venue. There are many reasons for this, most of which are cultural ones. Does this mean that you can't use Windows or that you'll be the only one doing it?

Although this book can be followed by utilizing any operating system of your choice, the assumption is that as a Microsoft developer, you're primarily familiar with Windows .NET, and other Microsoft developers often face a culture clash when trying to learn Rails. This book tries to minimize that by letting you take advantage of the tools and skills that you're already familiar with. For this reason, I've employed Windows to write this book, and the screenshots are from (the much debated) Vista.

Developing with Rails on Windows is usually not a problem, given that in the end we are just editing files, but it's a fair assessment to say that both Ruby and Rails work much better on Unix-like operating systems. For example, Ruby is significantly faster on Ubuntu, Fedora, or Mac OS X than it is on Windows XP (where it still performs better than it does on Vista).

Some people even go so far as to run Rails from within a virtual machine (using GNU/Linux or BSD) in Windows. There are also specific cases of libraries or particular deployment options that are well supported on, say, Linux, but not on Windows due to crashes and other problems. In general, it is recommended that you deploy your Rails applications on *nix systems, but it is understood that doing so is not always an option. You'll feel reassured to know that Rails can be deployed on Windows and that this is commonly done. Chapter 11 tells you how.

I wanted to give you a heads up about the special relationship between Ruby, Rails, their respective communities, and Windows, but please don't let this discourage you. Windows is a viable platform for Rails development and there are several initiatives to further improve the current situation. Rails' success and mainstream acceptance will also depend, in my opinion, on its ability to succeed on Windows, which is still the most popular operating system out there.

If you enjoy using Windows, I'll let you in on a surprising piece of information: Ruby is very popular on Windows. In fact, I'm going to prove its popularity in a somewhat scientific manner. Many Ruby and Rails projects are hosted at a site called RubyForge (http://rubyforge.org), the equivalent of SourceForge or CodePlex for Ruby. The most popular download is, surprise-surprise, a one-click installer for installing Ruby on Windows. As I write this, it has been downloaded about 3 million times. And the third most popular download is Instant Rails, a package that helps you to quickly get up and running with Rails on Windows (it's had more than 700,000 downloads so far). Rails on Windows might very well be a silent majority. In other words, and to quote Michael Jackson: you are not alone.

Installing on Windows

For this book you'll need to install the following components:

- ❑ **Ruby:** The Ruby interpreter plus its core and Standard Library. Ruby 1.8.6 or newer is required for modern versions of Rails (for example, 2.2.2 and newer).

- ❑ **RubyGems:** A packaging system used to install, update, and remove Ruby libraries and programs (packaged and distributed as "gems").

- ❑ **Ruby on Rails:** All the gems required to run Rails.

- ❑ **Mongrel:** A much faster server that we'll use in place of WEBrick.

- ❑ **SQLite3:** A lightweight, file based, ACID (Atomicity, Consistency, Isolation, Durability) compliant database that's available in the public domain.

- ❑ **sqlite3-ruby:** A gem used by Rails to access SQLite3 databases.

- ❑ **Subversion:** An open source version control system required to install many of Rails' plugins.

Installing the One-Click Ruby Installer

Windows is one of the easiest platforms on which to install such a complete Rails stack, thanks to the abovementioned One-Click Ruby Installer, which takes care of the first two elements in the preceding list.

To install it, follow these simple steps:

1. Visit the homepage of the project at http://rubyforge.org/projects/rubyinstaller and click Download on the right-hand side, half way through the page.

2. On the download page, there will be several versions available. Ensure that you download the latest one. At the time of this writing, the current stable version is ruby186-26.exe; click this or a more recent version if available.

3. Double-click the downloaded executable to start the setup wizard. Go through the installation process, accepting the default options (see Figure 1-1). The operation may take a few minutes to complete.

At this point Ruby, RubyGems, and a handy text editor called SciTE are all installed in c:\ruby (unless you specified a different location during the installation process).

To verify that the installation was successful, you can run a quick sanity check by opening the command prompt (cmd.exe) and running the following command:

```
ruby -v
```

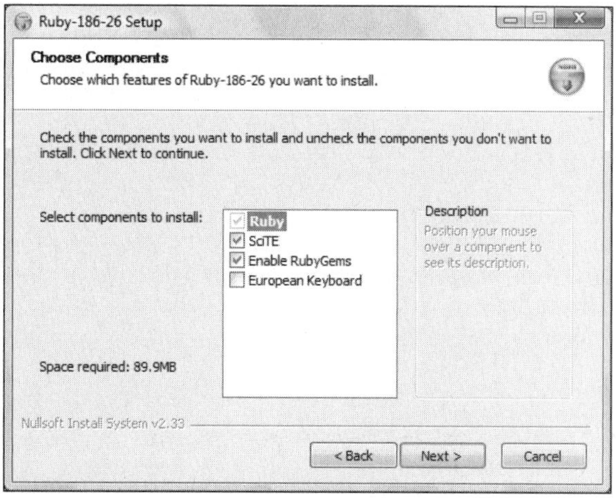

Figure 1-1

Ruby should reply, stating its version number to the prompt; for example, on my machine I obtain the following: ruby 1.8.6 (2007-09-24 patchlevel 111) [i386-mswin32]. Ensure that you have Ruby 1.8.6 or newer, because this is a requirement for Rails.

Updating RubyGems

The version of RubyGems that ships with the One-Click installer may not be the most recent one. You can verify the installed version number by running gem -v from the command line and upgrade to the latest version by issuing the following:

```
gem update — system
```

This will fetch and install the latest version of RubyGems from the RubyForge repository, so you'll need to be connected to the Internet. When the update is finished, you should get the message "RubyGems system software updated" or similar, as shown in Figure 1-2.

Running gem -v again will give you the peace of mind that the update was indeed successful and that the command is still working.

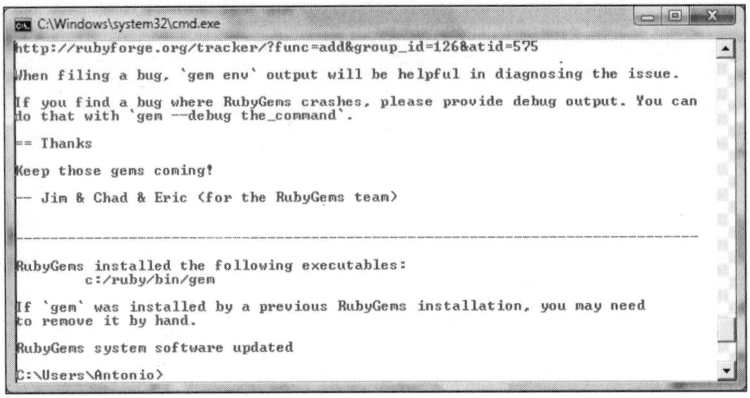

Figure 1-2

Now that you've updated the system, you can proceed to update the actual gems that came with the One-Click installer by running `gem update` from the command line. You can obtain a list of installed gems by running the following command:

```
C:\> gem list
*** LOCAL GEMS ***

fxri (0.3.7, 0.3.6)
fxruby (1.6.18, 1.6.12)
hpricot (0.6.164, 0.6)
log4r (1.0.5)
ptools (1.1.6)
rake (0.8.3, 0.7.3)
rubygems-update (1.3.1)
sources (0.0.1)
test-unit (2.0.2)
win32-api (1.3.0, 1.0.4)
win32-clipboard (0.4.4, 0.4.3)
win32-dir (0.3.2)
win32-eventlog (0.5.0, 0.4.6)
win32-file (0.6.0, 0.5.4)
win32-file-stat (1.3.2, 1.2.7)
win32-process (0.6.0, 0.5.3)
win32-sapi (0.1.4)
win32-sound (0.4.1)
windows-api (0.2.4, 0.2.0)
windows-pr (0.9.8, 0.7.2)
```

As you can see in the preceding output, when multiple versions of a gem exist, they are listed as well between parentheses.

Installing Rails

Now that the must-have RubyGems packaging system is installed, you can you use it to install a fresh copy of Rails by issuing the following command:

```
gem install rails -v 2.2.2
```

RubyGems Improvements

RubyGems has come a long way. In its previous versions, the developer had to indicate the gem version and platform required during the installation of a gem. If you want to install a specific version of a gem, you can now use the − version or -v option (for example, -v 2.2.2).

The dependencies weren't installed by default either, and the -y or − include-dependencies option was required to include them. Now that gem automatically installs the dependencies, you can specify the − ignore-dependencies option in the rare occurrence when you don't want them to be installed.

This command will fetch the rails gem version 2.2.2 and all its dependencies from the default source repository at http://gems.rubyforge.org (you can run gem source -l to see a list of sources used by the command). If you omit -v 2.2.2, the command will install the latest available version. This book uses version 2.2.2 so it's recommended that you follow along with the same version even if version 2.3 will be out by the time you read this.

No huge differences exist between Rails 2.2.2 and 2.3. At the time of writing 2.3's release date has not been announced but I will point out throughout the book when the known differences exist.

The installation process may take a while, as gem proceeds with installing Rails and five other gems plus their documentation, as shown in Figure 1-3.

To see a list of remote gems you can use the − remote option. When used in conjunction with list it can help you find gems by their name. For example, gem list sql − remote *will show you a list of gems that start with sql (it's not case sensitive).*

```
Administrator: C:\Windows\system32\cmd.exe

C:\Users\Administrator>cd ..

C:\Users>cd ..

C:\>gem install rails -v 2.2.2
Successfully installed activesupport-2.2.2
Successfully installed activerecord-2.2.2
Successfully installed actionpack-2.2.2
Successfully installed actionmailer-2.2.2
Successfully installed activeresource-2.2.2
Successfully installed rails-2.2.2
6 gems installed
Installing ri documentation for activesupport-2.2.2...
Installing ri documentation for activerecord-2.2.2...
Installing ri documentation for actionpack-2.2.2...
Installing ri documentation for actionmailer-2.2.2...
Installing ri documentation for activeresource-2.2.2...
Installing RDoc documentation for activesupport-2.2.2...
Installing RDoc documentation for activerecord-2.2.2...
Installing RDoc documentation for actionpack-2.2.2...
Installing RDoc documentation for actionmailer-2.2.2...
Installing RDoc documentation for activeresource-2.2.2...

C:\>
```

Figure 1-3

Gem places the rails command within c:\ruby\bin, which is in the Windows's Path environment variable and therefore executable from any command prompt.

Running rails − version (or its shorter version -v) tells you which version is currently active.

Installing Mongrel

It's nice that Rails ships with an HTTP server. Unfortunately, even strictly for development purposes, it's not very fast. Through RubyGems you can easily install a much faster replacement called Mongrel that, in more elaborate configurations, is often used to run some of the largest Rails websites out there.

To install Mongrel, simply run:

```
C:\> gem install mongrel
Successfully installed gem_plugin-0.2.3
Successfully installed cgi_multipart_eof_fix-2.5.0
Successfully installed mongrel-1.1.5-x86-mswin32-60
3 gems installed
Installing ri documentation for gem_plugin-0.2.3...
Installing ri documentation for cgi_multipart_eof_fix-2.5.0...
Installing ri documentation for mongrel-1.1.5-x86-mswin32-60...
Installing RDoc documentation for gem_plugin-0.2.3...
Installing RDoc documentation for cgi_multipart_eof_fix-2.5.0...
Installing RDoc documentation for mongrel-1.1.5-x86-mswin32-60...
```

This command installs the Windows version of Mongrel and the required dependencies as well.

> *A second gem,* `mongrel_service`, *exists for installing Mongrel as a Windows service. This is not needed for development but it's very useful when deploying an application, to ensure that Mongrel automatically starts if the machine reboots. You shouldn't worry about this gem until you are ready to deploy your application. This subject is discussed in Chapter 11.*

Installing SQLite3 and sqlite3-ruby

SQLite version 3 is a very nice, lightweight, file-based (like Microsoft Access) relational database. It's ideal for quick prototyping (in development mode) even though you'll probably want to use a data server when dealing with all but the smallest amount of traffic in a production setting.

MySQL used to be the default database system for Rails, but now SQLite has taken its place, lowering the entry barrier for developing in Rails even further and quickly allowing you to get started. There are no users, authentication, or ports to configure: just simple files. In this book, I decided to stick with the default database. Switching to a different database system is most often trivial.

Installing SQLite is a piece of cake. Just download the DLL contained in a zip file that's available from the official website at `http://www.sqlite.org/download.html`. The current version at the time of writing is 3.6.10, so I downloaded the file `sqlitedll-3_6_10.zip` containing `sqlite3.dll`. You should grab the most recent version available.

Extract the zip file and place the DLL in a location on your path. `c:\ruby\bin` is a good place, given that you're installing SQLite specifically for Rails development purposes.

You should also download the command-line program for accessing and modifying SQLite databases. It's available on the same download page, and its file name (as of this writing) is `sqlite-3_6_10.zip`. Again, extract it and place the `sqlite3.exe` file in `c:\ruby\bin`. From now on, running `sqlite3` from the command line opens the SQLite3 shell. Beginning with Rails 2.1, this shell can also be invoked using a Rails script (`dbconsole`), as explained in Chapter 5.

At this point you'll need to install the Ruby bindings through RubyGems as follows:

```
C:\> gem install sqlite3-ruby -v 1.2.3
Successfully installed sqlite3-ruby-1.2.3-x86-mswin32
1 gem installed
Installing ri documentation for sqlite3-ruby-1.2.3-x86-mswin32...
Installing RDoc documentation for sqlite3-ruby-1.2.3-x86-mswin32...
```

The preceding command specifies version 1.2.3 because it ships with the Ruby bindings in binary form. The latest release, 1.2.4, attempts to build the Ruby extension from source, which is more complicated on Windows because it requires Ruby's development headers and nmake, *Microsoft's version of* make.

Installing Subversion

Subversion (SVN) is a very popular open source version control system. Though it might not be very accurate from a technical viewpoint, it may help you to think about SVN as an efficient and whittled down version of Visual SourceSafe or Microsoft Team Foundation Server.

SVN and similar alternatives are crucial for working on real projects, but in this context I invite you to install the SVN client tools, because they're required for installing Rails plugins. When you attempt to install a plugin, Rails essentially performs a checkout from the given remote Subversion repository you specified.

On Windows, you can get SVN from the URL http://subversion.tigris.org/servlets/Project DocumentList?folderID=91. The most recent setup file in the download list will do (in my case, that's svn-1.4.6-setup.exe). All that's left to do is for you to double-click the downloaded installer and go through the default setup process.

Setup takes care of concatenating the SVN bin directory (for example, c:\Program Files\Subversion\bin) to your Path environment variable. Opening a new command prompt should now allow you to run svn and obtain in return a Type 'svn help' for usage message. It doesn't do anything too useful, but it's a good sanity check that guarantees you that svn.exe is available from the command prompt.

Many plugins are released on GitHub.com, *a site that hosts thousands of projects that use the Git distributed revision control system. For this reason, you may want to install a Git client as well. On Windows, you could install msysGit (*http://code.google.com/p/msysgit/*). If you are new to Git, you should also check out "An Illustrated Guide to Git on Windows" available at* http://nathanj.github.com/gitguide/tour.html.

Configuring Instant Rails

The original author of the One-Click installer (Curt Hibbs) created an alternative project called Instant Rails. Unlike the One-Click installer above, Instant Rails doesn't require any installation, nor does it modify your environment. You download a zip file, extract it to the folder of your choice, and you will automatically have a full Rails stack at your fingertips. The current version includes Ruby, RubyGems, Rake, Rails, Mongrel, support for SQLite3, MySQL, Apache, and PHP (for phpMyAdmin, which is used to manage MySQL), and a couple of sample Rails projects.

It essentially contains anything that'll you need to get started with Rails. You will need to manually install SVN, but other than that, you'll be all set (which helps explain the popularity of this package). Because it's such a great all-in-one package, it is very commonly used by Rails beginners who are working with Windows.

You could use Instant Rails while reading this book, but I don't recommend that you do so. Instant Rails is meant to be a development-only package, and it's not typically used in production environments. You're also somewhat tied to its management application (InstantRails Manager), even though you could manually configure the binaries to be accessible throughout the whole system. For as great as it is, Instant Rails remains a prepackaged solution that is not as flexible and "solid" as the manual installation previously discussed. On top of that, it could be using different version numbers and make this book harder to follow.

With that in mind, there are still times when you can't install software on your Windows system or, for whatever reason, prefer not to touch the existing environment. In such situations, Instant Rails is the right solution and you should have no qualms about giving it a spin. To install Instant Rails, follow these steps:

1. Download Instant Rails from `http://rubyforge.org/projects/instantrails/`. As usual, click Download and grab the latest stable version of the zip file that's available, which has the following format: `InstantRails-X.Y-win.zip`, where X and Y (obviously) make up the version number.

2. Extract the contents (see Figure 1-4) of the zip file to a convenient location, like `c:\ InstantRails`.

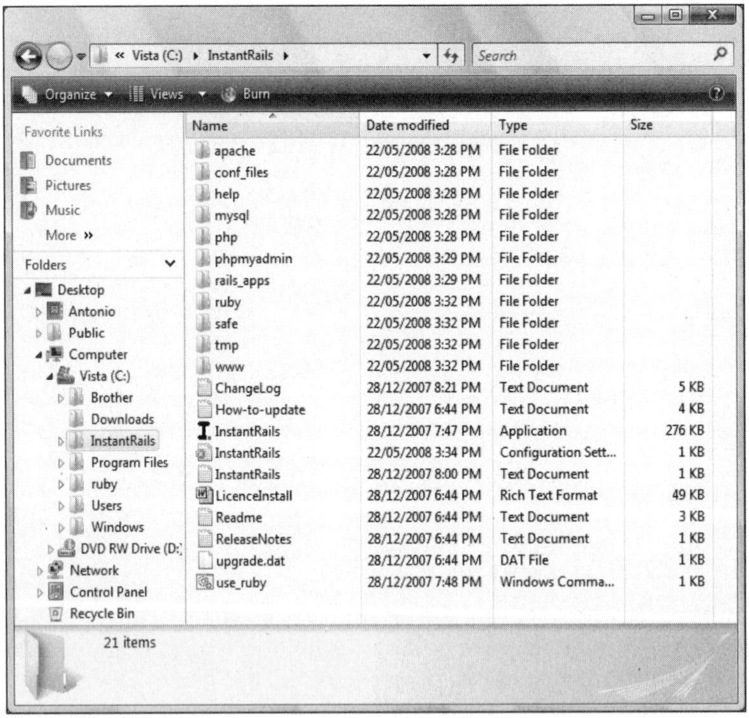

Figure 1-4

3. Double-click the InstantRails application and accept the configuration regeneration, as shown in Figure 1-5.

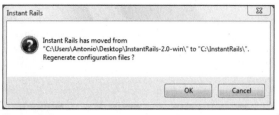

Figure 1-5

4 The Instant Rails management application now appears and attempts to start Apache and MySQL for you. The Windows Firewall may ask you to allow this. Feel free to keep blocking Apache, given that the combination of Apache and phpMyAdmin is not used throughout this book. You can even stop both services by selecting Stop (or Kill, if stop is not available) in the menu that appears after clicking respectively on the MySQL and the Apache buttons. Configuration and startup settings are available by clicking the I icon button within the interface, and selecting the (previously concealed) menu Configure ⇨ Instant Rails as shown in Figure 1-6.

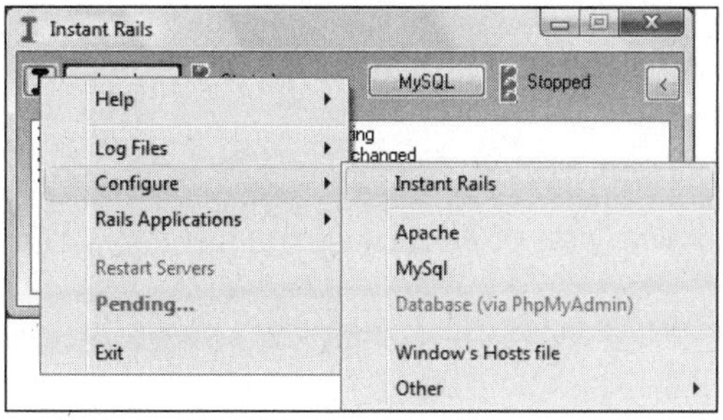

Figure 1-6

As per the "manual" installation through the One-Click installer, it is a good idea to update the installed gems, by issuing a gem update. In this case though, gem is not accessible from any command prompt, so you'll have to open the Ruby console from Instant Rails, by clicking Rails Applications ⇨ Open Ruby Console Window.

You can also create and manage your applications by selecting Rails Applications ⇨ Manage Rails Applications. The Rails Applications window will appear. To create a new application, you'd click the Create New Rails App button. What this does is simply open a command prompt, which is aptly located in (depending on the folder you picked in the beginning) c:\InstantRails\rails_apps.

These brief instructions should get you started on the right foot if you were not able to proceed with the recommended method in the previous section. Please note, however, that throughout the rest of the book, you won't find instructions that are specific to Instant Rails.

Installation on Other Platforms

This section is just a quick pointer in case you decide to get started with Rails on *nix systems rather than Windows.

Mac OS X

Apple has been shipping Ruby on its OS for some time now. The default Ruby installation on systems older than Mac OS X 10.4.6 doesn't work well with Rails. If this scenario applies to your system, you have a few options besides upgrading your OS.

You can download (http://www.ruby-lang.org/en/downloads/) and then compile and build from source code, if you are familiar with the process. If you're brave, this guide leads you through the installation step-by-step:

    http://hivelogic.com/articles/2005/12/ruby_rails_lighttpd_mysql_tiger

You can also simply use one of the popular distribution systems like MacPorts (http://www.macports.org) or Fink (http://www.finkproject.org). You should install the whole stack that I pointed out in the Windows section in order to successfully follow this book and start working with Rails projects.

The two preceding methods are only needed if you are running a Mac OS X version that's older than 10.4.6. But it's not uncommon for developers to install their own customized stack rather than to rely on Apple's copy.

A much easier alternative for beginners is Locomotive (http://locomotive.raaum.org), a popular project with similar aims (and arguably caveats) to those of Instant Rails, but targeted for Mac OS X.

If you are running Tiger, with a version number equal or greater than 10.4.6, your Ruby installation is good and you'll just need to update RubyGems, the pre-installed gems, and then proceed with the installation of Rails. Conversely, on Leopard (Mac OS X 10.5.x), Rails, Mongrel, and a series of other goodies are already included for you and you'll just need to update them to the latest version. In both cases, you can run the following commands from the Terminal:

```
sudo gem update —system
sudo gem install rails
sudo gem install mongrel
sudo gem update
```

GNU/Linux

If you are using GNU/Linux, you're aware of the many variants (aka distributions, or distros for short) available. It would be impossible for me to provide instructions on how to proceed for each of them. Chances are that no matter what package management system your GNU/Linux version adopts, Ruby 1.8.6 or later, RubyGems, SQLite3, and SVN will be around for you to work with. From RubyGems you can do the rest by updating RubyGems itself, installing (or updating) Rails and Mongrel (and optionally sqlite3-ruby if not available through the package management of your distro).

One of the most common distributions nowadays is Ubuntu (and its variants like Kubuntu and Xubuntu). As an example, I've provided the following instructions on how to set up a Rails stack on version 8.04 of K/X/Ubuntu:

```
sudo apt-get update
sudo apt-get install build-essential
sudo apt-get install subversion
sudo apt-get install ruby-full rubygems libsqlite3-dev libsqlite3-ruby1.8
```

```
sudo gem update — system
sudo gem install rails
sudo gem install mongrel
sudo gem update
```

You'll also have to add Gem's bin folder to your PATH, by adding the following line (or a similar one, if you're not using the default BASH shell) in your shell profile (for example, in ~/.bashrc):

```
export PATH=$PATH:/var/lib/gems/1.8/bin
```

By the time you read this book, things may have changed, but several people have reported a few issues with the RubyGems version installed through apt-get. *Alternatively, you could remove* rubygems *from the preceding instructions and install it manually by downloading and building its source code* (http://rubyforge.org/frs/?group_id=126) *before proceeding with the last four instructions.*

RubyStack

BitNami produces several open source multi-platform installers for popular development stacks. Among these, RubyStack installs Ruby, RubyGems, Rails, ImageMagick, Subversion, SQLite3, MySQL, Apache, PHP, and phpMyAdmin. Their installer works with Windows, GNU/Linux, and Mac OS X and, unlike Instant Rails, performs an actual installation and provides scripts to manage the various servers installed.

If you're struggling with alternative installation methods, you may want to give RubyStack, available at http://bitnami.org/stack/rubystack, a try.

Editors and IDEs

Talking about editors is like entering a minefield. As the Latin would say "De gustibus non est disputandum," which can be liberally translated as, "There's no arguing with taste." Editor and IDE preferences are highly personal, and I will therefore refrain from telling you which one you should use. I do, however, provide a list of a few popular choices, and I invite you to try them out at your leisure, until you find the one that's right for you.

IDEs Are Helpful, Not Necessary

Microsoft evangelists may occasionally use Notepad in their demos, but as a Microsoft developer you know all too well that without a serious IDE like Visual Studio, writing ASP.NET or .NET desktop applications would be a nightmare. Your proficiency in Visual Studio may make or break your productivity.

In the Rails world there isn't an official IDE and we're not big fans of drag-and-drop tools either. The truth of the matter is that Rails doesn't need either of these two things. Most Rails developers are very happy about using text editors. As a matter of fact, when programming in Ruby or in Rails, a good text editor is all you really need. Even something as simple as SciTE, which we installed through the One-Click Ruby Installer, is probably sufficient.

C# and Visual Basic are both relatively verbose languages that take advantage of a huge framework. Ruby is so expressive and concise that an IntelliSense system like the one you are used to in Visual Studio would be helpful, but it is not required to the same extent.

LIMERICK
COUNTY LIBRARY
00593678

Another great feature provided by IDEs is their ability to do the drudge work for you by generating a lot of code. This, again, is not necessary in Rails. The generation of controllers, models, or scaffold (aimed at rapid prototyping) to name but a few, are all carried out by simple scripts that you can run from the command line. And the generated code could be written (even in Notepad) in very little time. When dealing with Rails there simply isn't a need for a lot of code generation of the sort you'd expect with some other languages and frameworks.

> *Don't use Notepad as your editor. There are issues associated with the use of the Windows' end of line characters, which would cause trouble when deploying or committing your code to a non-Windows machine. If you must, at least consider Notepad++ (*`http://notepad-plus.sourceforge.net`*).*

IDEs help with the compilation of software, but Ruby is interpreted and, as such, the process is already much more straightforward. You write the code and then run it directly, plain and simple.

That said, IDEs can be helpful even when programming in Rails. But they are usually much lighter in terms of features (and responsiveness) when compared to Visual Studio and similar programs. A good Rails IDE needs first and foremost to have a solid editor. Syntax highlighting and auto indentation of the code are, in my opinion, a must. Not so much with Ruby, but Rails has a tendency to use very long method names, which can become quite tedious to type. An editor that enables fast typing and proposes contextual automatic completion of code can make your life easier.

I find that the most successful Rails IDEs (and some editors) tend to provide quick access to files and folders within your project, given that multiple folders and files are created when Rails generates the skeleton of an application. IDEs should also allow you to run shell commands directly within the environment, so that you aren't forced to switch between the editor and the command line. Some IDEs also provide support for refactoring, testing, and debugging/profiling of both Ruby and JavaScript.

Popular Choices

In an informal survey — admittedly not one of an overly scientific nature — performed by Tim Bray, the Ruby and Rails communities were asked to provide information about what tools they were using. I'm reporting the results of Bray's survey here because they definitely confirm the anecdotal evidence that I've gathered over the past few years in the Rails world.

Figure 1-7 shows a chart with the most popular choices for Rails, according to the survey available online at `http://www.tbray.org/ongoing/When/200x/2007/11/26/Ruby-Tool-Survey`.

Of the first 1,000 programmers who responded to the survey, 38.30% replied that TextMate was their Rails editor of choice. As you can see, text editors are very popular; in fact TextMate, Vi, Emacs, gedit, SciTe, jEdit, and E Text Editor are all editors. NetBeans, Eclipse, and IntelliJ are IDEs. ActiveState Komodo represents a mix of both, given that there is an Edit version and a commercial IDE. From these numbers, let's briefly consider the most popular choices.

TextMate: The King of Rails Editors

TextMate (`http://macromates.com`) is not an IDE, but a fast and extendable editor that is both very powerful and easy to use. It is a commercial product, but it's fairly inexpensive at about $63 US. TextMate's strength lies in its ability to employ user-contributed bundles, which are very easy to create and modify. It ships with a Ruby and a Rails bundle, among others, and new contributions, with improved features created by other open source developers, are often shared with the community.

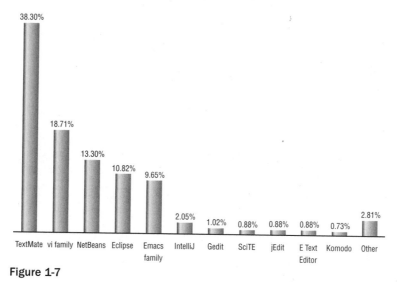

Figure 1-7

TextMate has a Drawer that can contain your project folder and file structure, multi-tabs, and the ability to quickly access a file by simply pressing a shortcut and typing the start of the file name. Among many useful features is the ability to trigger snippets of code (often, common idioms), which can save a lot of time and help you with Rails' long method names (for example, `validates_uniqueness_of`). The catch is that it's only available for Mac OS X.

E Text Editor (`http://www.e-texteditor.com`), used by less than 1% of the surveyed sample, is a clone of TextMate for Windows and its tagline is quite aptly "The Power of TextMate on Windows." It's cheaper than TextMate at about $35, and can take advantage of TextMate's bundles (see Figure 1-8), but you'll need Cygwin, a Linux-like environment for Windows, in order to get the best from its many features.

Cygwin and the One-Click Ruby Installer

The first thing I do whenever I need to work on a Windows box is to ensure that it has a POSIX emulation layer installed. I do this because I feel greatly incapacitated without being able to take advantage of the many powerful tools available in Unix-like systems.

The E Text Editor encourages you to install Cygwin upon startup and thanks to this you will be able to take advantage of TextMate bundles on Windows. Unfortunately, the native Ruby installed by the One-Click Ruby Installer and the emulated Ruby provided by Cygwin are not compatible. If you installed the One-Click Ruby Installer, and then tried to use Ruby or Rails from within Cygwin, you'd face all sorts of problems.

If you decide to uninstall the One-Click Ruby Installer and use the Cygwin version of Ruby, you will have to manually install RubyGems and then Rails through the gem command within the shell provided by Cygwin. Alternatively, by taking the E editor out of the picture, you can use the command-line tools provided by Cygwin (or similarly MinGW), but resist using the Ruby version they provide.

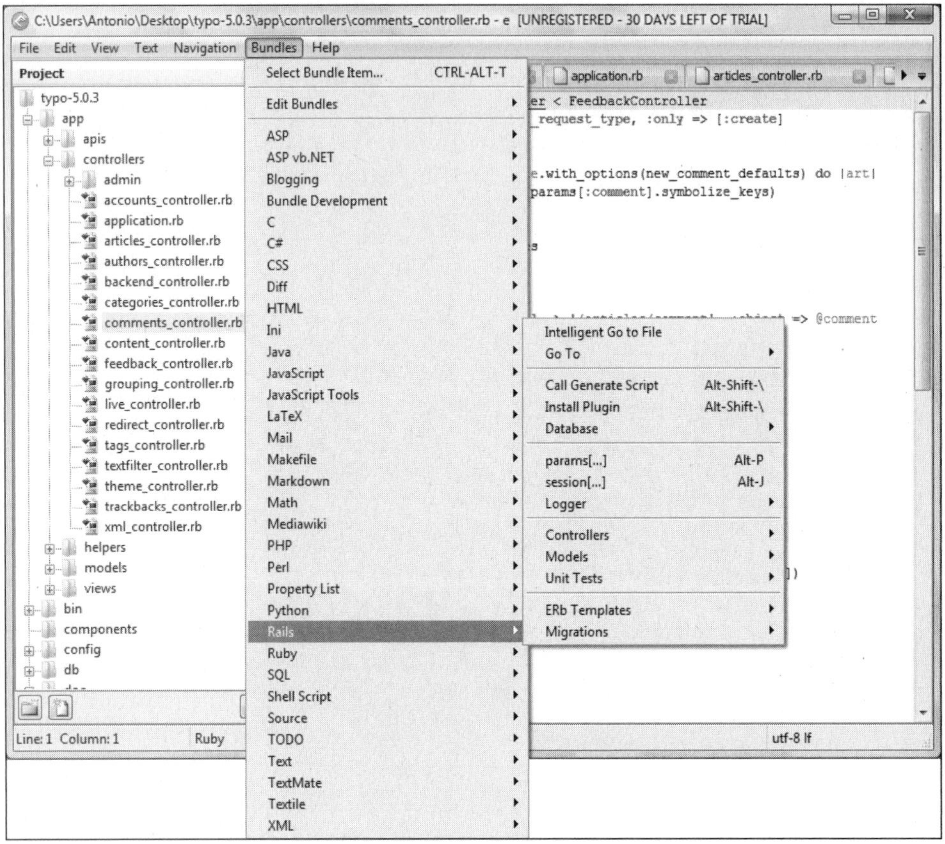

Figure 1-8

TextMate is what I personally use when I'm on a Mac, and I feel that the experience provided by TextMate on a Mac is hard to beat; but given that TextMate is not available for Windows, you may find E to be very useful. Expect it to be very different from what you're accustomed to with large IDEs. After all, it's still a text editor.

Vi and Emacs

Vi and Emacs, and all of their respective variants, are two powerful and very different text editors that have been popular for decades in the *nix world. They're free software and have Windows versions, but if you've never used them before, both will seem extremely complicated to you. In the Rails community Vi is the most used of the two, and in the Ruby community, according to that particular survey, members of the Vi family are even more popular than TextMate.

Some developers swear by either of them, whereas others consider them suboptimal for developing in Rails. It's true that Vi and Emacs are very extendable, powerful, and that there are all sorts of resources for using them for Ruby and Rails development, but unless you come from a Unix background, I don't particularly recommend you check them out. They are worth all the effort that's necessary to learn them, but I don't feel that you need extra obstacles while trying to learn Ruby, Rails, and a different culture.

NetBeans IDE

Sun Microsystems has vested a lot of interest in Ruby and RoR. One of the fruits of its involvement with the community is the NetBeans IDE. This multi-platform Java-based tool has been continuously improved to add new Ruby- and Rails-specific features and, in a short amount of time, it has gathered a growing following.

The tool works well and it even offers code auto completion as shown in Figure 1-9, but don't raise your hopes too high, because currently it's not nearly as refined and efficient as Microsoft's IntelliSense.

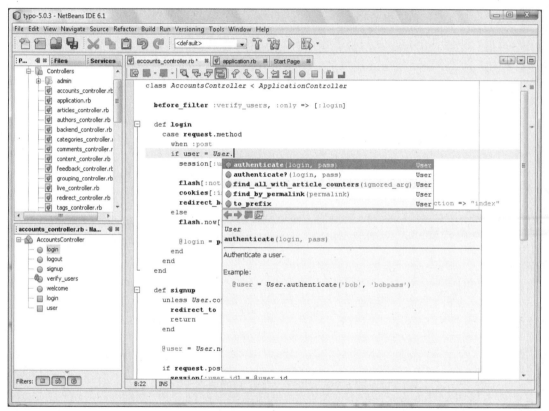

Figure 1-9

Aptana Studio and RadRails

Aptana RadRails is an award-winning open source plugin for Eclipse-based IDEs. It is available as a plugin for Eclipse and can also be installed from within the free-of-charge Aptana Studio, the community edition of a commercial IDE (Aptana Studio Pro). Aptana Studio is based on Eclipse, and once you've installed the RadRails plugin, it provides you with a very pleasant working environment, full of useful Rails features. This product is constantly being improved upon, has excellent support from the company, and it's one of the best liked and most used IDEs in the community.

Just like NetBeans, it offers basic support for code completion (see Figure 1-10) and many more features. You can see a feature comparison with NetBeans on Aptana's website (http://www.aptana .com/rails/).

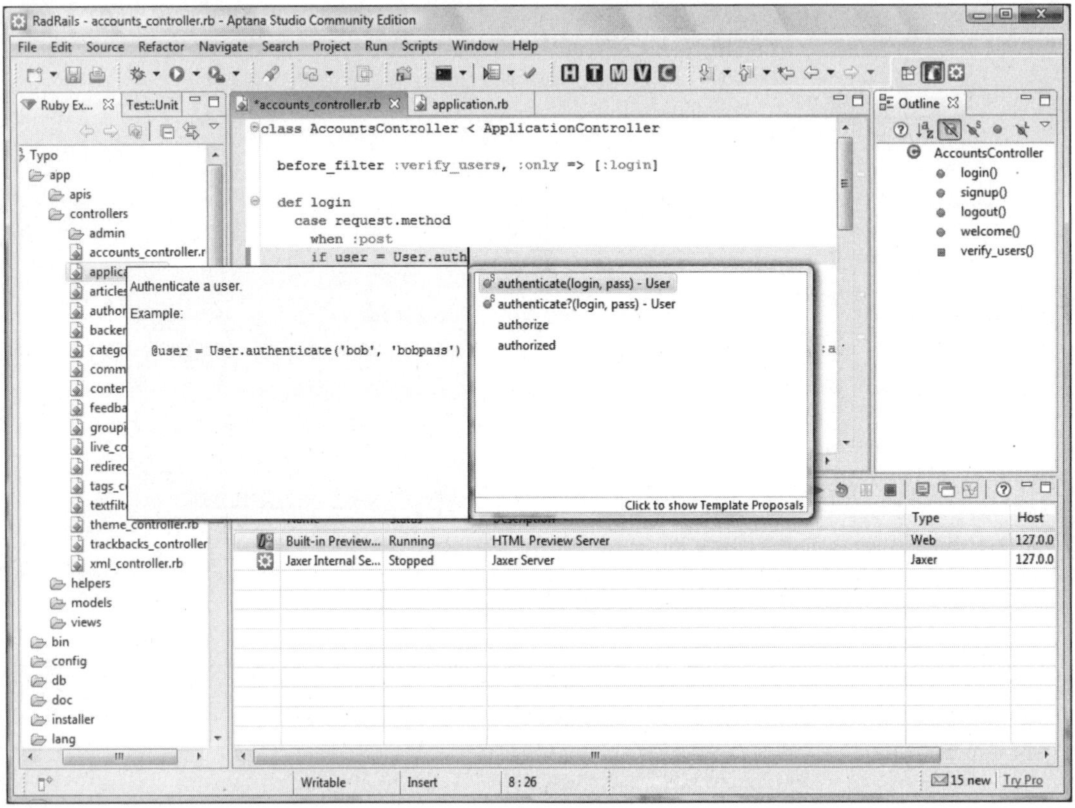

Figure 1-10

Out-of-the-box features aside, its real advantage over NetBeans is that it's part of the Eclipse ecosystem, where many useful plugins are available for Web developers. Of all the editors and IDEs presented here (which work on Windows), Aptana Studio plus the RadRails plugin are definitely one of the most valid choices (and what I use when I'm on a GNU/Linux or Windows workstation).

If you decide to try RadRails, install Aptana Studio (or Eclipse) and then click Install RadRails from the Aptana Start Page.

> ### RubyMine
>
> Currently available as a public preview release, RubyMine is a new Rails commercial IDE by JetBrains. Dubbed by its makers as "The Most Intelligent Ruby IDE," it's probably too early to establish the impact that it will have within the Rails community. The Java-based IDEs mentioned previously are quite smart in their own right and are available for free.
>
> Nevertheless, JetBrains has a reputation for creating great IDEs (it makes IntelliJ IDEA) and RubyMine 1.0 is scheduled to be released in the first quarter of 2009. By the time you read this sidebar, it will most likely have been released, and it may be worth checking out.

Ruby In Steel: I Still Want Visual Studio

Ruby In Steel is not on the list of the most common Rails tools. Still, in a book aimed at Microsoft developers, it's too important to be omitted.

You may spend a week or so trying out several of the recommended IDEs and notice that they all have little in common with the RAD tools you've spent most of your professional life working with. You may feel a bit lost, and would prefer to still work with something along the lines of Visual Studio 2008.

If that describes you, Ruby In Steel may be your best bet. It's not just similar to Visual Studio, it actually is Visual Studio! In fact, Ruby In Steel adds support for Ruby on Rails to Visual Studio 2005 and 2008. As such, this commercial IDE may greatly simplify your transition to the Rails world.

Four downloads are currently available (`http://www.sapphiresteel.com/spip?page=download`):

- ❏ **Ruby In Steel Developer 2005:** A plugin for Visual Studio 2005.
- ❏ **Ruby In Steel Developer 2008:** A plugin for Visual Studio 2008.
- ❏ **Ruby In Steel All-in-One Installer:** A complete package that installs Visual Studio 2008 Shell (integrated mode) with the Ruby In Steel Developer edition. This installer can also optionally setup Ruby, Rails, and MySQL for you.
- ❏ **Ruby In Steel Text Edition:** A lightweight entry level edition that can be installed in Visual Studio 2008 (standard and up) or in the Visual Studio 2008 Shell that is installed by the All-in-One Installer (but not with Visual Studio 2005).

Both versions (Developer and Text Edition) have a very fast debugger called "'Cylon" and provide support for IntelliSense (as shown in Figure 1-11). The Developer edition also features a Visual Rails WorkBench for drag-and-drop client-side design.

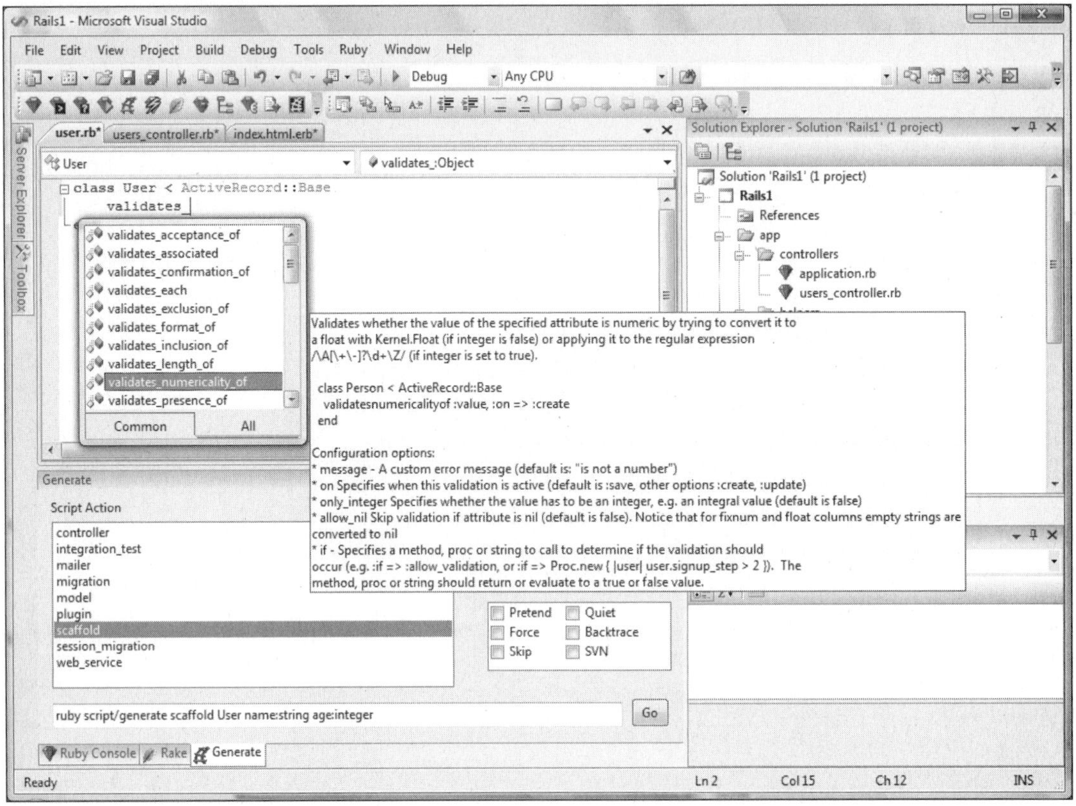

Figure 1-11

Ruby In Steel Developer (version 1.3) currently costs $199, and Ruby In Steel Text Edition is sold by Sapphire In Steel for $49. The trial versions will permit you to use them free of charge for up to 60 days. You may not be fond of Visual Studio in the context of Rails, but it's far more likely that you'll enjoy the familiarity of the environment.

Recently the company introduced a free edition known as Ruby In Steel PE 2008, which has most of the useful features offered by the commercial versions, but lacks the integrated debugger (available starting with the Text Edition), auto-expanding of code snippets, and technical support. Though not as useful as the commercial versions, it is still a good starting point nevertheless. You can find it online at `http://www.sapphiresteel.com/Ruby-In-Steel-New-Free-Edition`.

A fourth edition, Ruby In Steel IronRuby Edition — for Microsoft's implementation of Ruby on the Dynamic Language Runtime (DLR) — is free and currently in Alpha. I don't recommend that you install the Alpha version at this stage because neither IronRuby nor its VS plugin are currently suitable for developing Rails applications. This will probably change fast though, so feel free to check IronRuby's progress periodically at `http://www.ironruby.net`.

Spend some time exploring these tools; it's important to find the editor/IDE that you're most comfortable with. No matter what you choose, you'll be able to follow the rest of the book with ease.

Whetting Your Appetite

A "Getting Started" chapter would not be complete without an example to show you how quickly applications can be prototyped thanks to Rails. The aim of this section is truly to "whet your appetite" as opposed to provide extensive explanations of each step. In Chapter 5, after covering the Ruby language in Chapters 3 and 4, you'll create a more complex Web application and everything will be explained in detail. Here I'm going to provide you with a sneak preview. After all, Rails became so popular thanks also to its ability to create entire applications with just a few commands.

Begin by creating a Rails project that can hold your friends' addresses. From within a directory of your choice (for example, `c:\projects`), use the command prompt to run the following commands:

```
rails addressbook
cd addressbook
```

This generates an `addressbook` directory that contains the skeleton of your Rails application, and the second instruction makes it the current directory in your prompt.

This being Rails, you'll use a table within a database to store the data. This table will need fields like the person's name, address, phone number, and perhaps email and blog/site URL.

You can specify those fields and their data types thanks to the so-called `scaffold` generator, as follows:

```
ruby script/generate scaffold person name:string address:string phone:string
 email:string blog:string
```

This will generate a model, controller, and a series of view templates required to provide you with a basic application for performing CRUD operations.

Before you can see what it looks like, you will need to create a development database for the application as well as apply the table definition stored by scaffold in a migration file. The two tasks are achieved by a single command:

```
C:\projects\addressbook> rake db:migrate
(in C:/projects/addressbook)
==  CreatePeople: migrating ======================================================
— create_table(:people)
   -> 0.0660s
==  CreatePeople: migrated (0.0680s) =============================================
```

By convention the development database will be `db/development.sqlite3`; you didn't have to specify that nor provide a connection string. Also note how Rails is smart enough to figure out that a person's data should be stored in a `people` table (which is correctly pluralized).

Now that the database is taken care of, start the Web server:

```
ruby script/server
```

The Windows firewall may ask you to unblock the server, which you should agree to.

Point your browser to `http://localhost:3000/people` and you should see an interface for listing, creating, editing, and deleting entries in your address book. This also incidentally demonstrates Rails' cleverness in handling multiple versus singular terms, because the URL for the application is `http://localhost:3000/people` (where we'd expect to see a list of people). It's remarkable that no code was written to achieve all this.

Would you like to add validations to make the name and address mandatory? And how about ensuring that there are no duplicated names? Just add the following two highlighted lines within your `person.rb` model in the `app/models` directory:

```
class Person < ActiveRecord::Base
    validates_presence_of :name, :address
    validates_uniqueness_of :name
end
```

You now have a fully functioning, database-driven Rails Web application that has complete CRUD functionality. Into the bargain the application validates your input, checking that you have put in a name and address and checking that there are no duplicates (with nice friendly error messages if you get it wrong, as shown in Figure 1-12).

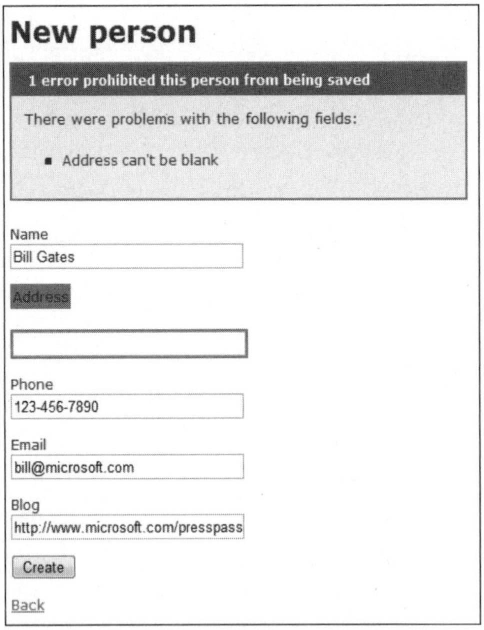

Figure 1-12

Summary

This first chapter provided a general introduction and overview of Ruby on Rails, highlighting part of its story, philosophy, and relevance to the current Web development world. Step-by-step instructions to set up a complete development environment as well as a quick glance at common editors completed the chapter.

Chapter 2 debunks common misconceptions, explores the concepts behind MVC, takes a closer look at the philosophical principles embraced by Rails, and finally, provides a macroscopic analysis of the differences between this and the ASP.NET world.

Understanding Rails

What sets this framework apart from all of the others is the preference for convention over configuration making applications easier to develop and understand.

— *Sam Ruby, Apache Software Foundation, Board of Directors*

After reading the first chapter you should have a clear mental picture of what Rails is. Unless you encountered unforeseen issues, you should also have your environment properly set up with Ruby, Rails 2.2.2, Mongrel, and SQLite3 with its Ruby bindings.

If you are experiencing difficulties while setting up your environment, feel free to ask for help in the p2p.wrox.com *forum for this book. I'll be glad to help you get started.*

This chapter delves further into the framework to provide you with more details and a better understanding of its main components and philosophies. Before diving in, though, some common misconceptions about Rails need to be debunked.

Months after I first wrote this chapter, David published a list of Rails Myths. You might consider reading them online at http://www.loudthinking.com/posts/29-the-rails-myths *in addition to the ones presented here. This note, of course, was added in during the chapter review phase.*

Misconceptions about Rails

When a new technology hits the spotlight, a lot people start talking about it. It's a given that not all of them are going to be fully aware of the subject, and new myths and misconceptions will inevitably spring forth. With Rails' exponential success and big promises of easier Web development, this phenomenon is particularly accelerated. In the past four years, all sorts of misinformed comments about Rails have popped up. The next few sections focus on some of the most common ones, but also on those that are very much worth clarifying from the get-go.

You Don't Have to Be a Programmer

Rails developers are often enthusiastic about their framework of choice. The fact that they like to stress how easy and productive Rails is, is very understandable given that programming in Rails is a joy and probably considered (by these developers) much easier and better than anything else they've tried before. In truth, to initially get started with Rails you don't really need to be an expert on how the Web works, nor proficient in SQL, HTML, or JavaScript. Rails takes care of a lot of small details for you.

The notion that you don't have to be a programmer to write Web applications with Rails, however, is false. All but the most trivial applications require a good dose of programming skills and design choices.

When you create a Rails application, one of the first tasks is to define the database structure. You'll have several tools that can help you with this, and you won't have to do it by specifying the SQL code in most cases, but you'll still have to fundamentally decide how the information is going to be stored in the database.

Most of the code that you'll be writing is going to be in Ruby, a full-fledged programming language. All of the most proficient Rails developers are excellent Ruby programmers as well, simply because Ruby is the key to getting the best out of Rails.

In other words, Rails is not a Content Management System (CMS) like DotNetNuke, Community Server by Telligent, or Drupal. Non-programmers are actually much better off with these highly modular CMS applications rather than with Rails, for the simple reason that these don't expect you to be a programmer, whereas Rails definitely does.

Rails makes Web development easier and much more accessible to newcomers, in the same way that programming in C# is more approachable than programming in, say, Assembler. But in both cases, it's still 100% programming.

Rails Is a Silver Bullet

In the famous paper "No Silver Bullet - Essence and Accidents of Software Engineering," Fred Brooks, author of *The Mythical Man-Month* (Addison-Wesley 1975), makes the following claim:

> *"There is no single development, in either technology or in management technique, that by itself promises even one order of magnitude improvement in productivity, in reliability, in simplicity. In this article, I shall try to show why, by examining both the nature of the software problem and the properties of the bullets proposed."*

> — *Fred Brooks*

You should take the time to read No Silver Bullet. You can find it online at `http://www.lips` `.utexas.edu/ee382c-15005/Readings/Readings1/05-Broo87.pdf`.

It is now well established in the software development industry that there are "no silver bullets," an expression that's loosely used today to indicate that no new technology is going to be the final solution to all of the problems of software design and productivity.

Yet Rails is often wrongly considered a silver bullet by some, because it is arguably much more productive than working with .NET or Java. As explained by Brooks in his essay, there are two types of complexities: accidental and essential. The former is caused by us developers and our approach, and the latter is intrinsic to the resolution of the problem.

Rails improves productivity by considerably reducing the accidental complexity, but it can't alter the essential complexity of Web development, hence Rails is no silver bullet and it never will be, no matter how much it improves.

This fact shouldn't concern you though, given that no other technology is going to be a silver bullet either. Rails is one of the best tools available today for aiding developers in managing complexity, but it's still just a tool, and one that doesn't aim at being the ultimate solution for every Web development problem and developer out there. Through this book, you'll understand Rails' strengths and weaknesses, and better evaluate when and if it's the right tool for you.

Rails Is Hard to Deploy

Deployment is the act of moving your Web application from your development machine to a production one, where it becomes accessible to your customers through their browser. Deploying Rails applications today is a fairly straightforward process. Several well-known configurations and a series of useful tools are available (for example, Capistrano) to help you out in the process. Many hosting companies have also heavily invested in improving their support for Rails and in providing easy "upload and go" solutions.

Admittedly in the past, especially before `mod_rails` for Apache was released in 2008, the experience of deploying Rails applications wasn't as pleasant as it was for the ubiquitous PHP. The most common solution was the adoption of a cluster of Mongrel instances, proxy balanced by a Web server like Apache. This configuration is not rocket science, and it's still the favorite one by many large sites, but it requires more configuration fiddling than some would like to do. This option also implies, in most cases, the use of a Virtual Private Server (VPS) or dedicated hosting solution, both of which are more expensive and require more attention than a shared hosting arrangement.

Today, the number of useful tools and hosting options has improved in number and quality, and there is no reason to believe in the myth that deploying Rails applications is hard. Chapter 11 guides you through some of the deployment tools and configurations, including hosting on Windows servers, and you'll realize how deploying Rails applications is generally not much more difficult than developing them.

Rails Doesn't Scale

To borrow an expression from Mark Twain, reports of Rails' scalability problems have been greatly exaggerated. One of the greatest myths surrounding Ruby on Rails is the claim that it doesn't scale. Whenever a large site written in Rails is having troubles (for example, like `twitter.com` did in 2008), misinformed pundits tend to immediately identify Rails as the culprit.

The reality is that there is nothing in Ruby or in Rails that makes them inherently non-scalable. Au contraire, Rails has a "share nothing" architecture, which allows you to plug in additional hardware with little extra configuration, as long as the data persistence mechanism adopted (for example, your database server) allows you to scale.

Scalability often has little to do with the given language or framework, and everything to do with the architecture and design choices made for the whole application stack.

The misconception that Rails doesn't scale probably originated due to a couple of existing issues surrounding Rails. First, the current main Ruby implementation is not fast. It is generally considered one of the slowest, even among other interpreted languages. Second, Ruby's adoption of green threads and ActiveRecord's historical lack of thread safety implies that Rails' concurrency support and ability to take advantage of multiple processors is limited. As explained in Chapter 4, several Ruby implementations exist with the aim, among others, to solve Ruby's performance issues. Conversely, Rails' performances have been improving with each new release.

> *ActiveRecord is currently thread safe; however, the C implementation of Ruby still uses threads that are not native to the operating system.*

The fact that Ruby is not as fast as C# — and even assuming that a Rails app is much slower than an equivalent one written in ASP.NET — doesn't imply that Rails doesn't scale. It only tells us that more hardware is required to handle a comparably large amount of Web traffic. You also need to keep in mind that often the real bottlenecks are elsewhere, and having a fast framework and language won't do you much good if, for example, caching and database optimization are not fine tuned.

Chapter 11 has further considerations on scaling but, for the time being, don't be too concerned about this aspect: many large sites employ Rails and are able to serve millions of requests on relatively inexpensive hardware.

Understanding MVC

The MVC architectural pattern is one of the most well-known and adopted patterns in the history of software engineering. When Trygve Reenskaug, a Norwegian computer scientist, first described it back in 1979, it aimed at favoring the development and maintainability of Smalltalk GUI applications by a clear division of business logic and presentation in three distinct types of components: the model, the view, and the controller.

> *You can find the original and revised documents describing the pattern online at* `http://heim.ifi.uio.no/~trygver/themes/mvc/mvc-index.html`.

The idea was general enough to be applied in any context that involved some form of user interaction. Thirty years later, the same architecture is in fact widely adopted for Web development. The monolithic approach taken by many in the early days of the Web was a regression over an older but well-proven pattern, especially if you consider that MVC is a particularly fitting abstraction of the underlying architecture provided by the Web. Although it's not the only valid option available, it is indisputably one of the most successful and, above all, the one chosen by the Rails framework.

Entire books could be written on the subject and some may like to indulge in sterile discussions about the purity and fidelity of the various MVC implementations when compared to the original idea. But this won't serve any concrete purpose and will not help you create better Rails applications. This section, therefore, concentrates on the MVC pattern as implemented by Rails.

Overview of the Architectural Pattern

As mentioned in the previous chapter, the model represents the data and the rules that guarantee the validity of the persisted data. The view handles the generation of the user interface, and the controller coordinates the application. It communicates with the model to retrieve and store data, while prompting the users with the right view based on their interaction with the Web application.

The real strength of the paradigm resides in the harmony of these three components, which is entirely handled by Rails for you, as long as you follow its sensible conventions. This facilitates development, testing, and maintenance, because you are able to focus on one component at a time. It also helps to separate the roles and responsibilities among the MVC components, clarifying what types of code belong where, as well as enabling developers to focus on the specific purpose of the code.

If you're not already familiar with the MVC architecture, the previous description may appear to be rather abstract, so let's move on to an example of the request/response life cycle as seen through the eyes of MVC. Figure 2-1 provides a high-level illustration of this process.

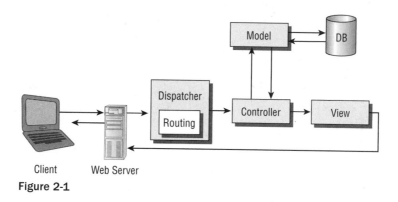

Figure 2-1

1. The user issues a request through his browser at the URL: `http://example.com/products/show/42`

Beautiful URLs

As you learn more about Rails, you'll realize how beautiful URLs are characteristic of Rails applications. You won't see the following:

`http://example.com/main.asp?type=product&action=show&id=42`

or similarly ugly query strings very often in the Rails world.

The issue of clean and beautiful URLs is not limited to aesthetics and Search Engine Optimization (SEO), but becomes a vital component of the application particularly when defining RESTful ones (which is a highly recommended style for CRUD-based applications) as explained in Chapters 5, 6, and 10.

---

2. The Web Server forwards the request for a dynamic page to Rails' dispatcher.

3. Rails' dispatcher invokes the routing component on the URL to determine what controller and *action* (Rails' speak for a public controller method) should handle the request. Routing uses a series of sensible conventions (configurable in `config/routes.rb` within a Rails application) to determine this information. By default, the `/controller/action/id` pattern applies; therefore, unless otherwise specified, the router determines that the request should be handled by the `show` action of the `Products` controller, using `id` 42 as a parameter.

4. The dispatcher loads the proper Ruby file for the controller at hand (`app/controllers/products_controller.rb`) and creates an instance of the controller class (`ProductsController`).

5. The `Products` controller's `show` action is called. This action typically interacts with the model layer by calling one or more methods of the `Product` model (note the singular form of the identifier).

6. The model translates the Ruby code into SQL and executes the query in order to retrieve the record with `id` 42 from the proper table (`products`) in the database. The information for the product is then returned to the controller, which stores it in an instance variable that will be accessible from the view.

7. The controller invokes the rendering of the proper view, which typically assembles an HTML template with the product information passed on by the controller.

8. The Web server uses this data to formulate a proper HTTP response to send to the user's browser.

9. Lastly, the user is presented with the page requested.

Of course many details are omitted from this simplified description, but this should suffice to provide you with an initial illustration of how model, view, and controller interact.

> *You may have noticed that despite the acronym MVC, the model, view, and controller don't work in that sequential order.*

As you can see, each of these three components has a specific set of responsibilities and Rails handles their coordination and cooperation automatically for you. You might also notice that Rails makes several assumptions along the way. For instance, as long as you have created a `Product` model, Rails knows by convention how to find the actual table in the database (the table `products`, unless otherwise specified). The Model-View-Controller set of layers combined with good conventions are crucial to Rails' incredible productivity.

Rails doesn't simply promote the MVC pattern, it actually enforces it from the moment you generate an application, creating empty folders for you that are ready to contain models, controllers, and each of the several templates that are part of the view layer.

Contrary to what the fashion industry would like you to believe, you should have "fat models." Conversely, you should aim to code "skinny controllers" and "dumb views." Models should do the heavy lifting as much as possible. Controllers should be thin and contain the bare essentials required to coordinate the action. And finally, views shouldn't house any but the most trivial business logic required to present the contents (for example, looping through a collection of objects that need to be presented).

Defining Models

In a typical Rails application, each model is a Ruby class that represents a table in the database. Rails provides a useful abstraction that enables you to think in terms of concepts and business objects, rather than tables and rows. To accomplish this goal, Rails employs ActiveRecord, an easy-to-use Object-Relational Mapper (ORM), which was briefly introduced in the previous chapter.

ActiveRecord is a powerful abstraction that greatly simplifies the development process. As an ORM, ActiveRecord maps a model to a table, the columns of the table to the model attributes, and the records within a table to instances of the corresponding model.

> *Martin Fowler described the Active Record ORM pattern as follows: "An object that wraps a row in a database table or view, encapsulates the database access, and adds domain logic on that data."*

One characteristic of ActiveRecord is that it works by making assumptions. Unless you need to over-write these assumptions, ActiveRecord won't require any configuration. This is in stark contrast with some other ORMs from the .NET and Java worlds, where the configuration is often performed within XML files, which is quite a tedious and time-consuming task.

When you create a `Product` model, ActiveRecord will automatically assume that it represents the table `products` in the database. You'll only have to specify otherwise if `Product` needs map to a different table, and even then this is done in Ruby within the model class with a single line of code: `set_table_name "myprodtable."`

ActiveRecord really simplifies working with databases. It provides a series of useful methods for querying tables, without having to specify any SQL code (in most cases), making basic CRUD (Create, Read, Update, and Delete) operations a breeze. ActiveRecord also handles the relationships between models and even validates the data, ensuring the correctness of the persisted data and disallowing the storage of information that doesn't respect the business rules that you've defined.

With a single line it's possible to retrieve the `product` with `id` 42 (to re-use the example mentioned previously) by running:

```
Product.find(42)
```

Behind the scenes, the `find` method searches for the product by issuing the query `SELECT * FROM "products" WHERE ("products"."id" = 42)`. If the product exists, an instance of the `Product` class is returned. This contains the information you are looking for. Often Rails developers are particularly fond of the notion of using Ruby, a single language, for all or at least most of their application. Therefore, minimizing the amount of SQL that needs to be written is seen as a good thing.

Similarly, in this hypothetical scenario, it's possible to obtain a list of all products that are no longer in stock, by running:

```
Product.find_all_by_quantity(0)
```

ActiveRecord is very flexible when it comes to providing you with finder methods to query the database. Likewise, assuming that the products table has name, quantity, and price columns, you can create a new record just as easily by running:

```
Product.create(:name => "iPhone", :quantity => 2000, :price => "199.99")
```

> *For the moment, don't worry about Ruby's syntax for hashes; it is thoroughly explained in Chapter 3.*

And of course, ActiveRecord has analogous methods for updating and deleting records, and even for specifying entirely customized SQL statements.

These methods are database agnostic, given that ActiveRecord uses the adapter for the database in use, in order to translate and execute the code into the specific SQL syntax requested. Aside from simplifying the development process, this implies that it's possible to switch from one database to another without changing any of the application's code.

In practice, there are more considerations to be made, due to the different levels of support for ActiveRecord's features provided by each adapter. But overall, a good code base can be switched from one adapter to another with minimal hassle.

Working with ActiveRecord models lets you focus on the domain logic without worrying about how the information is displayed. In fact, a model is entirely independent from the view and controller layers. The process of developing a model in Rails requires that you determine its name, its attributes/fields, and its associations with other model objects. It also requires that you define validations to ensure the validity of your data, and the definition of custom methods that encapsulate your domain logic and add the behavior you need to the model.

The model generator, scaffold generator, and migrations are all useful tools provided by Rails to facilitate this process by generating a skeleton and letting you fill the blanks to phase out the tedious work. You should take care to pay a lot of attention when developing your models, given that they'll end up being the heart of your applications.

What's Scaffolding?

It is worth spending a few moments to introduce this tool called scaffold generator, which aids you in creating Rails applications.

The scaffold generator is a tool that allows the automatic generation of a basic Web application for performing CRUD operations (as seen in Chapter 1). As a developer all you have to do is provide the specification, by indicating the name of the model (which in turn defines the name of the actual table in the database), its fields, and their data types.

Scaffolding takes care of the rest by generating the proper migration files (which define the table definition in Ruby code), the model, controller, view templates, routes, skeletons for the tests, and so on. The end result is the creation of a basic Web interface that can be used to insert, show, modify, and delete records from the database. All this without writing a single line of code.

Scaffolding is useful for rapid prototyping and for when you want to have a solid base upon which to customize and build more powerful features. It usually wows beginners because it gets you up and running in no time and the generated code is easy to understand and modify.

One of the easiest ways to understand how Rails applications work is in fact to analyze how the code generated by scaffolding works. When you create an actual application in Chapter 5, you'll take this approach and start by generating the basic components of the application by scaffolding.

Chapters 5, 6, and 7 provide you with more insight into model development and ActiveRecord.

Designing Views

The view represents the user interface. Of the three roles, the view is the one that requires the least amount of programming, and is in fact often delegated to the Web designer. It is important, though, not to underestimate the significance of this component in Rails applications.

The interface defines your software in the eyes of the user, given that it's the only layer the user will interact with directly. It is therefore your specification and a lot of attention should be paid to ensuring that the user is able to retrieve and store the information through a well-designed, intuitive, and logical UI.

> *A classic book on the subject of usability and Web design UI is Steve Krug's,* Don't Make Me Think! A Common Sense Approach to Web Usability *(Que 2000). This title is highly recommended for programmers and designers alike.*

The view layer renders the information to the user by assembling templates with the actual dynamic content provided by the action within the controller, which in turn obtains it (in most cases) directly from the model.

Rails offers three types of templates:

- ❏ **ERb:** Templates that embed Ruby code similarly to how it's done in ASP classic, PHP, or JSP. ERb templates aren't just used to generate XHTML, but can be employed so as to render emails, CSV files, and so on.

- ❏ **XML Builder:** Templates that are used to generate XML documents from Ruby code. They are often employed when creating Atom and RSS feeds.

- ❏ **RJS:** Templates employed to generate JavaScript from Ruby code. These, coupled with Rails' inclusion of the Prototype framework and the script.aculo.us library, enable you to create Ajax-powered user interfaces.

> **The view is not the spot to place application logic, so the presence of Ruby code should be kept to a minimum and strictly limited to what's required in order to properly present the data.**

ERb templates are the ones that you'll use most often, but the other two will be illustrated as well, particularly in Chapter 9.

The following code is an example of an ERb template (produced by the scaffold generator). The Ruby code is contained within the <% and %> tags:

```
<h1>Listing products</h1>

<table>
<tr>
<th>Name</th>
<th>Price</th>
<th>Quantity</th>
<th>Info</th>
</tr>
```

```
<% for product in @products %>
<tr>
<td><%=h product.name %></td>
<td><%=h product.price %></td>
<td><%=h product.quantity %></td>
<td><%=h product.info %></td>
<td><%= link_to 'Show', product %></td>
<td><%= link_to 'Edit', edit_product_path(product) %></td>
<td><%= link_to 'Destroy', product, :confirm => 'Are you sure?', :method => :delete
%></td>
</tr>
<% end %>
</table>

<br />
```

```
<%= link_to 'New product', new_product_path %>
```

Chapter 5 analyzes the code generated by scaffold in detail, so don't worry if the code doesn't make much sense to you at this stage. I only provided it as an example to help you picture what embedding Ruby code into XHTML can look like.

Ruby Template Engines

ERb is not the only Ruby template engine. There are in fact more than a dozen available choices that you can adopt in your Rails applications.

ERb is the default, mostly because it gets the job done and ships with Ruby, so no external dependencies are required. Two common alternatives are Erubis and Haml.

Erubis (`http://www.kuwata-lab.com/erubis/`) is an ERb-like engine whose main selling point is its rendering speed. According to a few benchmarks available on the official site, Erubis can be several times faster than ERb, a desirable trait for Web applications.

Haml (`http://haml.hamptoncatlin.com/`), on the other hand, is often adopted for its compact and beautiful style, which makes it very different (in a good way) from ERb. It's not everyone's cup of tea, but many developers and designers have expressed enthusiasm toward it.

Managing Controllers

Controllers coordinate the application. The importance of the controller in a Rails application can't be overstated, given that the interaction between the user and the view and model layers is controlled and coordinated by the controller.

A controller receives requests from the client, determines which action needs to handle the request, interacts with models to retrieve and store data in the database, and then invokes the view layer so as to render the results back to the user.

The areas of responsibility for the controller are far reaching and not limited to this; in fact, they include processing parameters, redirecting, handling errors, providing helpers for the view, managing caching for drastically improving performance, sessions for maintaining the user status as they inter-act with the application, and many other small errands that are further explained, predominantly, in Chapters 5 and 8.

A non-trivial Rails application has several controllers, each dedicated to a given area of functionality. For instance, an online store may have controllers for handling user accounts, displaying products, managing the inventory, and so on.

A controller Products for performing CRUD operations could have the following structure:

```ruby
class ProductsController<ApplicationController
def index
    # code for showing a list of products
end


def show
    # code for showing a given product
end


def new
    # code for the empty form for a new product
end


def edit
    # code for the editing form for a given product
end


def create
    # code for the creation of a new product
end


def update
    # code for updating a given product

End


def destroy
    # code for deleting a given product
end
end
```

Each of the public methods defined in the controller represents an action. When the routing component determines that the given request corresponds to a certain action, the Ruby code for that action is executed. From the controller, instance variables used by the view layer are set and the view itself is invoked, either explicitly or implicitly (in that case by a convention based on the action name).

Rails' Standard Packages

When you installed Rails in the first chapter, aside from the main Rails gem, several other gems were installed. All of these libraries together compose what is considered to be the Ruby on Rails framework. They are:

❑ **ActiveRecord:** The M of the MVC triad, which provides Object-Relational mapping for several RDBMS, as previously discussed.

❑ **ActionPack:** A very large library that handles the whole request-response cycle. It is composed of the **ActionController** library (the C of MVC) and the **ActionView** library (the V of MVC).

❑ **ActionMailer:** A small framework that adds email support to Rails applications. This can be used whenever the need for email notification arises, like in the case of sign ups or forgotten password requests. It greatly simplifies the process of sending out emails from Rails, and as such, can also be used to set up an admin notification every time the Rails application raises an exception.

❑ **ActiveSupport:** A series of utility classes and Ruby's Standard Library extensions used by Rails and in Rails applications.

❑ **ActiveResource:** A library that connects business objects to Representational State Transfer (REST) Web Services. Chapter 10 covers this subject in greater detail.

Understanding Rails' Main Principles

The Rails culture has adopted many of the good principles that derive from the world of Extreme Programming (XP) and the Agile movement in general. For example, though Rails doesn't force you to adopt Test-Driven Development (TDD), this is a popular practice in the Rails community. Also, Rails integrates, simplifies, and promotes testing. As briefly mentioned in the first chapter, YAGNI (You Ain't Gonna Need It) is also a principle that's been largely adopted by the community. There are, however, two mantras that characterize the Rails way of doing development above anything else: "Convention over Configuration" and "Don't Repeat Yourself (DRY)."

It can be said that Rails' strength comes from three components that fit together organically: the framework itself, its Agile philosophies and principles, and finally, the Ruby language. These Agile mantras are so important that it's worth spending some time to analyze them further; the next chapter takes care of providing you with all the essential Ruby skills that you'll need to understand and write Rails applications.

Convention over Configuration

Back in 2004, before Rails had garnered the popularity that it enjoys today, a nine-minute demo by David Heinemeier Hansson was recorded and placed online. The application he showcased was quick and simple: a bare-bones blog. Today, a second version (for Rails 1.0) is available online at http://rubyonrails.org/screencasts and, as you'll see for yourself if you decide to watch it for historical purposes (it's only 15 minutes long), there are no advanced features and even a few "whoops" here and there. Yet that seemingly plain video had a huge impact in contributing to Rails' popularity.

A third version covering Rails 2 has been recently released at the same URL.

> ## Extreme Programming vs. Agile Programming
>
> Agile development promotes iterations and incremental development, collaboration and adaptability to change. And so does XP. When talking about Rails' philosophy it's not unusual to see these two terms pop up almost interchangeably. So unless you're already familiar with the Agile world, you may be wondering what the difference between the two is.
>
> Extreme Programming is a specific Agile method that predates the Agile Manifesto. Agile is an umbrella term that covers several, somewhat similar, lightweight methodologies, which include, among others, the very popular Extreme Programming and Scrum.
>
> XP is by far the most applied Agile method and the one that includes software engineering practices such as Simple Design, Pair Programming, TDD, Continuous Integration, Refactoring, Coding Standards, and Collective Ownership. As a matter of fact, XP's engineering practices are often adopted within the context of Scrum, which acts in those cases as a management wrapper for XP.
>
> It's also worth noting the emergence of the so-called post-Agilism, which I believe represents several Rails programmers. Post-Agile developers are well aware of Agile methodologies, but don't identify themselves with them. They haven't reverted back to a waterfall, heavily processed approach, but rather try to apply the good, fundamental Agile principles to other development techniques as they fit, doing what works best for them, without being dogmatic about the approach taken. To learn more about post-Agilism, you can read the FAQ at `http://www.kohl.ca/blog/archives/000184.html`.

The reason for its success was that in its simplicity, the video gave away the fact that Rails was extremely productive. It was more than just productive; it was magical. The application was only 58 lines (in the case of the video from 2005, referenced previously). In virtually no time at all, there it was, a working, albeit basic, Web log engine.

Admittedly, part of the magic was due to the fact that David employed dynamic scaffolding, a feature that allowed him to add columns to the tables and see the forms in the browser automatically update to accommodate the new columns. But from Rails 2.0 onward, this feature no longer exists. When it was included, it made for some great demos, but was usually not suitable and flexible at all for real-world projects. At the time, even the normal (static) scaffold wasn't a particularly good starting point for real applications, so when they wrote the new one, they got rid of dynamic scaffolding as well.

The point was that Rails brought productivity to a whole new level with its lack of configuration. David didn't have to write a connection string that was a few hundred characters long, he didn't have to use an IDE to pre-generate a lot of code for him, and he didn't have to specify the mapping between tables and the Ruby code anywhere either. He was just a guy with a text editor (TextMate), a command line, and a browser.

The only piece of configuration required was to add his password for the database to a file (`config/database.yml`) that was generated by the `rails` command at the beginning. In the video you can hear David point this out: "Look at all the things I'm not doing, look at all the configuration I'm not writing."

Developers (and their managers) love to hear that a new framework will make them much more productive. When the productivity claim is found to be true, as intuitively shown by David's demo, the effort and time investment required to learn a new framework becomes both justified and welcomed.

Rails tackles the problem of increasing productivity from several angles. But at its heart, the philosophical principle of favoring Convention over Configuration is fundamental to Rails' productivity and hassle-free development.

Frameworks are supposed to make your life easier, allow you to write better and more maintainable code, and improve your productivity by letting you focus on the logic of your application rather than repetitive, dreary details (for example, configuration). Far too many frameworks fall short of this goal, because they don't endorse the principle of Convention over Configuration nearly enough.

Frameworks need to have a set of sensible defaults straight "out of the box," and they should force you to resort to configuration only when strictly necessary, because their defaults are not suitable for your specific project requirements. When naming conventions fail, the framework should be flexible enough to allow you to add in your own configuration.

Ruby on Rails empowers developers to get started quickly by just learning a few naming conventions and, as they become more experienced, allows them to overrule these conventions through configuration for unconventional scenarios and edge cases. As such, it becomes particularly productive if you follow its conventions whenever possible, in order to reduce the amount of configuration required. In other words, try not to contradict Rails.

> If you think about it, Convention over Configuration is a universally good software design paradigm. If you're defining an API, library, or framework of your own, always provide defaults that make sense and allow these conventions to be easily overwritten, if the need arises.

As mentioned a few times now, a model's identifier should be singular (for example, `Project`), and in turn it is automatically mapped to a table of the same name, only pluralized (for example, `projects`). Each table is supposed to have an auto-incrementing field called `id`. Associations between models assume that the naming convention for foreign keys is adopted. For example, the foreign key in the `tasks` table referencing the `projects` table will be called by convention `project_id`. You get the idea.

Understanding how ActiveRecord works is one of the most direct ways of experiencing the power of Convention over Configuration, so pay close attention to Chapters 5, 6, and 7. Rest assured that naming and other useful conventions, which you'll need to know, are explained throughout this book as they are introduced.

Don't Repeat Yourself (DRY)

Try to think about any software project you've worked on in the past. How long did it take before you had to go back and start making changes, essentially switching to maintenance mode programming? Contrary to popular belief, maintenance programming doesn't start after the first release is out. It usually begins much sooner: a few minutes after you wrote that initial line of code.

Programming is maintenance programming, even when you start with a fresh new project. The reality of this fact can be easily verified empirically if you sit down and try to come up with any program or Web application, no matter how small. You will start defining a few classes, some methods, and then you'll realize that something is not working right. You'll go back and make changes to the code to fix the bug that you just introduced a few minutes earlier. After a while you'll realize that certain portions of the code can be refactored and improved, and there you are, half an hour after you started writing your program, already doing maintenance work.

Maintenance and change can't be avoided, so why not embrace them? That's what Rails does by incarnating and promoting the Don't Repeat Yourself (DRY) principle, and the direct consequence is better applications that can easily accommodate change. DRY is about removing duplication and encouraging loosely coupled designs by ensuring that the ties between unrelated layers of an application are kept to a minimum (a concept sometimes referred to as *orthogonality*). The DRY principle promotes the localization of change, so that whenever requirements change (and that will definitely happen) the developer can respond to them by simply changing the application in one place rather than several.

What this means in practice is that you shouldn't repeat your code in several places, but rather find a single authoritative location in the application. For example, if several pages share a common element, you could "copy and paste" the code for that element onto each page, but if you ever need to change it, you'd have to go back to edit each applicable page. That's not DRY that's a mess. The proper way to do it would be to define a reusable component (for instance, using what Rails calls *partials*) that can be included on the desired pages, so that if you need to change it, you can do so in just one spot.

And the principle of not repeating yourself extends far beyond your application's code. A software project will typically have code, a database schema, tests, and documentation. If your coding style and the framework that you use don't endorse the DRY principle, you will find yourself juggling each of the components of your system, in an attempt to keep them all in sync.

Rails offers you plenty of tools to prevent this from happening. The MVC architecture neatly separates concerns; ActiveRecord's Object-Relational mapping creates a correspondence between your business and database objects; the migration system allows you to keep the database schema and its evolution under control; excellent testing capabilities are available "out of the box" so that you can have more confidence in accommodating changes; and the documentation can be automatically generated from the code, hence, if you change the code and its comments, this is automatically reflected when you generate the documentation.

When developing Rails applications you should always keep the DRY mantra in mind. Thankfully, Rails was designed from the ground up in a manner that allows you to espouse these philosophies. As you gain more knowledge about the framework, you'll realize how many options are available to keep things DRY and avoid the need to write similar code more than once.

That said, remember that the best tool against coupling and duplication is your brain. No matter how good a framework is at promoting superior development practices (and Rails is definitely excellent in this regard), there is no substitute for the developer actively pursuing the application of the principles illustrated to obtain productivity and code that is maintainable and easy to change.

Rails vs. ASP.NET vs. ASP.NET MVC

If you are reading this book, you're probably an ASP.NET developer. However, even if you aren't, the Rails versus ASP.NET diatribe that's raised every so often in online forums and groups is worth addressing before wrapping up this "philosophical" chapter.

The "versus" question is often asked by developers who'd like to learn the "next big thing" in Web programming, be prepared for the evolution of the job marketplace, or, even more commonly, by programmers who're looking for the best tool for a certain project.

Becoming proficient in a new framework can take at least a few months, so it is understandable that most people don't want to bet "on the wrong horse."

Choices exist that are bound to become more popular and that better suit certain types of projects or development philosophies, just like there are options that are more productive than others. Switching to Rails from an ASP.NET background makes a lot of sense in most cases, so this section will help you to better understand how these two different frameworks compare from a macroscopic perspective.

A 10,000-Foot Comparison

From a technical standpoint Microsoft ASP.NET and Ruby on Rails are very different. They have so little in common that, at a microscopic level, a detailed list of differences would be huge. It is truly comparing apples to oranges; they are both round fruit, just like Rails and ASP.NET are both Web application frameworks, but they don't have too much in common beyond that. Taking into consideration the Rails notions introduced so far, a high-level comparison based on several aspects of the two worlds is going to be the most beneficial.

Albeit very different, whenever the occasional similarity exists between the two, this is pointed out (throughout the book) as Rails concepts are introduced, in order to make them seem less foreign. For instance, the concept of layouts in Rails is very similar to that of MasterPages in ASP.NET. Or again, the controller layer can be intuitively seen as the Rails (loose) equivalent of the Code-Behind model in ASP.NET.

Political Matters

Microsoft ASP.NET is a proprietary solution for Web development, whereas Ruby on Rails is entirely open source and ships with a very liberal license (MIT). Microsoft is slowly embracing openness, but it is far from being able to claim that ASP.NET is open source. ASP.NET works on Windows only, if we exclude the Mono project (http://mono-project.com). Mono allows you to run ASP.NET applications on operating systems like Linux and *BSD, but being a part of Microsoft's implementation, it usually plays the "catch up game" with the latest version that's been released by Microsoft. Rails and Ruby are, on the other hand, both cross-platform.

The implication is that Rails developers tend to opt for open source tools, operating systems, databases, and Web servers, whereas ASP.NET developers will usually employ Visual Studio, Windows, SQL Server, and IIS. They are two different breeds of developers living in different cultures.

The open nature of Rails-based stacks is a strong advantage that shouldn't be ignored when choosing between the two platforms; but it's up to you to decide whether these somewhat "political" considerations matter or are entirely irrelevant.

A very practical implication that comes to mind is that ASP.NET development is tied to Windows and has (with the exception of Mono) a single deployment stack that is centered around IIS. As you will learn in Chapter 11, Rails has many possible deployment stacks, most of which separate the Web server from the application server, giving you a greater deal of flexibility in deciding how the request-response cycle should be handled.

Who Uses What?

ASP.NET has the advantage of being a few years older than Rails, plus the backing of a giant corporation like Microsoft. Despite the David (literally) versus Goliath scenario, Rails is the tool of choice that's favored by most startups and independent Software as a Service (SaaS) vendors, especially in Silicon Valley, which, as we all know, is the biggest startup hub.

Its exponential growth in the marketplace implies that today Rails has even attracted the attention of the corporate world. Its market share will continue to grow, but realistically though, ASP.NET along with Java remain the most widely used solutions in the Enterprise world. In these environments, big projects carried out by large teams of developers still favor ASP.NET over Rails any day.

This has certain implications in the job marketplace. Currently there are far more job ads for ASP.NET developers than there are for Rails ones (at least outside of Silicon Valley). On the other hand, Ruby and Rails skills are very much in demand, given that there are relatively fewer developers than the fierce competition that exists in the .NET world. If you are a manager, please be advised that Rails developers are not hard to find (and visiting `http://WorkingWithRails.com` is a good starting point for finding talents).

The working environments in which these two frameworks are utilized are also very different. It's a good bet that Dilbert-esque scenarios are much more common among ASP.NET corporate jobs than they are in Rails startups or corporate teams that are brave (and smart) enough to adopt Rails.

Learning Curve

Based on experience, it's far easier and faster to teach developers Rails than it is to teach them ASP.NET. The technology is much simpler and more intuitive. The .NET Framework alone is a huge body of concepts and namespaces that heavily affect one's ability to get started quickly.

Try to remove Visual Studio from an ASP.NET developer and then ask him to code with Notepad. He'll probably be unable to do so. A Rails developer, on the other hand, would have no problem using just Notepad. It would be less convenient, but not worth sweating over. I think this speaks volumes about the relative complexity of the two frameworks and their reliance on RAD tools.

Even if you take the frameworks out of the picture, C# and Visual Basic.NET are much more complex to learn than a "programmer friendly" language like Ruby. Anyone who can program in both is bound to confirm this point.

Rails requires only a decent understanding of Ruby and a few specific concepts and conventions. As such, even existing .NET teams can switch over to Rails in a relatively short amount of time. And this book should help you to do just that.

> *Anecdotal evidence is not conclusive, but should help illustrate this point. A couple of years ago in IBM I had three bright students doing an internship. These students had never seen Ruby or Rails code before, so I trained them on both Ruby and Rails, for three days in a row. After that they started working on a project, while I provided them with mentoring support.*

> *They wrote all the code, and after only 10 weeks, they had a complex Ajax-enabled application up and running. Those who saw the application couldn't believe that it had been developed in so little time by a trio of students. And what's more important — you guessed it — they absolutely loved working with Ruby on Rails.*

Performance Considerations

Rails is written in Ruby and as such is interpreted, whereas ASP.NET is compiled. It can't be denied that this difference has repercussions when considering performance. ASP.NET tends to be faster than Rails. Just as C# is a relatively fast programming language, whereas Ruby is a slow one.

This aspect is worth keeping in mind, but not worth getting paranoid about. It only means that if you're ever going to handle very large volumes of traffic with a Rails application, it is plausible to assume that you may need slightly more hardware than if you implemented the same application in ASP.NET.

What's more important though, is that Rails allows you to develop applications faster (and simplify their maintenance) than ASP.NET can. That's your crucial gain. After all, hand-coded Assembler is drastically faster than C#, but that's not a good enough reason to favor it over C# in most contexts. There is a clear trend in the industry and it's that very high-performing, dynamic languages are here to stay.

The Issue with ASP.NET

Beyond language choices and culture diversity, which could certainly be discussed at length, a fundamental issue distinguishes ASP.NET from Rails.

ASP.NET is based on the very bad assumption that Web development should mimic desktop application development as much as possible. But desktop applications and Web applications are fundamentally different.

The act of dragging and dropping controls on WebForms made ASP.NET relatively easy for MFC and Windows Forms programmers, but it was also a terrible decision that has had far-reaching consequences. ASP.NET's evolution has been continually forced to work around that initial mistake.

For instance, it greatly complicated the request-response life cycle and forced a paradigm that is essentially event driven upon Web developers. You drag and drop the control, double-click it, and then proceed to describe what it should do when the associated event is triggered. That's not how the HTTP protocol or the Web naturally works.

That same assumption also led to abominations like the ViewState, in order to store the state of these fancy controls on the client side through a hidden HTML field. ViewState can easily be abused, and accidentally introduce serious problems. Even when Microsoft introduced the ASP.NET Ajax extensions (formerly known as Atlas) in order to inject Ajax functionalities into ASP.NET development, it was forced to do so in a control-centric manner.

Many ASP.NET developers create Ajax-powered applications by essentially dragging and dropping controls within the UpdatePanel, enabling portions of the page to be partially rendered without the need for a postback. That's very different from how the overwhelming majority of other Ajax frameworks work and it's arguably a much less flexible approach. Of course, ASP.NET Ajax provides more than just "ajaxified" controls, but many developers will still probably end up using and abusing the drag-and-drop approach due to its familiarity and ease of use.

If you'd still like the convenience of dragging and dropping controls from within an IDE into an ERb template, you can use the Ruby In Steel IDE described in the first chapter. This offers a Visual Rails Workbench, which enables drag-and-drop design without the negative consequences of ASP.NET server controls.

Rails avoids all these headaches by simply opting not to force an abstract, event-driven, and control-based approach onto developers. Through ERb templates and the information provided by the controller, the view can render HTML which, along with JavaScript and CSS, is all you really need to generate Web pages. No special server controls, a straightforward request-response cycle, and a clean separation of content and presentation through the MVC paradigm greatly simplifies development and has the added bonus of facilitating the testing of each layer. In particular, Unit Testing in Rails is fairly easy, whereas all the complications mentioned previously (which are due to that initial assumption) imply that the same can't be said for ASP.NET. Data access becomes extremely easy too, thanks to ActiveRecord. And there's no need to bind controls to a given DataSet or to follow other approaches that are typical of the desktop development arena.

Rails lets you be "closer to the metal" and gain flexibility without being unnecessarily complicated.

When to Use ASP.NET Instead of Rails

Learning to program in Rails doesn't have to be a religious conversion. In many cases developers realize how much more enjoyable Rails is and prefer to switch from ASP.NET entirely. But that's not always an option. Learning Rails will therefore, in most cases, be the equivalent of adding a useful tool to your toolbox.

Though it's possible to use Rails for just about any project, there are still times when ASP.NET would work fine and be even less problematic than Rails. To distinguish what this sort of case is, you need to learn where ASP.NET has the advantage over Rails:

❑ **Performance:** The performance issue was mentioned earlier. If you need to develop a Web application whose performance is critical, ASP.NET may be the right solution. Just don't be too quick to jump to the conclusion that this applies to your application. The average social networking site, blog engine, Content Management System, or online store is in no way a performance-crucial application. As a matter of fact, these are all areas where Rails would excel.

❑ **Unicode support:** Great progress has been made in the area of internationalization and Unicode support by both Ruby (particularly since the 1.9 development release) and Rails. To be fair, though, these are still far behind what the .NET Framework has to offer. If this topic is critical for the success of your application, you should carefully evaluate whether Rails' current support (including its plugins) satisfies your needs well enough.

❑ **Legacy databases:** Rails' Convention over Configuration approach implies that it really works best when you follow its conventions. If you are dealing with legacy databases that diverge a lot from the standard Rails conventions, you may find yourself "fighting" with Rails and spending far too much time configuring and "convincing" ActiveRecord to work with your data. In instances like these, ASP.NET can be more productive and less of a headache.

❑ **Enterprise features:** Though the number of libraries for Ruby, and plugins for Rails, is constantly growing, large and complex projects that require a lot of integration with an existing Enterprise infrastructure are probably better left to ASP.NET. For example, the .NET transaction model and message queue capabilities are far more advanced than what you can currently find in Ruby-land. Chapter 11 provides a few pointers to articles about Rails and the Enterprise.

ASP.NET MVC and Other .NET Frameworks

Many Web developers have come to appreciate the MVC paradigm thanks to Rails. It shouldn't be too much of a surprise, then, that so many MVC frameworks are inspired by Rails or, in some instances, are even clones of Rails, for languages other than Ruby. The .NET world wasn't immune to this influence either.

MonoRail

Several MVC frameworks are available for .NET, but the most popular open source one comes from the Castle Project. Castle (for short) includes, among other components, MonoRail and ActiveRecord. MonoRail is a clone of ActionPack for .NET. You can think of it as the VC part of the MVC triad. ActiveRecord is, as you would expect, an implementation of the Active Record pattern for the .NET Framework, and covers the M layer of MVC. Castle's ActiveRecord leverages the NHibernate ORM, but it doesn't require XML configuration.

A few .NET developers have expressed enthusiasm toward the combination of MonoRail and ActiveRecord, and opted for this alternative, as opposed to switching to a new language (Ruby) and framework (Ruby on Rails). But many who tried this approach eventually ended up opting for Rails, because it's more polished, robust, and well-documented than its .NET clone. "Why not use the real deal?" is an argument often heard, and many admit that by not using Ruby, these frameworks lose a lot of their appeal.

With this and other Rails inspired projects, you need to take into consideration that they were started later than Rails itself and have received much less attention and time in the limelight. As such, their maturity in the face of real-world projects is usually inferior to that of a well-tested framework with thousands of contributions, like Rails. For example, these frameworks may lack a few generators (one of Rails' killer features) or other particular features (for example, according to the FAQ, the current version of MonoRail doesn't offer support for caching).

That being said, and despite this being a book about Rails, you are absolutely encouraged to try out MonoRail and other .NET alternative frameworks if you are an ASP.NET developer. There is no reason why you couldn't take your knowledge and apply it to both MonoRail and Ruby on Rails. In life, as in programming, it's always worth being open minded and ready to try out possible alternatives.

> In the .NET culture, developers who keep an eye open for a better way, independently from where it's coming from (Microsoft or not) are part of the so called ALT.NET movement. David Laribee coined the term in his original post that you can read at http://laribee.com/blog/2007/04/10/altnet/.

ASP.NET MVC

Following Rails' success even Microsoft took note and decided to come up with the ASP.NET MVC project, which adds an MVC framework that's similar to Rails, on top of ASP.NET, wherein the controller takes the place of the typical postback model.

This is definitely a huge step in the right direction for Microsoft and, if you're an ASP.NET developer, you may really want to try it out. It provides some of Rails' strong selling points, including the ability to delineate beautiful URLs by defining routes in your `Global.asax.cs` file. The same considerations made in the previous section for MonoRail apply to this project too, though, even if it's probably going to become the de facto standard in the .NET world. A lot of Rails' productivity and wow factor is directly related to the fact that the Ruby language is employed. Consequently, ASP.NET MVC applications still feel different and much more verbose than Rails ones (at least until IronRuby will be ready for prime time).

ASP.NET MVC is often considered a clone of Rails, but this is not entirely fair. It's very likely that Microsoft started the project in order to offer to .NET developers the advantages of a framework like Rails. And yes, perhaps it also did it to prevent many .NET developers from switching to Rails. Rails and other open source MVC frameworks heavily inspired Microsoft. But the final product includes bits of Microsoft's own approach to MVC and Web development, and as such it ends up being different enough so as to not feel like one's developing in Rails when using it.

Consider these alternatives, particularly the promising ASP.NET MVC, but please read on and give Rails and Ruby a shot. You may find, as many did before you, that Rails has a unique chemistry, which is hard to duplicate even in very similar frameworks.

Summary

Congratulations, you've reached the end of Rails' Philosophy 101. More seriously, Rails' MVC architecture, its culture, and development philosophies are fundamental parts of the framework and it was worth spending time exploring them further to truly "understand Rails."

Now that you are equipped with enough background information, you can start digging into the Ruby language in the next two chapters, as well as creating a sample Rails application in Chapters 5 and 6.

3

Ruby's Data Types

Ruby is designed to make programmers happy.

— *Yukihiro Matsumoto, Creator of Ruby*

Ruby on Rails lets you create Web applications in Ruby. Working with Rails without a proper understanding of the essentials of the Ruby language is akin to creating ASP.NET applications without possessing any knowledge of .NET-enabled languages. In both cases, the language used in order to work with the framework is a strict prerequisite.

Many beginners try this approach because they're eager to get started with Rails. Unfortunately for them, they end up wasting more time than if they'd picked up the basics of the language first, and then moved on to Rails.

Trying to learn both Ruby and Rails at the same time can work for some, but passing over Ruby altogether is a huge mistake. For this reason, unless you are already well versed in Ruby, it's recommended that you don't skip over this and the next chapter.

What's Ruby?

As briefly discussed in the first chapter, Ruby is a modern object-oriented programming language that was first released by its author, Yukihiro Matsumoto, back in 1995. Despite being older than C#, and just as old as Java, Ruby's recognition outside of Japan has been undeservedly very limited for many years.

Over the past few years, Ruby has been one of the fastest growing languages in the world. Rails made this popularity possible, but as many developers have discovered, Ruby is a language whose value stands on its own. And it's very much worth knowing independently from your interest in Rails.

Ruby is fully object-oriented (everything is an object), but it is also considered multi-paradigm, because it allows for a procedural style (useful for scripts) and has support for several elements that are typical of the functional programming world.

Clearly Ruby has been influenced by many languages, but it can be said that it combines an object model, which is heavily inspired by Smalltalk, with the immediacy, pragmatism, and text processing ability of Perl (which also influenced its syntax), plus the expressive nature of Lisp.

Ruby is often referred to as a scripting language, but what's more important is that it's a very high-level language that's both powerful and concise. It was created with the intention of being programmer-friendly, focused on simplicity and productivity, and as such it is often associated with the principle of least surprise (POLS). This principle implies that Ruby, unlike languages like C++, tends to be less confusing and more predictable for experienced developers (but also for beginners). Ruby code is therefore easy to read and to write, and it features an arguably elegant syntax.

> *If you head over to the official website at* `http://www.ruby-lang.org` *you'll notice that Ruby's tagline is A Programmer's Best Friend. An apt description in my opinion.*

There isn't a universally accepted definition of *strongly typed*. Nevertheless it is generally fair to say that Ruby is both dynamically and strongly typed. What this means is that with Ruby you don't need to explicitly declare your variables' type, but at the same time, Ruby will only perform trivial automatic conversions for you (for example, you can't sum a string with a number directly, like you can in some other languages). Ruby adopts the so-called *Duck Typing*, which makes working with types less restrictive and allows for polymorphism independently from inheritance. Duck Typing is further explained in the next chapter.

Ruby implements native regular expression support, a large Standard Library, a wide array of third-party code and libraries, and is easily extensible in C. Like C#, Visual Basic, and Java, Ruby features automatic memory management through Garbage Collection. It also provides support for operator overloading, introspection, reflection, blocks, closures, and metaprogramming. If these terms don't make sense to you now, fear not. The foundations of what you need to know to use Ruby in your Rails applications are housed in this and the next chapter.

Last but not least, the main implementation of Ruby is a single-pass interpreter that's available for several platforms, and it's free software with a very liberal license.

But enough with notional descriptions, let's get started.

Hello, Ruby!

You have to start somewhere, so I won't break the tradition of using a *Hello world* program as the first example.

Place the following lines into a file called `hello.rb` as shown in Listing 3-1.

Listing 3-1: Hello world in Ruby

```
# Saying hello the Ruby way
puts 'Hello, Ruby!'
```

To run this, execute `ruby hello.rb` from the command line. Not surprisingly, Ruby displays the string `Hello, Ruby!` as shown in Figure 3-1.

Figure 3-1

When working with single Ruby files on Windows, it is convenient to use the SciTE editor (shown in Figure 3-2) that gets installed with the One-Click Ruby Installer. By default, this is located in `c:\ruby\scite\SciTE.exe`. If you opt to do the same, press F5 to run the `hello.rb` program or reach for the Tools menu.

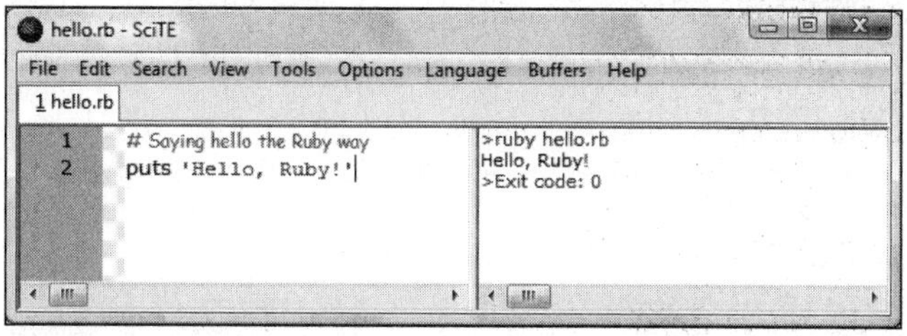

Figure 3-2

In its extreme simplicity, this example already offers grounds for a few important considerations.

You run your program by simply invoking the Ruby interpreter (aptly named `ruby`). Being an interpreted language, you didn't have to compile it first, obtain an executable, and then run it.

From the first line you can see how Ruby comments begin with a # character and continue for the rest of the line. You can also place comments in line with code:

```
puts 'Hello, Ruby!' # Saying hi from Ruby
```

When commenting multiple lines you can either have a series of # characters or opt for embedded documents, which start with `=begin` *at the beginning of a line, and end with* `=end` *at the beginning of another:*

```
=begin This is an embedded document.
Anything in here is considered a comment.
No matter how many lines it spans.
=end
```

In this example, you are passing a string to the `puts` method. As you can see, in Ruby the parentheses around the arguments of a method are optional, even though they are highly recommended in all but the most trivial cases (`puts` is an example of a method for which it is usually considered okay to omit the parentheses). One clear exception is for methods that don't accept any parameters; in this case the parentheses should be omitted (for example, use `my_method` not `my_method()`).

> **Ruby is a case-sensitive language. Don't capitalize method names.**

Literals delimited by single quotes are instances of the class `String`. Double quotes can be used as well (for example, `"Hello, Ruby!"`), but in Ruby there are a couple of fundamental differences between the two. If a double-quoted string includes an escape sequence, for example, the newline (that is, `\n`), this is correctly interpreted as a single character, which moves the cursor to the next line in the case of newline. With strings defined through single quotes, the newline is considered by Ruby to be a sequence of two regular characters (the backslash and the letter n, respectively). String literals defined with double quotes can also be used for string interpolation, a concept explained later on in this chapter.

> **Unlike C# and Visual Basic, Ruby doesn't have a special data type reserved for single characters. Characters are just strings of length one (for example, `'a'` or `"a"`).**

This example uses the method `puts`, which is the most commonly used by Rubyists for printing to the standard output. A couple of common alternatives are `print` and `printf`. The difference between `puts` and `print` is roughly equivalent to the difference between `Console.WriteLine` and `Console.Write` in .NET. But there is a twist. `puts` is smart enough to place the cursor on a new line after printing each of its arguments, but only when the argument needs it because a `\n` is missing at the end (`print` doesn't do this).

```
print "Hello, Ruby!\n" # Equivalent to: puts 'Hello, Ruby!'
```

`printf` is a more advanced method that is used in order to apply a format string to a list of arguments:

```
printf("$%.2f", price) # e.g. prints $48.95
```

If you've ever programmed in C or C++, you should already be familiar with this method.

You may also notice that there is no need for semicolons at the end of the line, as is the case with Visual Basic as well. Semicolons can still be useful though, such as whenever you feel the need to place several statements on the same line:

```
puts 'Hello, Ruby!'; puts 'Hello again!' # Two statements on the same line
```

One final consideration it is important to make is the immediacy of the program. Yes, it's one of the most trivial programs you could possibly write, but it's already much more concise than its equivalents in compiled languages such as C# and VB.NET.

Visually compare them:

Ruby

```
puts 'Hello, Ruby!'
```

C#

```
using System;
```

```
class Hello
{
static void Main(String[] args)
    {
Console.WriteLine("Hello, Ruby!");
    }
}
```

VB.NET

```
Imports System

Class Hello

    Shared Sub Main()
Console.WriteLine("Hello, Ruby!")
    End Sub

End Class
```

There's certainly no need to create wrapping methods and classes just to print a string. And unlike the C# and VB.NET examples, the Ruby Hello world reads like English. The general idea is that Ruby tries to remove obstacles from the developer and strives not to get in the way.

Your New Best Friends

In the preceding section, you wrote a tiny script and then ran it by passing the name of the file to the Ruby interpreter. If you think about it, you already cut the typical development cycle in half by skipping the compilation portion. That's good, for sure, but you still have a couple of issues to deal with.

Imagine that you are writing a large program and would now like to incorporate a new functionality. Wouldn't it be nice to be able to try it out before you actually start to change your program? You could create a new file, write the snippet of code to test, and then run it as usual through your editor. That works, but Ruby is all about having fun and that approach sounds a bit tedious and not so immediate. A better way to go is to use a tool called `irb` (Interactive Ruby).

Our second point to consider is that you are brand new to the world of Ruby. You don't know what methods are available for a given class or how to use them. You could use Google, and the API for Ruby's Core and Standard libraries is available online in several places (for example, `http://www.ruby-doc.org`). But it's not as immediate. To help you out, there's `ri` (Ruby Interactive).

The two tools have very similar names, which can be quite confusing. Most rubyists prefer to simply call them irb and ri.

irb and ri should become "your best friends" if you wish to learn Ruby. But don't think that they're only for beginners. They are used by Rubyists of all levels and even by Matz himself.

Interactive Ruby (IRB)

Interactive Ruby is an invaluable tool for the Ruby programmer. It's a Ruby shell that lets you evaluate expressions in interactive mode and is ideal for trying out snippets and experimenting with Ruby. When you start `irb` from the command line, you'll be greeted by the prompt shown in Figure 3-3.

Figure 3-3

You can now insert Ruby code and see it evaluated in "real time." To get started, use `irb` as a powerful calculator. Try inserting the following expressions:

```
irb(main):001:0> 3+3
=> 6
irb(main):002:0> 4-9
=> -5
irb(main):003:0> 7*8
=> 56
irb(main):004:0> 10/3
=> 3
irb(main):005:0> 3**100
=> 515377520732011331036461129765621272702107522001
```

The values following `=>` are the output provided by `irb`. You can see that as you enter more expressions, the counter in the prompt increases as well. If you don't really care about this kind of information you can opt for a simplified prompt that can be obtained by running `irb −simple-prompt` (a −no-prompt option exists as well). The prompt in this case looks like the following:

```
>> 8 % 3
=> 2
```

If you are using Terminal on a Mac, the simple prompt is displayed by default.

From now on I'll use `>>` and `=>` to indicate the input and output in an `irb` session.

The expressions inputted so far should all be familiar to you: you added, subtracted, multiplied, divided, performed exponentiation, and calculated a remainder (using the modulo operator).

The section on numbers provides more details about numeric operations, but it's important to note immediately how the division between two integer numbers results in another integer number (expression 4), and how Ruby is able to handle arbitrarily large numbers (expression 5).

In reality, even arbitrary numbers have their limits when dealing with ridiculously large numbers. For example, if you tried to calculate 2 to the power of 1000000000, you'd obtain the following:

```
>> 2 ** 1000000000
(irb):1: warning: in a**b, b may be too big
=> Infinity
```

`irb` can be used to evaluate any Ruby code, so don't assume that it's limited to calculations. For instance, the following concatenates my first name, with a space, and my last name:

```
>> "Antonio" + " " + "Cangiano"
=> "Antonio Cangiano"
```

Interactive Ruby also provides you with information about exceptions that are raised during the execution of your snippets as shown here:

```
>> 3 / 0
ZeroDivisionError: divided by 0
        from (irb):1:in `/'
        from (irb):1
```

Familiarize yourself with this handy tool; you'll be using it on a regular basis.

Ruby Interactive (RI)

A second "tool of the trade" is Ruby Interactive, a command-line tool for viewing Ruby's documentation.

It is not universally accepted what `ri` *stands for. Ruby Interactive is fairly common, but Ruby Index and Ruby Information are not unheard of. Again, calling it just* `ri` *works best.*

`ri` provides you with information about Ruby's Core and Standard libraries, as well as other libraries that you may have installed on your system.

To obtain a list of classes and modules that `ri` *is aware of, you can run* `ri  -c` *from the command line.*

The command-line tool accepts the name of a module, class, or method and displays information about it. You can also provide a partial name and when more than one match exists, you are prompted with a list of options.

You may be curious to learn more about the previously mentioned `String` class. If so, run the following from the command line:

```
ri String
```

The output of the command is partially shown in Figure 3-4.

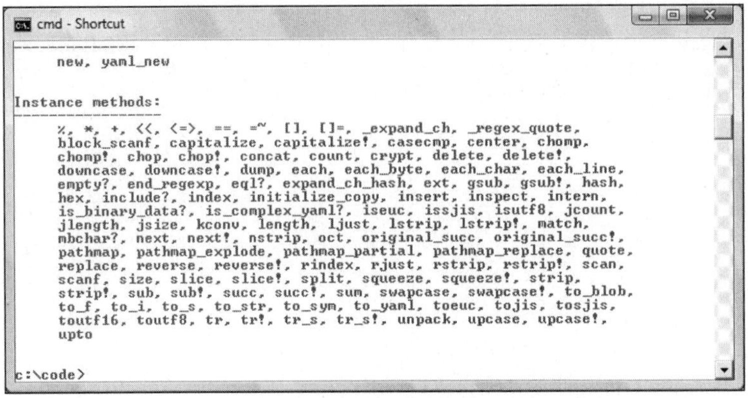

Figure 3-4

Now imagine that from that list, you'd like to learn how to use the downcase method. You can simply run:

```
ri String.downcase
```

Figure 3-5 shows the output of the command. As you can see, in this particular case, aside from a brief explanation, there's also a usage example.

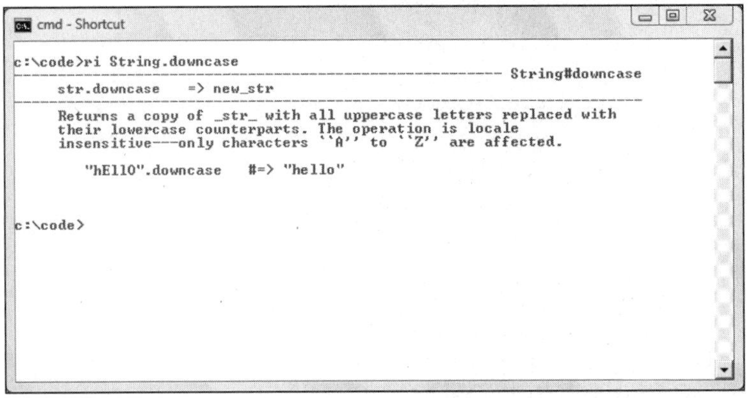

Figure 3-5

Omitting the name of the class or module, or providing a partial name for methods, works too, but usually yields a list of possible matches. For example, if you run:

```
ri F.tim
```

ri displays:

```
More than one method matched your request. You can refine
your search by asking for information on one of:

    File::atime, File::ctime, File::mtime, File::utime, File#atime,
    File#ctime, File#mtime
```

All the methods that match the search pattern are returned. The methods `atime`, `ctime`, and `mtime` of the `File` class appear twice, once separated by `::` and a second time by `#`. The reason for this is that each of these three methods exists as both a class method and an instance one. Please note that the `Class#method` notation is conventionally used by the `ri` tool to indicate instance methods but it's not valid Ruby syntax.

> *It's also worth noting that when using the `ri` tool you can be more specific than simply using the dot to separate classes (or modules) and methods. You can use `::` for methods that you already know are class methods, and `#` for instance methods. For example, if you run `ri Complex.polar` you'll be prompted with both versions of the method and the message "More than one method matched your request...". If you run `ri Complex#polar` (for the instance method) or `ri Complex::polar` (for the class method) you'll bypass the list of methods and be taken straight to the documentation of the right version of the method. Of course, there will be times when you don't know if the method you are looking for is an instance or class method, in which case using the dot is a safer bet. FastRI is a significantly faster and more advanced implementation of `ri`. The RubyForge project is located at* `http://rubyforge.org/projects/fastri`.

Ruby's Essential Data Types

Ruby offers a wide range of data types that you can use in your programs and Rails applications. Being a dynamic language, when it comes to types, Ruby is slightly different from what you may have seen in compiled languages such as C, C++, C#, Visual Basic, or Java. Fortunately, working with Ruby data types tends to be much easier.

Everything Is an Object

.NET developers are familiar with the Common Type System (CTS), in which there are two broad categories of types: *Value* types and *Reference* types. Among the Value types there are the built-in value types such as `System.Int32`, `System.Double`, or `System.Boolean`.

Other languages like C, C++ (outside of the .NET Framework), and Java may use different names and a different terminology, but they all essentially distinguish between "primitive" types and actual full-fledged classes. In these languages, there are objects, like instances of the class Array, and then there are primitive types that you can't inherit from, call a method on, retrieve or set a property for, and so on.

Forget all that. In Ruby that distinction doesn't exist. Here are a few examples of perfectly valid Ruby code:

```
3.zero?      # Equivalent to 3 == 0
-5.abs       # 5
12.to_f      # 12.0
15.div(3)    # 5
9.9.round    # 10
true.to_s    # "true"
nil.nil?     # true
```

This example just called methods on simple numbers, `true`, and even `nil` (Ruby's version of `null`). How is that possible? In Ruby every value is an object!

Ruby methods can end with a question mark, as shown in the example with zero? *and* nil?. *Such methods should always return a Boolean value. The general idea behind this nomenclature is that it increases the readability of the code.*

To verify this further you can use the method class available for any object in Ruby. As you can imagine this method tells you the class of a given instance:

```
3.class          # Fixnum
-273.15.class    # Float
true.class       # TrueClass
false.class      # FalseClass
nil.class        # NilClass
"hello".class    # String
```

All those values, except for "hello," may appear "primitive" to you, but they really aren't. As you can see 3 is an instance of the Fixnum class. -273.15 is an object of the Float class. Even "special" values (they are keywords) such as true, false, and nil represent (the sole) instances of the classes TrueClass, FalseClass, and NilClass, respectively.

Identifiers and Variables

Identifiers are case-sensitive names for entities like variables, methods, and classes. There's nothing weird about identifiers in Ruby, but there are conventions and rules to follow when defining them. Conventions make your code nicer and more understandable to other Rubyists, but by the same token, they won't break your program if ignored. Rules, on the other hand, affect the semantics of your program and are definitely a deal-breaker and can't be ignored.

Convention: Adopt snake_case

As a Microsoft developer you're probably used to adopting camelCase (or CamelCase) for multi-word variables and methods. In Ruby the convention is to use the so called snake_case instead. Conventionally, the underscore sign is used to separate words in variables and methods. For example, use file_name, not fileName. Though this may appear bizarre at first, you'll soon realize how it makes your code easier to read and introduces fewer accidental mistakes (for example, due to the fact that filename and fileName are distinct). This is not a rule; Ruby works fine with CamelCase variables and methods, but nothing screams "newbie" as much as employing this type of naming style in Ruby. Code is written for both humans and machines; the former will certainly appreciate any effort to keep your code as idiomatic as possible.

Abelson and Sussman remarked in their classic textbook Structure and Interpretation of Computer Programs *(The MIT Press 1996, also known as the SICP) that "Programs must be written for people to read, and only incidentally for machines to execute." Truer words have rarely been written.*

Convention: Don't Switch Types of a Variable

Ruby is a dynamically typed language and as such, you don't need to declare a variable's type. Aside from all the disputes about the merits of static versus dynamic typing, most people agree that dynamically typed languages tend to be more immediate, less verbose, and, ultimately, easier to program.

This is how you declare and assign a value to the following three variables in C#:

C#
```
int age = 100;
string name = "Antonio";
MyObject obj = new MyObject();
```

In Ruby this simply becomes:

```
age = 100
name = "Antonio"
obj = MyObject.new
```

Notice how the left-side type declarations (and the semicolon) have disappeared. In Ruby, you use variables without having to declare their type. Whenever you introduce a new variable without assigning a value to it, its default value is `nil`.

> Ruby provides you with several methods to verify the type of a given variable. The most common ones are `class`, `is_a?`, and `kind_of?`.

The fact that variables don't have a fixed type implies that you could first assign an integer value to a variable, then assign it a string literal, and, finally, assign it the instance of a given object:

```
# Don't do this
my_var = 100
my_var = "Antonio"
my_var = MyObject.new
```

Though this is possible, it's highly discouraged. If you start assigning different types of values to the same variable throughout your program, you'll easily introduce bugs and greatly impair the readability of your code.

Ruby's dynamic nature has several (positive) consequences. Aside from being a more immediate, easier, concise, and readable programming language which doesn't get in the way, its dynamism implies that many features and design patterns that are required in other languages are already incorporated in Ruby and its Standard Library. For example, think of .NET Generics; in Ruby, there's no reason for them to exist.

Rule: Define Scope Using Sigils

Ruby makes use of *sigils*, which are symbols attached to an identifier to indicate its scope or data type. In Ruby's specific case, they don't offer any data type information, but they do fundamentally define the scope of the variables.

Local variables don't have any sigils attached to their names, and as such, they start with a letter or an underscore. Identifiers starting with an @ character are instance variables. Those starting with @@ are class variables. Finally, global variables start with a dollar sign ($).

The following summarizes this:

```
price      # local variable
@price     # instance variable
@@price    # class variable
$price     # global variable
```

The next chapter explains Ruby's object model, so the differences between the scopes of these variables will become evident.

Convention: Append ! and ? to Certain Methods

Ruby methods can end with a special character, like an equal sign, an exclamation mark (sometimes referred to as *bang*), or a question mark (as mentioned before). The final equal sign is used for setter methods, as you see in the next chapter. The other two, ! and ?, are appended to method names to increase the readability of code and to distinguish methods that behave differently despite having an otherwise identical name.

Many methods from the Core and Standard libraries adopt this convention and so should you. Whenever you define a new method, you need to decide if using one of them is appropriate, based on the behavior of the method. The rule of thumb is that methods that "answer a question" and return a true or a false value should be defined with a question mark at the end. For example:

```
"    ".empty?          # Evaluates to false, because spaces are characters
"".empty?              # It's the empty string, so the returned value is true
```

Methods that don't answer any questions, but rather perform certain actions on copies of the receiver object should not have any special ending signs. The method upcase of the class String is a perfect example:

```
name = "Matz"          # "Matz"
new_name = name.upcase # new_name's value is "MATZ"
name                   # name's value is still "Matz"
```

Finally, methods that directly alter the object that they were called on should be defined with an exclamation mark as the last character. Methods such as these that alter the receiver carry an ! as a warning for the developer, because they can modify or destroy the receiver object, as shown in the following snippet:

```
name = "Matz"           # "Matz"
new_name = name.upcase! # new_name's value is "MATZ"
name                    # name's value is "MATZ" as well
```

There are a few exceptions. For example, the element assignment of a string doesn't have an exclamation mark, yet it still alters the string. Whenever you're in doubt, you can consult the documentation (for example, through the ri tool) and verify Ruby's behavior from irb.

When working with these kinds of methods, you should be cautious and also keep in mind that they typically return nil when the method doesn't make any changes to the receiver object. Here is a practical example:

```
my_string = "1234"                 # "1234"
new_string = my_string.downcase!   # new_string's value is nil
my_string                          # my_string's value is still "1234"
```

The string `"1234"` can't be transformed into lowercase, because it's composed entirely of digits which are, in their nature, neither upper- nor lowercase. Hence, the `downcase!` method does not alter the receiver (`my_string`), and therefore, returns `nil` as a result. `my_string` will contain the original value and `new_string` will contain `nil`. This behavior is expected.

> **Be careful when assigning the return value of a method that ends with an excla-mation mark. In this example, you may have mistakenly assumed that** `downcase!` **would still assign the original string to a** `new_string` **like** `downcase` **would. But this is clearly not the case.**

Using this set of conventions, you could theoretically have three versions of the same method name (for example, `read`, `read!`, and `read?`). This doesn't happen very often, but it isn't uncommon to have classes that offer some methods in both a "plain" version that returns a properly modified copy of the receiver, and one that ends with an exclamation mark, which actually modifies the original object.

Rule and Convention: Naming Constants

Identifiers that start with an uppercase letter are constants. Once you set the value of a constant, you're not really supposed to change it in your application. However, Ruby doesn't strictly enforce this, and instead of raising an exception, it issues a warning:

```
>> ALMOST_PI = 22/7.0
=> 3.14285714285714
>> ALMOST_PI = 355/113.0
(irb):2: warning: already initialized constant ALMOST_PI
=> 3.14159292035398
```

It's idiomatic to use all uppercase letters for the name of constants. For multiword constants, use the uppercase SNAKE_CASE naming convention. This is not a requirement though, given that Ruby will recognize a constant based solely on the case of its first letter. Yet it's still a good convention to adhere to. One exception is the case of class and module names (which are constants too); you would typically use `MyName` rather than `MY_NAME`.

Modules are formally introduced in the next chapter. For the time being, simply think of them as namespaces.

Working with Numbers

It's already established that numbers are objects. Ruby provides several classes for working with numbers. Some of these are part of the Core Library, while others are included in the Standard Library. The first are "built-in" or readily available, whereas files containing the classes that belong to the Standard Library need to be loaded explicitly into the program. Figure 3-6 shows the inheritance hierarchy for Ruby's numeric classes. Similar to .NET, there is an `Object` class from which each class inherits.

There are quite a few classes, but arithmetic operations in Ruby couldn't be easier. The following list analyzes each of the classes that you'll be using in your programs:

❑ `Fixnum`: Integer numbers that can be represented on a machine word, minus 1 bit. This typically means 31 bits. In Ruby though, you never have to worry about overflows and rarely have to think in terms of bits. If the number becomes too big to be represented as a `Fixnum`, it is auto-matically converted to `Bignum`.

❏   `Bignum`: Arbitrarily large integer numbers outside of the range of `Fixnum`. When a `Bignum` object becomes small enough to fit in a `Fixnum`, it automatically gets converted.

❏   `Float`: Real numbers in double-precision floating-point representation.

❏   `BigDecimal`: Real numbers with arbitrary precision. They can be seen as the equivalent of `Bignums` for the floating-point world.

❏   `Complex`: Complex numbers.

❏   `Rational`: Rational numbers (fractions).

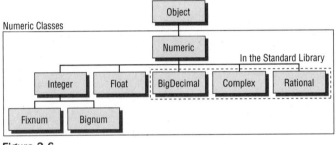

Figure 3-6

`BigDecimal`, `Complex`, and `Rational` are far less common and are part of Ruby's Standard Library. As such, if you wanted to use rational numbers, for example, you would need to require the proper file from the Standard Library. The following `irb` session should clarify this requirement:

```
>>r = Rational(2,6)
NoMethodError: undefined method 'Rational' for main:Object
        from (irb):1
>>require 'rational'
=>true
>>r = Rational(2,6)
=>Rational(1, 3)
>>r.to_f
=> 0.333333333333333
```

As you can see, this example first tries to create a `Rational` object (corresponding to the 1/3 reduced fraction), but it can't because Ruby doesn't have `Rational` in its Core Library. When you require rational, `irb` tells you that it was successfully loaded and from then onward, you'll be able to use `Rational`.

> `require` *loads a Ruby file only once. If a file is already loaded,* `require` *returns* `false`.

You assign a rational number to the variable `r` and then call its instance method `to_f` to obtain its floating-point representation. On a side note, rational numbers created in this way are reduced to their lowest terms.

At this stage you should really just worry about understanding how integer and floating-point numbers work in Ruby. And the easiest way to do that is with a few examples.

Fixnums and Bignums

Conversions between `fixnums` and `bignums` are usually automatic, and you can practically ignore the difference between the two in most cases. As previously mentioned, fixnums are stored in a native word, which is 4 bytes on most architectures. Bignums, on the other hand, can be arbitrarily large. If you wish to verify this and would like to see how much space an integer occupies, you can use the method `size`, which is available for both classes:

```
x = 2302
y = 150
x.class        # Fixnum
x.size         # 4 (bytes)
power = x**y
power.class    # Bignum
power.size     # 212 (again, bytes)
```

When dealing with large numbers, for legibility purposes, Ruby allows you to separate the digits with an underscore. For example, you can use `award = 1_000_000` *instead of* `award = 1000000`, *if you wish (yes, some may even opt for* `award = 10**6` *in this particular case).*

`Fixnum` and `Bignum` numbers support all the basic arithmetic operations that you would expect as follows:

```
a = 4
b = 5
sum = a+b
subtraction = a-b
product = a*b
power = a**b
division = a/b
modulus = a%b
```

Be Aware of the Differences

Ruby behaves very differently from C, C++, Java, C#, and Visual Basic when it comes to divisions where at least one operand is negative. In such instances, Ruby rounds the quotient to minus infinity, whereas C# and the other compiled languages that have already been mentioned round to zero. What this means is that, for example, `13/(-4)` would return -3 in these languages, whereas it's -4 in Ruby.

The same care should be applied when dealing with modulo operators. A different quotient obviously affects the remainder. Moreover, in C# or VB the sign of the remainder (determined through the modulo operator) is provided by the sign of the first operand. In Ruby, in such circumstances, it's the second operator that determines the sign of the result. For instance, `13%(-4)` is 1 in C#, but -3 in Ruby.

You should keep this consideration in mind whenever you use the `modulo` method, its equivalent `%` operator (syntax sugar), and the `divmod` method, which returns both the quotient and the modulus as elements of an array. The method `remainder` returns results consistent with C, C#, and all the other languages mentioned. So `13.remainder(-4)` returns 1, as you would expect.

For further examples regarding this issue, please consult the documentation for `divmod` (with `ri Numeric#divmod`).

Shortcut assignments are available as well as shown here:

```
a = 4
a += 2    # Equivalent to a = a+2
a -= 2    # Equivalent to a = a-2
a *= 3    # Equivalent to a = a*3
a /= 6    # Equivalent to a = a/6
a %= 2    # Equivalent to a = a%2
```

Unlike C++ and C#, Ruby doesn't provide a ++ (increment) or − (decrement) operator. But just as you would in Visual Basic, you can use a shortcut assignment (for example, i += 1 or i -= 1). In Ruby, the need for these two operators is even less prominent, given that programs tend to rely on higher-level control structures (such as iterators) when looping, as opposed to the typical loop of C-like languages.

Ruby allows you to convert an integer number into a string through the to_s method. Not surprisingly, this is the Ruby equivalent of the Object.ToString method provided by the .NET Framework. As such, it's not exclusive to numbers; you'll find that it's available for any object and you can customize it within your own classes. When dealing with integers, it can do more than a plain conversion to string, as shown here:

```
42.to_s       # "42"
42.to_s(2)    # "101010"
42.to_s(8)    # "52"
42.to_s(16)   # "2a"
```

Notice how when passing an integer argument (the radix), you specify that the string should represent the receiver (42) in binary, octal, or hexadecimal notation. The base that you select is not limited to 2, 8, and 16, and can be any positive number between 2 and 36 ("z" would be the last admissible digit in that case).

Integer literals can also be written in binary, octal, or hexadecimal by prefixing them with a 0b, 0, or 0x, respectively:

```
0b110    # Binary, equivalent to 6
0177     # Octal, equivalent to 127
0xfff    # Hexadecimal, equivalent to 4095
```

Finally, you can use the chr method to obtain a string containing the equivalent ASCII character that is represented by a given integer as shown here:

```
59.chr     # ";"
65.chr     # "A"
93.chr     # "]"
200.chr    # "\310"
3000.chr   # RangeError: 3000 out of char range
```

Floats

Floats are numbers with a decimal point as in the following examples:

```
22/7.0    # 3.14285714285714
49.99
-273.15
```

```
2.1e3       # 2100.0
0.1010101
0.3333333
```

Unlike integers, the chr method doesn't exist and the to_s method on floating-point numbers doesn't accept any parameters:

```
65.0.chr                    # NoMethodError: undefined method 'chr' for 65.0:Float
345_002_132.1932.to_s       # "345002132.1932"
345_002_132.1932.to_s(2)    # ArgumentError: wrong number of arguments (1 for 0)
```

All the basic operations that you saw in the "Fixnums and Bignums" section are available for floats too, but it's worth nothing that whenever one of the operands is a float, the result will be a float because Ruby performs an automatic conversion. For example:

```
1/3     # Evaluates to 0. Integer division between two fixnums.
1/3.0   # 0.333333333333333
1.0/3   # 0.333333333333333
```

You should use the to_f method on one of the operands whenever you want to divide two integer numbers to obtain a float.

The Float class implements all the useful methods that you'd expect, and that you can find in any other modern programming language. You can use the methods to_i, to_int, or truncate to convert a float into an integer by eliminating the decimal part of the number. Similarly, you're able to use the methods floor, ceil, and round as shown here:

```
1.8.to_i      # 1
2.1.ceil      # 3
2.9.floor     # 2
1.8.round     # 2
1.3.round     # 1
1.5.round     # 2
```

Aside from regular "finite" floats, two special numbers exist: NaN (short for Not a Number) and Infinity. A float is represented with NaN when the number is not defined, and it is Infinity (or -Infinity) when it's extremely large. The following example should help demonstrate this:

```
1.0/0     # Infinity
-1.0/0    # -Infinity
0.0/0     # NaN
```

You can use the nan?, finite?, and infinite? methods to verify whether or not a float is a regular number.

Floats are not immune to accuracy errors, but as a developer, you should already be aware of this:

```
x = 0.4 - 0.3    # 0.1
y = 0.1          # 0.1
x == y           # false
```

This is due to their different representation. Using the "format % value" shorthand, you can verify this as follows:

```
>> "%.20f" % (0.4 - 0.3)
=> "0.10000000000000003000"
>> "%.20f" % (0.1)
=> "0.10000000000000001000"
```

In Ruby, the machine epsilon is available through `Float::EPSILON`. The two colons act as a scope resolution operator, and allow you to access the `EPSILON` constant within the `Float` class. Using this, you can perform relative comparisons and work around the accuracy issue:

```
x = 0.4 - 0.3
y = 0.1
epsilon = Float::EPSILON    # 2.22044604925031e-016
(x - y).abs <= epsilon      # true
```

You are probably very aware of this, but it's worth repeating: do not use floats for financial and monetary calculations! Whenever accuracy is a must, use the `BigDecimal` class (similarly to how you'd use `decimal` in .NET):

```
require 'bigdecimal'

x = 0.1
bx = BigDecimal(x.to_s)            # #<BigDecimal:28d6128,'0.1E0',4(8)>
by = BigDecimal((0.4 - 0.3).to_s)  # #<BigDecimal:28d1894,'0.1E0',4(8)>
bx == by                           # true
```

You can also automatically convert from floats to decimals in this way:

```
require 'bigdecimal'
require 'bigdecimal/util'

x = 0.1.to_d
y = (0.4 - 0.3).to_d
x == y   # true
```

Booleans

`true` is a keyword that evaluates to the only instance (known as a *singleton* instance) of the `TrueClass`; similarly, `false` is a keyword that evaluates to the only instance of the `FalseClass`. Ruby provides you with the usual operators for Boolean expressions:

```
true and false    # false
true and true     # true
true && false     # false
true && true      # true
```

The and and && operators are very similar but it's recommended that you use the latter, because it has higher precedence and is the one that's recommended for Rails' internal code. Note that the && operator applies a short-circuit evaluation; therefore, if the first operand evaluates to `false`, the second won't be calculated at all, no matter what it is:

```
false && 3/0    # Evaluates to false with no exceptions raised
```

Similarly, you have the `or` and `||` operators:

```
true or false     # true
false or false    # false
true || false     # true
false || false    # false
```

For the same reasons just mentioned, use `||` whenever you can. This performs the same short-circuited evaluation, so if the first operand is `true`, there is no reason to calculate the second one:

```
true || 3/0    # Evaluates to true with no exceptions raised
```

Ruby also has the & and | operators (single character as opposed to double), but these are, respectively, the bitwise AND and bitwise OR.

To no one's surprise, `not` and `!` are also available:

```
not true # false
!false    # true
```

Most classes provide operators for comparing instances.

These classes use the `Comparable` mixin as explained in the next chapter.

`<`, `<=`, `==`, `>`, `>=`, and `between?` are the most common ones:

```
3 < 5               # true
4 <= 4              # true
5 == 3              # false
9 > 3               # true
9 >= 10             # false
3.between?(3,8)     # true
```

Only the `between?` method should be new to you and it can really come in handy at times.

Boolean expressions are often used in control structures, like `if` or `while` statements, so it's important to point out that any expression can be evaluated as a Boolean by Ruby.

When Ruby requires a Boolean value, everything but `nil` and `false` evaluates to `true`. This implies that 0, an empty string, or even `NaN` will all evaluate to true when a Boolean value is required. The following will print `"Zero!"` and `"Empty String!"`:

```
if 0
  puts "Zero!"
end
```

```
if ""
  puts "Empty String!"
end
```

For the time being, ignore the specific syntax of the if *statement in Ruby. It is formally introduced in the next chapter along with other control structures.*

The && and || shortcut evaluation's nature can (sometimes) be used even when you don't need a Boolean value. In fact, && returns the second operand as long as the first is not false or nil, whereas the || operator returns the first operand if this is true, otherwise the second operand is returned:

```
10 && 20            # 20
"hello" && "Ruby"   # "Ruby"
false && Time.now   # false

10 || 20            # 10
"hello" || "Ruby"   # "hello"
false || Time.now   # Thu Jun 19 23:12:47 -0400 2008
false || nil        # nil
```

There is one particular idiom that is very common in Ruby programs:

```
x ||= y
```

If x evaluates to false, y gets assigned to x. If x already has been assigned a value other than false or nil, no assignment is performed. This is very efficient because if the expression on the right side of ||= is expensive (like retrieving data from a database) it gets executed only once in the life cycle of the variable on the left (assuming that this expensive calculation doesn't return false or nil). It's an easy way of achieving memorization.

Strings

Strings are the data type that you'll be dealing with the most. String objects can be created by explicitly calling String.new. As you've seen so far, string literals can also be defined with double quotes or with single quotes, and there is an important distinction between the two. Double-quoted literals interpret escape sequences and allow substitutions, whereas single-quoted literals do not.

Let's see this is in action:

```
name = "Antonio"
"Name:\t#{name}"    # Name:       Antonio
'Name:\t#{name}'    # Name:\t#{name}
```

During the evaluation of the second line, which is a double-quoted literal, the \t sequence was interpreted as a tab. The variable name was also substituted with its actual value "Antonio." Whereas when the third line was evaluated, no interpretation of \t or substitution of name occurred.

This substitution process is called *String Interpolation*. Ruby recognizes #{expression} patterns inside double-quoted strings and substitutes the value of the expression in the string. This is usually much cleaner than concatenating values. For example, in the following snippet, the string "My name is

`Antonio Cangiano.`" gets printed twice. Both approaches work, but the string interpolation one is definitely the way to go:

```
name, lastname = "Antonio", "Cangiano"   # Parallel assignment

# Don't do this
puts "My name is " + name + " " + lastname + "."

# Do this instead
puts "My name is #{name} #{lastname}."
```

It is worth noting that the substituted expressions are not limited to simple variables but can be arbitrarily complex as follows:

```
x = 3
y = 4
"Hypotenuse: #{Math.sqrt(x**2 + y**2)}" # "Hypotenuse: 5.0"
```

When dealing with long strings that span several lines it's convenient to use the `%q` and `%Q` literal constructors as shown here:

```
%q{
This is a long string that spans multiple lines.
Any line within the matching brackets will be part of the string.
}

%Q{
This is a long string that spans multiple lines.
Any line within the matching brackets will be part of the string.
I can include expressions like this #{expression} and escape sequences as well.\n
}
```

Using `%q` is equivalent to using single quotes, and `%Q` is the same as creating the string literal and surrounding it with double quotes. The curly brackets are arbitrary, given that other matching special characters could be used as well (for example, `%Q( )`, `%Q[ ]`, or `%Q! !`).

Aside from concatenating strings through the addition operator or through string interpolation, you can also "multiply" them:

```
"abc" * 5 # "abcabcabcabcabc"
```

Ruby is very flexible when it comes to working with strings. You can treat them as arrays and access substrings directly. For example, assume that you have the following string:

```
string = "Ruby on Rails for Microsoft Developers"
```

If you want to retrieve the first character, you can use `string[0]`. Unfortunately, passing a single `Fixnum` argument to the `[]` method returns the numeric representation of the ASCII character, which is not what you want (in most cases, at least). To obtain the actual character you would have to either concatenate the `chr` method to `string[0]` or slice the string by passing two `Fixnum` arguments to `[]`:

```
string[0]      # 82
string[0].chr  # "R"
string[0,1]    # "R"
```

This behavior has been fixed in the upcoming version of Ruby, which will most likely be released in its stable form as Ruby 1.9.1. By the time you read these words, the release should already be out but this is not something that should concern you. It will take a long time for the community, and all the useful gems and plugins, to move to this new version. For the relatively near future, Ruby 1.8 is the version in use for Rails programming.

Passing two `Fixnum` arguments (call them a and b) tells Ruby that we requested a substring, which starts at the a position and continues on for a number b of characters. Negative indexes can be used as well, with –1 representing the last character of a string, –2 the one before it, and so on. If you want to obtain the last 10 characters from the preceding string, you could use the following:

```
string[-10,10]   # "Developers"
```

Running `ri "String#[]"` provides you with a lot more information and available options.

Use the `length` method (or its alias `size`) to determine the length of a string:

```
string.length   # 38
```

Another common method is `chomp` (or its `chomp!` version), which removes the separator, specified as an argument, from the end of the receiver. When the method is called without parameters, Ruby will remove carriage return characters from the end of the string if they exist:

```
input = gets    # "example\n"
input.chomp!    # "example"
```

`gets` *is Ruby's equivalent of .NET's* `Console.ReadLine`.

You can also substitute strings using the `sub` or `gsub` method:

```
"hello".gsub('h', 'Oth')   # Othello
```

The `String` class offers a wide range of methods to manipulate strings. It is far easier to work with strings in Ruby than it is in C#. It's strongly advised that you run `ri String` to familiarize yourself with the many methods available. There is no reason to "reinvent the wheel" and with Ruby, for any given micro-task, there is often a built-in method ready to help you out.

An important distinction exists between Ruby's strings and C# strings. In C# or VB.NET, strings are immutable. In Ruby they are not (like C and C++). It's important to keep this in mind. The following example should help clarify this further:

```
first = "Ruby"
second = first

first.reverse!

puts first     # "ybuR"
puts second    # "ybuR"
```

Notice how `reverse!` is able to modify the first string, and how this affects the second variable that references it as well.

Whenever you need to render an instance unmodifiable, you can use the `freeze` method and verify if an instance is currently frozen through the `frozen?` method.

```
string = "Ruby"
string.frozen?    # false
string.freeze     # Freezes the object referenced by the variable string
string.frozen?    # true
string[0] = "N"   # `[]=': can't modify frozen string (TypeError)
```

Symbols

Not only Ruby's strings are mutable, but two different `String` instances with the same identical value are stored in memory as two distinct objects. This means that strings aren't the best choice when you need to use and reuse some form of identifiers that won't change over time.

Ruby finds an answer to this point in symbols. A symbol is an instance of the `Symbol` class. Symbol objects are used by the Ruby interpreter to represent names and certain strings. What's more important, only one instance exists for a given symbol.

Using the `object_id` method, you can determine if two instances are the same actual object in memory. Compare the different behavior between strings and symbols shown here:

```
# Strings
"Rails".object_id   # 21103620
"Rails".object_id   # 21103600
"Rails".object_id   # 21103580

# Symbols
:rails.object_id    # 99298
:rails.object_id    # 99298
:rails.object_id    # 99298
```

Symbols can be defined as `:name` or `:"name"` literals or created by `to_sym` methods available in a few classes (including `String`, of course). Some people like to think of symbols as lightweight strings, but it's much better to distinguish them in terms of when their usage is appropriate. When the focus is on the name itself — and this can be used over and over — symbols are favored over strings.

Symbols are ideal for keys of associative arrays (or Hashes, in Ruby speak) and are widely used when programming in Ruby on Rails. This is an example, taken straight from the Rails documentation:

```
link_to "Profile", :controller => "profiles", :action => "show", :id => @profile
```

As you can see the symbols `:controller`, `:action`, and `:id` are the keys of the hash passed to the `link_to` method (a Rails helper).

Regular Expressions

Ruby has built-in support for regular expressions, which are instances of the class `Regexp`. Regular expressions are essentially patterns used to match and extract information from text. They are a very powerful and useful tool, even though they can easily get complex and hard to understand.

In Rails they are often used to validate user input. For example, you may want to verify that a phone number is in the right format. Regular expressions allow you to do this, even if they appear to be very complex to the untrained eye.

Instances of `Regexp` can be created by delimiting the pattern between forward slashes `/pattern/`, through the `%r{pattern}` literal, or by passing the pattern to the `Regexp` constructor (for example, `Regexp.new(pattern)`).

Ruby has two built-in operators to test whether or not a given regular expression matches a string: `=~` and its opposite `!~`. The first is the most common one and returns the index of the first matching character if there is a match, or `nil` if there's not:

```
'A long string with some text' =~ /long/   # 2
/Microsoft|Rails/ =~ "Ruby on Rails"       # 8
/\s+/ =~ "The answer is 42"                 # 3
/\d+/ =~ "a word"                           # nil
```

As you can see the order of the operands is not important (such as if the string is on the left or on the right of the operator).

In case you are new to the world of regular expressions, the first one indicates that the word `"long"` has to appear in the string (and it does on the third character), the second that the string needs to contain either `"Microsoft"` or `"Rails"` for a match to exist, the third that the string needs to contain at least one space, and the last one that the string needs to contain one or more digits (and it doesn't, so `nil` is returned).

Ranges

Instances of the class `Range` represent a set of values defined by their start and their end. As usual, they can be defined through `Range.new` or through literals as shown here:

```
Range.new('a', 'z') # "a".."z"
'c'..'k'  # "c".."k"
-10...10  # -10...10
```

The difference between literals defined with the two dots and literals defined with the three dots is that ranges defined with the three dots won't include the last element. So `-10...10` will include consecutive numbers from `-10` to 9.

Ranges are not limited to single characters and integers. If a class, whether user-defined or built-in, satisfies two specific requirements, ranges can be constructed using its instances. The two requirements are: 1) The class instances can be compared using the special `<=>` operator, which unequivocally allows for a comparison of the elements, and 2) The class needs to implement a method called `succ`, which returns the next instance in a sequence.

Don't worry about the details of these requirements; they essentially mean that to create a range with an arbitrary object type, these objects need to be comparable (for example, 4 < 8) and that there must be a way to obtain the next number (for example, 6 following 5, 7 after 6, and so on). The second requirement is not a strict one; in fact you could create a range of floats. However, a range loses a lot of its usefulness if it can't be iterated over.

You can convert ranges to arrays, using the `to_a` method:

```
(1..10).to_a    # [1, 2, 3, 4, 5, 6, 7, 8, 9, 10]
```

Or through the so called *splat* operator, which "expands" the range into the array:

```
[*1..10]        # [1, 2, 3, 4, 5, 6, 7, 8, 9, 10]
```

Iterating over ranges is fairly easy, because they are essentially collections of consecutive objects. The following snippet loops through a range and prints the whole English alphabet, with one character per line:

```
for c in 'a'..'z'
  puts c
end
```

On a side note, idiomatic Ruby code uses two-space indentation.

This is perfectly fine and somewhat friendly to C# and VB programmers. However, the true "Ruby way" is to put aside the "syntax sugar" provided by the `for` loop and opt for the `each` iterator instead as shown here:

```
('a'..'z').each {|x| puts x }
```

To understand that one-liner, a few concepts need to be introduced. The next chapter tells you all you need to know about blocks and iterators, including how to create your own iterators for your classes and for built-in ones.

It may seem quite surprising, but Ruby allows you to reopen classes, including core ones, and define additional methods of your own or overwrite existing ones. This is a powerful feature of the language, though you do need to be careful not to abuse it. The next chapter covers this topic as well.

Arrays

Arrays in Ruby are instances of the `Array` class. They are collections of objects, whose integer index starts at 0, like in most other languages. These objects can be of any type and don't have to be homogeneous. A single array could contain numbers, strings, ranges, Booleans, and nil values. An array of arrays is perfectly fine as well. Of course, it usually makes sense to collect elements of the same type, but this is not enforced by the interpreter. With no set type and size, arrays don't require any special declarations.

`[]` and `Array.new` can both be used to create arrays, for example:

```
a = []                  # []
b = Array.new           # []
c = Array.new(5, 0)     # [0, 0, 0, 0, 0]
d = [2, 3, 7, 9, 18]    # [2, 3, 7, 9, 18]
```

As you can see, when you pass two parameters to the `Array.new` method, you are specifying the number of elements (in this case 5) "to initialize" and their value (in this case 0). Again, this doesn't mean that the array can contain only the specified number of elements. It's just an available initialization option that can be convenient in a few circumstances.

In the "Strings" section of this chapter, you've already seen how you can access individual characters by referring to their index, as well as how to select a substring, by specifying an offset and the number of characters required. The same rules apply to arrays, and this shouldn't come as a shock if you consider that strings are essentially sequences of bytes, for example:

```
array = ['Matz', 'David', 'Antonio']
array[0]                 # "Matz"
array[-1] == array[2]    # true
array[2] = 'Tony'        # "Tony"
array                    # ["Matz", "David", "Tony"]
array[1, 2]              # ["David", "Tony"]
array[0, 2]              # ["Matz", "David"]
```

puts vs. p

If you are trying out these lines of code for yourself through `irb`, you will see the same properly formatted results that I've indicated in the inline comments. If, on the other hand, you are trying them out from a Ruby file, prefixing the expressions with `puts`, you may have noticed the following:

```
array = ['Matz', 'David', 'Antonio']
puts array   # Prints Matz, David and Antonio, one per line
```

That's not very nice, especially when dealing with large and complex arrays. In order to visualize arrays, the way you did in the inline comments, and the way `irb` displays them, you should use the method `p` rather than `puts`.

This method is very handy not only with arrays, but whenever you need to analyze objects. What this does is print the object's data based on the return value of its `inspect` method.

Even with simple strings, the difference between `puts` and `p` is evident: `puts "hello\n"` prints "hello" whereas `p "hello\n"` prints the actual stored value `"hello\n"`. If you are troubleshooting a problem, the second is definitely preferable.

If you decide to assign a value to the 50th element in an array (for example, `array[49] = 'Something'`), and there are currently only three elements, the assignment will be successful and the values from the 4th element to the 49th one will be `nil`.

Similarly, you can add elements:

```
a = [3, 10, 20, 44]
p a << 5                 # [3, 10, 20, 44, 5]
p a.push(2)              # [3, 10, 20, 44, 5, 2]
```

And remove them:

```
a = [1, 2, 3, 4]
a.pop                    # 4
a                        # [1, 2, 3]
a.delete_at(1)           # 2
a                        # [1, 3]
```

The following snippet shows a few of the many methods available for Array objects:

```
numbers = [9, 5, 3 , 4, 2, 8, 1, 6, 7]

numbers.first              # 9
numbers.last               # 7
numbers.length             # 9

numbers.max                # 9
numbers.min                # 1

numbers.join               # "953428167"
numbers.join(", ")         # "9, 5, 3, 4, 2, 8, 1, 6, 7"

numbers.sort               # [1, 2, 3, 4, 5, 6, 7, 8, 9]
numbers                    # [9, 5, 3 , 4, 2, 8, 1, 6, 7]

numbers[0] = nil           # nil
numbers[3] = nil           # nil
numbers                    # [nil, 5, 3, nil, 2, 8, 1, 6, 7]
numbers.compact!           # [5, 3, 2, 8, 1, 6, 7]

numbers << 9 << 4 << 10    # [5, 3, 2, 8, 1, 6, 7, 9, 4, 10]
numbers.sort!              # [1, 2, 3, 4, 5, 6, 7, 8, 9, 10]

numbers += [20]            # [1, 2, 3, 4, 5, 6, 7, 8, 9, 10, 20]
numbers - [1,2,3,4]        # [5, 6, 7, 8, 9, 10, 20]
numbers.reverse!           # [20, 10, 9, 8, 7, 6, 5, 4, 3, 2, 1]
numbers                    # [20, 10, 9, 8, 7, 6, 5, 4, 3, 2, 1]
```

The few isolated `numbers` variables in the snippet are there to show you once again what methods modify the original array and which ones leave it unaltered. As usual, `ri Array` is your friend.

In the next chapter, when iterators and blocks are introduced, you will see some of the most useful methods of Array objects. Meanwhile, just as you can with ranges, you are able to loop through arrays too, for example:

```
# Prints 2, 4, 6, 8 one per line
for i in [1,2,3,4]
  puts i*2
end
```

Hashes

Hashes are associative arrays. They are essentially arrays that allow any type of keys to be used, as opposed to consecutive integer ones, which start from zero. Another important distinction is that Hashes, unlike Arrays, are not ordered.

Hashes are somewhat similar to Hashtables or `Dictionary<TKey, TValue>` *in .NET. Like Hashtables, which return* `null` *if the key is not found, Ruby's Hashes return* `nil` *by default, unless a different value has been specified as a parameter of the* `Hash.new` *method.*

You can use two curly brackets to create an object of the Hash class or (as usual) Hash.new:

```
h1 = {}                        # {}
h2 = Hash.new                  # {}
h1 == h2                       # true
h1.object_id == h2.object_id   # false
```

Once a variable has been assigned a reference to an empty hash, you can add entries (key-value pairs):

```
h1["name"] = "George"     # "George"
h1["age"] = 71            # 71
h1                        # {"name"=>"George", "age"=>71}
h1["name"]                # "George"
h1["age"]                 # 71
```

Ruby offers a much friendlier syntax for initializing hashes, and if you consider (as mentioned before) that symbols are a better choice for hash keys, you get the following:

```
h = {:name => "George", :age => 71}
h[:name]                   # "George"
h[:age]                    # 71
```

If you have a hash with strings as keys and would like to switch to symbols, you can always use the symbolize_keys! method.

Looping through the keys and values of a hash can be easily accomplished through a for loop or more idiomatically through an each iterator, for example:

```
h = {:name => "George", :age => 71}

for key, value in h
  puts "#{key} = #{value}"
end

# More idiomatic
h.each {|key, value| puts "#{key} = #{value}" }
```

This snippet prints the following output:

```
age = 71
name = George
age = 71
name = George
```

Hashes are widely used by Rails, so it's important that you understand their basic workings.

Again, ri Hash gives you more details about the class and the available methods. Most of the fun methods, just as was the case for Array, require knowledge of blocks and iterators. Further examples are therefore provided in the next chapter.

Summary

This chapter provided you with a quick introduction to some of the essential data types and how they work. You should have a clearer picture of what Ruby code looks like and how to manipulate basic objects. The fun really starts in the next chapter, however, which explores actual object-oriented programming in Ruby.

4

Programming Ruby

I learned very early the difference between knowing
the name of something and knowing something.

— *Richard Feynman*

The previous chapter introduced the Ruby language by briefly surveying its syntax and the fundamental data types that you'll encounter over and over again as you learn about and develop more with Rails.

Chapter 3 started by introducing you to common tools of the trade like irb and ri, the concept that everything is an object, the conventions and rules for identifiers and variables, as well as essential types like numbers, Booleans, strings, symbols, regular expressions, ranges, arrays, and hashes.

This chapter brings your Ruby knowledge to the next level by exploring the essential aspects of object-oriented programming, the Ruby way. It does so by first covering basic concepts like defining methods, using conditional and looping statements, and handling exceptions, only to focus in the second half of the chapter on objects, classes, and modules. Finally, at the very end of the chapter, you'll find a short overview of a few available Ruby implementations.

Chapters 3 and 4 are therefore your Ruby tutorial before you begin to truly work with Rails in Chapter 5. With this roadmap in mind, let's get started.

Defining Methods

Every object and class exposes several methods. Class methods are methods that can be invoked directly on classes, for example ActiveRecord's finders:

```
author = Author.find_by_last_name("Ginsberg")
```

Similarly, there are instance methods that can be invoked on any object of a given class, like the down-case method of a `String`, or to keep in line with ActiveRecord's example:

```
books = author.books
```

Then there are the so-called singleton methods, which are a special type of method that can be defined, and which exist only for a specific instance of a class:

```
my_string.my_method     # my_string has a singleton method
my_string2.my_method    # Raises a NoMethodError
```

Ruby doesn't really differentiate between the three of them when you call a given method on a class or an object. The interpreter only cares about determining whether or not the receiver exposes that method. When you use the syntax `receiver.method`, Ruby is actually sending a message with the name of the method, and its arguments, to the receiver object (be it an object, class, or module). As a matter of fact, the following two are equivalent, and the dot notation is just sugar syntax for the developer:

```
"antonio".capitalize         # "Antonio"
"antonio".send(:capitalize)  # "Antonio"
```

You can see the advantages of the dot notation when chaining multiple method calls together as shown here:

```
puts "$32.90".sub('$','Ð')                         # Prints Ð32.90
Kernel.send(:puts, "$32.90".send(:sub, '$', 'Ð'))  # Prints Ð32.90
```

As a reminder, the values placed in the inline comments can either refer to the output of an expression or the value it evaluates to. If a method like puts, p, *or* print *is used, the output is shown in the comment (as opposed to the return value). If you were to run either of the two lines above in irb, you would see* Ð32.90 *printed, as well as a* => nil *to notify you of the much less interesting return value.*

The method `puts` that you've used so far (as though it were a function rather than a method) is in reality a `Kernel` method. `Kernel` is a module included in `Object`, and as such its methods are available everywhere within Ruby programs. Remember, Ruby is purely object-oriented and as such every function is a method and it's defined, implicitly or explicitly, within an object, a class, or a module.

Using existing methods won't get you too far, so you can move on to creating methods of your own.

You define methods through the `def` statement and terminate the method definition with end:

```
def hello_antonio
  puts "Antonio"
end

hello_antonio    # Prints Antonio
```

You can create an alias method by writing alias :new_method_name :old_method_name *outside of the method definition. Oddly enough, Ruby provides you with* undef *as well, so you could theoretically define a method, use it and then "undefine" it (for example,* undef hello_antonio*).*

Methods can also accept one or more arguments as shown here:

```ruby
def hello(name)
   puts name
end

def sum(x, y)
   x + y
end

hello("Antonio")      # Prints Antonio
puts sum(5, 3)        # Prints 8
```

Notice how there is no need to declare variable types and, as such, the `hello` method is able to print any type of argument that you pass to it. Similarly, the `sum` method works with any parameters whose class implements the + method/operator, be it numeric, string, array, or what have you. Note also how the `sum` method did not use the `return` keyword. This is optional in Ruby, given that by default the last evaluated expression in the method body is returned. This also means that the `hello` method defined in the preceding code returns `nil`, because that's the returning value of the `puts` method (which is the last, and only, expression that's evaluated in the body of the method). At times it's still useful to use `return` to make the returning value stand out or to insert multiple exit points within the method.

Ruby methods also support default arguments:

```ruby
def greet(user = "guest")
   puts "Welcome #{user}!"
end

greet                 # Prints Welcome guest!
greet("Matz")         # Prints Welcome Matz!
```

Methods can only have one default argument, and this has to be the last argument:

```ruby
def power(x, y = 2)
   return x**y
end

puts power(5)         # Prints 25
puts power(5, 3)      # Prints 125
```

Unlike C# and VB, Ruby does not support method overload. This is to say that Ruby won't accept two identical identifiers with the same scope, which accepts different arguments. The polymorphic nature of Ruby's methods ensures that you don't have to create copies of the same method to handle integers, floating-point numbers, and so on, as you would in most compiled languages. The issue of variable arguments passed to the method still exists though, and you may want your method to accept one, two, or even three arguments. In Ruby you can use the splat operator (*) to define a method that accepts a variable number of arguments that are stored in an array:

```ruby
def my_print(*list)
   p list
end
```

```
my_print                            # Prints []
my_print("a string")                # Prints ["a string"]
my_print(2, 5, 9)                   # Prints [2, 5, 9]
my_print("user", "pass", true)      # Prints ["user", "pass", true]
```

This can also be used to define a list of mandatory arguments along with optional ones:

```
def collect_data(name, last_name, *info)
  # code...
end
```

You learn much more about methods later on in this chapter.

Conditionals

Ruby offers several conditional statements and control structures for managing the flow of your applications. In the previous chapter you had a sneak peak at the `if` and `for` statements; here they are introduced more formally, among others useful statements.

if / elsif / else / unless

The following illustrates the usage of the `if` conditional statement in Ruby:

```
if temperature < 0
  puts "Freezing!"
end
```

Visual Basic programmers will find this syntax quite natural, and it shouldn't be too foreign to C# programmers either.

Any code between the `if` and the `end` line is executed unless the tested expression evaluates to `false` or `nil`. The `if` statement also accepts the `then` token separator (as opposed to the newline alone), so you could have written the same code as follows:

```
if (temperature < 0) then
  puts "Freezing!"
end
```

Parenthesis around expressions within conditional statements are optional in Ruby, but it may not be a bad idea to include them when they're helpful in clarifying the meaning of the code. Or even as a single line:

```
if temperature < 0 then puts "Freezing!" end
```

Ruby 1.8 allows semicolons as token separators as well, but Ruby 1.9 doesn't.

Listing 4-1 shows a recursive version of the factorial in Ruby.

Listing 4-1: Naïve Factorial in Ruby

```ruby
# Naive, recursive implementation of the factorial in Ruby

def fact(n)
  if n <= 1
    1
  else
    n * fact(n-1)
  end
end

n = (ARGV[0] || 10).to_i
puts fact(n)
```

Copy the code into a `fact.rb` file (or whatever you wish to call it), and then run `ruby fact.rb`. The result should be `3628800`, which is the factorial of 10. You can also pass an argument to the program by running (for example) `ruby fact.rb 5`, obtaining `120`.

Line 11 shows you a little trick: `n = (ARGV[0] || 10).to_i`. *ARGV is an array of arguments passed to the program, so* `ARGV[0]` *retrieves the first argument as a string or* `nil` *if no arguments were passed.* `ARGV[0] || 10` *returns the first argument if different than* `nil` *or 10 if* `nil`. *The result is then converted to an integer (because* `ARGV[0]` *is a string when it exists). This idiom is an easy way to specify a default number when no arguments are passed to the program, while still accepting an argument from the user.*

Ruby also offers the possibility of using the `if` statement as an expression modifier. So you can rewrite the line from the earlier example as:

```ruby
puts "Freezing!" if temperature < 0
```

This notation offers a clear gain in readability for simple one-liners (try reading it out loud), but for non-trivial statements it's far better to use the "traditional" multiple-line `if`.

`if` statements may also include the optional `elsif` and `else` clauses using the following syntax:

```ruby
if expression1
  code
elsif expression2
  code
elsif expression3
  code
else
  code
end
```

From now on, in these snippets, `code` *is used as a single, generic term that indicates one or more lines of code.*

There can be several `elsif` clauses but only one final `else`. Please pay attention to the peculiar syntax of the `elsif` clause. It's not `ElseIf` of VB, nor `else if` of C#.

Perhaps surprisingly, Ruby also offers an unless statement:

```
unless sold_out
  place_order
end
```

As you can imagine, unless is the opposite of if, and the preceding code delimited within unless and end is executed only when the condition tested is nil or false. unless can also be used as an expression/statement modifier:

```
place_order unless sold_out
```

unless supports an else clause, but unlike the if statement, it doesn't accept elseif clauses. Depending on the situation, you may opt for if or prefer unless; Ruby provides both for the sake of convenience and readability.

Though if and unless have been viewed as "statements" so far, in Ruby there's a twist: they too are expressions. Unlike C# and VB, in Ruby everything is an expression, so even if and unless return values. If you run the following snippet, the variable state is set to the returning value of the if expression, in this particular case "Gas," before being printed to the console:

```
h2o_temp = 130

state = if h2o_temp < 0
  "Solid"
elsif h2o_temp > 100
  "Gas"
else
  "Liquid"
end

puts state
```

The Ternary Operator

Like C#, and many other C-derived languages, Ruby also supports the ternary operator. The ?: operator returns the first value unless the condition is false or nil, in which case the second value is returned:

```
value = condition ? val1 : val2
```

The preceding line is a much more succinct way of writing the following if statement:

```
value = if condition
  val1
else
  val2
end
```

For example, you could write:

```
ticket = (age < 18) ? "child" : "adult"
```

The case Statement

In most languages, whenever you need to verify multiple conditions, you'd employ the "switch" statement. Ruby calls it the case statement and it's far closer to what Visual Basic developers — as opposed to C# ones — are accustomed to. That said, Ruby's case statement is much more powerful than what you may expect at first.

There are two ways of using the statement. The first, without passing an argument, is equivalent to using an if statement with a series of elsif clauses:

```
case
  when condition1
    code
  when condition2
    code
  when condition3
    code
  when condition4
    code
  else
    code
end
```

And the second, which passes an argument:

```
case expression
  when value1
    code
  when value2
    code
  when value3
    code
  when value4
    code
  else
    code
end
```

In both usages, the case statement can have multiple when clauses, and an optional else clause for code that should be executed if no other previous condition has been successful. This is equivalent to the default clause in C# and the Case Else in VB.NET.

Please note that case has no fall-through behavior, so if one of the conditions is met, no other attempts to evaluate other conditions are carried out by the interpreter. This implies that, just as in VB.NET, there's no need for break statements of any sort. Still similarly to Visual Basic, it is possible to combine multiple conditions on the same line by separating them with a comma:

```
case expression
  when value1, value, value3
    code
  when value4, value5
    code
```

```
  when value6, value7, value8
    code
  when value9
    code
  else
    code
end
```

Just like if *and* unless, *the* case *statement returns the last evaluated expression if any code is executed, or* nil *if no condition was successful and no* else *clause was defined. Conversely, like* if *and* unless, *the* when *clause supports the* then *token separator as well.*

The case statement in Ruby is very powerful because it's able to use not only integers, strings, or what other languages consider "primitive types," but any type of expression, even when the value is determined during runtime. What's more, it works by using the so-called "case equality" operator (that is, ===). Though several classes make no distinction between this operator and the simple equality one (that is, ==), many classes implement the case equality operator in a somewhat intuitive and logical manner. The class Regexp implements the === operator to check if there is a match for the given pattern, whereas the Range class implements it in order to check whether the element is contained within the given range, and so forth. For example, the following snippet prints "Senior" to the console.

```
age = 85

puts case age
        when 0..12 then "Child"
        when 13..19 then "Teenager"
        when 20..65 then "Adult"
        else "Senior"
     end
```

Another common idiom takes advantage of the equality operator implemented by the Class class. This verifies that the given expression is an instance of the specified class:

```
Numeric === 3        # true
String === "Rails"   # true
Array === {}         # false, because an empty hash is not an instance of Array
```

Within the context of the case statement, you could then write the following:

```
case my_expression
  when Numeric
    # Handle number
    code
  when String
    # Handle String
    code
  when Array
    # Handle Array
    code
  when Hash
    # Handle Hash
    code
```

```
  when TrueClass, FalseClass
    # Handle Boolean
    code
  else
    # Handle any other type
    code
end
```

Looping

The Ruby language offers two categories of looping statements: "built-in loops" and iterators. Ruby has three types of built-in loops: `for`, `while`, and `until`. A few differences aside, these are constructs that you should already be accustomed to from other languages.

Ruby also offers an infinite loop construct, through the `loop` method.

Despite being employed at times, idiomatic Ruby code tends to favor iterators that can also be customized to reflect the needs of your code.

The for/in Loop

The `for` statement in Ruby iterates over a collection of elements. To be more exact, it enables you to iterate through enumerable objects such as arrays, hashes, and ranges. This is its basic syntax:

```
for element in collection
  # Do something with element
  code
end
```

Notice that the statement requires both the `for` and `in` keywords, and as such it acts similarly to the `For Each` in Visual Basic, and `foreach` in C#, not their simple `For` and `for` versions.

These are a few examples that use `for` to loop through collections:

```
# Prints the integers between 0 and 10
for i in 0..10
  puts i
end

# Prints each element of the array
for el in [2, 4, 6, 8, 10]
  puts el
end

# Prints each key-value pair in the hash
h = { :x => 24, :y => 25, :z =>26 }
for key, value in h
  puts "#{key} => #{value}"
end
```

Similarly to `if`, `unless`, and `case`, `for` is terminated by `end`, and it accepts an optional separator token. Only, instead of being `then`, `do` is the keyword as shown here:

```
for c in 'a'..'z' do
   puts c
end
```

This is useful when a newline or a semicolon (in Ruby 1.8's case) is missing, but usually otherwise omitted.

The while and until Loops

The `while` loop in Ruby acts just as you'd expect. When the tested condition is not `false` or `nil`, the body of the loop gets executed. Here is the basic syntax:

```
while expression
   code
end
```

The `until` statement is the opposite. It continues to loop when the condition evaluates to `nil` or `false` and stops when it evaluates to `true` (remember that anything but `false` and `nil` evaluates to `true`):

```
until expression
   code
end
```

The following example would probably never be written by a savvy rubyist in a real program, but it illustrates the difference between the two:

```
# Prints integers from 0 to 10
i = 0
while (i<= 10)
  puts i
  i += 1
end

# Prints integers from 0 to 10
i = 0
until (i> 10)
  puts i
  i += 1
end
```

Like the `for`/`in` *loop,* `while` *and* `until` *accept an optional* `do` *keyword.*

There is nothing particular about `while` and `until` in Ruby, except that they too can be used as expression modifiers. Here again this increases readability for trivial one-liners, as shown by these two equivalent, hypothetical lines of code:

```
battery.charge! while !battery.full?
battery.charge! until battery.full?
```

Blocks and Iterators

Ruby methods can have regular parameters, and can accept a block as well. A block is one or more statements grouped together, which act as nameless (or anonymous) functions. They don't exist on their own, but need to be associated with a method. Iterators are methods that accept an associated code block of this type. They usually iterate over a collection of elements, but the definition is broad enough to include methods that don't do that. For this reason, some people prefer not to refer to methods that don't iterate as iterators, but simply as methods that accept an associated block.

If you've ever worked with the `IEnumerable` and `IEnumerator` interfaces (and their generic forms) the iterator pattern shouldn't feel new to you. In the .NET world, LINQ to Objects introduced a few generators to simplify the process further. In Ruby, things are much simpler and concise, though undisputed that iterators and blocks were not invented by Ruby, but they are a distinctive feature of the language.

Numeric Iterators

Take a look at one of the simplest iterators, the method `times` of the `Integer` class:

```
5.times { puts "Ruby" }
```

This iterator accepts a block of code that prints the `"Ruby"` string literal and executes it a number of times, as specified by the receiver object (5 in this case). In short, this prints the code between the curly brackets five times.

Blocks can be defined between curly brackets or through the `do`/`end` notation, for example:

```
5.times do
  puts "Ruby"
end
```

The convention is to use curly brackets for one-line blocks and a `do`/`end` pair for blocks that contain multiple lines of code.

When the iterator has a regular argument, this should be surrounded by parentheses when adopting the curly brackets style for blocks, given that they have high precedence and would end up calling the block over the argument (a generally meaningless operation), instead of the method.

At each iteration, `times` passes a value to the associated block. That value is accessible from within the block as an iterator parameter/variable that you define by specifying an arbitrary identifier between pipes (for example, `|identifier|`):

```
5.times {|x| print x }
```

At each iteration the value of x is set as an incremented number (in the case of `times`), starting from zero. This line of code therefore prints `01234`.

The class `Integer` offers another two common iterators, `upto` and `downto`:

```
1.upto(10) {|n| puts n }     # Returns 1 and prints integers from 1 up to 10
10.downto(1) {|n| puts n }   # Returns 10 and prints integers from 10 down to 1
```

For the sake of simplicity, this example uses the `puts` method, but blocks can contain any arbitrarily complex code as shown here:

```
fact = 1
2.upto(10) {|n| fact *= n }
puts fact                    # Prints 3628800
```

The `Numeric` class offers a `step` iterator as well, which invokes the block with the sequence of numbers that begins with the number that the method is invoked on. It's also incremented by the specified step on each call, until the limit is exceeded:

```
# Prints a table of squares for numbers
# between 0 and 10, in increments of 0.1
0.step(10, 0.1) do |n|
  puts "#{n}\t#{n**2}"
end
```

The each Method

Perhaps the most common iterator that's available for many objects is the `each` method, as you briefly saw in the previous chapter when you used it as a more popular alternative to the `for` loop.

The following snippet shows its usage with arrays:

```
sites = ["reddit.com", "dzone.com", "digg.com"]
sites.each {|site| puts "<a href=\"http://#{site}\">#{site.capitalize}</a>" }
```

Blocks can perform any action on the data iterated over, but the returning value of each *is generally the receiver itself (the array* sites *in the preceding example).*

This outputs:

```
<a href="http://reddit.com">Reddit.com</a>
<a href="http://dzone.com">Dzone.com</a>
<a href="http://digg.com">Digg.com</a>
```

It is common for classes that implement the `each` method to include the `Enumerable` module as well, which provides a series of useful traversal and search methods. For example, `Array` also has the method `each_with_index`, which passes the actual element and its index to the two block parameters:

```
["a","b","c"].each_with_index {|elem, index| puts "#{elem}: #{index}" }
```

*Again, the names of the block parameters (*elem *and* index *in this example) are entirely up to you. It is often useful to use short, meaningful ones though.*

This prints:

```
a: 0
b: 1
c: 2
```

The `each` iterator can be used with ranges as well:

```
('abc'..'xyz').each {|s| puts s }
```

This prints all the strings between `'abc'` and `'xyz'` in alphabetical order:

```
abd
abe
abf
abg
abh
...
...
xyv
xyw
xyx
xyy
xyz
```

And hashes:

```
author = { :name => "Kurt Vonnegut", :site => "vonnegut.com", :books =>14 }
author.each {|k, v| puts "#{k} => #{v}" }
```

This prints each key-value pair. Hashes are not ordered and, as such, the output may appear in a different order:

```
site => vonnegut.com
books => 14
name => Kurt Vonnegut
```

The `String` class has an `each` method as well (also available as `each_line`). It accepts an optional argument (the string separator) that defaults to the newline:

```
"this is\na string\non multiple\nlines".each {|line| puts line }
```

The output of this one-liner is:

```
this is
a string
on multiple
lines
```

This is perhaps not exactly what you expected from the `each` method when it's applied to strings. Perhaps you were expecting to be able to iterate over every single character. Doing so is possible by employing the `each_byte` iterator:

```
"just a string".each_byte {|c| print c, " " }
```

which prints:

```
106 117 115 116 32 97 32 115 116 114 105 110 103
```

This is probably still not what you want. So you need to convert the numbers to their ASCII character representation through the `chr` method:

```
"just a string".each_byte {|c| print c.chr, " " }
```

And obtain:

```
just    a    string
```

Yes, the preceding example adds a final space at the end of the output.

Alternatively, you could have used the `printf` method passing it the argument `"%c."`

The `each` method is particularly useful when dealing with files:

```
# A very simple quine

File.open("quine.rb") do |f|
    f.each {|line| puts line }
end
```

If you save the code of that snippet in a file called `quine.rb` and run it, the program prints its own source code. This is a very straightforward form of *quine* (a program that prints its own source code).

You might also notice that blocks are often employed when working with files by passing them to the class method `File.open`. In a similar way, you could write to a file:

```
File.open("myfile.txt", "w") do |f|
    5.times { f.puts "Let's add a string" }
end
```

The `"w"` specifies that the file is accessible for writing and it should be created if it doesn't exist. If the file already exists, it is overwritten. If you'd like to append instead, use the `"a"` argument.

The `each_with_index` iterator exists for files as well:

```
File.open("myfile.txt") do |f|
    f.each_with_index do |line, index|
        puts "#{index}: #{line}"
    end
end
```

This prints each line contained in the `myfile.txt` file with its index. For example, if you ran the previous "write on file" snippet from the same folder, you'd obtain:

```
0: Let's add a string
1: Let's add a string
2: Let's add a string
3: Let's add a string
4: Let's add a string
```

ri `File` *will tell you a whole lot more about the* `File` *class.*

When working in Ruby on Rails you will often deal with arrays. So the next section takes a closer look at some other common iterators that are available for instances of `Array` (and in most cases, `Hash`).

Common Iterators

Array objects have a map method (alias for collect) that creates a new array containing the values returned by the associated block:

```
[1,2,3,4].map {|n| n**2 }      # [1, 4, 9, 16]
[1,2,3,4].collect {|n| n** 2 }  # [1, 4, 9, 16]
```

It is the Ruby equivalent of Enumerable.Select in .NET. This is particularly useful when you want to obtain a new array by uniformly altering each element of another array as shown here:

```
def capitalize_names(list)
   list.map {|name| name.capitalize }
end

names = ["matz", "david", "antonio"]
cap_names = capitalize_names(names)   # ["Matz", "David", "Antonio"]
```

Notice how map doesn't alter the original names array because, as is common in Ruby, it works on a copy of the receiver. The equivalent methods map! and collect! actually modify the receiver:

```
names.map! {|name| name.capitalize }
p names                               # Prints ["Matz", "David", "Antonio"]
```

Using the select iterator, you can create a new array by selecting elements based on the given criteria:

```
numbers = [*1..10]               # [1,2,3,4,5,6,7,8,9,10]
evens = numbers.select {|x| x % 2 == 0 }
p evens                          # Prints [2, 4, 6, 8, 10]
```

If you are an efficiency geek, in Ruby you can use x & 1 == 0 *when testing for evenness, too.*

The select method can be employed to implement the classical Quicksort algorithm, as shown in Listing 4-2 (quicksort.rb).

Listing 4-2: Quicksort Using Array#select

```
def qsort(array)
   return [] if array.empty?
   pivot, *tail = array
   less = tail.select {|el| el < pivot }
   greater = tail.select {|el| el >= pivot }
   qsort(less) + [pivot] + qsort(greater)
end

a = [2, 7, 9, 1, 3, 5, 2, 10]
p qsort(a)                       # Prints [1, 2, 2, 3, 5, 7, 9, 10]
puts qsort(a) == a.sort          # Prints true
```

The third line assigns the first element of the array to pivot, and the rest of the array to the variable tail.

If you are not familiar with the Quicksort algorithm, feel free to skip this example.

The opposite of select is reject, which returns only elements for which the block is not true. Somewhat similarly, arrays have the delete_if method that removes elements for which the block evaluates to true (from the receiver array, not a copy):

```
numbers = [*1..10]
numbers.delete_if {|x| (x&1).zero? }  # Returns [1, 3, 5, 7, 9]
p numbers                             # Prints [1, 3, 5, 7, 9]
```

The Enumerable module also provides the Array class with the partition method, which returns two arrays: the first array contains the elements of the array for which the block evaluates to true, and the second one, for which the block is false:

```
numbers = [*1..10]
p numbers.partition {|x| (x&1).zero? } # Prints [[2, 4, 6, 8, 10], [1, 3, 5, 7, 9]]
```

You can use this method to make Listing 4-2 even more concise as shown in Listing 4-3 (quicksort2.rb).

Listing 4-3: Quicksort Using Enumerable#partition

```
def qsort(array)
  return [] if array.empty?
  pivot, *tail = array
  less, greater = tail.partition {|el| el < pivot }
  qsort(less) + [pivot] + qsort(greater)
end

a = [2, 7, 9, 1, 3, 5, 2, 10]
p qsort(a)                 # Prints [1, 2, 2, 3, 5, 7, 9, 10]
puts qsort(a) == a.sort    # Prints true
```

tail.partition creates an array containing two arrays: the first with elements less than the pivot, and the second with elements greater or equal to the pivot. The parallel assignment assigns the first element (an array) to the less variable, and the second element (an array as well) to the greater variable.

Another iterator worth mentioning is Enumerable#inject, which is sometimes known as reduce, fold, or aggregate in other languages. As a matter of fact, it's the Ruby equivalent of Enumerable.Aggregate in .NET 3.5.

This is the description of the method taken from the output of ri Enumerable#inject:

```
- - - - - - - - - - - - - - - - - - - - - - - Enumerable#inject
enum.inject(initial) {| memo, obj | block }   => obj
enum.inject            {| memo, obj | block }   => obj
- - - - - - - - - - - - - - - - - - - - - - - - - - - -
   Combines the elements of _enum_ by applying the block to an
accumulator value (_memo_) and each element in turn. At each step,
   _memo_ is set to the value returned by the block. The first form
lets you supply an initial value for _memo_. The second form uses
the first element of the collection as a the initial value (and
skips that element while iterating).
```

The description is exact, but may still appear somewhat confusing unless you're well-versed in functional programming languages. A few examples should help illustrate its usage.

Take this line into consideration (it uses a range, but works equally well with arrays):

```
puts (0..100).inject {|sum, n| sum + n }   # Prints 5050
```

The great mathematician Gauss didn't need inject *to calculate this. When he was a schoolboy he came up with a formula that easily added up arithmetical series.*

The sum parameter is first set to the first element of the receiver (0 in this case). At each iteration n is set to the current element, and the returning value of the block is stored in sum. This means that the first iteration sum is set to 0+1, then 1+2, then 3+3, then 6+4, and so on, until the last element (100) has been added.

You could very easily rewrite the factorial (seen before), through the inject method (the factorial of 0 and 1 is 1, so you can pass 1 as an argument for inject, and this will work as the initial value for the calculation):

```
(2..n).inject(1) {|fact, x| fact * x }
```

Running ri Hash will tell you which iterators are available for Hash objects. collect, select, reject, delete_if, and partition, to name but a few, are all available. They usually accept two block parameters/variables instead of one. Of these, one is for the key and the other for the value. The following is an example of Hash#select and Hash#delete_if usage:

```
hash = { "a" => 1, "b" => 2, "c" => 3, "d" => 4 }
p hash.select {|k,v| k > "b" }    # Prints [["c", 3], ["d", 4]]
p hash.select {|k,v| v < 3 }      # Prints [["a", 1], ["b", 2]]
p hash.delete_if {|k,v| v < 3 }   # Prints {"c"=>3, "d"=>4}
```

Array and Hash both include the Enumerable module, or in Ruby speak, they "mix in" its methods. Many instance methods are made available by Enumerable, but the following is a list (almost complete) of common ones:

- ❑ **Plain iterators:** each_with_index, each_cons, and each_slice.
- ❑ **Methods that return** true **or** false: include? (and member?), any?, and all?.
- ❑ **Filter methods:** detect (and find), select (and find_all), reject, and grep.
- ❑ **Methods that transform a collection by either directly modifying it or by returning an altered copy of the receiver:** map (and collect), partition, sort, sort_by, zip, and to_a (and entries).
- ❑ **Aggregators:** inject and sum.
- ❑ **Summarizers:** max and min.

Use the ri tool to look up those that haven't been illustrated in this and the previous chapter (for example, ri Enumerable#find).

Before moving on to the creation of your own iterator methods, think about how you'd implement all these little snippets of code in C#, Visual Basic, or on any other language you're accustomed to. Chances are that you'll find Ruby far more direct, concise, and easy to use.

Defining Your Own Iterators

A common characteristic of all the iterator methods seen so far is that they invoke the associated block of code for each element of a given sequence. As mentioned before, there can also be methods that expect and invoke the execution of a block of code, but don't actually loop (and they too are sometimes broadly and improperly called iterators).

At the heart of both, there is the `yield` statement, which enables the invoked method to temporarily pass the control to the block for execution. For example, the following method executes the associated block three times:

```
def three_times
  yield
  yield
  yield
end

three_times { puts "hello" }
```

It is important to understand that `yield` temporarily passes the control to the block of code, but when the last line of code in the block gets executed, the control is passed back to the method. The following modified version of the preceding example illustrates this:

```
def three_times
  puts "In the method"
  yield
  yield
  yield
  puts "In the method again"
end

three_times { puts "In the block" }
```

which prints:

```
In the method
In the block
In the block
In the block
In the method again
```

Remember the previous snippets in which most iterators allowed you to use one argument in the block (or two in the case of hashes)? You can pass argument values to the associated block by following your `yield` statements with a list of values (or expressions, to be more exact):

```
def three_times
  yield 1, 2
  yield 3, 4
  yield 5, 6
end

three_times {|a, b| puts a + b }
```

And this prints to the standard output:

```
3
7
11
```

This example illustrates the point, but it's rather silly, given that your real code will most likely need to perform something much more useful than that. So assume for a moment that you'd like to have an iterator for ranges that pass only even argument values to the associated block. You can easily implement it as follows:

```
def each_even(range)
  range.each do |n|
    yield n if (n&1).zero?
  end
end

each_even(1..10) {|x| print x, " " }   # Prints 2 4 6 8 10
```

It is worth noting that the class Range *has an instance method called* step, *which could be used instead.*

You can verify if a block was passed to the method through the block_given? method (globally accessible, because it's defined in Kernel) as shown here:

```
def n_times(n)
  if block_given?
    n.times { yield }
  else
    puts "I'm blockless"
  end
end

n_times(5) { puts "oh hi" }            # Prints 5 times oh hi
n_times(5)                             # Prints "I'm blockless"
```

The n.times *passes an argument whose value goes from zero to* n-1 *during the execution, as seen before, but in this specific case, it was ignored. Changing the line* n.times { yield} *to* n.times {|val| yield val } *makes that value available to your custom-defined version (for example,* n_times(5) {|x| puts x }).

yield also has a rough equivalent that can be utilized by specifying a block argument explicitly then prefixing it with an ampersand character (&), before invoking it through the call method. The previous range example can therefore be written as follows:

```
def each_even(range, &block)
  range.each do |n|
    block.call n if (n&1).zero?
  end
end

each_even(1..10) {|x| print x, " " }   # Prints 2 4 6 8 10
```

It is usually fine to opt for `yield` instead, but the "`&block` and `block.call`" approach has an advantage in situations where you need more control, given that you have an actual object (a `Proc` one) to use as a point of reference, rather than just relying on a keyword (`yield`) to handle control from the method.

Proc.new and lambda

As mentioned before, blocks are essentially subroutines that are associated with a method and as such, cannot exist on their own:

```
my_block = { puts "don't do this" }    # syntax error
```

Thankfully, Ruby offers a way to explicitly convert a "standalone block" into an actual `Proc` object through the `Proc.new` and `Kernel#lambda` methods.

When a block is passed to a method, this gets instantiated as a `Proc` object as well.

Take a look at the following example:

```
add = lambda {|x, y| x + y }       # #<Proc:0x03c1926c@myfile.rb:1>
sum = Proc.new {|x, y| x + y }     # #<Proc:0x03c190b4@myfile.rb:2>
puts add.call(3, 5)                # Prints 8
puts sum.call(3, 5)                # Prints 8
```

Both methods are used to create anonymous methods (or functions, if you prefer) that can be invoked (with parameters in this case) and reused in your programs. When in the previous section you gave a name to the block, specifying it as an argument prefixed by an ampersand character, and then you called it with `block.call`, you were working with a `Proc` object.

You can use `Proc` objects as arguments for iterators that expect a block, by prefixing them with an ampersand:

```
addition = Proc.new {|sum, x| sum + x }
puts [1,2,3,4,5].inject(&addition)    # Prints 15
```

Blocks and procs act as *closures* because they can access variables that have been defined outside of their scope (or to clarify this further, outside of the curly brackets or the do/end pair). This means that they're able to access and modify objects that were defined in the context that invoked them (their *binding*).

There is actually a method called `binding` that returns a `Binding` object. This describes the variables and methods' context when called.

Behind the scenes, Ruby associates a binding with any block or proc that it creates. This implies that you can have the following:

```
sum = 0
1.upto(100) {|n| sum += n }
puts sum                          # Prints 5050
```

Notice how the sum variable can be accessed and modified from within the block. Variables defined inside the block are local to the block and not accessible outside of it:

```
1.upto(100) {|n| var = n }
puts var                                # Raises a NameError
```

Please bear in mind that block scoping will be substantially revisited in the next version of Ruby (Ruby 1.9).

In the following example, you can see how the method n_power returns a Proc object, created through lambda. When this proc gets invoked, the value (3) of the argument n originally passed to the n_power method is retained by the proc and is used along with the val parameter (whose value is 5), passed to the call method, in order to execute the actual calculation in the body of the proc:

```
def n_power(n)
  lambda {|val| val ** n }
end

cubed = n_power(3)
puts cubed.call(5)                      # Prints 125
```

The following shows how a Proc "remembers" and can modify its binding, even when invoked several times:

```
def make_counter(n = 0)
  lambda { n += 1 }
end

c1 = make_counter
c1.call                     # 1
c1.call                     # 2
c1.call                     # 3
```

Note how the counter gets incremented because lambda created a closure that's able to keep the state of the argument n (assigned to 0 by default when executing c1 = make_counter) and increment its value at each call. If you were to create a second closure, its local variables would be independent from c1, which has a different binding:

```
c2 = make_counter
c2.call                     # 1
c2.call                     # 2
```

Both Proc.new and Kernel#lambda return a Proc instance and can usually be used almost interchangeably. It's important to be aware of two fundamental differences between these two methods though.

The first difference concerns the returning behavior. Using return within the block of a proc created with lambda returns control back to the calling method. Using return with a proc created with Proc.new tries to return from the calling method. The following example shows these different behaviors:

```
def process_lambda
  puts "In the method"
  p = lambda { return "In the block" }
  puts p.call
```

```
    puts "Back in the method"
  end

  def process_procnew
    puts "In the method"
    p = Proc.new { return "In the block" }
    puts p.call
    puts "Back in the method"
  end
```

Executing `process_lambda` produces:

```
In the method
In the block
Back in the method
```

which is what you would expect in most cases. Executing `process_procnew` prints the following:

```
In the method
```

This surprising result is due to the fact that `return` within the `Proc.new` block returns `"In the block"` as the returning value for the calling method, which exists de facto from the earlier method.

Not only that, but if the proc were to be called outside of a method, it would raise a `LocalJumpError` error:

```
p = Proc.new { return "In a block" }
p.call                                # Raises unexpected return (LocalJumpError)
```

The second difference, perhaps with far fewer implications, is that `Proc.new` tends to be more liberal in terms of argument passing, whereas `lambda` acts like a regular method that expects an exact number of arguments (unless the splat operator is used to pack a variable number of arguments into an array). You can see the different behavior in the following example:

```
p1 = Proc.new {|x, y| x + y }
p2 = lambda {|x, y| x + y }

# 2 arguments as expected
puts p1.call(1,2)       # 3
puts p2.call(1,2)       # 3

# A third unexpected argument
puts p1.call(1,2,3)     # 3
puts p2.call(1,2,3)     # Raises wrong number of arguments (3 for 2) (ArgumentError)
```

At this point you may wonder why so many pages have been devoted to covering concepts like blocks, iterators, procs, and closures. It's because these are so fundamental to Ruby (and Rails) programming, that if the chapter were to abruptly end here, understanding these concepts would still place you ahead of many Rails beginners.

It was important to spell out a few more advanced details. That said, this section is admittedly quite heavy in terms of details and you should be able to get by even if you don't remember all of them, as long as you get the general idea. You can breathe a sigh of relief as the chapter progresses toward other topics.

Exception Handling

In the previous examples, it was casually mentioned how Ruby raises this or that type of error, if you perform an illicit operation. Just like C#, VB, and any other respectable modern programming language out there, Ruby offers full support for handling exceptions.

This is how you would typically "catch an exception" in C# and VB:

C#

```
int a = 5;
int b = 0;
int div;

try
{
    div = a / b;
    Console.WriteLine("This is never written");
}
catch (Exception ex)
{
    Console.WriteLine("Oops... {0}", ex.Message);
}
```

VB

```
Dim a As Integer = 5
Dim b As Integer = 0
Dim div As Integer

Try
    div = a / b
    Console.WriteLine("This is never written")
Catch ex As Exception
    Console.WriteLine("Oops... {0}", ex.Message)
End Try
```

In both cases a division by zero is attempted within the try statement, and the exception raised is caught by the catch clause, which prints "Oops... Attempted to divide by zero." in C#'s case and "Oops... Arithmetic operation resulted in an overflow." for VB. Ruby works in the same way through begin/rescue as shown here:

```
a = 5
b = 0

begin
  div = a /b
  puts "This is never written"
rescue Exception => ex
  puts "Oops... #{ex.message}"
end
```

The rescue clause sets the variable ex to reference an instance of the given error class. The Exception class is the root of all error classes in Ruby, and as such it catches any errors that can possibly be raised.

It is generally a bad idea to rescue all the exceptions in a single catch *clause.*

If you didn't specify Exception at all (that is, rescue => ex) this would still handle most errors in a program because the rescue clause would default ex to an instance of StandardError. There are, however, errors that are not subclasses of StandardError. For example, ScriptError (and its LoadError, NotImplementedError, and SyntaxError subclasses), NoMemoryError, and other low-level errors.

Please also keep in mind that there will be a few rearrangements to the exception hierarchy in the next version of Ruby (1.9), but this shouldn't really affect you too much.

Conversely, as long as you don't need a variable representing the just caught exception, you could remove the => ex part as well, reducing the basic begin/rescue statement to:

```
begin
  3/0
rescue
  puts "There was an error!"
end
```

Similarly to C# and VB, you can be more specific and only handle a certain type of exception as follows:

```
begin
  5.a_non_existing_method
  3/0
rescue ZeroDivisionError
  puts "You divided by zero!"
end
```

This snippet raises the following error:

```
errors.rb:2: undefined method 'a_non_existing_method' for 5:Fixnum (NoMethodError)
```

errors.rb is just the file that was running the snippet and the 2 afterwards indicates that the second line was the culprit behind the error. If you were to run the same from an irb session, you'd get an error message along the lines of:

```
NoMethodError: undefined method 'a_non_existing_method' for 5:Fixnum
        from (irb):2
```

Regardless of how you ran the snippet, the reason why Ruby raised an unhandled exception is that the rescue clause was ready to handle ZeroDivisionErrors, but not NoMethodErrors. Aside from providing you with a "catch-all" exception class, you can also chain multiple rescue clauses together to handle several exceptions differently, just like you would in C#, VB, and many other programming languages.

Ruby also supplies you with an else clause that is executed when no errors are raised in the begin/end block of code, and an ensure clause that is executed no matter what, for example:

```
begin
  # ... some error prone code
  # ...
```

```
rescue SystemCallError => ex
  puts "A system call failed: #{ex.message}"
rescue ZeroDivisionError
  puts "You divided by zero!"
rescue NoMethodError => ex
  puts "That method doesn't exist: #{ex.message}"
rescue Exception => ex
  puts "Error: #{ex.message}"
else
  puts "Yay! No errors!"
ensure
  puts "Error or not, this is always printed!"
end
```

ensure *is, of course, the equivalent of* finally *in C# and VB.*

As usual, Ruby also provides you with an inline option:

```
File.read('non_existent_file.txt') rescue puts "You need an existing file!"
```

When defining methods you can also skip begin and the final end:

```
def with
  begin
    #...
  rescue
    #...
  end
end

def without
  # ...
rescue
  # ...
end
```

Raising Errors

At times you may need to raise errors. In Ruby this is done through the Kernel#raise method. Try the following sessions in irb:

```
>> raise
RuntimeError:
        from (irb):1
```

As you can see, called on its own without arguments, it raises a RuntimeError with an empty message. Now add a message to the error, for example:

```
>> raise "A generic error message"
RuntimeError: A generic error message
        from (irb):2
```

Now you have a `RuntimeError` with a custom message. This works fine as long as the error that you want is a generic `RuntimeError`. But what if you want a `ZeroDivisionError`, `ArgumentError`, or `ThreadError`? You can pass the error type to `rescue`:

```
>> raise ZeroDivisionError, "Don't divide by 0, mkay?"
ZeroDivisionError: Don't divide by 0, mkay?
        from (irb):3
```

Perfect. Now you can use it to make your methods a little more robust as shown in Listing 4-4.

Listing 4-4: Factorial Method That Can Raise an ArgumentError

```
def fact(n)
  if n >= 0
    (2..n).inject(1) {|f, x| f * x }
  else
    raise ArgumentError, "The factorial is defined for non-negative integers only."
  end
end

(0..10).each {|n| puts "#{n}:\t#{fact(n)}" }
```

This prints the following table:

```
0:      1
1:      1
2:      2
3:      6
4:      24
5:      120
6:      720
7:      5040
8:      40320
9:      362880
10:     3628800
```

The method `fact` can now raise exceptions, so passing a negative number executes the `else` clause of the `if` statement within the method, therefore raising an `ArgumentError`.

If you place the following within the same file (`fact2.rb`):

```
puts fact(-5)
```

this prints to the standard error output stream (`stderr`):

```
fact2.rb:5:in `fact': The factorial is defined for non-negative integers only.
(ArgumentError)
   from fact2.rb:10
```

Objects and Classes

Ruby wouldn't be much of an object-oriented language if you weren't able to define your own classes and objects. The next few sections show you how.

Defining and Instantiating Classes

Classes are defined through the class keyword, followed by the capitalized name of the class. The name needs to be capitalized because, as mentioned before, classes in Ruby are constants:

```
class Account
end
```

As usual, the definition is terminated by end, and any line of code contained between class and end forms the body of the class. From the defined class you can obtain an object by invoking the new method:

```
account = Account.new
account.class              # Account
```

By employing the Object#is_a? method, you can determine whether or not an object is an instance of a given class:

```
account.is_a? Account      # true
```

The same method can also be used to verify if a class is a superclass of the class of an instance (or an ancestor class in the inheritance hierarchy):

```
account.is_a? Object       # true
```

The preceding line tells you that Object is a superclass or an ancestor for the Account class. It's actually a superclass as you can see if you run the following:

```
account.class.superclass   # Object
```

You may notice that no method is specified in the Account class, but it was still possible to instantiate it thanks to the fact that the constant Account is a Class object, and as such, it has access to a new method for creating instances.

The initialize Method

An empty class defined in this manner won't be very useful, so the next step is to specify an initialize method for the class. This method is private by default, and therefore cannot be called directly as you would with a constructor in C# or VB (but you can call it from within the class implementation). If an initialize method exists, this will automatically be called by the method new when it creates an instance of the given class.

For the sake of simplicity, assume that in order to open an account, all that's required is a name and Social Security number:

```
class Account
  def initialize(holder, ssn)
```

```
      @holder = holder
      @ssn = ssn
      @balance = 0
    end
end
```

Note that the method requires two arguments. The arguments passed to the new method will be passed to the initialize method. Therefore, by requiring two arguments for the initialize method, you are essentially specifying that the new method will require two arguments as well:

```
account = Account.new("Jane Smith", "123-45-6789")
```

By default, whenever you define a method with the def keyword followed by a simple identifier inside a class, this is an instance method. As such, it is accessible only to objects of that class (and its subclasses).

self

Within the body of the initialize method, you set three instance variables. Instance variables are prefixed by an @ symbol and can only be accessed by instance methods of that object. Ruby uses self as a reference to the current object. This is somewhat similar to this in C# and Me in VB, but can be used anywhere in the code of your program. To clarify this, take a look at how self changes depending on where you are in the execution of the code:

```
class A
  puts self

  def initialize
    puts self
  end
end

a = A.new
```

This will print A first, and then something along the lines of #<A:0x3e09054>. Within the class definition, but outside of any method, self references the class itself, whereas inside an instance method, self references the current instance. It is important to point this out because as a .NET developer, you may be inclined to "declare" your instance variables at the beginning of the class outside of any method, which would not be what you intended.

Attributes and Accessor Methods

Now that you've specified a more meaningful initialization, you can inspect the object that you've created and verify that the instance variables are being set correctly:

```
account = Account.new("Jane Smith", "123-45-6789")
# Prints #<Account:0x3c18ed4 @balance=0, @ssn="123-45-6789", @holder="Jane Smith">
puts account.inspect
```

Now think about adding a couple of instance methods for depositing and withdrawing money from the account as shown in Listing 4-5 (account.rb).

Listing 4-5: Adding Deposit and Withdrawal to the Account Class

```ruby
class Account
  def initialize(holder, ssn)
    @holder = holder
    @ssn = ssn
    @balance = 0
  end

  def deposit(amount)
    @balance += amount
    puts "You deposited #{amount} dollars."
  end

  def withdrawal(amount)
    new_balance = @balance - amount
    if new_balance >= 0
      @balance = new_balance
      puts "You withdrew #{amount} dollars."
    else
      puts "Your account doesn't allow overdrafts."
    end
  end
end

account = Account.new("Jane Smith", "123-45-6789")
account.deposit(100)      # Prints You deposited 100 dollars.
account.withdrawal(20)    # Prints You withdrew 20 dollars.
account.withdrawal(100)   # Prints Your account doesn't allow overdrafts.
```

Note that if you tried the following:

```ruby
puts account
```

you'd get an unconvincing `#<Account:0x3c18678>` written to the console. This is due to the fact that `puts` is using the default `Object#to_s` method, thereby printing the object's class and the encoding of its object id.

Change this by overwriting the default with your own `to_s` instance method:

```ruby
def to_s
  "#{@holder}'s account has #{@balance} dollars."
end
```

Now, `puts account` prints `"Jane Smith's account has 80 dollars."` Note how easy it is to overwrite methods defined in the parent class: you simply redefine them.

You may also be tempted to read the balance with the dot notation directly from your instance, but this won't work:

```ruby
account.balance   # Raises a NoMethodError
```

Instance variables are associated with a given instance, but are not directly accessible.

Instance variables are essentially private, unlike constants, which are practically public.

This guarantees proper encapsulation while still allowing instance methods to be read and modified. If you want to be able to read the balance of a given account, you could define a getter method in the class. Getter and setter methods in Ruby can be declared as normal instance methods. In the case of `@balance` you don't want to change it directly, so it will be the equivalent of a read-only property:

```
def balance
  @balance
end
```

You may also want to retrieve the name of the account holder. Assume for a moment that Jane Smith is getting married to John Doe, and opts to change her surname. To handle this occurrence as well, you should be able to define a getter and a setter method for the `@holder` variable. This is easy enough and can be done as follows:

```
def holder
  @holder
end

def holder=(new_name)
  @holder = new_name
end
```

> You may be tempted to use the newly defined setter method from within other instance methods. For example, instead of using `@holder = new_holder` **you may opt for** `holder = new_holder`. **Don't do that. This will only create a** `holder` **local variable, not actually set the value of the instance variable** `@holder`. **For simple scenarios stick with** `@holder = new_holder`. **If the setter method does a lot of heavy lifting for you and you'd like to reuse it, use** `self.holder = new_holder` **instead.**

Now you can do the following:

```
puts account.holder    # Prints Jane Smith
account.holder = "Jane Doe"
puts account.holder    # Prints Jane Doe
```

This is okay; it works as expected, and it wasn't too much of a hassle. You essentially defined the equivalent of traditional properties in C# or VB, with a much cleaner and concise syntax. Ruby pushes the envelope further when it comes to attributes though, and provides a series of methods to automate this extremely common process, whenever the logic of the getter and setter are trivial (as it was in this case). C# 3.0 assumes a similar approach with its recently introduced *auto-implemented properties*.

An attribute is Ruby-speak for an instance variable that is available through a getter or setter method. They are what C# and Visual Basic programmers call properties, and have nothing to do with the word "attribute" in the .NET world.

You can specify that an attribute should be read only (a getter) through the `attr_reader` method, written only (a setter) through the `attr_writer` method, and readable and writable (an accessor) through the `attr_accessor` method. All three methods accept a list of symbols that specify the attributes that should be defined. They can also — but much less conventionally — accept a list of strings.

These methods are defined by the `Module` class, which is a superclass for the `Class` class. As such they are available for every class in Ruby. This is an example of Ruby's powerful metaprogramming abilities. With a single method you're able to dynamically create instance variables, plus getter and setter methods.

In the wake of this new knowledge, you can rewrite your class as shown in Listing 4-6 (`account2.rb`).

Listing 4-6: Using attr_reader and attr_accessor in the Account Class

```ruby
class Account
  attr_reader :balance, :ssn
  attr_accessor :holder

  def initialize(holder, ssn)
    @holder = holder
    @ssn = ssn
    @balance = 0
  end

  def deposit(amount)
    @balance += amount
    puts "You deposited #{amount} dollars."
  end

  def withdrawal(amount)
    new_balance = @balance - amount
    if new_balance >= 0
      @balance = new_balance
      puts "You withdrew #{amount} dollars."
    else
      puts "Your account doesn't allow overdrafts."
    end
  end

  def to_s
    "#{@holder}'s account has #{@balance} dollars."
  end
end

account = Account.new("Jane Smith", "123-45-6789")
puts account
puts account.balance
account.deposit(1000)
puts account.balance
account.withdrawal(100)
puts account.balance
puts account.holder
account.holder = "Jane Doe"
puts account.holder
puts account.ssn
```

This prints to the standard output:

```
Jane Smith's account has 0 dollars.
0
You deposited 1000 dollars.
1000
You withdrew 100 dollars.
900
Jane Smith
Jane Doe
123-45-6789
```

Methods Visibility

Ruby's methods can be public, protected, or private. Methods are by default public, with an exception for the `initialize` method and methods defined globally, outside of a class definition. What this means is that whenever you define a new method in a class, be it an instance method or a class method (as shown later on), these can be invoked on the object and on the class, respectively.

Private methods are methods intended for use from within the class or its subclasses, and as such cannot be invoked outside of the class (or its subclasses). Even from within the class or object implementation, these are implicitly invoked on `self` (for example, `my_private_method` not `self.my_private_method` or `obj.my_private_method`).

Protected methods are a middle ground. They can only be used from within the class and its subclasses, and allow for invocation on a receiver other than the implicit `self`, as long as the objects they are invoked on are the same class or subclass of `self`'s class. Of the three visibility levels, protected is by far the least commonly used (being utilized in practice only for instance methods).

Method visibility can be set in two ways. You can use the `private`, `public`, and `protected` methods without arguments, for example:

```
class A
  def a
  end

  def b
  end

  protected

  def c
  end

  def d
  end

  def e
  end

  private
```

```
    def f
    end
end
```

a and b will be public by default; all the methods underneath `protected` and up to `private` will be protected (meaning c, d, and e). f will be private. You'll be able to run:

```
obj = A.new
obj.a
obj.b
```

but not so with any of the other methods previously defined:

```
obj.c # protected method `c' called for #<A:0x3d68a50> (NoMethodError)
```

The second way to set method visibility is by specifying arguments for any of three methods seen previously:

```
class A
  def a
  end

  def b
  end

  def c
  end

  def d
  end

  def e
  end
  protected :c, :d, :e

  def f
  end
  private :f
end
```

Ruby's reflective nature and metaprogramming capabilities actually allow you to work around the method visibility limits and access methods that are defined as private (and instance variables). Exploring these capabilities is outside the scope of this book, but keep in mind that the encapsulation provided by these three levels of visibility does not limit Ruby's incredibly reflective and open nature.

Single Inheritance

Ruby supports single inheritance. A class has only one direct parent. Every class you define is implicitly a subclass of the `Object` class and, therefore, its instances are provided with a whole set of features out of the box (for example, you already saw the `to_s` method).

When programming in C# or VB you have the concept of "multiple implementations" through interfaces, to emulate the benefits of multiple inheritance. Ruby uses something called mixins, as explained later on.

If you want to specify that class `Child` inherits from class `Parent`, you can use the < operator:

```
class Child < Parent
end
```

If `Parent` exposes many useful methods and attributes, `Child` will automatically inherit them "for free." This is what Rails uses for controllers and models. A controller looks like the following when you've just created it:

```
class PostsController < ApplicationController
end
```

And this is an Active Record model:

```
class Post < ActiveRecord::Base
end
```

Now imagine that you have two classes, `Child` and `Parent`, defined as follows:

```
class Parent
  def my_method
    puts "I'm in Parent and self is #{self}"
  end

  def parent_method
    puts "I'm in the method defined in Parent only and self is #{self}"
  end
end

class Child < Parent
  def my_method
    puts "I'm in the overwritten Child method and self is #{self}"
  end
end
```

The `parent_method` is defined by `Parent` only, but it's still accessible by instances of its subclass `Child`. The fact that `my_method` is defined by both the `Child` class and its superclass (`Parent`) implies that the respective objects call the version defined by their own class:

```
child = Child.new
parent = Parent.new

child.my_method
child.parent_method

parent.my_method
parent.parent_method
```

This prints:

```
I'm in the overwritten Child method and self is #<Child:0x3e08a28>
I'm in the method defined in Parent only and self is #<Child:0x3e08a28>
I'm in Parent and self is #<Parent:0x3e089d8>
I'm in the method defined in Parent only and self is #<Parent:0x3e089d8>
```

Also notice how `self` is always a reference to the current object, no matter where the method that is invoked from is defined.

In the previous section you defined a bank account class. This was the definition of its `initialize` method:

```ruby
class Account
  # ...

  def initialize(holder, ssn)
    @holder = holder
    @ssn = ssn
    @balance = 0
  end

  # ...
end
```

If you were to define a class to represent a credit card account, you could inherit from the more generic `Account`, but you would have to specify an Annual Percentage Rate (APR) for the account (obviously, this is really simplifying the banking system here). So you might be tempted to write the following:

```ruby
class CreditCard < Account
  # ...
  def initialize(holder, ssn, interest_rate)
    @holder = holder
    @ssn = ssn
    @balance = 0
    @apr = interest_rate
  end
  # ...
end

cc = CreditCard.new("Jane Smith", "123-45-6789", 12.99)
```

This works but it's not very DRY. The two `initialize` methods would be essentially identical if it wasn't for the `@apr` assignment. If the logic of the method changes in the future, you'd have to go and change the same code in both classes. Ruby's solution to this is the method `super`, as shown here:

```ruby
class CreditCard < Account
  # ...
  def initialize(holder, ssn, interest_rate)
    super(holder, ssn)
    @apr = interest_rate
  end
  # ...
end
```

When you specify `super(holder, ssn)` in the `initialize` method, Ruby looks for an `initialize` method in the superclass, and passes the two arguments specified to it. In this case it executes the code within `Account`'s `initialize` method, which sets both `@holder` and `@ssn`, and then "comes back" to the method that called it, to continue the execution (in this case, by performing an assignment to the instance variable `@apr`). When the method that Ruby is looking for does not exist in the immediate superclass, Ruby continues to search for it in each ancestor within the inheritance hierarchy until it finds one that implements it (and raises an error if there are no classes that implement it). The exact method resolution algorithm is more complex than this, though, and is explained in detail later in this chapter.

Monkey Patching

If you've worked with .NET, you're probably familiar with the concept of sealed classes. C# uses the `sealed` modifier, whereas Visual Basic .NET uses `NotInheritable`; they both mean the same thing: this class shall not be inherited from.

In Ruby things are much more open and dynamic. Not only can you inherit from any user-defined class, core classes, and classes defined in the Core and Standard libraries, but you can actually reopen classes and redefine existing methods or add your own methods and attributes, without touching the initial definition of the class.

> **ActiveSupport**
>
> Rails' internal code relies heavily on ActiveSupport, a collection of utility classes and Ruby's Standard Library extensions, which contains numerous useful features. ActiveSupport is possible thanks to Ruby's ability to reopen classes. The following are a few basic examples of methods that are available only when the ActiveSupport library has been loaded into your Ruby programs (and of course, ActiveSupport is automatically available in Rails applications):
>
> ```
> require 'rubygems'
> require 'activesupport'
>
> puts "my_table".classify    # Prints MyTable
> puts "author_id".humanize   # Prints Author
> puts "mouse".pluralize      # Prints mice
>
> puts 2.days.ago             # Prints something like Mon Jun 30
> 19:02:29 -0400 2008
> puts 3.hours.from_now       # Prints something like Wed Jul 02
> 22:02:29 -0400 2008
> ```
>
> As you can see ActiveSupport is not only for Rails' internal code, but you can use it in your own programs and in Rails applications whenever it is convenient to do so.

Remember the `Integer` class (inherited by both `Fixnum` and `Bignum`) discussed in the previous chapter? Now add an `even?` instance method to it:

```
class Integer
  def even?
    self & 1 == 0
  end
end
```

Believe it or not, you can now do the following:

```
puts 10.even?   # Prints true
puts 15.even?   # Prints false
```

Notice how `self` is used to refer to the current instance within the method `even?`, to verify whether or not it's an even number.

Perhaps you'd like a `squares` iterator:

```
class Integer
  def squares
    self.times {|x| yield x**2 }
  end
end

10.squares {|n| print n, " " } # Prints 0 1 4 9 16 25 36 49 64 81
```

Or plug that `each_even` iterator you defined before for ranges, directly into the `Array` class (for a bit of variety):

```
class Array
  def each_even
    self.each do |n|
      yield n if (n&1).zero?
    end
  end
end

[1,1,2,4,5,6,8,9,10,11,15].each_even {|x| print x, " " }   # Prints 2 4 6 8 10
```

As you can see, this can be a very powerful feature and most people who learn about it for the first time think it's extremely cool. Most Rails plugins rely on this technique (called *Monkey Patching*) to modify the core behavior of Rails, which would otherwise be hard to customize. Monkey Patching is a useful technique and in the Ruby community, unlike the Python one, it is usually not frowned upon. As a developer you should always keep a balanced approach to programming though.

This technique can be easily abused, thus making it hard to find bugs. For example, a library could change the behavior of a core method and your program — which loads the library and relies on the standard behavior of the method — will start to act differently from what you expected, for no apparent reason.

With great power comes great responsibility. Always try to see if other techniques are suitable before blindly applying Monkey Patching, which may appear to be the "easy way out."

Singleton Methods and Eigenclasses

In Ruby you can define methods that exist only for a specific instance. These methods are called singleton methods, for example:

```
str = "A string"
```

```
def str.print
  puts self
end
```

```
str.print  # Prints A string
```

```
# Raises a NoMethodError
"a different one".print
```

Duck Typing

Monkey Patching is only one of the unusual names that you'll hear in the Ruby community. Another common one is Duck Typing.

The gist of it is that in Ruby there is a tendency to consider objects based on their behavior, as opposed to their type. In other words, more often than not, we care more about what an object can do and what methods it implements, instead of its type. The saying goes, "If it walks like a duck, and it talks like a duck, then it's a duck." It may not be an actual duck, but Ruby is able to treat it as such.

If you define the following method:

```
def put_them_together(a, b)
  a + b
end
```

it doesn't particularly matter if a and b are two integers, two floats, an integer and a float, two complex numbers, two points of a plane, two strings, two arrays...as long as they can be "added" through the + method/operator.

At times you may want to be more mindful and verify that a given object responds to a certain method before trying to invoke it. The method respond_to? does just that:

```
10.respond_to?(:find)         # false
"a string".respond_to?(:find) # true
[1,2,3].respond_to?(:find)    # true
(5..50).respond_to?(:find)    # true
```

As you can see, the method name is prefixed by the actual object that you're defining it for (plus a dot). If you define such a method for a particular object and then try to call it for a different instance of the same class, the method won't be available and a NoMethodError will be raised.

Please note that the main Ruby implementation treats fixnums and symbols as immediate values (they are still objects, but are treated as values as opposed to references). This generally doesn't affect you in any way, but there is a small caveat; being immediate values, you won't be able to define a singleton method for any of their objects. What's more, for consistency reasons, the same is extended to any instance of the Numeric class, thus:

```
a = 3
```

```
def a.print
  puts self
end
```

```
a.print   # Raises a TypeError
```

Class Methods

Having introduced singleton methods naturally brings us to class methods. Class methods are singleton methods defined for an object that happens to be a class (or a module). In fact, in Ruby, even classes are objects, because they are themselves instances of the `Class` class. What does this mean in practice?

Class methods must be invoked on a class (or a module), instead of an instance of the class. For example, when you invoke `File.open` you are requesting the `open` class method on the class `File`, similarly to how `Math.cos` means invoking the class method `cos` defined by the module `Math`. On the other hand, `"a string".reverse` or `["a", "string"].join(' ')` are calls to instance methods on receivers that are "regular objects."

Class methods in Ruby are essentially the same as `static` methods in C# and `shared` methods in VB.NET. Given that class methods are just a particular form of singleton methods, the syntax for defining them is quite different from the one in those languages though. You can define them as follows:

```ruby
class MyClass
  def self.my_name
    puts self.to_s
  end
end
```

```ruby
MyClass.my_name    # Prints MyClass
```

The object you are defining the singleton method `my_name` for is referenced by `self`. But as you have seen before, `self` inside of a class and outside of an instance method refers to the class itself. So what you are doing is the equivalent of saying: `def MyClass.my_name` (which would work as well, by the way). Now you can call the `my_name` method on `MyClass`. Note also how `self` within the class method just defined is still referencing `MyClass`, because there is no instance, and the "current object" is the class itself, which acts as the receiver of the method invocation.

Class Variables Considered Harmful

Similarly to "static methods," Ruby provides "static fields" as well. Ruby offers class variables, which are variables defined at class level and prefixed by two `@@` symbols (for example, `@@counter`).

Whenever a subclass modifies the value of a class variable though, this is changed for the base class and all of its subclasses as well; this is not always the desired outcome and this lack of encapsulation can accidentally introduce hard-to-trace bugs into the program.

Their usage is often discouraged in the Ruby community, and many avoid them altogether, opting for class instance variables instead. These are instance variables (a single `@`) that are defined at class level. Googling the subject should bring up a series of discussions on the topic.

On a side note, global variables prefixed by the `$` sign (for example, `$my_directory`) are accessible in any scope within an application and their use tends to be discouraged as well.

You can use class variables if you have to, even Rails uses them internally, but do so with care.

As you would probably expect, invoking a class method of a class on an instance of that class raises an error:

```
m = MyClass.new
m.my_name   # Raises a NoMethodError
```

Eigenclasses

Whenever you define a singleton method for a particular object, this gets stored in an anonymous class associated with that object. This special type of class is often called eigenclass, but can also be referred to as singleton class, metaclass, or even ghost class.

Ruby offers a shorthand notation for explicitly opening the eigenclass of a given object:

```
class << obj
  #...
end
```

Any method defined within that eigenclass will of course be a singleton method for `obj`, as shown in the following example:

```
beats = ["Ginsberg",  "Kerouac",  "Burrough",  "Corso"]
```

```
class << beats
  def list
    self.join(", ")
  end
end
```

```
puts beats.list     # Prints Ginsberg, Kerouac, Burrough, Corso
puts [1,2,3].list   # Raises a NoMethodError
```

This is a handier way of defining several singleton methods at once without having to prefix each definition with `obj.` (for example, `obj.method1`, `obj.method2`, and so on).

A distinction between singleton methods defined on common objects and those defined on class objects (hence class methods) is that the eigenclasses associated with a class object can have a superclass, plus ancestor classes. Understanding this distinction will help you better understand Ruby's lookup method algorithm, as explained later in this chapter.

The same technique can be applied to define class methods en masse (remember, class methods are singleton methods for a class object). Assuming that you defined a `MyClass` class, you can define new class methods for it by opening its eigenclass:

```
class << MyClass
  def method1
    # ...
  end

  def method2
    # ...
  end
```

```
      def method3
        # ...
      end
   end

MyClass.method1
MyClass.method2
MyClass.method3
```

Or perhaps more commonly:

```
class MyClass
   # ...
   # Some instance methods
   #...

   # Class methods
   class << self
      def method1
         # ...
      end

      def method2
         # ...
      end

      def method3
         # ...
      end
   end
end

MyClass.method1
MyClass.method2
MyClass.method3
```

Notice how class << self is equivalent to class << MyClass because self within that point of the class definition references to MyClass.

Again, this is shorthand that spares you from defining each class method by prefixing it with self.:

```
# Equivalent to the previous definition
class MyClass
   # ...
   # Some instance methods
   # ...

   # Class methods
   def self.method1
      # ...
   end

   def self.method2
      # ...
   end
```

```
        def self.method3
            # ...
        end
end

MyClass.method1
MyClass.method2
MyClass.method3
```

The `class << self` idiom is extremely common, but a style consideration is in order. When you define several singleton methods at once directly in the eigenclass, you may have code that spans many lines, so it may not be so obvious that a method you're looking at is a class method (because it's defined between `class << self` and `end`) and not an instance method. For the sake of readability it is usually better to define class methods explicitly by prefixing them with `self`.

As you advance with your knowledge of Ruby, you'll realize that the ability to open eigenclasses still comes in handy on a few occasions, especially when doing metaprogramming.

Modules and Mixins

The word "module" has been mentioned here and there a few times so far. It's time to take a closer look at a fundamental part of Ruby programming.

As mentioned before, modules serve two purposes. They act as namespaces that prevent name collision and are used as a way to add functionalities to classes that would otherwise be limited by the single inheritance nature of Ruby's object model.

A series of similarities between classes and modules are as follows:

❑ Classes are constants and so are modules.

❑ Classes are defined through the `class` keyword and modules are defined with the `module` keyword.

❑ Classes are instances of the `Class` class, and modules are instances of the `Module` class.

❑ Classes act as namespaces. Two identical methods defined within two unrelated classes are not going to pose a problem. The same is true for modules.

❑ Classes can be nested, and so can modules.

❑ The `Class` class inherits from the `Module` class, so it can be said that every class is also a module.

On the other hand, a few fundamental differences also exist:

❑ Classes can be instantiated. Modules cannot.

❑ Classes can have a superclass and subclasses; as such they yield a hierarchy tree. Modules do not, because they don't have a parent or any children.

❑ Modules can be used as mixins, but classes cannot.

Modules Act as Namespaces

If you are a .NET developer, you are no doubt familiar with the concept of namespaces. The basic idea is to group constants, variables, methods, and classes into well-organized units. In C# and VB you'd use `namespace`, in Ruby you use `module`:

```
module MyModel
end
```

Modules, like classes, are constants, and as such need to start with a capital letter. It is also customary to adopt the CamelCase notation for module names (just as it is for classes).

Now define a module and a constant as follows:

```
module Physics
  EARTH_MASS = 5.9742e24 # In Kg
end
```

How do you access that constant now? In Ruby you access methods through a dot operator and constants through `::`. This means that you'll have access to the value of that `EARTH_MASS` constant in the following way:

```
puts Physics::EARTH_MASS   # Prints 5.9742e+024
```

You could start to add a series of constants to the module; in fact, given its name, it is plausible to assume that the module would take care of a lot of physics-related functionalities. Imagine that this module would be developed to contain dozens of physics constants, a few classes, and many methods. It would be much better to organize all the physics constants into a module called `Constants`.

Modules can be nested, so you can achieve this quite easily. For example:

```
module Physics
  module Constants
    EARTH_MASS = 5.9742e24 # Kg
    # ...
    AVOGADRO = 6.0221415e23 # mol^-1
    # ...
  end
end
```

Now how can you get access to the value of `EARTH_MASS` or `AVOGADRO`? Again, in Ruby you access constants through the `::` operator; it doesn't matter if the constant happens to be a numeric one, a class, or a module. You start with the name of the outermost module (`Physics`), add a couple of colons to access the constant/module `Constants`, and finally, add another pair of colons to gain access to the two constants `EARTH_MASS` and `AVOGADRO`:

```
puts Physics::Constants::EARTH_MASS   # Prints 5.9742e+024
puts Physics::Constants::AVOGADRO     # Prints 6.0221415e+023
```

You can nest modules by simply nesting their definitions:

```
module A
  # ... A ...
  module B
    # ... B ...
    module C
      # ... C ...
      module D
        # ... D ...
      end
    end
  end

  module F
    # ... F ...
  end
end
```

As long as the intermediary modules are already defined (`A::F` in this case), you can also define a nested module in this way:

```
module A::F::G
  # ...
end
```

Generally speaking you wouldn't want to overdo it, but two or three nested namespaces are not uncommon.

"Standalone" class methods can be defined within modules in the usual "singleton manner":

```
module MyModule
  def self.method1
  end

  def self.method2
  end

  def self.method3
  end
end
```

Or alternatively:

```
module MyModule
  def MyModule.method1
  end

  def MyModule.method2
  end

  def MyModule.method3
  end
end
```

In both equivalent cases, the dot operator is used to access the method directly contained in a namespace:

```
MyModule.method1
```

If `MyModule` were a module nested within, say, `AnotherModule`, then `method1` would be accessible through `MyModule::AnotherModule.method1`. `AnotherModule::MyModule` is the receiver for the method.

> *Class methods defined within modules, just like class methods defined for classes, can share data through class variables (for example, @@var). Modules don't inherit from each other, so using them inside of the definitions of class methods within modules (but outside of classes) makes them less risky.*

Modules can also contain classes, as you'd probably expect if you are coming from a .NET background.

> *Just as for the classes, you can reopen modules as well, and monkey patch them if needed.*

Before moving onto the real deal with modules (their usage as mixins) you should know how you can load Ruby files (including those that contain modules). Assume that you defined the `Physics` module within a `physics.rb` file.

> *The name of a file can be arbitrary and contain any Ruby code you like. If your file contains only one main module (and its possible nested modules and classes) though, it is customary to call the file with the name of that module (in lowercase).*

To load it from a program in the same directory, you can run:

```
require 'physics'
```

The file will actually be loaded only once, and all of its content (modules, classes, methods, and so on) will be available in your program.

> `require` *accepts absolute paths as well. See* `ri Kernel#require` *for more information about this.*

Modules Act as Mixins

Modules are a powerful tool in the hands of a competent Ruby programmer, because they can act as mixins. You won't find "mixins" in the dictionary, but the term comes from "mix" and "in," which is a very apt description of what modules can do; they can add functionalities to existing classes by "mixing in" a series of methods.

Mixins are modules whose code can be included in a class (and in another module). Consider a basic example. The following is a module with a method:

```
module Logger
  def log
    puts "#{Time.now}: #{self.inspect}"
  end
end
```

All the `log` method does is print the current time and object. Note how this method is not a class method (because it wasn't defined as `self.log` or `Logger`). `log` is an instance method and you can't really instantiate modules. What this means is that you are not able to invoke `Logger.log`. What you can do, though, is to add the functionalities of the `Logger` module to a class, by adding its instance methods to the class. In this example, the added feature will just be the `log` method, but the same principle applies to arbitrarily complex code as well.

You can `include` the module within any class:

```ruby
class Array
   include Logger
end
```

This adds the instance method `log` to the class `Array`. Now you can run:

```ruby
array = []
10.times { array << rand(100) }
array.sort!
array.log
```

and obtain something that resembles this in your output:

```
Wed Jul 02 00:31:32 -0400 2008: [5, 38, 47, 51, 63, 73, 83, 84, 90, 95]
```

Interestingly, you can verify that `array.is_a? Logger` *evaluates to* `true`, *whereas* `array.instance_of? Logger` *will return* `false`.

Notice that the method is general enough to be used by any class. By defining it in a mixin, instead of a specific class, you can include that functionality in any class that may need it. This turns out to be extremely powerful, even if the simplicity of the example may be misleading and cause you to think otherwise. A class can include several mixins, and as such obtain functionalities derived from several modules. This approach is simple, flexible, and essentially provides the benefits of multiple inheritance.

Classes like `Range`, `Array`, and `Hash` all include the `Enumerable` module, whereas `String` (at least in Ruby 1.8) includes both `Comparable` and `Enumerable`. `Enumerable` is definitely one of the most used mixins. The reason for this is that it provides many iterators "for free" to your classes, as long as you implement a required `each` method. If you do, `Enumerable` can infer the right behavior for its iterators.

To include multiple mixins, you can pass a list to `include`:

```ruby
class MyClass
   include Enumerable, Comparable, MyCustomMixin
end
```

include Versus extend

A lot of concepts were introduced in the past couple of sections, so let's recap the type of methods that you can define directly inside of a module. If you define a singleton method in the module (for example, `def self.my_method`), you can then invoke it like a utility function, with the module as a receiver (for example, `MyModule.my_method`) acting mainly as a namespace for logically similar functions/methods. If you define an instance method in the module (for example, `def my_method`), you can then add it to classes as an instance method by passing the mixin (that is, the name of the module) to `include` within the definition of the class.

You may notice that a third type of method is missing. What about actual singleton methods that can be invoked on a specific object, or perhaps more interestingly, on a class object? Yes, having arrived at this point, you are essentially missing a way to define class methods that are invoked on actual classes.

Ruby provides you with `extend` exactly for that purpose:

```
class MyClass
    extend Logger
end
```

```
MyClass.log
```

Notice how the method `log`, defined as an "instance method" in the module `Logger`, becomes a class method of the `MyClass` class. Behind the scenes, all the instance methods defined in `Logger` get added to the eigenclass of `MyClass`. This means that, if instead of doing it with a class object, you added `extend Logger` to a specific instance of an object, the methods would become regular singleton methods for that object. For most practical purposes, just remember: use `include` to obtain instance methods, and `extend` to get class methods for your class.

> *Investigate the* `module_function` *method if you'd like to automatically obtain a method that can be called on a module (for example,* `MyModule.my_method`*) from an instance method that you defined in the module. This way, you'll be able to obtain mixin behavior with* include/extend *in your classes, while still being able to access the methods like you would with a module that acts purely as a namespace.*

Metaprogramming

Metaprogramming is defined as the act of programming code that is able to manipulate itself (or other code). A practical example of this showed up a few sections ago when you used methods such as `attr_accessor` to dynamically obtain getter and setter methods for instance variables. The ability to reopen classes, define classes and methods conditionally, and call methods that get defined when first invoked, are all good examples of Ruby's metaprogramming abilities.

Metaprogramming is generally encouraged within the Ruby community partially because it's particularly useful when defining Domain Specific Languages (DSLs). Most Ruby developers would agree that powerful metaprogramming techniques should not be abused when writing code that may end up becoming "too clever for its own good," but that a decent mastery of the subject can really separate a beginner from a pro Ruby programmer.

Rails makes extensive use of metaprogramming in its implementation, and you are encouraged to explore the topic further on your own once you've gained more confidence with Ruby and Rails. Even as a Rails developer (as opposed to a Rails implementer), metaprogramming can be very useful, particularly when you want to start creating and publishing your own plugins. It's important to provide you with one quick example though, in order to understand how ActiveRecord's dynamic finders work. If you have a User model with a `user_name` and a `password` attribute, in ActiveRecord you could issue the following:

```
@user = User.find_by_user_name_and_password("acangiano", "secret")
```

131

No matter where you look in ActiveRecord's code you won't find a `find_by_user_name_and_password` method. This method gets created on the spot, the first time that it's invoked. This is mainly possible thanks to two metaprogramming features of Ruby: `method_missing` and the ability to dynamically define methods (this can be accomplished in more than one way).

`method_missing` is a special method that gets invoked whenever a requested method cannot be found by the receiver. By default `method_missing` will just raise a `NoMethodError` error, but it can be overwritten and customized to implement your own logic. The following example verifies that `method_missing` gets invoked when you send an undefined method name to the receiver:

```
class String
  def method_missing(method_id, *args)
    puts "Don't know how to handle #{method_id}."
  end
end

"A string".matz
```

The `"A string"` object doesn't know how to handle the method `matz`, so `method_missing` (the overwritten version) is invoked. This is the output of the preceding snippet:

```
Don't know how to handle matz.
```

The first argument of `method_missing` is a symbol that represents the name of the unknown method, and the second argument stores a variable number of arguments in the `args` variable (here they are called `method_id` and `args`, but they are just parameters; you can call them however you please). If you wanted to handle a possible block passed to the method, you could use the usual third `&block` parameter.

This example kept things simple and printed a message, but within that `method_missing` method you could write elaborate logic to handle situations where a method is unknown to its receiver. Behind the scenes that's exactly what ActiveRecord does with dynamic finders, and it employs `class_eval`, a method used to dynamically add methods to classes.

Method Name Resolution

Instance methods, singleton methods (including class methods), objects, classes, eigenclasses, modules that act as mixins, `super`, `method_missing`... How does a receiver know where to find a method? The Ruby interpreter uses a specific algorithm to look up methods. Consider the following method invocation:

```
[1,2,3].method1
```

Assume that we haven't defined `method1` anywhere for that array.

Ruby will follow each step until it finds a matching method:

1. Look into the eigenclass of that particular instance. Is `method1` defined in there?

2. Is there an instance method `method1` defined by the `Array` class?

3. Does the mixin `Enumerable`, included in the class `Array`, have a `method1`?

4. Does the superclass of `Array` (that is, `Object`) include a `method1`?

5. Does the mixin `Kernel`, included by the superclass `Object`, include `method1`?

6. Starting from the eigenclass, and through all the classes and modules in the order presented here (`eigenclass`, `Array`, `Enumerable`, `Object`, `Kernel`), is `method_missing` defined? Yes, the first `method_missing` is defined by the `Kernel` mixin and can therefore be invoked. `method_missing` will raise a `NoMethodError` error.

If you were to run `[1,2,3].length`, the method name resolution algorithm would stop at the second step.

> *You can see the ancestor of a class, including its mixins, through the* `ancestors` *method. For example* `String.ancestors` *returns* `[String, Enumerable, Comparable, Object, Kernel]`.

Class method lookup works in almost the same manner, which is not surprising if you consider that a class method is just a singleton method where the associated object is an instance of `Class`. As mentioned before, the main difference is that class methods are defined in eigenclasses that can have superclasses. So if you define a class method in `Object` and a class method in `Array`, `Object`'s eigenclass is going to be a superclass of `Array`'s eigenclass. As such, instead of going from step 1 to step 2, the algorithm introduces an intermediary step, which is used to search for a singleton method (a class method) within the superclass of the eigenclass associated with the receiver, and all of the ancestor eigenclasses in the hierarchy tree, before moving on to step 2 (which becomes step 3, as a matter of fact).

> *Realistically, this is more than you need to know at this stage. But it's included so that you can come back to it at a later stage.*

Alternative Ruby Implementations

When we talk about Ruby it's common to assume that we are referring to the latest stable version of Matz's interpreter. It is important to keep in mind that Ruby is a programming language, not a single implementation. Several alternative implementations have popped up over the past few years, thanks to the incredible success that Rails brought to the language. Most of them were aimed toward fixing Ruby's main Achilles' heel, the speed of its most commonly used interpreter. But the world of alternative implementations is so much more than that, and each of them is characterized by particular strengths and weaknesses. Every year new implementations are released and thus there is a form of natural selection in place, which will end up whittling the selection down to a few established players that will become somewhat commonly used. In their wake, many others will fall to the wayside and end up being used far less routinely. The following list introduces you to the ones that are today's main players:

> *I periodically run shootouts among all these implementations. You can find them on my blog at* http://antoniocangiano.com.

❑ **Ruby 1.9** is the next version of Ruby. In this version, the heart of Ruby has been replaced with a bytecode interpreter known as YARV (Yet Another Ruby VM). It has support for Rails and it's about three times faster than Ruby 1.8.6, according to a series of micro-benchmarks that I run periodically. Unfortunately other benchmarks have shown that Rails applications running on Ruby 1.9 don't gain nearly as much speed. But that said, it's still a huge improvement over the current interpreter nevertheless, especially if you consider that a few design flaws of the language are being addressed as well.

❏ **JRuby** is an implementation of Ruby for the JVM, which is aimed at being fast and providing integration with the Java world. It is the oldest and probably most mature alternative implementation, and it has been able to run Rails since 2006.

❏ **Rubinius** is a compiler and Smalltalk-like virtual machine for Ruby. The focus of this VM is on correctness, extensibility, and speed. The development team, joined also by other VM implementers, did a great job in creating specs for the Ruby language (which unfortunately, lacks a formal grammar). In 2008, Rubinius was able to introduce preliminary support for Rails applications.

❏ **MagLev** is the youngest of the lot, but was able to wow the audience at RailsConf 2008, thanks to its impressive results during a series of micro-benchmarks. At the time of this writing it is not yet publicly available, or able to run Rails. But I have tried it and can confirm that it's a promising project with the potential to do very well in terms of performance. It's developed by Gemstone, a well-known company in the world of Smalltalk, and may become a commercial product with a free version available as well. The basic idea behind this project is that Ruby is not all that different from Smalltalk, and as such, Gemstone should be able to leverage their experience in delivering a fast and scalable platform for Smalltalk, even when applied to Ruby.

❏ **MacRuby** is an implementation of Ruby 1.9 in Objective-C, developed by Apple, Inc. Its goal is to become a fast replacement for RubyCocoa when it comes to writing Ruby applications for Mac, and at the time of this writing, is not able to run Rails applications yet.

❏ **IronRuby** is a version of Ruby implemented by Microsoft. It's built on top of the Dynamic Language Runtime (DLR), which in turn sits atop of the CLR. If you are a .NET developer, this is the alternative implementation that should interest you the most, given that when a stable version is released, it will allow you to write Rails applications that can take advantage of Silverlight and the .NET Framework. This would be the best of both worlds, as long as you haven't decided to abandon the .NET ship altogether. At the time of this writing, IronRuby has added preliminary support for both Rails and Silverlight.

A similar project that was sponsored by Microsoft is Ruby.NET (based on the CLR). Though it is clear that IronRuby is going to become the de facto standard for Ruby on .NET, particularly after the head of the project left Ruby.NET and joined IronRuby, few developers do try to actively keep the Ruby.NET project alive, but its future is uncertain at best. I recommend that you explore the IronRuby possibility first, if you are interested in the interoperability between Ruby and the Microsoft world.

Summary

Hefty tomes have been written on the subject of Ruby programming (see Appendix A), and this and the previous chapters alone cannot possibly do Ruby full justice, particularly when it comes to advanced topics (such as metaprogramming).

Ruby's coverage within this book is meant to be a solid language foundation upon which you can approach the world of Rails. Whenever the need for further Ruby-specific knowledge arises throughout the book, I have ensured that I've covered it by augmenting topics that have already been covered in the current and prior chapter.

In the next chapter you finally get to play with Rails, and I'll guide you step-by-step as you create a basic sample application to illustrate how Rails is used and how it works in practice.

5

A Working Sample

Ruby on Rails is astounding. Using it is like watching a kung-fu movie, where a dozen bad-ass frameworks prepare to beat up the little newcomer only to be handed their asses in a variety of imaginative ways.

— Nathan Torkington, O'Reilly Program Chair for OSCON

The first two chapters provided an overview of Rails, and the last two gave you a good taste of what programming in Ruby is like. In this chapter the action begins and you start creating a simple blog engine in Rails. It's admittedly not a very original project, but it's a great example for learning Rails' basics. It's simple enough to be explained in a chapter or two, and substantial enough to explore a lot of Rails concepts and how to apply them in practice to write real Web applications.

Creating a New Rails Application

If you were to create a new ASP.NET application, you would typically reach for Visual Studio or its free counterpart Visual Web Developer 2008 Express Edition, in order to produce a new ASP.NET website. The solution and project generated would essentially be an almost empty container for the items that you'd add as you developed the application.

With Rails you reach for the command line and invoke the `rails` command, unless you are using one of the available IDEs that does that behind the scenes for you. Unlike Visual Studio, this command generates several folders and files that act as the skeleton of your application.

> **In Rails there is a lot of magic going on. This improves productivity but can also be intimidating to newcomers. When doing Rails development, always keep a tab open on the official API documentation** (http://api.rubyonrails.org) **or equivalent sites such as** http://apidock.com/rails.

LIMERICK
COUNTY LIBRARY

The rails Command

You can use the `rails` command to create your blog application:

```
C:\projects> rails blog
```

This creates a `blog` directory in the current one (`C:\projects` in this case) and also prints a list of directories and files that are generated, as shown in Figure 5-1.

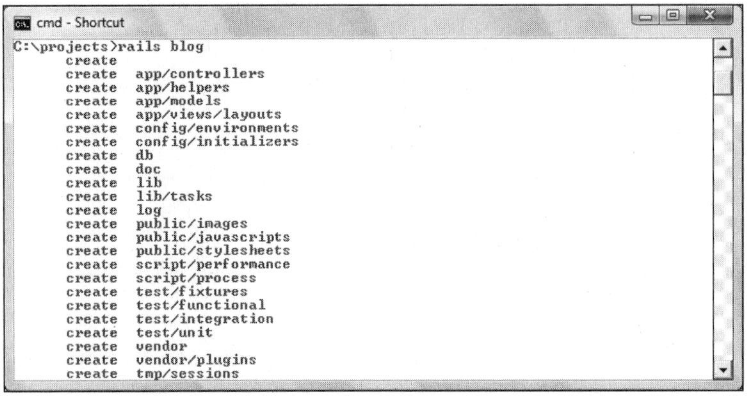

```
C:\projects>rails blog
      create
      create    app/controllers
      create    app/helpers
      create    app/models
      create    app/views/layouts
      create    config/environments
      create    config/initializers
      create    db
      create    doc
      create    lib
      create    lib/tasks
      create    log
      create    public/images
      create    public/javascripts
      create    public/stylesheets
      create    script/performance
      create    script/process
      create    test/fixtures
      create    test/functional
      create    test/integration
      create    test/unit
      create    vendor
      create    vendor/plugins
      create    tmp/sessions
```

Figure 5-1

You use `cd` to step into the `blog` directory that was just generated by the `rails` command:

```
C:\projects> cd blog
```

The directory structure is shown in Figure 5-2. In this chapter you get to interact with several of these directories, in particular with `app`, where most of the application resides, and `config`, where the configuration of the application is found. The next chapter presents a more systematic explanation of all the remaining folders.

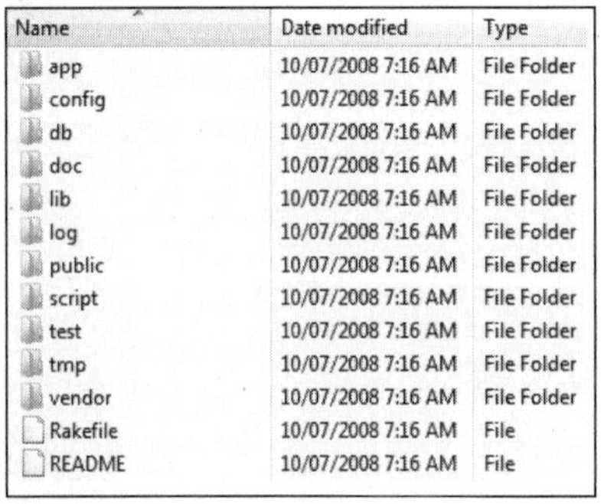

Name	Date modified	Type
app	10/07/2008 7:16 AM	File Folder
config	10/07/2008 7:16 AM	File Folder
db	10/07/2008 7:16 AM	File Folder
doc	10/07/2008 7:16 AM	File Folder
lib	10/07/2008 7:16 AM	File Folder
log	10/07/2008 7:16 AM	File Folder
public	10/07/2008 7:16 AM	File Folder
script	10/07/2008 7:16 AM	File Folder
test	10/07/2008 7:16 AM	File Folder
tmp	10/07/2008 7:16 AM	File Folder
vendor	10/07/2008 7:16 AM	File Folder
Rakefile	10/07/2008 7:16 AM	File
README	10/07/2008 7:16 AM	File

Figure 5-2

Forward Slash Versus Backslash

If you are using Windows, the path to the `database.yml` file is `config\database.yml`. If you happen to use a *nix system, the path will be `config/database.yml`. This raises the issue of forward slash (which is cross-platform) and backslash (which is Windows specific).

Given the target audience for this book I will adopt the following convention: I'll use the backslash when describing folder and file paths in the text, and use the forward slash in the commands. The reason for this is that I'd like to keep the commands cross-platform, in case you are following the book from GNU/Linux or a Mac.

In reality Rails' scripts understand both type of slashes, so as you type along on your Windows machine, it may be easier to use the backslash rather than forward slash, because the command prompt will give you proper auto-completion by pressing the Tab key.

---

config\database.yml

The database credentials in a Rails application are stored in `config\database.yml` by default. Listing 5-1 shows the one generated by the previous `rails` command (available for download as `listing0501.yml`).

Listing 5-1: Default config\database.yml for SQLite3

```
# SQLite version 3.x
#   gem install sqlite3-ruby (not necessary on OS X Leopard)
development:
  adapter: sqlite3
  database: db/development.sqlite3
  pool: 5
  timeout: 5000

# Warning: The database defined as "test" will be erased and
# re-generated from your development database when you run "rake".
# Do not set this db to the same as development or production.
test:
  adapter: sqlite3
  database: db/test.sqlite3
  pool: 5
  timeout: 5000

production:
  adapter: sqlite3
  database: db/production.sqlite3
  pool: 5
  timeout: 5000
```

As you can see this is not XML but a very readable YAML (recursive acronym for *YAML Ain't a Markup Language*) file. Ruby ships with support for reading and writing YAML files and this format is often favored over XML in the Ruby and Rails communities.

You'll also notice that `adapter`, `database`, and `timeout` are provided for each of the three environments: `development`, `test`, and `production`. These three environments are independent of each other, so in theory you could use SQLite3 for development, SQL Server for production, and MySQL for testing. Of course this doesn't generally make much sense and it's not recommended, but it illustrates how each environment can be treated as a separate world independently from the others. Furthermore, it clearly highlights how Rails' database abstraction allows you to write Ruby code while all the heavy lifting is done for you, regardless of what database environment you ultimately end up using.

Depending on whether you're in development mode, production mode, or test mode, Rails will employ the right database and other supported options, as specified (for example, the 5 seconds `timeout` or the size of the connection `pool`). In this particular case, given that `sqlite3` is Rails' default adapter, there isn't very much to specify, because you don't have to provide a username and password, nor the details to reach a remote host that is running your databases.

Had you decided to employ MySQL instead, you would have run the `rails` command with the `-d` option and passed the name of the adapter required (that is, `-d mysql`). Even though SQLite, MySQL, and PostgreSQL are the only databases for which the adapter ships directly with Rails, the `-d` option currently accepts the following adapters: `mysql`, `sqlite2`, `sqlite3`, `postgresql`, `oracle`, `frontbase`, and `ibm_db` (for DB2). If you are using SQL Server, for example, you will have to skip the `-d` option and manually modify the `database.yml`.

Running `rails blog -d mysql` would have generated the `database.yml` as shown in Listing 5-2 (available for download as `listing0502.yml`) for you.

> *Listing 5-2 strips all the comments from the file for improved clarity on the printed page.*

Listing 5-2: Default config\database.yml for MySQL

```
development:
  adapter: mysql
  encoding: utf8
  database: blog_development
  pool: 5
  username: root
  password:
  host: localhost

test:
  adapter: mysql
  encoding: utf8
  database: blog_test
  pool: 5
  username: root
  password:
  host: localhost

production:
  adapter: mysql
  encoding: utf8
  database: blog_production
  pool: 5
  username: root
  password:
  host: localhost
```

The database name for each of the three environments is automatically generated based on the name of the application and the environment at hand. The default host name is `localhost`, and in the specific case of MySQL there is an `encoding` parameter set to `utf-8` to support internationalization.

If you were using a remote MySQL database, you could specify the host IP or name and optionally its port number.

Compare this approach with the option of adding a connection string to a `Web.config` XML file and you'll start to realize how Rails consistently tries to make things easy for the developer from the beginning. You provide the user credentials, specify the database and its location, and you're set. In this case, using SQLite3 practically means that you don't even have to touch the `database.yml` file at all.

Creating Databases

Rails generates and populates a configuration file for your databases, but it doesn't automatically create the actual databases for you. In order to create the databases you have two options. You could create them independently from Rails, for example, by using the `sqlite3` command for SQLite3 databases, or SQL Server Management Studio for SQL Server databases. This approach works, but Rails provides a handier option when the databases that need to be created are local to the machine that's running Rails. You can create local databases using a Rake task.

Rake is a build tool, just like Microsoft `nmake` and `NAnt`. It allows you to define a series of tasks in Ruby that perform certain actions for you. As you can imagine, Rails ships with a whole set of useful Rake tasks to help out while developing applications. To create all the local databases specified in the `database.yml` file, run the following:

```
C:\projects\blog> rake db:create:all
```

Similarly, you can drop all the local databases with `rake db:drop:all`. If you want to create or drop the database for a specific environment only, use `rake db:create` and `rake db:drop`, respectively. In Rails, the default environment is development, so if you execute those two Rake tasks without specifying an argument, they will create and drop the local development database, respectively. If you want to explicitly specify that, say, the production database should be created or dropped (be careful with dropping actual production databases), you can pass a `RAILS_ENV=production` argument to the tasks (for example, `rake db:create RAILS_ENV=production`).

To display a complete list of Rake tasks that are available in a given Rails application, you can run `rake -T`. You can also limit the list of tasks to those that contain a given word as shown here:

```
C:\projects\blog> rake -T notes
(in C:/projects/blog)
rake notes            # Enumerate all annotations
rake notes:custom     # Enumerate a custom annotation, specify with ANNOTATI...
rake notes:fixme      # Enumerate all FIXME annotations
rake notes:optimize   # Enumerate all OPTIMIZE annotations
rake notes:todo       # Enumerate all TODO annotations
```

By the way, the tasks in the output are used to retrieve all the FIXME, OPTIMIZE, and TODO or custom comments embedded in your Rails application's code, in a similar manner to how you'd use the Task List in Visual Studio.

Scaffolding and Migrations

You can get a head start on building your simple blog engine by employing the `scaffold` generator. The guiding idea behind scaffolding is that you can use it to obtain a basic CRUD application that displays and manipulates the data within a table, without having to write a single line of code (as briefly seen in Chapter 1). This then becomes a foundation that can be customized and which allows you to build a more complex application that looks and behaves the way you want it to.

As a bare minimum your blog will need to allow you to list, show, create, delete, and edit articles. For each article, you should keep track of its title (which is a string), body (which is a bunch of text), whether or not it is published already (so a Boolean) and its publication date and time. To translate this idea into an actual application, go ahead and run the following command:

```
C:\projects\blog> ruby script/generate scaffold article title:string body:text
published:boolean published_at:datetime
```

`article` is the resource, and the pairs `title:string`, `body:text`, `published:boolean`, and `published_at:datetime` specify its attributes and their data types.

The output of this command resembles the following (except that the `exists` lines have been removed for clarity):

```
        create  app/views/articles
        create  app/views/articles/index.html.erb
        create  app/views/articles/show.html.erb
        create  app/views/articles/new.html.erb
        create  app/views/articles/edit.html.erb
        create  app/views/layouts/articles.html.erb
        create  public/stylesheets/scaffold.css
        create  app/controllers/articles_controller.rb
        create  test/functional/articles_controller_test.rb
        create  app/helpers/articles_helper.rb
         route  map.resources :articles
    dependency  model
        create     app/models/article.rb
        create     test/unit/article_test.rb
        create     test/fixtures/articles.yml
        create     db/migrate
        create     db/migrate/20080710224642_create_articles.rb
```

The `scaffold` generator creates folders and files for the `ArticlesController`, the `Article` model, and the view layer. It generates a few basic functional tests (for testing the controller) and unit tests (for testing the model), and modifies the `config\routes.rb` file to map URLs to actions in the controller. Each of these are analyzed in detail, but focus first on the last two highlighted lines.

Migrations

The `scaffold` generator created a `migrate` directory inside the `db` one. Within it, it placed a file called, in this specific case, `20080710224642_create_articles.rb`.

The file name is determined by a timestamp of the UTC time of creation, and the name of the table it will create, based on the resource (for example, `article`) you passed as an argument to the `scaffold` generator. The numeric part of your file name will therefore definitely be different. If it isn't, two of the following things are possible. Your computer time is wrong and you miraculously managed to get the same timestamp, in which case I suggest that you buy a lottery ticket; or you're a time traveler and I suggest that you go back to mid 2004 and start studying Rails back then. That too is arguably one way to win a lottery of sorts.

Using Ruby to Define Tables

This file defines the structure of the `articles` table with Ruby code. Take a look at the code of the `20080710224642_create_articles.rb` file, which is automatically generated for you:

```ruby
class CreateArticles < ActiveRecord::Migration
  def self.up
    create_table :articles do |t|
      t.string :title
      t.text :body
      t.boolean :published
      t.datetime :published_at

      t.timestamps
    end
  end

  def self.down
    drop_table :articles
  end
end
```

The `create_table` method on the third line is used in its block form. It accepts the table name as a symbol (that is, `:articles`) or a string (that is, `"articles"`), a series of options (missing in this particular case), and a block in which you can define columns by using the syntax `t.datatype :column_name`, where `t` is the argument of the block and it represents the table definition. Each column definition can have a series of options as well (not shown in this snippet of code).

You may notice that the `scaffold` generator added a `t.timestamps` line as well. This adds two special columns called `created_at` and `updated_at` that are automatically handled by Rails. The first stores the date and time for when an instance of the `Article` model (a row) gets created, and the second one stores the date and time of its last update. You can remove this feature if you wish, but there is usually no harm in keeping it.

You might be wondering why we needed to specify a `published_at` attribute, if we have a `created_at` column "for free." In general we don't, but in this particular case I wanted to provide the author of the blog with the ability to schedule the publication of a post in the future, as you'll see later on.

Rails Data Types

The mapping of Rails data types with the actual database types is defined within the Active Record's adapter for the database that's in use. For example, the DB2 adapter I created for IBM supports an `xml` data type, but this will not be available for your SQLite3 database.

A few exceptions aside though, the following data types are native: `binary`, `boolean`, `date`, `datetime`, `decimal`, `float`, `integer`, `string`, `text`, `time`, and `timestamp`. There is also a special type called `primary_key`.

> `string` *is usually implemented as a* `varchar` *(or equivalent) with a default limit of 255 characters. This limit can be overwritten by passing a hash of options containing the* `:limit` *symbol as a key to the column definition method (for example,* `t.string :name, :limit => 80`*) to the string.*

The following are the available options when it comes to defining columns:

- ❑ `:limit` defines the maximum length for the column. This option is supported by default by the following data types: `string`, `text`, `integer`, and `binary`.

- ❑ `:default` defines the default value for the column. If NULL is the desired default value, use `:default => nil`.

- ❑ `:null` defines whether or not null values are accepted in the column. By default they are (except for `primary_key`, of course), but you can specify `:null => false` if you wish to not permit them.

- ❑ `:precision` and `:scale` are two options for `decimal` columns. They can be used independently, but often go together (for example, `t.decimal :budget, :precision => 15, :scale => 2`).

You may be confused by `date`, `datetime`, `timestamp`, and `time` all being very similar data types. The `sqlite3` adapter, for example, maps all of them, except `date`, to the SQL `datetime` data type, so you might as well consider `timestamp` and `time` as aliases for `datetime`. Other adapters (like `mysql` and `postgresql`) may map `datetime` and `timestamp` to the same SQL data type, but have `date` and `time` mapped to distinct SQL data types. Don't worry too much about this though, because you can always inspect a table to verify what these "abstract" data types actually map to in the definition of your table in the database.

As a Microsoft developer you are probably interested in the mapping of the data types from Active Record to Microsoft SQL Server. The following table describes mapping between Active Record and the SQL Server Adapter.

Active Record	Microsoft SQL Server
primary_key	int NOT NULL IDENTITY(1, 1) PRIMARY KEY
binary	image
Boolean	bit
date	datetime
datetime	datetime
decimal	decimal
float	float
integer	int

Active Record	Microsoft SQL Server
string	varchar
text	text
time	datetime
timestamp	datetime
rake	db:migrate

Remember how the `rails` command generated a `config\database.yml` file, but you had to use a Rake task to create the actual databases? The same principle applies here. The `scaffold` generator created a migration file containing the table definition, but didn't actually create the table in the database. To do that you'll need to use the Rake task `db:migrate`. So run the following to create the `articles` table:

```
C:\projects\blog> rake db:migrate
(in C:/projects/blog)
== 20080710224642 CreateArticles: migrating =====================================
- create_table(:articles)
   -> 0.1090s
== 20080710224642 CreateArticles: migrated (0.1250s) ===========================
```

The preceding output shows that the table was created and there were no errors whatsoever. Once again, given that you didn't specify otherwise with a `RAILS_ENV` argument, the table was created in the development database.

Open the SQLite3 console as follows (also available through `sqlite3 db/development.sqlite3`):

```
C:\projects\blog> ruby script/dbconsole
SQLite version 3.6.10
Enter ".help" for instructions
Enter SQL statements terminated with a ";"sqlite>
```

Now you can show the tables within the database with `.tables`:

```
sqlite> .tables
articles          schema_migrations
```

And see the table definition for the `articles` table with `.schema`:

```
sqlite> .schema articles
CREATE TABLE "articles" ("id" INTEGER PRIMARY KEY AUTOINCREMENT NOT NULL, "title"
varchar(255), "body" text, "published" boolean, "published_at" datetime,
"created_at" datetime, "updated_at" datetime);
```

Use `.exit` *to get out of the SQLite3 console.*

As you can see in the SQL query, all the columns for the attributes specified as arguments of the `scaffold` generator, plus `created_at` and `updated_at`, are there; no surprise. The table also has a primary key called `id`. As mentioned before, this is an ActiveRecord convention, and it's automatically defined whenever you create tables by specifying their definition with the `create_table` method. This method allows you to overwrite the convention by either specifying `:id => false` or by indicating a different name for the primary key (for example, `:primary_key => 'guid'`). It's worth repeating that unless you have a good reason for overwriting a given convention (and occasionally you will), it's better to stick with what ActiveRecord, and more generally Rails, expects.

The schema_migrations Table

When you listed the tables in the SQLite3 console, you may have noticed that there was a `schema_migrations` table next to `articles`. This table is created by the `db:migrate` task if it doesn't already exist. If it does exist, it's used by the task to determine which migration files need to be applied to the current schema in the database. The table `schema_migrations` has a single column called `version` and every time a migration file is applied, the timestamp within its name gets stored as a string in the table.

When I ran `rake db:migrate` on my machine, the table `schema_migrations` was first created, then the class method `up` defined in `20080710224642_create_articles.rb` was invoked, creating therefore the table `articles`, and lastly the value `20080710224642` was inserted into the `schema_migrations` table.

> `SELECT version FROM schema_migrations` *gets executed before and after each migration. This helps, for example, to ensure that a file hasn't already been migrated meanwhile by a different developer in your team.*

Migrating Up and Down

Let's try to better understand how migrations work and why they are a very useful tool. In a traditional ASP or ASP.NET environment, you would define the database objects through a series of SQL scripts (T-SQL if using SQL Server) or directly from a GUI application. Any change or rollback to the database schema would typically have to be performed "manually."

Rails believes in the idea of defining database objects through Ruby code as much as possible, so migrations are a way to define and manipulate tables through Ruby instead of SQL as seen earlier (well, at least, in most cases). But migrations are much more than that.

Every time a migration file is generated (through `scaffold` or not) its name will be "timestamped." In this case, for example, the timestamp was `20080710224642`, which is the UTC time in the year, month, day, hour, minute, and second format.

If at a later stage you add a second migration file that adds a column to the existing table, the timestamp for this file will be successive to the previous one. What this means is that the `db:migrate` task will execute them in succession, which is what you want.

> `scaffold` *is not the only generator that creates migration files. Any generator, whether it's built-in or provided by a plugin, that requires an alteration of the database somehow, will generate migration files. There is also a* `migration` *generator, which simply creates a migration file for you. We talk more about this in Chapter 7.*

The fact that `schema_migrations` holds all the timestamps for the migration files already migrated means that the `db:migrate` can compare them with the files within the `db\migrate` directory and determine which migration files need to be migrated. It will pick up migrations that are newer as well as migrations that have older timestamps, but which have not been run yet perhaps because they were committed at a later stage by a different developer in the team or are being merged from a different branch.

Running `rake db:migrate` runs all the migrations that haven't been executed yet, but you can also migrate or rollback up to a specific version (for example, `rake db:migrate VERSION=20080711104321`). You can rollback to the previous migration level if you realize you made a mistake by using `db:rollback` too. Specifying a `STEP=` argument, you can rollback a number of steps in the migration history, instead of passing a specific version number (for example, `rake db:rollback STEP=3`). Every time you migrate up or down, the entries within the `schema_migrations` change to keep track of which migration files were applied to the current schema.

Old Style Migrations

Before Rails 2.1 was released, migrations worked in a similar fashion (aside from a few methods introduced by Rails 2.1) but were not time-stamped and as such were more susceptible to collisions. The first migration file of a project had the `001` prefix instead of a timestamp, and each new migration file had a prefix that was incremented by one. At the time there was a `schema_info` table that kept track only of the latest version you'd migrated to, as opposed to `schema_migrations` in Rails 2.1 and successive, which keep tracks of every migration that you've run.

The problem with this approach was that it introduced unnecessary collisions. For example, say that the last migration file committed to the repository of the project is `011_create_users.rb`. Now if you add a migration file to your local copy of the repository, this will be, say, `012_create_assets.rb`. If another developer needs to add a new table called `tasks`, he will create, say, `012_create_tasks.rb` in his local copy of the repository. Then you both commit to the repository. When migrating up, you'll encounter a conflict because both of your commits will be prefixed by `012`, which is the version that `db:migrate` is supposed to migrate to (given that 11 is the version stored in the `schema_info` table).

In reality your changes may be entirely independent, so it wouldn't really matter whether or not your migration gets executed first. With timestamp-based migrations á la Rails 2.1, the probability of this type of collision is exceptionally slim, so the migrations for adding `assets` and `tasks` would have a different timestamp and could be migrated without encountering any problems.

Unnecessary collisions, where the order of the two migrations is irrelevant, are removed, but even the timestamp-based migrations can still have collisions that need to be resolved manually. For example, if a migration drops a certain table, and a second migration (from another developer who doesn't know about your change) adds a column to that table, the order of execution matters. If your migration has a timestamp older than the one of the other developer, you'll encounter a conflict when migrating up, because `rake db:migrate` will drop a table and then attempt to add a column to that table that was just dropped, resulting in an error.

Conceptually unavoidable conflicts aside, migrations are still much more convenient than modifying the database directly through SQL scripts. With that in mind, developing in Rails without using migrations is still perfectly possible.

The up and down Class Methods

If you take a look again at the migration file for the creation of the `articles` table, you'll notice that the `CreateArticles` migration inherits from `ActiveRecord::Migration` and defines two class methods, `up` and `down`:

```
class CreateArticles < ActiveRecord::Migration
  def self.up
    create_table :articles do |t|
      t.string :title
```

```
      t.text :body
      t.boolean :published
      t.datetime :published_at

      t.timestamps
    end
  end

  def self.down
    drop_table :articles
  end
end
```

If `db:migrate` determines that this file should be included in the migration to evolve the schema of the database, `CreateArticles.up` gets invoked. When you are migrating down or rolling back to a schema version that predates this file, the effect of the `up` method gets cancelled out by invoking the `CreateArticles.down` method. You can also explicitly invoke the `up` and `down` methods of a specific migration by using the `db:migrate:up` and `db:migrate:down` tasks and passing a `VERSION=` argument to it (for example, `rake db:migrate:down VERSION=20080711104321`).

It is important that you define the opposite action of what you're doing in the `up` method in the `down` method of the migration, so that it can be safely rolled back. If you are adding a column through the `add_column` method, then in the `down` method you should use `remove_column`. If, like in this case, you are creating a table `articles` in the `up` method, then to restore the database to its previous state in case of a rollback, a `drop_table :articles` within the `down` method is required. If you are changing a column in the `up` method, change it back in the `down` method. You get the idea.

Migrations offer several handy methods to manipulate database objects. We cover them in Chapter 7.

Migrations are a concept that sounds complicated in theory, but that is very simple in practice. You ran `rake db:migrate` to create the `articles` table, but as you work with the application, you'll use migrations again to evolve the schema and add, at a bare minimum, a second table. You'll see that it couldn't be easier and migrations are a great tool for handling the incremental evolution of the schema in an "as automated as possible" way.

Putting It All Together: Creating a Rails Application

Before showing you (in the browser) what the `scaffold` generator actually accomplished, let's recap the steps that were required to achieve this. Migrations were discussed at length and introduced several new concepts, but don't get the false impression that scaffolding is hard. It's not. So far you haven't actually written a single line of code, and the following table shows you the commands employed up to this point.

Command	Meaning
`rails blog`	Generates a blog folder that contains the skeleton of the Rails application.
`rake db:create:all`	Creates all the local databases defined in `config\database.yml`.

Command	Meaning
`ruby script/generate scaffold article title:string body:text published:boolean published_at:datetime`	Generates an entire basic application for handling CRUD operations on the `articles` table.
`rake db:migrate`	Runs the migration file defined by scaffold, creating the `articles` tables.
`ruby script/server`	Runs the Web server to serve the Rails application.

The last step in the table should be new to you. This is used to start a Web server to serve your Rails application. By default this is WEBrick, but if you installed Mongrel in the first chapter, it will automatically be picked up, providing you with a smoother and quicker experience as you try out the application in development mode.

> *If you are not using Windows, you can simply run* `./script/server` *from the main folder of your project.*

Go ahead and start the Web server in development mode:

```
C:\projects\blog> ruby script/server
=> Booting Mongrel (use 'script/server webrick' to force WEBrick)
=> Rails 2.2.2 application starting on http://0.0.0.0:3000
=> Call with -d to detach
=> Ctrl-C to shutdown server
** Starting Mongrel listening at 0.0.0.0:3000
** Starting Rails with development environment...
** Rails loaded.
** Loading any Rails specific GemPlugins
** Signals ready.  INT => stop (no restart).
** Mongrel 1.1.5 available at 0.0.0.0:3000
** Use CTRL-C to stop.
```

> *If you are using Windows Vista you may have to approve the operation in a security popup that appears.*

This will make the application available in development mode, on the `localhost`, on port `3000`. These defaults can be changed of course, as shown by the output here:

```
C:\projects\blog> ruby script/server -help
=> Booting Mongrel (use 'script/server webrick' to force WEBrick)
Usage: server [options]
    -p, -port=port              Runs Rails on the specified port.
                                Default: 3000
    -b, -binding=ip             Binds Rails to the specified ip.
                                Default: 0.0.0.0
    -d, -daemon                 Make server run as a Daemon.
    -u, -debugger               Enable ruby-debugging for the server.
    -e, -environment=name       Specifies the environment to run this server
```

```
under (test/development/production).
                                    Default: development

    -h, —help                       Show this help message.
```

Now that you have the server up and running, take a look at your application. Direct your browser to http://localhost:3000. You should see the Rails' welcome message as shown in Figure 5-3.

If you are using Internet Explorer, you may be prompted with an information bar warning you about intranet settings. Click it and follow the instructions to make it disappear.

Figure 5-3

If you can see it on your screen, congratulations, it means that you are up and running with Rails. There is however, a problem: this has nothing to do with your articles table. The reason why this page is being served instead of the promised application, which is supposed to handle articles, is that the rails command generates a public\index.html static file. By the same token, scaffolding mapped the address /articles, not /, to ArticlesController. Long story short, head over to http://localhost:3000/articles and you should be able to see a page that lists articles as shown in Figure 5-4.

If you take a look at the command prompt where you are running Mongrel, you'll notice a few pieces of information that have been logged for the request it just served. In this case:

```
Processing ArticlesController#index (for 127.0.0.1 at 2008-07-11 05:12:38) [GET]

  Ð[4;36;1mArticle Load (0.0ms)Ð[0m   Ð[0;1mSELECT * FROM "articles" Ð[0m
Rendering template within layouts/articles
Rendering articles/index
Completed in 16ms (View: 0, DB: 0) | 200 OK [http://localhost/articles]
```

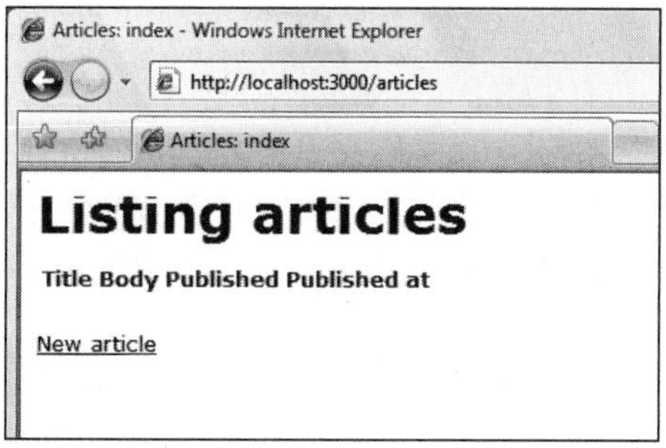

Figure 5-4

Being able to see all this information is great when trying to figure out why something isn't working as expected. And given that you are in development mode, the file log\development.log will contain the same (and more) information as well. If you were in production mode, the actual SQL query would not be logged.

Click New Article and you should see a form as shown in Figure 5-5.

Figure 5-5

It may not be the prettiest form that you've ever seen, but it's fully functional, and again, you didn't have to write a single line of code. Notice also how the URL changed from `http://localhost:3000/articles` to `http://localhost:3000/articles/new`. Let's add a title, some text, mark off the published checkbox, and click the Create button. This will create a record in the `articles` table and redirect you to `http://localhost:3000/articles/1`, where the record (which has `id` 1 in the table) is shown, as you can see in Figure 5-6.

Figure 5-6

Also notice how a confirmation message, "Article was successfully created." appears on the page.

Again, perhaps it's not the presentation that you intended for the final application, but it works and the aesthetics can always be customized later. If you click the Edit link you're brought to the address `http://localhost:3000/articles/1/edit`, from which you can update the record. Clicking Back brings you back to `http://localhost:3000/articles`, which lists all the records (well, you only have one record so far) as shown in Figure 5-7.

Figure 5-7

From there you can show records (Figure 5-6 without the "Article was successfully created." message), edit them, and even destroy them (upon clicking OK on a confirmation message box). So there you have it, not a single line of code (so far) and you have a front-end that's ready to perform CRUD operations on the back-end.

It doesn't look or behave like a blog quite yet, but that's not a problem; to fix that you can use incremental development. You can use this base and customize it for your needs. Furthermore, scaffolding doesn't just create a bunch of forms for you; it enables an application to work as a Web Service (a RESTful one, as you'll see in the next section). In fact, if you append an `.xml` to `http://localhost:3000/articles/1` you'll obtain an XML representation of the first record in the `articles` table, as shown in Figure 5-8.

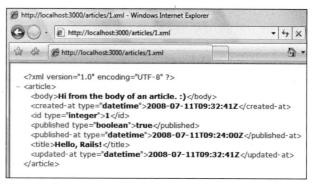

Figure 5-8

Before explaining the code that makes all this magic possible, there is one thing that annoys me. When I head over to `http://localhost:3000` I don't want to see a welcome page, but would prefer to get a list of all the articles. This can be accomplished in two steps. First you can edit your `config\routes.rb` file in order to include the highlighted line:

```
ActionController::Routing::Routes.draw do |map|
  map.root :controller => "articles"
  map.resources :articles

  # ...
```

This maps the root path of the application (that is, `/`) to the `Articles` controller. The second step is to delete the `public\index.html` file, because being a static HTML file it would have precedence over the `index` action of the `Articles` controller (which gets invoked by default when you visit `/articles` or, from now on, when you visit `/` as well).

> *It is customary to say "`Articles` controller," even if the actual name of the class is "`ArticlesController`." They are used interchangeably throughout this book.*

A RESTful Application

The file `config\routes.rb` defines how URLs are mapped to controllers and their methods (*actions*, in Rails speak). For example, in the previous paragraph you mapped the controller `Articles` with the root of your Rails application.

In traditional Rails applications — if the word "traditional" can be used for such a young framework — URLs have the following format by default `:controller/:action/:id`, as briefly discussed in Chapter 2.

So `/articles/show/3` would trigger the `show` action defined within the `ArticlesController` and pass a parameter `id` to it, whose value is 3. Similarly, `/articles/edit/3` would trigger the `edit` action of the same controller on the same object, and `/articles/update/3` would do the same for the `update` action.

Defining URLs in this manner is still possible today with the current version of Rails, but it means thinking in terms of pages that you access and upon which you perform certain actions that send a request and receive a response back. This approach works and it's the traditional way of doing Web development. Even the ASP.NET event-based model, despite its many differences, essentially leads developers to think in terms of pages (WebForms).

What's REST?

Rails has clearly embraced "the REST way" of doing Web development. REST stands for *REpresentational State Transfer* and it's a set of principles that define the style of software architecture for distributed networks such as the Web. What this means in practice is that you think in terms of resources that are accessible by a Uniform Resource Identifier (URI). Each resource is the source of the information, and it exposes a series of functions to the Web clients, so that they can read and manipulate the resource. The communication between the server and the client happens over the HTTP protocol.

The server determines what to do based on the identifier of the resource and the HTTP method (often referred to as *verb*) that's being used for the request. Resources in Rails are usually exposed by seven CRUD actions defined in the controller, but you can define additional custom actions when needed.

The URI also provides the representation requested for the resource (essentially its format). The actual information could be stored in the database within a table, but the client ignores all this. For example, the client will send a request for a given URI (for example, `http://localhost:3000/articles/1.xml`), with a certain HTTP verb (for example, `GET`) and will obtain the resource associated with that URI in the XML format back in return.

> *As you'll see in a moment, Rails knows that a* `GET` *request with that URI should be handled by the* `index` *action of* `ArticlesController` *and will respond to the request with XML data.*

If you omit the `.xml` part, the HTML representation will be transferred to the client instead. It's important to understand that even though HTML and XML are the most common formats for most requests, a resource could be programmed to present the information in a number of representations, including, but not limited to, JavaScript Object Notation (JSON), plain text, one of the many image formats, a comma-separated list of values, or iCalendar. The information in the model remains the same, but its representation (which is sent to the client) varies depending on the URL of the request. You'll see later on what formats are available out of the box in Rails and how to define custom ones.

Applications that follow REST principles are commonly known as RESTful. And because Rails is continually becoming a more RESTful framework (a trend that started in 2006), you'll develop your blog the REST way. As a matter of fact, given that you employed the `scaffold` generator as the base of your application, you've already started doing RESTful development.

> *You may have noted that I initially, somewhat casually, used the word "resource" to identify the* `article` *argument that I passed to the* `scaffold` *generator. Now you know that scaffolding effectively builds a basic resource-based application, which exposes the seven actions mentioned previously.*

Mapping Routes to Actions

In an earlier section, you saw a few CRUD operations, which are made available by scaffolding. These were possible because the `scaffold` generator added `map.resources :articles` in `config\routes.rb`. That single line defines a series of named routes and maps pairs of URLs and HTTP verbs to actions within the `ArticlesController`.

What's more, that line also instructs Rails to provide you with a series of helper methods, so that you can easily refer to these named routes from the controller and the view layer.

The following table shows you the mapping of a URL and an HTTP method to a controller action for all seven of the CRUD actions of the `Articles` controller. The number 1 is used as an example of the `id` parameter.

URL	HTTP Method	Controller Action
/articles	GET	index
/articles	POST	create
/articles/new	GET	new
/articles/1	GET	show
/articles/1	PUT	update
/articles/1	DELETE	destroy
/articles/1/edit	GET	edit

As you can see, four HTTP verbs are employed: GET, POST, PUT, and DELETE. When you send a GET request for the path /articles, the index action of ArticlesController is executed. When you send a POST request for the resource located at /articles, the create action is run instead; and so on for the other five actions.

> In earlier versions of Rails, the path mapping to the edit action was /articles/1;edit. Nobody really liked this though and it caused problems when dealing with caching, so a forward slash was employed instead of a semicolon.

If you are familiar with the HTTP methods and current Web browsers, you may spot a problem with this, though. In fact, though it's not hard to create a client for a Web Service that sends PUT or DELETE requests, the major browsers support only two verbs: GET and POST.

If REST is going to be the future for many Web projects, it is likely that the PUT and DELETE methods will see their way into the browser — eventually. In the meantime though, Rails cheats. PUT and DELETE requests in the browser are handled by placing a hidden _method field. When Rails sees that field, it correctly interprets the request as if it was a genuine PUT or DELETE request. And with Rails being Rails, specifying that a link should send the request in a particular HTTP method is a snap, as you'll see later on in this chapter.

There are seven default CRUD actions, but some of the routes also accept an optional format. In fact, a single resource can have many representations. When you factor this in, remembering all the routes may be a bit tricky. That's where the `routes` task comes in handy. If you run `rake routes` in your project, you will obtain the following output:

```
C:\projects\blog> rake routes
(in C:/projects/blog)
                      root        /
{:controller=>"articles", :action=>"index"}
              articles GET     /articles
{:controller=>"articles", :action=>"index"}
    formatted_articles GET     /articles.:format
{:controller=>"articles", :action=>"index"}
                       POST    /articles
{:controller=>"articles", :action=>"create"}
                       POST    /articles.:format
{:controller=>"articles", :action=>"create"}
           new_article GET     /articles/new
{:controller=>"articles", :action=>"new"}
 formatted_new_article GET     /articles/new.:format
{:controller=>"articles", :action=>"new"}
          edit_article GET     /articles/:id/edit
{:controller=>"articles", :action=>"edit"}
formatted_edit_article GET     /articles/:id/edit.:format
{:controller=>"articles", :action=>"edit"}
               article GET     /articles/:id
{:controller=>"articles", :action=>"show"}
     formatted_article GET     /articles/:id.:format
{:controller=>"articles", :action=>"show"}
                       PUT     /articles/:id
{:controller=>"articles", :action=>"update"}
                       PUT     /articles/:id.:format
{:controller=>"articles", :action=>"update"}
                       DELETE /articles/:id
{:controller=>"articles", :action=>"destroy"}
                       DELETE /articles/:id.:format
{:controller=>"articles", :action=>"destroy"}
                               /:controller/:action/:id
                               /:controller/:action/:id.:format
```

The output will appear with the same line wraps, unless you set the width of your command prompt to be very large.

Despite the output being poorly formatted (due to the limited width of the page), you can see how each line maps an HTTP verb and a URL to a controller and an action. These are all RESTful routes, except for three routes for which no HTTP verb is specified:

```
root / {:controller=>"articles", :action=>"index"}
/:controller/:action/:id
/:controller/:action/:id.:format
```

All the routes but these three were defined by that `map.resources :articles` line in `config\routes.rb`, which was placed there by the `scaffold` generator. So where do these three non-RESTful routes come from? The first of the three is the `root` named route. You defined it earlier in the chapter in order to map / with the `index` action of the `Articles` controller. To find out more about the other two, take a look at the routes file once again (stripped of most of its comments for brevity):

```
ActionController::Routing::Routes.draw do |map|
  map.root :controller => "articles"
  map.resources :articles

  # Install the default routes as the lowest priority.
  map.connect ':controller/:action/:id'
  map.connect ':controller/:action/:id.:format'
end
```

Notice how the last two highlighted lines define the two routes you were looking for. These are default routes and are defined by three parameters: a `:controller`, an `:action`, and an `:id`. In the case of the second route, there is also a `:format` parameter. The existence of those two `map.connect` calls in the `config\routes.rb` file implies that traditional non-REST mapping is still allowed.

So if you were to point your browser to `http://localhost:3000/articles/show/1` (or `1.xml`) you'd still get the desired outcome. Even the controller is a parameter in these default routes; therefore if you reach `http://localhost:3000/account/list`, Rails tries to map that URL with the `list` action of the `Account` controller. In this case, there is no `Account` controller, so an `ActionController::RoutingError` exception is raised.

The sample blog is going to be a purely RESTful one, so you can go ahead and comment those two lines out (never expose more than you need to):

```
ActionController::Routing::Routes.draw do |map|
  map.root :controller => "articles"
  map.resources :articles

  # Install the default routes as the lowest priority.
  #map.connect ':controller/:action/:id'
  #map.connect ':controller/:action/:id.:format'
end
```

Named route Helpers

The following is one of the routes printed out by the `rake routes` command:

```
articles GET /articles     {:controller=>"articles", :action=>"index"}
```

`articles` represents the named route, which is also the stem for a series of handy helpers. Appending `_url` or `_path` to a named route will give you a method that returns that route's address. For example, given that you have a named route `articles`, you can use `articles_url` and `articles_path`, which will return `http://localhost:3000/articles` and `/articles`, respectively. The difference between the two pretty much means that helper methods suffixed with `_url` are often used within the controller, and those postfixed by `_path` are often employed in the view layer.

From the output of the `rake routes` command, you'll notice that `:id` and `:format` are often parameters. `:id` identifies the resource needed by its id (for example, 1), and `:format` is an optional parameter that specifies the representation required (for example, .xml). For instance, when you send a GET request for the URL http://localhost:3000/articles/1.xml, the params hash is:

```
{ "format"=>"xml", "action"=>"show", "id"=>"1", "controller"=>"articles" }
```

Named routes that allow you to specify a format begin with the word formatted. In our case, these are: formatted_articles, formatted_new_article, formatted_edit_article, and formatted_article. The presence of that initial token affects the name of the dynamically generated helpers.

For example, you can have articles_url and articles_path as you saw before, as well as their "formatted" counterparts, such as formatted_articles_url and formatted_articles_path. These formatted helpers accept the format requested as an argument. For example, if in a view you were to use formatted_articles_path(:xml), the value returned by the helper would be the string literal "/articles.xml," which would invoke the index method of the Articles controller, and respond to the request with an XML representation of the resources (rather than the default HTML that's returned if no other format is explicitly requested).

Likewise, in the view layer you could use formatted_article_path(@article, :xml), where @article is an instance variable that is defined in the show action of ArticlesController, and it refers to an instance of the Article model. The helper is smart enough to extract the id attribute from the @article object and assign it to the id parameter. It also assigns :xml as the value for the key :format in the parameters hash. The end result would be the path: /articles/1.xml.

After this overview of the config\routes.rb file, which was generated through scaffolding, you can move on to briefly analyzing the code in the model, controller, and view, which allows you to perform CRUD operations of the articles table.

Analyzing the Model

Rails' models are stored in the app\models directory of the project. The Article model is therefore defined in the file app\models\article.rb. This is the code contained within it:

```
class Article < ActiveRecord::Base
end
```

That's it. At this stage the model is just a class definition. The class Article inherits from ActiveRecord::Base and this is sufficient enough to obtain a fully functional model that maps an articles table in the current database.

The database in use is always (by default) the one specified in config\database.yml *for the current environment mode.*

Please pay attention to singulars and plurals in Rails. The model should be singular and automatically map to a plural table name. Rails is smart enough to understand that the model Mouse maps to the table mice and not (sic) mouses. The mapping for very uncommon irregular plurals may not always be correct, but you can customize the inflection rules and also set the table name manually through the set_table_name method, as explained in Chapter 7.

Analyzing the Controller

Controllers are stored in `app\controllers`, so you can find your `Articles` controller in `app\controllers\articles_controller.rb`.

Note how the singular resource (that is, article) passed to the `scaffold` generator created a model that is singular and a controller that is plural. It is customary for RESTful controllers to be plural, because when you send a GET request for `/articles` or `/articles.xml` you are expecting to get a collection of items in return. Issuing a `/article` or `/article.xml` to obtain a series of articles doesn't seem as logical.

All of the code for your controller exists within the following class definition:

```
class ArticlesController < ApplicationController
  # ...
end
```

As you can see, the class `ArticlesController` inherits from `ApplicationController`. The `Application` controller is an application-wide controller, and all the controllers that you define inherit from it. You can find its definition in `app\controllers\application.rb`. `ApplicationController` in turn inherits from `ActionController::Base`.

Let's tackle each action within `ArticlesController`, one at a time.

index

The `index` action is there to list all the existing articles. This is how it is defined:

```
# GET /articles
# GET /articles.xml
def index
  @articles = Article.find(:all)

  respond_to do |format|
    format.html # index.html.erb
    format.xml  { render :xml => @articles }
  end
end
```

The two comments are there to remind you that a GET /articles or GET /articles.xml request would lead to this method being invoked.

The first line of the method retrieves a list of all the records that are available in the `articles` table and stores them in the `@articles` instance variable:

```
@articles = Article.find(:all)
```

The `find` class method will return an array of `Article` objects because the `:all` argument was passed to it. Every instance variable that you define in an action becomes available in the corresponding view that gets rendered by Rails. By assigning an array of articles to `@articles`, you can use this instance variable to loop through the records in the view.

If you were to serve HTML only, the code of your action would be that single line and no further code would be required, because Rails knows, by convention, which files in the view layer need to be rendered. The controller definition that's generated through scaffolding also has Web Service support, as you saw when you rendered XML instead of HTML. For this reason, you need the following snippet as well:

```
respond_to do |format|
  format.html # index.html.erb
  format.xml  { render :xml => @articles }
end
```

> Note that # index.html.erb *is just a comment; it's not necessary. It's usually included for the sake of clarity.*

Within the block passed to the respond_to method, you specify what to do depending on the format that's requested. Rails determines what format was requested by the client by analyzing the HTTP Accept header that it submitted.

If the format requested is HTML, Rails just renders the default view template associated with this action (which is index.html.erb in this case). If XML was requested by the client instead, Rails renders the list of articles retrieved, but in XML format. The block { render :xml => @articles } is actually smart enough to invoke the to_xml method on the @articles instance variable, and is therefore equivalent to { render :xml => @articles.to_xml }.

Supported Formats

So far you've seen format.html and format.xml. Other request formats are available out of the box in Rails: js, atom, rss, text, yaml, and ics (for iCalendar).

If you'd like to define your own format for a MIME type that is not supported by default, you can do so in config\initializers\mime_types.rb. For example, if you add Mime::Type.register "text/richtext", :rtf to that file, you will then be able to use format.rtf within the block of the respond_to method.

---

show

This is the definition of the show action:

```
# GET /articles/1
# GET /articles/1.xml
def show
  @article = Article.find(params[:id])

  respond_to do |format|
    format.html # show.html.erb
    format.xml  { render :xml => @article }
  end
end
```

This snippet of code looks very similar to the one shown for the index action. However, this time you only need to hand back one record. You start by finding the record and assigning it to the @article instance variable:

```
@article = Article.find(params[:id])
```

params is a hash that stores the parameters passed to this action by the request. The path that triggers this action is either going to be /articles/:id or /articles/:id.:format, therefore params[:id] will store the value of the id contained in the URL. If the request is http://localhost:3000/articles/10, then params[:id] will be 10.

When you just pass a numeric value to the find method, this will return the record whose id is the same as that number. Hence, Article.find(10) will return the Article object whose id attribute is equal to 10. In short, Article.find(params[:id]) will retrieve the record associated with the id requested in the URL.

The respond_to method will do the same thing as the index method, with the sole exception being that only one record (that is @article) will be rendered as XML (not an entire list of them). Also, the name of the action is show this time, so the associated template that will be rendered if the requested format is HTML will be show.html.erb.

new

The definition of the new action is very similar to the show one:

```
# GET /articles/new
# GET /articles/new.xml
def new
  @article = Article.new

  respond_to do |format|
    format.html # new.html.erb
    format.xml  { render :xml => @article }
  end
end
```

The only obvious difference is that you assigned a new Article object to the @article instance variable, instead of finding a record, like you did for show.

> *As explained in a later section, whether the instance variable @article is a new object or an existing one will be an important distinction for Rails, because it uses it for deciding whether a "new" form or an "edit" one should be generated in the view.*

Not surprisingly, new.html.erb gets rendered when the requested format is HTML.

edit

The `edit` action is the simplest of the lot, because by default it handles HTML requests only and, as such, doesn't need a `respond_to` method. The associated `edit.html.erb` template will be rendered automatically (which is Rails' default behavior). Here is the method definition:

```
# GET /articles/1/edit
def edit
  @article = Article.find(params[:id])
end
```

The requested record is retrieved and assigned to the `@article` instance variable. `edit.html.erb` provides the user with an input form to update the record. If the object referenced by `@article` contains any values in its attributes, these will already be pre-filled in the input form (this magic is possible thanks to helpers like `form_for`).

create

The `create` action gets a little trickier because it handles HTML and XML requests, plus it deals with two different cases, depending on whether or not the record was successfully saved. This is its definition:

```
# POST /articles
# POST /articles.xml
def create
  @article = Article.new(params[:article])

  respond_to do |format|
    if @article.save
      flash[:notice] = 'Article was successfully created.'
      format.html { redirect_to(@article) }
      format.xml  { render :xml => @article, :status => :created, :location => @
article }
    else
      format.html { render :action => "new" }
      format.xml  { render :xml => @article.errors, :status => :unprocessable_
entity }
    end
  end
end
```

In order to understand this action, let's try to see when this gets invoked for HTML requests. Before when you clicked the New Article link, you were redirected to `/articles/new`. That in turn invokes the `new` action and renders an empty form that allows you to input the details of an article you want to create. When you click the Create button, a `POST /articles` request is sent for you.

At this stage, the `create` action is invoked but you don't have an `id` in the `params` hash. What you have is an `article` parameter that contains all the attributes of the object that you'd like to create as inserted in the form. Hence, the first line of this action creates a new object with this data and assigns the object to `@article`:

```
@article = Article.new(params[:article])
```

Notice that at this point the record has not been saved yet in the database.

Then the method invokes the `respond_to` method in order to handle both HTML and XML requests as follows:

```
respond_to do |format|
  if @article.save
    flash[:notice] = 'Article was successfully created.'
    format.html { redirect_to(@article) }
    format.xml  { render :xml => @article, :status => :created, :location => @article }
  else
    format.html { render :action => "new" }
    format.xml  { render :xml => @article.errors, :status => :unprocessable_entity }
  end
end
```

Here is what happens within the block. You first try to save in the database the object you created by calling the `save` instance method.

Behind the scenes this calls a `create_or_update` method, which will do exactly that, create the record if it's new or update it if this already exists.

If the record is successfully saved, the user is prompted with the message "Article was successfully created." as was shown in Figure 5-6. `flash` is a special type of hash (whose class is `ActionController::Flash::FlashHash`) that allows you to store data that will be exposed in the next action. In practice this means that you can store your message in `flash[:notice]` within the `create` action, and you'll be able to retrieve and display it when you're redirected to the `show` action (after the record is saved). As soon as you move onto yet another action or refresh the page, the `flash` content is discarded.

After storing your message in the `flash`, you can handle the HTML and XML cases separately. When the client wants HTML, you can redirect to the `show` action for the article you just created. Notice that the `redirect_to` method is smart enough to figure out that passing a single `Article` object implies that you want to show it. This would be equivalent to using `redirect_to(article_url(@article))`, but much more concisely. In the case of an XML request, you send the XML encoded object and pass a pair of headers back to the client.

If the record isn't able to be saved, as in the case of HTML requests, you can render the template for the action `new`. Notice that you don't have to perform a full redirect to the `new` action, because this would clear out all the data that the user just tried to save. If the requested format is XML, you can return the errors in XML format back to the client, and set the `:status` header to `:unprocessable_entity`.

This may appear complicated at first, but it's all very easy once you get the hang of it, and it's important to remember that you didn't actually write this code, but that it's there for you to build upon.

update

The update `action` is defined as follows:

```
# PUT /articles/1
# PUT /articles/1.xml
def update
  @article = Article.find(params[:id])
```

```
      respond_to do |format|
        if @article.update_attributes(params[:article])
          flash[:notice] = 'Article was successfully updated.'
          format.html { redirect_to(@article) }
          format.xml  { head :ok }
        else
          format.html { render :action => "edit" }
          format.xml  { render :xml => @article.errors, :status => :unprocessable_
entity }
        end
      end
    end
  end
```

This action is very similar to the `create` one except that it calls the method `update_attributes` instead of `save`, and passes it through the `params[:article]` argument. You'll also notice that upon successfully updating the record, in the XML response block there is simply a `head :ok`. This is a method that returns only headers and not content. The logic behind this is that if the update was successful, you'd inform the Web Service client of this with a `200 OK` response. You can use symbols (for example, `:ok`) or status code (for example, `200`).

A list of all the status codes is available (depending on your version and installation path) at `C:\ruby\lib\ruby\gems\1.8\gems\actionpack-2.2.2\lib\action_controller\ status_codes.rb`.

If the update isn't successful, you can render the `edit.html.erb` template by issuing `render :action => "edit"` if the response requested is HTML, or you can provide the same error you saw for the `create` action if XML was requested.

This shouldn't be too confusing if you look at it from a user's standpoint. The user reaches the URL `/articles/1/edit` to edit a record, makes a few changes, and clicks the Update button. This sends a request that gets handled by the `update` action, which in turn tries to update the record. If it's able to do so, the user is redirected to `/articles/1` and shown the updated record and a confirmation message (through `flash`). If it's not able to be saved for some reason, the user is sent back to the editing form (which hasn't been cleared of the existing data that he has already inserted).

destroy

Finally, the `destroy` action is defined as such:

```
# DELETE /articles/1
# DELETE /articles/1.xml
def destroy
  @article = Article.find(params[:id])
  @article.destroy

  respond_to do |format|
    format.html { redirect_to(articles_url) }
    format.xml  { head :ok }
  end
end
```

You first find the record that needs to be deleted and then invoke the `destroy` method. Then if the requested format is HTML, you then redirect the user to the list of all articles using the `articles_url` helper as an argument for the `redirect_to` method. This list will show that the deleted record is no longer there. If the request format was XML, you can simply confirm that the request was successful by calling `head :ok`.

Analyzing the View Layer

So far you have analyzed the model and the controller, now let's complete the MVC triad. The files constituting the view layer are all enclosed within folders located in `app\views` as shown in Figure 5-9.

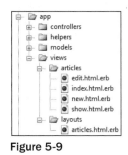

Figure 5-9

As you can see, inside `app\views` are two folders, `articles` and `layouts`. The `articles` folder is there to contain all the view templates and partials that are associated with the `Articles` controller.

> *Notice how each of the view files generated by the* `scaffold` *generator has the format* `name.html.erb`. *This indicates that ERb should be used as a template engine to produce HTML.*

The `layouts` folder hosts, as the name implies, layouts. Rails knows by convention that the `ArticlesController` should render the layout `app\views\layouts\articles.html.erb`. This convention can of course be overwritten and you could, for example, decide to reuse the same layout for multiple controllers.

Rails' Layouts vs. ASP.NET's Master Pages

There is a striking similarity between ASP.NET's master pages and Rails' layouts. Both are aimed at sharing the same layout, structure, and style among pages that should have a similar look and feel. The first benefit in both cases is therefore the ability to automatically obtain a consistent style and structure for all the pages that are supposed to have a specific theme.

Both Rails' layout and ASP.NET's master pages help to guarantee that the code is DRY and that you don't have to repeat, for example, the same header and footer for each view template (in Rails' case) or .aspx page (in ASP.NET's case).

Layouts in Rails are contained in the `app\views\layouts` folder, but their extensions are no different than those of a normal view template. They are, in fact, a view template themselves and as such can embed Ruby code and define the presentation logic in them. Master pages use the `ContentPlaceHolder` control to indicate the place where the content (the `.aspx` page) should be wrapped at runtime. Rails' layouts work in a similar fashion, but the `yield` keyword is used instead.

In ASP.NET, you would have to set the `MasterPageFile` property to indicate the name of the master page file associated with a page. Unlike ASP.NET, in Rails each view template doesn't need to be aware of the existence of a layout. They get "included into the layout" dynamically at runtime and there is no need to specify anything.

Rails' layouts can be specific to one or more controllers as mentioned before, but it's also possible to define an application-wide controller. If you add an `application.html.erb` layout, by default it will apply to all of the application's controllers. If a controller specifies otherwise in its code (for example, `layout "my_layout"`) or there's already a layout for a specific controller (for example, `articles.html.erb`), these take precedence over `application.html.erb` and will instead be rendered when rendering an action of that controller.

Rails 2 also introduces the concept of partial layouts, as explained in Chapter 9.

The articles.html.erb Layout

This is the code of the `articles.html.erb` layout:

```
<!DOCTYPE html PUBLIC "-//W3C//DTD XHTML 1.0 Transitional//EN"
        "http://www.w3.org/TR/xhtml1/DTD/xhtml1-transitional.dtd">

<html xmlns="http://www.w3.org/1999/xhtml" xml:lang="en" lang="en">
<head>
<meta http-equiv="content-type" content="text/html;charset=UTF-8" />
<title>Articles: <%= controller.action_name %></title>
<%= stylesheet_link_tag 'scaffold' %>
</head>
<body>

<p style="color: green"><%= flash[:notice] %></p>

<%= yield %>

</body>
</html>
```

Applications that are based on the output of the `scaffold` *generator are by default XHTML Transitional, but this can easily be changed by specifying something else in each layout.*

I've highlighted the interesting bits so as to analyze them line by line. The following code uses the `controller.action_name` to retrieve the name of the action that's being rendered:

```
<title>Articles: <%= controller.action_name %></title>
```

Notice how the tags for embedded Ruby code are `<% %>`, which should be familiar to you. Whenever you want the calculated expression to be rendered in the page, as opposed to just being interpreted, you place an equal sign after the opening tag (for example, `<%= 2 + 2 %>`).

Sometimes you'll see a closing tag with a minus sign (that is, -%>), which removes any unnecessary empty lines in the output.

The second highlighted line uses the `stylesheet_link_tag` helper to include the scaffold stylesheet file, which is located in `public\stylesheets\scaffold.css`. As always with helpers, they are there to make your life easier, but you could have skipped the helper and written HTML to link to the stylesheet if you were so inclined.

The third highlighted line is interesting because it shows how the `flash[:notice]` you set in a few actions gets retrieved in the view. And now you also know why the confirmation messages from scaffolding are green:

```
<p style="color: green"><%= flash[:notice] %></p>
```

The fact that the flash notice is retrieved from within the article's layout implies that it will be available in every action of that controller (unless you specify otherwise in the controller).

Finally, the most important line of all is: `<%= yield   %>`. This tells Rails to enclose any view template rendered inside the layout.

For example, if you visit `/articles/1` you should obtain the following HTML code:

```
<!DOCTYPE html PUBLIC "-//W3C//DTD XHTML 1.0 Transitional//EN"
        "http://www.w3.org/TR/xhtml1/DTD/xhtml1-transitional.dtd">

<html xmlns="http://www.w3.org/1999/xhtml" xml:lang="en" lang="en">
<head>
<meta http-equiv="content-type" content="text/html;charset=UTF-8" />
<title>Articles: show</title>
<link href="/stylesheets/scaffold.css?1215730002" media="screen" rel="stylesheet"
type="text/css" />
</head>
<body>

<p style="color: green"></p>
```

```
<p>
<b>Title:</b>
  Hello, Rails!
</p>


<p>
<b>Body:</b>
  Hi from the body of an article. :)
</p>


<p>
<b>Published:</b>
  true
</p>


<p>
```

```
<b>Published at:</b>
  2008-07-11 09:24:00 UTC
</p>


<a href="/articles/1/edit">Edit</a> |
<a href="/articles">Back</a>
```

```
  </body>
</html>
```

The final document combines the rendering of the outer layout discussed earlier, with the view template, which in this case is show.html.erb.

As was shown in Figure 5-9, the articles folder contains four templates: index.html.erb, new .html.erb, edit.html.erb, and show.html.erb. Each of these is automatically rendered when the corresponding action is invoked and the requested format is HTML. There are three actions that don't have an associated template and these are create, update, and destroy.

The index.html.erb Template

The index.html.erb template contains the following code:

```
<h1>Listing articles</h1>

<table>
<tr>
<th>Title</th>
<th>Body</th>
<th>Published</th>
<th>Published at</th>
</tr>

<% for article in @articles %>
<tr>
<td><%=h article.title %></td>
<td><%=h article.body %></td>
<td><%=h article.published %></td>
<td><%=h article.published_at %></td>
<td><%= link_to 'Show', article %></td>
<td><%= link_to 'Edit', edit_article_path(article) %></td>
<td><%= link_to 'Destroy', article, :confirm => 'Are you sure?', :method => :delete
%></td>
</tr>
<% end %>
</table>

<br />

<%= link_to 'New article', new_article_path %>
```

The instance variable @articles defined in the index action is used here to loop through all the articles. Inside the loop, several attributes of the article object are rendered (one per column). article .title is a string containing the title of the given article object, article.body is a string containing the text, and so on.

You'll notice that there is an h after the equal sign. That's a special helper that is an alias for the ERB::Util method html_escape. This escapes HTML tags transforming the less than and greater than signs into their HTML characters. For example, h("<p>hi</p>") will return "<p>hi</p>." This helper is used whenever you need to display potentially unsafe content (the rule of thumb is that any content provided by the user cannot be trusted).

The scaffold generator tries to be security conscious and strips any tags by employing the h helper. That said, in this specific case, you're the only one who is entering articles (once the app has an authentication system), so there isn't a concrete need to sanitize your own input. There's no harm in leaving them in there though.

link_to is a helper for producing HTML links. To provide a link to the show action for a given article you can use:

```
<%= link_to 'Show', article %>
```

The link_to method — like redirect_to(@article) did in the controller — understands that if you pass the article object to the helper as its second argument, you intend to obtain the URL for the show action. This is equivalent to passing article_path(article), but is easier to remember and more concise.

The named route helpers mentioned before still come in handy though. For example, for the Edit link, you would use:

```
<%= link_to 'Edit', edit_article_path(article) %>
```

The Destroy link is rather different given that you need to perform a request through the DELETE HTTP method. As mentioned before, Rails emulates this by inserting a hidden form field _method. To make this happen then, the third argument (a hash) needs to have a :method key whose value is set to :delete. Given that you're deleting a record, you want to provide a confirmation step too, as shown in Figure 5-10. All this is accomplished by the following line:

```
<%= link_to 'Destroy', article, :confirm => 'Are you sure?', :method => :delete %>
```

The fact that a DELETE HTTP verb is required to delete a record ensures that a record is never accidentally deleted by simply sending a GET request to a given URL from your browser. Adding a confirmation message box makes accidental deletion even less likely.

It's also worth pointing out that the :comfirm and :method keys are part of the same hash, which is the third parameter you pass to the link_to method.

The last link that was generated takes advantage of the new_article_path route helper:

```
<%= link_to 'New article', new_article_path %>
```

Figure 5-10

The new.html.erb Template

The template for the new action is very straightforward:

```
<h1>New article</h1>
```

```
<% form_for(@article) do |f| %>
<%= f.error_messages %>

<p>
<%= f.label :title %><br />
<%= f.text_field :title %>
</p>
<p>
<%= f.label :body %><br />
<%= f.text_area :body %>
</p>
<p>
<%= f.label :published %><br />
<%= f.check_box :published %>
</p>
<p>
<%= f.label :published_at %><br />
<%= f.datetime_select :published_at %>
```

```
</p>
<p>
<%= f.submit "Create" %>
</p>
<% end %>

<%= link_to 'Back', articles_path %>
```

The `form_for` helper is a method that is able to create a form for a given model object. In this case the model object is `@article`, which was set in the `new` action of the `Articles` controller, to be a brand new `Article` object. The `form_for` helper understands that the object it's creating the form for is a new object, so it generates an empty input form.

> Notice that the action that needs to process the form is not explicitly specified; this is because the helper is aware of REST and can yield a RESTful form automatically for you.

Inside the associated block, the `f` block argument is used to give scope to each of the fields that correspond to the attributes of the given object (except for its `id`). This allows you to write a very concise line, such as:

```
<%= f.text_field :title %>
```

This is equivalent to using the following, less succinct method:

```
<%= text_field :article, :title %>
```

During runtime, both translate into this XHTML code:

```
<input id="article_title" name="article[title]" size="30" type="text" />
```

If you visit `http://localhost:3000/articles/new` and view the source code that's been generated, you'll see how each of the fields is transformed from the DSL (Domain Specific Language) methods provided by ActionView to XHTML. You'll quickly notice how these methods are very convenient.

The `form_for` line gets translated into:

```
<form action="/articles" class="new_article" id="new_article" method="post">
```

A `POST /articles` request will be handled by the create action, which is exactly what you want when the Submit button is clicked.

---

form_for in a non-RESTful Context

If `config\routes.rb` didn't identify the articles as a resource with `map.resources :articles`, you would be doing "traditional" development in a non-RESTful way. In that case the `form_for` arguments would have to be more verbose and explicit as follows:

```
<% form_for :article, :url => { :action => "create" } do |f| %>
```

The syntax for the Submit button is just as succinct:

```
<%= f.submit "Create" %>
```

The scope around `@article` that's provided by the block enables that generic line to be rendered in XHTML as follows:

```
<input id="article_submit" name="commit" type="submit" value="Create" />
```

You'll notice that this is a very different approach than using special controls, as ASP.NET does, but it's just as convenient.

In this form, the `scaffold` generator uses the `label`, `text_field`, `text_area`, `check_box`, `date-time_select`, and `submit` methods inside the block associated with the `form_for` helper. Other methods are available as well though, such as `file_field`, `hidden_field`, `password_field`, and `radio_button`.

On the first line inside the block there is a mysterious <%= f.error_messages %>. This is used to display any possible errors for the model object. The requirement for this will become clear as validations are introduced later on.

Finally, the `new.html.erb` template provides a "Back" link to a list of all the articles. As usual, the `link_to` URL helper is used, this time in conjunction with the named route helper `articles_path`.

The edit.html.erb Template

The `edit.html.erb` file contains the following code:

```
<h1>Editing article</h1>

<% form_for(@article) do |f| %>
<%= f.error_messages %>

<p>
<%= f.label :title %><br />
<%= f.text_field :title %>
</p>
<p>
<%= f.label :body %><br />
<%= f.text_area :body %>
</p>
<p>
<%= f.label :published %><br />
<%= f.check_box :published %>
</p>
<p>
<%= f.label :published_at %><br />
<%= f.datetime_select :published_at %>
</p>
<p>
<%= f.submit "Update" %>
</p>
```

```
<% end %>

<%= link_to 'Show', @article %> |
<%= link_to 'Back', articles_path %>
```

If you exclude the h1 tag and a "Show" link at the bottom, this is identical to new.html.erb. The reason for this is that as a matter of fact, the new and edit forms have the same fields. On top of that, the form_for method is smart enough to figure out that this time around the Article object — assigned to @article in the controller — is not empty and that it should pre-fill the fields for the existing attributes of the object as shown in Figure 5-11.

Figure 5-11

If you think that all this repetition directly violates the DRY principle, you're absolutely correct. You are definitely repeating yourself in the new.html.erb and edit.html.erb templates. To fix this you'll need to use partials, as explained in a subsequent section.

The show.html.erb Template

The template for the show action is defined as follows:

```
<p>
<b>Title:</b>
```

```
        <%=h @article.title %>
        </p>

        <p>
        <b>Body:</b>
        <%=h @article.body %>
        </p>

        <p>
        <b>Published:</b>
        <%=h @article.published %>
        </p>

        <p>
        <b>Published at:</b>
        <%=h @article.published_at %>
        </p>


        <%= link_to 'Edit', edit_article_path(@article) %> |
        <%= link_to 'Back', articles_path %>
```

You don't need a `form_for` helper because you are just displaying data. The `@article` instance variable was set in the `show` action, so you can now display its attributes (highlighted in the preceding code).

Adding Partials

`new.html.erb` and `edit.html.erb` both have the code that generates their forms in common. Rails provides partials in order to reuse code and remove repetition, thereby allowing you to include a partial in other view templates. Partials can be spotted thanks to the underscore prefix on their file name (for example, `_person.html.erb`).

Go ahead and create an empty `_form.html.erb` file in `app\views\articles`. In this file you'll want to include the common snippet of code between the new and edit forms. As such you could copy in `_form.html.erb` the following code:

```
    <% form_for(@article) do |f| %>
      <%= f.error_messages %>

      <p>
        <%= f.label :title %><br />
        <%= f.text_field :title %>
      </p>
      <p>
        <%= f.label :body %><br />
        <%= f.text_area :body %>
      </p>
      <p>
        <%= f.label :published %><br />
        <%= f.check_box :published %>
```

```
  </p>
  <p>
    <%= f.label :published_at %><br />
    <%= f.datetime_select :published_at %>
  </p>
  <p>
    <%= f.submit "Update" %>
  </p>
<% end %>
```

The only problem with this is the value of the Submit button, which is different in the two forms. One is Create and the other says Update. To solve this you can use a local variable (that is, button_value) instead of a string literal (for example, "Create"). You can also change the instance variable @article into a simple variable that's local to the partial, to improve encapsulation.

Copy the following code into _form.html.erb:

```
<% form_for(article) do |f| %>
  <%= f.error_messages %>

  <p>
    <%= f.label :title %><br />
    <%= f.text_field :title %>
  </p>
  <p>
    <%= f.label :body %><br />
    <%= f.text_area :body %>
  </p>
  <p>
    <%= f.label :published %><br />
    <%= f.check_box :published %>
  </p>
  <p>
    <%= f.label :published_at %><br />
    <%= f.datetime_select :published_at %>
  </p>
  <p>
    <%= f.submit button_value %>
  </p>
<% end %>
```

Now you can remove the existing form from new.html.erb and edit.html.erb and include the partial you just defined. Go ahead and change the new.html.erb template to look like this:

```
<h1>New article</h1>

<%= render :partial => "form", :locals => { :article => @article, :button_value =>
'Create Article' } %>

<%= link_to 'Back', articles_path %>
```

Similarly, replace the content of edit.html.erb with this:

```
<h1>Editing article</h1>

<%= render :partial => "form", :locals => { :article => @article, :button_value =>
'Save Changes' } %>

<%= link_to 'Show', @article %> |
<%= link_to 'Back', articles_path %>
```

As you can see, the highlighted lines render a partial through the render method. The :locals option allows you to specify the value of local variables inside of a hash. In this case you used it to set the variable button_value to "Create Article" when rendering new.html.erb, and to "Save Changes" when rendering edit.html.erb. That value will be rendered as the value of the button in the partial. You also passed to the partial the @article object, which is assigned to its local variable article.

> *Using* :locals *to assign values to variables local to the partial is conceptually similar to passing arguments to a method.*

In this way the repetition is eliminated, and any changes to the _form.html.erb partial will be reflected automatically in the templates for the new and edit actions. That's DRY.

Adding Validations

Validations are a mechanism provided by Active Record to ensure that the data conforms to certain business rules. The forms generated by the scaffold generator don't perform any validations by default. For example, you could create an article that had an empty title and empty body, and these would be stored in the database as empty strings. Similarly, you may decide that you don't want to allow articles to have the same exact text, therefore eliminating duplicates. Validations are the answer.

Change the Article model to look like this (app\models\article.rb):

```
class Article < ActiveRecord::Base
  validates_presence_of :title, :body
  validates_uniqueness_of :body
end
```

Those two highlighted lines indicate that an article's title and a body are required and that the body of an article needs to be different from any others that already exist. Save the file, head over to /articles/new, and try to click Create Article with the title and body left empty. You should see an error report similar to the one shown in Figure 5-12.

> **Unlike ASP.NET validation controls, Rails validations are always server-side and defined in the model, as opposed to the page that gets rendered.**

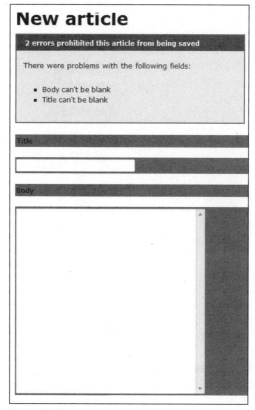

Figure 5-12

That was quite effortless! If you take a look at the source of the generated page, you will see that the `<%= f.error_messages %>` inside the partial was transformed into *(reformatted for clarity)*:

```
<div class="errorExplanation" id="errorExplanation">
<h2>2 errors prohibited this article from being saved</h2>
<p>There were problems with the following fields:</p>
<ul><li>Body can't be blank</li><li>Title can't be blank</li></ul>
</div>
```

You'll notice also that the affected fields are now surrounded by a `<div>` tag, which highlights them:

```
<p>
<div class="fieldWithErrors"><label for="article_title">Title</label></div>
<br />
<div class="fieldWithErrors"><input id="article_title" name="article[title]"
size="30" type="text" value="" /></div>
</p>

<p>
<div class="fieldWithErrors"><label for="article_body">Body</label></div>
```

```
<br />
<div class="fieldWithErrors"><textarea cols="40" id="article_body"
name="article[body]" rows="20"></textarea></div>
</p>
```

The CSS classes errorExplanation and fieldWithErrors are defined in the scaffold.css file in public\stylesheets, so you can customize the look and feel of error reporting to suit your own tastes. You can also define your own custom messages by passing the :message option to the validation. For example, you can specify that the report should print "Body is a required field" and "Title is a required field" instead of the default "can't be blank," as follows:

```
validates_presence_of :title, :body, :message => "is a required field"
```

Notice that even though the two attributes that you are trying to validate are passed to the method on the same line, their validation is independent from each other. This means that if you tried to submit an article with a non-empty body but an empty title, you'd get an error message about the missing title only. Similarly, if you tried to create a duplicate post with the exact same text as a previous one, a message would inform you that this is not allowed.

Chapter 7 explains many more useful validations.

Adding a Bit of Style

One of the main reasons why you still can't quite call the output of the scaffold generator a blog is that it doesn't look like one. Create a couple more articles in order to have at least three of them to work with, and let's add some style.

To get a nice looking blog, you'll need a few stylesheet files and a few images. In a real-life scenario these would be provided to you by your Web designer. In order to follow along, download the code for this chapter from the wrox.com site and copy the stylesheets contained in the project_files folder, into the public\stylesheets directory of your project. Similarly, copy over the three images from the project_files folder you just downloaded into your public\images directory. Also delete rails.png from that same directory, and public\stylesheets\scaffold.css because you won't need them anymore.

You'll start your customization by modifying the articles.html.erb layout. In this example I call the blog "The Rails Noob," so the first thing you can do is change the title tag:

```
<title>The Rails Noob</title>
```

Next, you need to link to the main stylesheet, which is going to be site.css:

```
<%= stylesheet_link_tag 'site' %>
```

You can add a logo (linked to the homepage) in plain HTML or by using the image_tag helper:

```
<%= link_to image_tag('logo.png', :width => '350', :alt => "The Rails Noob"), root_
path %>
```

You'll also need to add a few tags, and ids and classes attributes to give the blog a bit of structure and style. Listing 5-3 shows the full code of the `articles.html.erb` layout. Ensure that your layout looks the same by either typing the difference from Listing 5-3 or by copying the file from the downloaded directory (the file is named `listing0503.html.erb`).

Listing 5-3: app\views\layouts\articles.html.erb Customized

```
<!DOCTYPE html PUBLIC "-//W3C//DTD XHTML 1.0 Transitional//EN"
        "http://www.w3.org/TR/xhtml1/DTD/xhtml1-transitional.dtd">

<html xmlns="http://www.w3.org/1999/xhtml" xml:lang="en" lang="en">
<head>
  <meta http-equiv="content-type" content="text/html;charset=UTF-8" />
  <title>The Rails Noob</title>
  <%= stylesheet_link_tag 'site' %>
</head>
<body>
  <div id="header" class="container">
    <div id="logo">
      <%= link_to image_tag('logo.png', :width => '350', :alt => "The Rails Noob"),
  root_path %>
    </div>

    <ul id="nav" class="clear">
      <li><%= link_to 'Home', root_path %></li>
      <li><%= link_to 'New Article', new_article_path %></li>
    </ul>
  <!— /header —>
  </div>

  <div id="main" class="container">
    <p style="color: green" id="notice"><%= flash[:notice] %></p>
    <%= yield  %>
  </div>

  <div id="footer" class="container clear">
    <div class="column span-6">
       
    <!— /column —>
    </div>

    <div class="column span-4 last">
      <p>
          Lorem ipsum dolor sit amet, consectetuer adipiscing elit.
          Nullam sed lectus ut nisi hendrerit congue.
      </p>
    <!— /column —>
    </div>
  <!— /footer —>
  </div>
</body>
</html>
```

Now you can tackle the `index.html.erb` template as shown in Listing 5-4.

Listing 5-4: app\views\articles\index.html.erb Customized

```erb
<% for article in @articles %>
  <div class="article clear">
      <h2><%= link_to h(article.title), article %></h2>
      <div  class="column span-6">
          <div class="entry">
              <%=h article.body %>
          </div>
      <!- /column ->
      </div>

      <div  class="column span-4 last">
          <div class="meta">
              <h3>About this article</h3>
              Published on <%= article.published_at.to_s(:long_ordinal) %>
          </div>

          <div class="tools">
              <h3>Tools</h3>
              <%= link_to 'Edit', edit_article_path(article) %> &middot;
              <%= link_to 'Destroy', article, :confirm => 'Are you sure?', :method
=> :delete %>
          </div>
      <!- /column ->
      </div>
  <!- /article ->
  </div>
<% end %>
```

Note in the following line that the date and time format are set to appear in the long ordinal format:

```erb
Published on <%= article.published_at.to_s(:long_ordinal) %>
```

Time and dates can be easily formatted using one of the existing format types and you can even define your own formats as explained later on in the book.

The end result of the cosmetic changes that you've applied so far is shown in Figure 5-13.

That looks much better! But notice how the oldest post (the one that you initially created) appears first, which is the opposite of how a blog normally works. You can fix this by modifying the `index` action in the controller and specifying the order of the retrieved articles as follows:

```ruby
def index
    @articles = Article.find(:all, :order => "published_at DESC")

    respond_to do |format|
```

```
        format.html # index.html.erb
        format.xml  { render :xml => @articles }
    end
end
```

Figure 5-13

ActiveRecord's finders are extremely flexible and accept many options including `:order`. This fixes the order issue as shown in Figure 5-14.

Now that you've embellished the layout for the `Articles` controller and the template for the `index` action, you can customize the `_form.html.erb` partial slightly, for the `new` and `edit` actions as shown in Listing 5-5.

Figure 5-14

Listing 5-5: app\views\articles_form.html.erb Customized

```erb
<% form_for(article) do |f| %>
  <%= f.error_messages %>
  <% field_set_tag do %>
    <div class="field">
      <%= f.label :title %>
      <%= f.text_field :title %>
    </div>

    <div class="field">
      <%= f.label :body %>
      <%= f.text_area :body %>
    </div>
```

Listing 5-5: app\views\articles_form.html.erb Customized *(continued)*

```erb
    <div class="field">
       <%= f.label :published_at %>
       <%= f.datetime_select :published_at %>
    </div>

    <div class="field">
       <%= f.check_box :published %>
       <%= f.label :published %>
    </div>
  <% end %>

  <% field_set_tag do %>
    <%= f.submit button_value, :class => "button" %>
  <% end %>
<% end %>
```

Notice how `f.submit` *accepts a* `:class` *optional argument to specify the CSS class of the button.*

Showing the articles, creating, and editing them is all good, but what about the show action? Figure 5-15 shows you a less than satisfactory default look.

Figure 5-15

You can change this by modifying the `show.html.erb` template as shown in Listing 5-6.

Listing 5-6: app\views\articles\show.html.erb Customized

```
<div class="article clear">

  <h1><%= h(@article.title)%></h1>

  <div  class="column span-6">
      <div class="entry">
          <%=h @article.body %>
      </div>
  <!- /column -->
  </div>

  <div  class="column span-4 last">
      <div class="meta">
          <h3>About this article</h3>
          Published on <%=h @article.published_at.to_s(:long_ordinal) %>
      <!- /meta -->
      </div>

      <div class="tools">
          <h3>Tools</h3>
          <%= link_to 'Edit', edit_article_path(@article) %> &middot;
          <%= link_to 'Destroy', @article, :confirm => 'Are you sure?',
                                    :method => :delete %> &middot;
      <!- /tools -->
      </div>
  <!- /column -->
  </div>

<!- /article -->
</div>
```

The result of this cosmetic change is shown in Figure 5-16.

Setting a Default Time Zone

Every time a model's datetime attribute is saved in the database, this becomes stored as a UTC time. The problem is that the dates and times presented to the visitor and the blog author are UTC times, rather than a predefined local time zone. When you click New Article you'll see that the default date and time selected are based on UTC, not the local time zone. This implies that if you want to schedule a post in the future for a certain "local time," you'll have to offset it (in your head) to obtain the UTC time. Likewise, having chosen the "long ordinal" presentation of the date and time, when showing an article the readers of your blog will just see an absolute numeric representation of the time and won't assume that it's a UTC time.

Figure 5-16

Depending on your application's requirements, this may or may not be a big deal. Luckily for you, Rails 2.2.2 provides excellent support for time zones and setting a predefined time zone for your application is extremely easy. I live in Toronto, so my time zone is `Eastern Time (US & Canada)`. You can see a list of local time zones by running the rake task `time:zones:local`:

```
C:\projects\blog> rake time:zones:local
(in C:/projects/blog)

* UTC -05:00 *
Bogota
Eastern Time (US & Canada)
Indiana (East)
Lima
Quito
```

You can use `rake time:zones:us` to obtain only the US time zones matching the local time on your machine. If you'd like a list of all the time zones supported by Rails, run `rake time:zones:all`.

Once you've determined the time zone that you'd like to apply — usually the time zone of your computer or of your deployment server — you need to tell Rails that you'd like to use this instead of UTC for your dates and times. In the `config\environment.rb` file change this line:

```
config.time_zone = 'UTC'
```

With the following or the time zone you're in:

```
config.time_zone = 'Eastern Time (US & Canada)'
```

Restart Mongrel, refresh the `/articles` page, and you will see that the times are now presented in the local time zone. Furthermore, if you head over to `/articles/new` the default time for the `published_at` field will be the current time in your local time zone as well.

Rails will still store the date and time values as UTC in the database, but will perform an automatic conversion for you when retrieving them from, or storing them in, the database. To verify this fire up the Rails console:

```
C:\projects\blog> ruby script/console
Loading development environment (Rails 2.2.2)
>>
```

This console works similarly to `irb` but it already has Rails' current environment loaded for you.

Try to evaluate the following expression:

```
>> Article.find(1).published_at
=> Fri, 11 Jul 2008 05:24:00 EDT -04:00
```

The result I obtained is local to my machine (which is what I'm after), however this may trick you into believing that the database holds that local date and time as well. This is not the case, as you can confirm by appending `before_type_cast` to the attribute `published_at` to obtain the date and time before the automatic conversion:

```
>> Article.find(1).published_at_before_type_cast
=> "2008-07-11 09:24:00"
```

Adding Support for Textile

Despite having separate paragraphs in the text area for the `body` attribute as shown in Figure 5-17, these newlines (that is, \n) are not rendered as line breaks or new paragraphs when the template is rendered in HTML.

You could use the helper `simple_format`, which appends a linebreak (that is, `<br />`) to each newline. When two consecutive newlines are found, the text before them, and the text after them, is wrapped in two separated pairs of paragraph tags. This fixes the "wall of text" issue, but you'd still be left with the issue of safely allowing innocuous HTML tags.

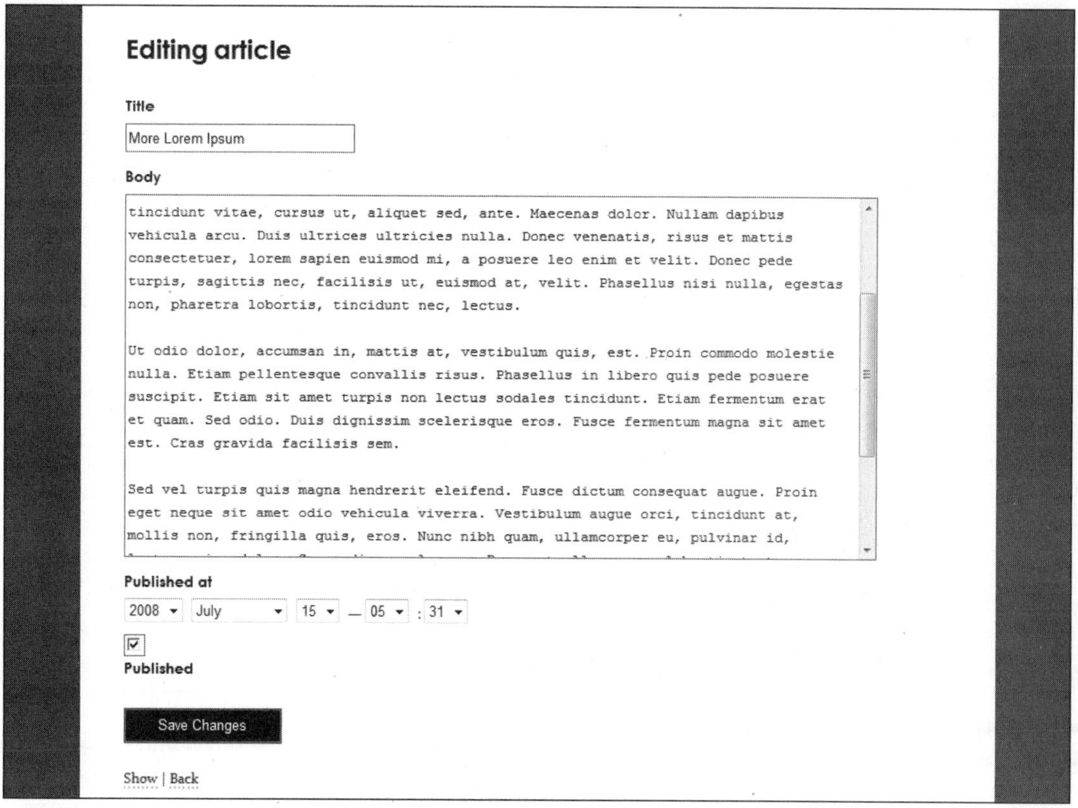

Editing article

Title

More Lorem Ipsum

Body

```
tincidunt vitae, cursus ut, aliquet sed, ante. Maecenas dolor. Nullam dapibus
vehicula arcu. Duis ultrices ultricies nulla. Donec venenatis, risus et mattis
consectetuer, lorem sapien euismod mi, a posuere leo enim et velit. Donec pede
turpis, sagittis nec, facilisis ut, euismod at, velit. Phasellus nisi nulla, egestas
non, pharetra lobortis, tincidunt nec, lectus.

Ut odio dolor, accumsan in, mattis at, vestibulum quis, est. Proin commodo molestie
nulla. Etiam pellentesque convallis risus. Phasellus in libero quis pede posuere
suscipit. Etiam sit amet turpis non lectus sodales tincidunt. Etiam fermentum erat
et quam. Sed odio. Duis dignissim scelerisque eros. Fusce fermentum magna sit amet
est. Cras gravida facilisis sem.

Sed vel turpis quis magna hendrerit eleifend. Fusce dictum consequat augue. Proin
eget neque sit amet odio vehicula viverra. Vestibulum augue orci, tincidunt at,
mollis non, fringilla quis, eros. Nunc nibh quam, ullamcorper eu, pulvinar id,
```

Published at

2008 ▾ July ▾ 15 ▾ — 05 ▾ : 31 ▾

☑
Published

Save Changes

Show | Back

Figure 5-17

The helper method `santize` does exactly that. It strips all the attributes that aren't explicitly allowed, while encoding the ones that are permitted. The method accepts two arguments, the HTML text that needs to be "sanitized," and a hash of options. `santize` can be considered as a more advanced replacement of `h`. If you were to adopt this strategy, `simple_format` and `sanitize` could be used together to obtain paragraph separation from newlines first, and then strip all the non-allowed tags and attributes. This approach would work but would require the blog's author to manually insert HTML.

It is customary for blog engines to provide a friendly markup language like Textile or Markdown, instead of requiring HTML code to be written. Assume that in your blog you'll opt for Textile, which is a very readable and easy to remember markup language.

> *A textile reference is available online at* `http://hobix.com/textile`. *For converting Markdown, you can use the BlueCloth plugin instead.*

The user will insert textile text, which will be stored in the database. The only conversion required is in the view layer, where you want to transform the retrieved body attribute in textile format into HTML that can be rendered by any browser.

Ruby offers a library called RedCloth that is able to perform this conversion for you. As long as the RedCloth gem is installed, Rails' helper method `textilize` can be used. The first thing you'll need to do is add a requirement for the RedCloth gem in `config\environment.rb`, as follows:

```
Rails::Initializer.run do |config|
  # ...
  # ...
  config.gem "RedCloth", :version => ">= 3.301", :source => "http://code.
whytheluckystiff.net"
  # ...
  # ...
end
```

As you can see, this specifies that the application depends on the RedCloth gem, that the version installed should be 3.301 or greater, and that it should be fetched directly from the website of the developer. This third option is not strictly required, but for this particular gem it is highly recommended, given that the gem that's available from RubyForge is not the most up-to-date one and an important release (nicknamed Super RedCloth) was recently put out by the developer on his own repository.

Once you have added this `config.gem` line, save the file and run the `rake gems:install` task to install the required gem as follows:

```
C:\projects\blog> rake gems:install
(in C:/projects/blog)
gem.bat install RedCloth −version ">= 3.301" −source http://code.whytheluckyst
iff.net
Successfully installed RedCloth-3.301-x86-mswin32
1 gem installed
```

Now you need to employ the `textilize` helper provided by Rails into the templates for the `index` and `show` actions.

> *You could also use* `RedCloth.new(text).to_html` *where* `text` *is the textile text that needs to be converted.*

This is easily done by replacing the following snippet in `index.html.erb`:

```
<div class="entry">
<%=h article.body %>
</div>
```

with:

```
<div class="entry">
<%= textilize(article.body) %>
</div>
```

And similarly, replace the following in `show.html.erb`:

```
<div class="entry">
<%=h @article.body %>
</div>
```

with:

```
<div class="entry">
<%= textilize(@article.body) %>
</div>
```

This will convert the textile markup into HTML code.

> ### Regarding the Security of textilize
>
> The `textilize` helper doesn't sanitize the text passed to it, and as such is susceptible to cross-site scripting (XSS) attacks. If the input is coming from the end user, such as in the case of a comment, the output of the `textilize` method needs to be explicitly sanitized using the `santize` method or another white listing filter.
>
> In this specific case, as mentioned before, you are the only one who will have access to the form for entering and editing articles (once the app has authentication in place), so it is not strictly necessary to sanitize your own input. Things would be very different for forms that accept textile comments from visitors. Chapter 11 has more security considerations.

Restart Mongrel, and load `http://localhost:3000` into your browser. This time around, you should be able to see that `textilize` has converted each chunk of text into a paragraph of its own.

Now create a new article by employing a bit more textile markup. Use the following text for the body:

```
Hi there!

If you don't know what %{color:red}Rails% is, you can read more about it on the
"official website":http://rubyonrails.org and then buy Antonio Cangiano's book.
It's *highly recommended*. ;-)

By the way, did you know that Ruby on Rails(TM) is a trademark of "David Heinemeier
Hansson":http://loudthinking.com?
```

This will be converted into the following HTML code by the `textilize` helper:

```
<p>Hi there!</p>
<p>If you don&#8217;t know what <span style="color:red;">Rails</span> is, you can
read more about it on the <a href="http://rubyonrails.org">official website</a>
and then buy Antonio Cangiano&#8217;s book. It&#8217;s <strong>highly recommended</
strong>. ;-)</p>

<p>By the way, did you know that Ruby on Rails&#8482; is a trademark of <a
href="http://loudthinking.com">David Heinemeier Hansson</a>?</p>
```

The rendered page for the `show` action is shown in Figure 5-18.

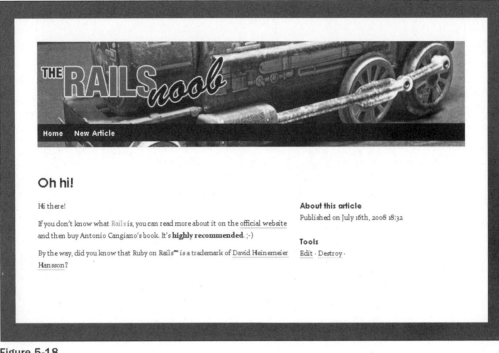

Figure 5-18

Another easy way to handle textile in Rails is to use the `acts_as_textiled` *plugin.*

Using named_scope

At this stage your *The Rails Noob* blog publishes every single article in the database regardless of its published or unpublished status. This is because in the `index` action you used a finder method, which retrieves all the records from the `articles` table:

```
@articles = Article.find(:all, :order => "published_at DESC")
```

You can change this in order to select only published articles by specifying a condition in the query:

```
@articles = Article.find(:all, :conditions => { :published => true }, :order =>
"published_at DESC")
```

This is converted into the SQL query:

```
SELECT * FROM "articles" WHERE ("articles"."published" = 't') ORDER BY published_at
DESC
```

You don't want to show all the published articles though. For example, if an article is set as published, but its publication date is in the future, that article is scheduled and should be shown only when its publication date is presently due or if it was in the past. You need to indicate two conditions to the `find` method, then, as shown here:

```
@articles = Article.find(:all, :conditions => ["published = ? AND published_at <=
?", true, Time.now], :order => "published_at DESC")
```

Notice how you specify the conditions by assigning an array to the `:conditions` key. This array contains the SQL condition, and the two parameters that the condition requires, in the order that they appear within it. The resulting SQL query will resemble the following:

```
SELECT * FROM "articles" WHERE (published = 't' AND published_at <= '2008-07-16
21:49:52') ORDER BY published_at DESC
```

This is almost what you want, except that there's a problem: `Time.now` is a local time and it gets compared to UTC times in the database. To fix this you need to convert it to UTC through the `utc` instance method:

```
@articles = Article.find(:all, :conditions => ["published = ? AND published_at <=
?", true, Time.now.utc], :order => "published_at DESC")
```

This, at the time I ran the query, was converted into:

```
SELECT * FROM "articles" WHERE (published = 't' AND published_at <= '2008-07-17
02:01:22') ORDER BY published_at DESC
```

This is exactly the query you were aiming for. In theory you could have gone ahead and applied the new finder options in your `index` action and everything would work as expected. There is, however, a consideration to be made.

If you were to develop your blog in the real world, so as to include many typical blog features, it's very possible that you'd find yourself refining your query further in different ways. For example, in an action you may want to retrieve a list of published articles for a given month, whereas in another you may wish to get a list of articles that have been published within a certain range of dates. All these finders, which can become visually quite busy, will have a lot of common code because they all need to retrieve a list of published posts.

One approach to deal with this repetition, and adhere to the DRY principle, would be to create a class method in the model as follows:

```
# Returns published articles excluding scheduled ones
def self.published(options)
    find(:all, options.merge(:conditions => ["published = ? AND published_at <= ?",
true, Time.now.utc]))
end
```

This solution enables you to call `Article.published` as well as pass a few finder options to the method from your controller:

```
Article.published(:order => "published_at DESC")
```

Since version 2.1, Rails offers an even better solution that is more concise and far more flexible: named scopes. These were introduced into Rails' core with the 2.1 release, but were already available before thanks to a plugin called has_finder. The idea behind named scopes is that it's possible to attribute a name to a customized finder much as you would with a class method. Unlike a class method though, these can be chained with other ActiveRecord methods so that they become a very easy way to reuse the finder logic that they encapsulate. Within your models you can define a named scope with the method named_scope. Go ahead and add the following named scopes to the Article model (in app\models\article.rb):

```
# Finds all the published posts excluding scheduled ones
named_scope :published, :conditions => ["published = ? AND published_at <= ?",
true, Time.now.utc]

# Finds all the drafts and scheduled posts
named_scope :unpublished, :conditions => ["published = ? OR published_at > ?",
false, Time.now.utc]
```

Now you'll be able to run Article.published and obtain a list of published (excluding scheduled ones) articles. Likewise, you can use Article.unpublished to get an array of scheduled articles and drafts. You can also transparently chain a finder method to it (or any Article class method or Array instance method) to refine the select conditions further.

Change the finder in the index action within the Articles controller from:

```
@articles = Article.find(:all, :order => "published_at DESC")
```

to:

```
@articles = Article.published.find(:all, :order => "published_at DESC")
```

Reload http://localhost:3000 and you should see that only published, non-scheduled articles appear.

Feel free to change the publication status or scheduled dates of a few articles of your own to see how this is properly reflected on the articles (as shown on the blog's homepage). You can also use the Rails console introduced previously, which is also a quick way to modify the status of a record as shown in the following Rails console session:

```
C:\projects\blog> ruby script/console
Loading development environment (Rails 2.2.2)
>> a = Article.published.first
=> #<Article id: 1, title: "Hello, Rails!", body: "Hi from the body of an articl
e. :)", published: true, published_at: "2008-07-11 09:24:00", created_at: "2008-
07-11 09:32:41", updated_at: "2008-07-11 09:32:41">
>> a.published
=> true
>> a.published = false
=> false
>> a.save
=> true
>> a
=> #<Article id: 1, title: "Hello, Rails!", body: "Hi from the body of an articl
```

```
e. :)", published: false, published_at: "2008-07-11 09:24:00", created_at: "2008
-07-11 09:32:41", updated_at: "2008-07-17 03:18:28">
```

Like irb, enter exit *and hit the Return key to quit the console.*

Notice that there is no collision between the named scope published and the attribute published. The first is accessed from the Article class (like a common class method), whereas the second is only defined by Article instances.

Adding a Custom REST Action

At this point in time, any scheduled article or draft will be excluded from the homepage. You could edit them from the console or access them by placing their id in the URL, but this is far from convenient. What you can do is create a custom action called unpublished. Add the following action to your ArticlesController:

```
# GET /articles/unpublished
# GET /articles/unpublished.xml
def unpublished
  @articles = Article.unpublished.find(:all, :order => "published DESC, published_
at DESC")

  respond_to do |format|
    format.html { render :action => "index" }
    format.xml  { render :xml => @articles }
  end
end
```

To retrieve the list of unpublished articles, you can chain the unpublished named scope with a finder that sorts them to display scheduled articles first and drafts second. Furthermore, you keep the inverse chronological order for each of the two "groups."

The template for the unpublished action would be identical to the one of the index action because they both display a bunch of articles, no matter what these are.

> *Truth be told, the* destroy *action redirects every HTML request to the* index *action. This means that if you delete an article from the "unpublished page" you'll be redirected back to the* index *action, not to* unpublished. *It's a minor nuisance that can be fixed by improving the redirecting logic inside the* destroy *action, to make it aware of the previous action (for example,* index *or* unpublished). *To do so, replace* redirect_to(articles_url) *in* destroy *with* redirect_to(:back).

Rather than fostering repetition by copying the index.html.erb template into a unpublished.html.erb file, it's far nicer to simply render the template of the index action via render :action => :index.

> **Unlike** redirect_to, **using** render **implies that only the** index.html.erb **template will be rendered and there is no risk that the** index **action will be executed, thereby assigning the wrong array of articles to the** @articles **variable.**

If you try to access `http://localhost:3000/articles/unpublished` you'll get an ugly error message:

```
Couldn't find Article with ID=unpublished
```

The reason for this is that you are using a custom REST action that is not automatically mapped by `map.resources :articles` in `config\routes.rb`. Therefore routing assumes that `unpublished` is the `id` of the record that you are looking for, not the name of an action.

You'll just have to plug the new action into the collection of REST actions within the routes file. Change it as follows:

```
map.resources :articles, :collection => { :unpublished => :get }
```

Restart Mongrel, because you've modified the routes file, and visit `http://localhost:3000/articles/unpublished` again. This time you should see a list of scheduled and drafted articles. Likewise, visiting `http://localhost:3000/articles/unpublished.xml` will return the same articles (encoded in XML format) to you.

Beautiful! Now that it works, you can add a link (the highlighted line) in the `articles.html.erb` layout:

```
<li><%= link_to 'Home', root_path %></li>
<li><%= link_to 'Unpublished Articles', unpublished_articles_path %></
li><li><%= link_to 'New Article', new_article_path %></li>
```

Notice that when you added your custom REST action to the collection in the routes file, you essentially created a named route for it, so you can also use the handy "url" and "path" helper methods (for example, `unpublished_articles_path`). If you reload the homepage, you should now see that the new menu bar includes a working link to the unpublished articles.

When adding some form of authentication to the blog, it will be necessary to hide this link from the general public.

A final touch would be the ability to distinguish drafts from scheduled posts. You could, for example, provide this bit of information in the "About this article" section on the right side of the article's body. Instead of saying "Published on" all the time, you could distinguish and use "Scheduled for" and "This is still a draft." when appropriate.

Defining a Helper Method

One way to do this is by defining a `status` instance method in the `Article` model that returns a string indicating the status of the article object. You would then need to use this value to create a full string that includes the proper "for" or "on" preposition, plus the publication date and time in the view layer. If you take this approach, you could even think of formulating the whole string, as it needs to appear to the user, directly in the `status` method from within the model. This latter idea is a very bad one! You shouldn't include presentation logic in the model, because a distinct separation of concerns is king when it comes to Rails development.

A much more straightforward approach consists of simply defining a custom helper method that receives the article object as an argument and returns the desired string. You can define helper methods in the app\helpers directory of your project. If you take a look in that folder, you'll find two files, applica-tion_helpers.rb and articles_helpers.rb. The naming convention has the same logic as that of controllers and layouts. Methods defined in application_helpers.rb will be available site-wide, whereas those defined in articles_helpers.rb will be accessible only from the article templates.

In this case the helper method that you need is highly specific to articles, so go ahead and change your app\helpers\articles_helpers.rb file to look like this:

```ruby
module ArticlesHelper
  def publication_status(article)
    publication_time = article.published_at.to_s(:long_ordinal)

    if article.published
      if article.published_at <= Time.now
        "Published on #{publication_time}"
      else
        "Scheduled for #{publication_time}"
      end
    else
      "This article is still a draft."
    end
  end
end
```

Notice how this uses the attributes of the article object passed as an argument to determine its status and in turn decides which string to return. In the case of a draft, it doesn't make much sense to publish the publication date, so the string literal "This article is still a draft." is returned.

Now you need to use the helper publication_status in both the index.html.erb and show.html.erb templates. Before doing that though, you need to make an important consideration. This isn't the first time that you had to change the code in both templates. When this happens, it's a surefire giveaway that the code could adhere more to the DRY principle by employing a partial template. Effectively, if you take a look at the code of index.html.erb and show.html.erb you'll notice that they are virtually the same, except that the template associated with the index action loops through the list of articles.

More about Partials

To solve this, create a partial in the app\views\articles directory and call it _article.html.erb.

Place the following code, cut and pasted from the index.html.erb template, inside the partial you just created:

```erb
<div class="article clear">
    <h2><%= link_to h(article.title), article %></h2>
    <div  class="column span-6">
      <div class="entry">
        <%= textilize(article.body) %>
      </div>
    </div>
    <!-- /column -->
    </div>
```

```
<div  class="column span-4 last">
  <div class="meta">
    <h3>About this article</h3>
    Published on <%= article.published_at.to_s(:long_ordinal) %>
  </div>

  <div class="tools">
    <h3>Tools</h3>
    <%= link_to 'Edit', edit_article_path(article) %>&middot;
    <%= link_to 'Destroy', article, :confirm => 'Are you sure?', :method =>
:delete %>
  </div>
  <!- /column ->
  </div>
<!- /article ->
</div>
```

You can immediately modify it to use the `publication_status` helper you defined before. Replace the following line in the `_article.html.erb` partial:

```
Published on <%= article.published_at.to_s(:long_ordinal) %>
```

with:

```
<%= publication_status(article) %>
```

Now that you have created this partial, go ahead and remove the entire content of `show.html.erb`, replacing it with the following line:

```
<%= render :partial => @article %>
```

The render method is smart enough to figure out the partial name, inferring it from the name of the class of the object, `@article`. In our case, it will render `_article.html.erb`. That method also makes the object assigned to the `@article` instance variable available through the `article` local variable in the partial.

> *Some people prefer to avoid all this magic and opt instead to specify the name of the partial and the local variables explicitly. Another common option is* `:object`, *which passes the value assigned to it down to the local variable that matches the name of the partial. For example:* `render :partial =>"article",` `:object => @article` *will accomplish the same results as* `render :partial => @article`, *but in a less concise way. Be careful though, because* `render :partial =>"my_partial", :object` `=> @article` *would assign the value of* `@article` *to the local variable* my_partial, *not* article.

You made the `show.html.erb` template as DRY as possible, however you still need to address the `index.html.erb` one. The peculiarity of this template is that it loops through a collection of articles, so you'd have to render the partial you saw before (within a loop).

Thankfully, the `render` method is flexible and smart enough to infer from an `@articles` collection of `Article` objects assigned to `:partial`, that the partial `_article.html.erb` should be rendered once for each object in the array. Every time the partial is rendered, the current object in the array will be assigned to the local variable `article` in the partial. This syntax is much more concise. What's more, the local variable `article_counter` will be set to store the current position in the list of records (starting from 1, not 0).

Replace the entire contents of the `index.html.erb` file with the following:

```
<%= render :partial => @articles %>
```

Earlier you saw that `:partial => @article` *could be rewritten using the* `:object` *option if you wanted to. Similarly,* `:partial => @articles` *could be rewritten using the* `:collection` *hash. For example,* `render :partial => "article", :collection => @articles` *is equivalent to* `render :partial => @articles`, *which you used in* `index.html.erb`. *Just like* `:object`, `:collection` *defines the local variable based on the name of the partial. In the case of collections, this can be overwritten with the option* `:as` *introduced in Rails 2.2.*

Assuming you followed each step carefully, everything should be working now, just as planned, and the code that you've got in your hands here definitely applies the Don't Repeat Yourself principle. Figure 5-19 shows you the "Unpublished Articles" page for the articles I created on my machine (I highlighted the rendered output of the `publication_status` helper with a rectangle).

Figure 5-19

195

Summary

Now your blog looks sufficiently presentable. There are still a few missing features though, before you can rightfully consider it a full-fledged simple blog:

1. You lack pagination. If your blog had 50 currently published articles, all of them would appear on the front page. I like the idea of having only one post on the front page (or if you wish, more) and being able to click a navigation menu to see the previous posts.

2. Some blogs opt not to have comments enabled, but in your blog you'll allow them and this provides the opportunity to introduce a few more Rails concepts.

3. Any respectable blog should allow content syndication; hence you need to add an RSS and Atom feed.

4. You should throw in a bit of Ajax in order to provide a more responsive experience when using your application.

In the next chapter you address the first two points, adding pagination and comments to your blog. In Chapter 8 you evaluate a few options for easily adding authentication and authorization to the application, and in Chapter 9 you add RSS and Atom feeds, as well as throwing in a sprinkle of Ajax.

What's key is that you are doing incremental development, so as new concepts are explained in the coming chapters, you'll add a few features to the application when doing so fits.

## 6

Incremental Development, Logging, and Debugging

The wages of sin is debugging.

— Ron Jeffries, Co-founder of the XP methodology

The previous chapter laid the foundation for your undemanding *The Rails Noob* blog application, but you currently lack pagination and the ability to add comments. In this chapter, you add these functionalities and also take a closer look at a few other aspects of the framework, including logging and debugging.

Adding Pagination

As seen before, when you visit / or /articles all the currently published posts are shown. If you are a regular blogger you'll probably post at least an article each week. At that pace, the front page would soon become an exceedingly long scroll of content. To work around this issue, you are going to add pagination, which is the ability to define a set number of articles that will appear per page. Here it is assumed that you want to display only the latest post on the homepage.

You could implement this feature yourself, given that ActiveRecord's finders allow you to specify :limit and :offset conditions for SELECT queries, but why should you reinvent the wheel? Pagination is an extremely common requirement for Web applications, and several plugins are available that can be readily used.

> *In earlier versions of Rails, pagination was a feature that was included by the framework, but its implementation and performance were less than satisfactory, so it has since been removed.*

Installing the will_paginate Plugin

The most commonly used pagination plugin is `will_paginate`. This excellent plugin makes adding pagination to your applications a joy. The recommended way of installing it is through RubyGems. The first thing that you need to do, then, is to add a requirement for the gem in `config\environment.rb`.

Add to that file the following line:

```
config.gem 'mislav-will_paginate', :version => '>= 2.3.2',
                             :lib => 'will_paginate',
                             :source => 'http://gems.github.com'
```

This should be placed after the existing `config.gem` *line in the* `Rails::Initializer.run` *block.*

You need to specify the `:lib` key/option because the name of the gem is `mislav-will_paginate`, whereas the name of the actual library that needs to be loaded is `will_paginate`. GitHub is a very popular and highly appreciated site for Ruby projects and libraries, and as such it's common for many gems and plugins to be hosted there.

Not all plugins are available as gems, and many of them need to be installed by running ruby `script/plugin install http://example.org/repository/name_plugin`, *which copies the plugin to the* `vendor\plugins` *directory of the project.*

So far, you've only specified what's required for loading a specific gem when the HTTP server starts up; you've yet to actually install the gem though. Let's do that next.

From the main directory of your project, run `rake gems:install`. You should see a reassuring message that confirms that the gem was correctly installed. Now you can restart Mongrel, wherein you shouldn't see any warnings about missing gems.

Using the Plugin

Now that the plugin is properly installed, you'll need to do two things. The first is to specify the number of articles per page that you'd like to retrieve. The second is to modify the `index.html.erb` template so that it contains a page menu that will allow you to navigate between pages. The `will_paginate` plugin makes both of these steps incredibly straightforward.

You're interested in paginating the main page of your site, so you'll need to modify the finder used in the `index` action of the `Articles` controller. The plugin you just installed adds a `paginate` class method to `ActiveRecord::Base`, which is essentially a finder with two additional options: `:page` and `:per_page`.

Replace the existing finder in the `index` action with the following:

```
@articles = Article.published.paginate(:page => params[:page],
                                 :per_page => 1,
                                 :order => "published_at DESC")
```

With that line you specified that only one record per page should be fetched. The method `paginate` knows which record should be retrieved based on the `:per_page` setting and the `page` parameter (with 1 being the default for page if no parameter is given). As you can verify by visiting http://localhost:3000/, in this case loading the homepage would lead to the retrieval of only the last published, non-scheduled article.

Don't forget to have the Web server running with ruby script/server.

Upon visiting http://localhost:3000/?page=2 in your browser, you'd assign the value 2 to the page parameter, trigger the index action, and obtain the second page that should be rendered. Because you specified that you'd like to see only one article per page (with :per_page => 1), that request will lead you to the second record. Had you specified :per_page => 5, the second page would have displayed records from the 6th to the 10th post (based on the order condition "published_at DESC").

Before proceeding to add a convenient pagination menu to move between pages, let's think this one through. Is the index action the only action that should be paginated? It could be argued that any page that needs to display a series of articles should have pagination. In this scenario, this assumption leads us to consider pagination for the unpublished action as well.

Replace the existing finder in the unpublished action with the following:

```
@articles = Article.unpublished.paginate(:page => params[:page], :per_page => 1,
  :order => "published DESC, published_at DESC")
```

If you now load http://localhost:3000/articles/unpulished in your browser, you'll see only the latest unpublished article.

The problem with what you just did is that you need to repeat how many records you want per page in both actions. With only two existing actions, this is not a big violation of the DRY principle, but every time you need to add a new action that's able to display a collection of articles, you'll face this same repetition (assuming that they all share the same per_page setting).

Truth be told, some may opt for a larger number of articles per page for the unpublished page, in which case no repetition occurs when specifying the per_page *option.*

Setting per_page in the Model

Thankfully, the will_paginate plugin provides a way to specify this option model-wide. All you need to do is define a class method called per_page that returns the number of records that you want to render on each page.

Sometimes you'll see code that looks like the following:

```
cattr_reader :per_page
@@per_page = 1
```

This works too. cattr_reader *is a method provided by ActiveSupport, which adds the equivalent of* attr_reader *to class variables. Using the preceding code in a class will define a class method and an instance method called* per_page. *Both will return the value of the class variable* @@per_page.

You can improve your code slightly then, so go ahead and change your `Article` model by adding the following class method to its definition:

```
def self.per_page
  1
end
```

Having defined the `per_page` option in the model, you can now remove it from the two actions. The "final" finders appear as follows:

```
# In index
@articles = Article.published.paginate(:page => params[:page], :order =>
"published_at DESC")

# In unpublished
@articles = Article.unpublished.paginate(:page => params[:page], :order =>
"published DESC, published_at DESC")
```

Adding a Pagination Menu to the View

Now that the model and controller have done their part, you'll need to modify the view layer to include a pagination menu. Edit the `index.html.erb` template (used by both `index` and `unpublished`) so that it looks like the following:

```
<%= render :partial => @articles %>
<%= will_paginate @articles %>
```

Save the file and reload the homepage; you should see the pagination menu at the bottom as shown in Figure 6-1. The number of pages will depend on the quantity of published articles that already exist.

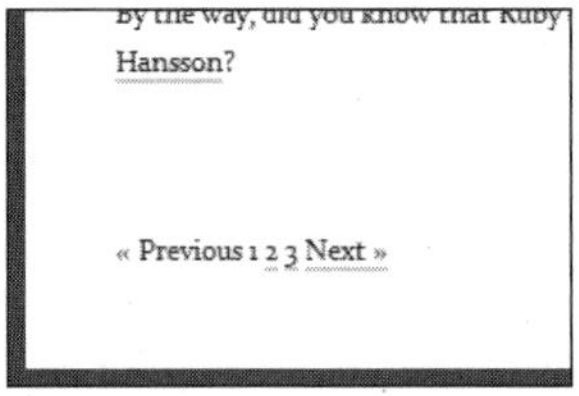

Figure 6-1

If you visit `http://localhost:3000/articles/unpublished` you can obtain a similar menu that may have a different number of pages, depending on the number of scheduled and drafted articles.

> The plugin repository for the plugin is located at `http://github.com/mislav/will_paginate/`. Within the file `examples/pagination.css` are a few predefined CSS classes that you can use to customize the look of the output of the `will_paginate` helper.

Try to think about what you just did and you'll realize how adding pagination was very straightforward and much easier than what you would have to do if you were implementing it in ASP or ASP.NET.

Adding Comments

Your visitors should be able to read articles and comment on them. The information that you need from each commenter is their name, their email address (which you won't display), and the body of their comment. Let's create a new resource for this.

Go ahead and run the following:

```
C:\projects\blog> ruby script/generate scaffold comment article:references
name:string email:string body:text
```

This is analogous to what you already did before for the article resource. The only part warranting explanation is `article:references`. It indicates that you need a foreign key that references the primary key of the `articles` table so that you can establish a one-to-many relationship between the `articles` table and the `comments` table. The foreign key in the `comments` table will be `article_id`. It will be an integer (just as the referenced `id` is).

> `references` has an alias called `belongs_to`. Using `article:belongs_to` would have been acceptable as well.

The migration file looks like this:

```
class CreateComments < ActiveRecord::Migration
  def self.up
    create_table :comments do |t|
      t.references :article
      t.string :name
      t.string :email
      t.text :body

      t.timestamps
    end
  end

  def self.down
    drop_table :comments
  end
end
```

It is usually a very good idea to add indexes to foreign key columns. This can drastically improve performance. Before proceeding with the creation of the table, you should modify the migration file to add an index as shown here:

```
class CreateComments < ActiveRecord::Migration
  def self.up
    create_table :comments do |t|
      t.references :article
      t.string :name
      t.string :email
      t.text :body

      t.timestamps
    end
```

```
      add_index :comments, :article_id
  end

  def self.down
    drop_table :comments
  end
end
```

Please note that `add_index` has an opposite method, called `remove_index`. For example, in the `down` method you could write `remove_index :comments, :column => :article_id`. This is not necessary, however, given that you already have `drop_table :comments`. When the table is dropped, the index you defined will be removed as well.

Now you need to evolve the current schema, which includes the `articles` table only, to a version that will include the new `comments` table as well. To do this, run `rake db:migrate` as you did in the previous chapter. If you look at the `log\development.log` file, you'll see that the generated SQL query creates a `comments` table that includes an `article_id` column, the `name`, `email`, and `body` fields that you specified, plus the usual `created_at` and `updated_at`. You'll also see the following query for the index you defined:

```
CREATE INDEX "index_comments_on_article_id" ON "comments" ("article_id")
```

You can also see this in Ruby code if you take a look at the contents of the file `db\schema.rb`, which is generated after executing rake tasks that affect the schema (for example, `db:migrate`):

```
ActiveRecord::Schema.define(:version => 20080723022822) do

  create_table "articles", :force => true do |t|
    t.string   "title"
    t.text     "body"
    t.boolean  "published"
    t.datetime "published_at"
    t.datetime "created_at"
    t.datetime "updated_at"
  end

  create_table "comments", :force => true do |t|
    t.integer  "article_id"
    t.string   "name"
    t.string   "email"
    t.text     "body"
    t.datetime "created_at"
    t.datetime "updated_at"
  end

  add_index "comments", ["article_id"], :name => "index_comments_on_article_id"
end
```

This file can also be explicitly generated by running `rake db:schema:dump` and loaded into an empty database by running `rake db:schema:load`. `schema.rb` is essentially a translation, in Ruby code, of the database schema. This uses the ActiveRecord adapter for the specific database system to determine how to map SQL data types with Rails data types.

Because `schema.rb` is relied upon for generating the test database, if your database has database-specific column types that are not supported by the adapter or that use other db-specific features, which won't be "dumped" by the `db:schema:dump` task, it's far better to switch to an SQL-based creation of the test database by uncommenting the existing line in `config\environment.rb`:

```
# Use SQL instead of Active Record's schema dumper when creating the test database.
# This is necessary if your schema can't be completely dumped by the schema dumper,
# like if you have constraints or database-specific column types
config.active_record.schema_format = :sql
```

Fortunately, you don't need to do that in your case.

If you head over to `http://localhost:3000/comments`, you will probably be quite disappointed by the bare-bones look that is typical of the `scaffold` generator, as shown in Figure 6-2.

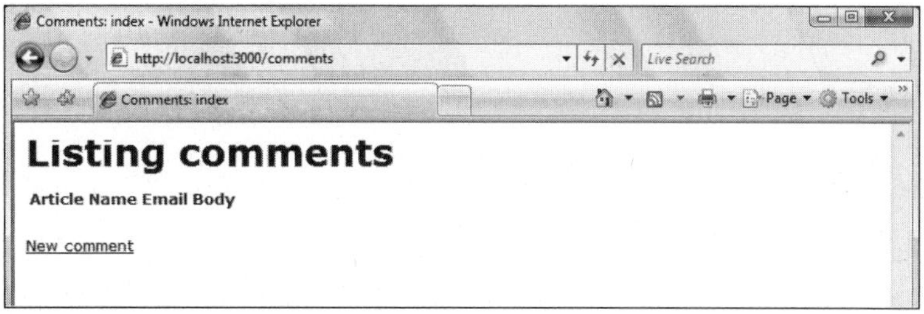

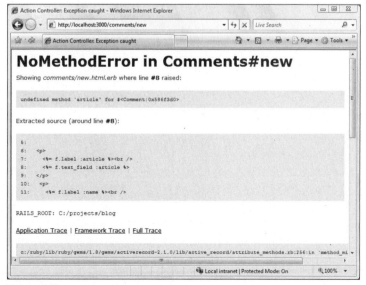

Figure 6-2

The reason for this is that the actions of the `Comments` controller are rendered using the `comments .html.erb` layout and not the `articles.html.erb` one that you've customized so far.

Things get even worse if you decide to accept the open invitation to click "New comment" as shown in Figure 6-3.

Figure 6-3

Defining Associations

That doesn't look too good, now, does it? The problem lies in the fact that the app\views\comments\ new.html.erb template that's generated by scaffold expects Comment model objects to have an article method. This is not automatically the case because you have not specified an association between the Article and Comment models. To do that, edit the Article model to include the following highlighted line:

```
class Article < ActiveRecord::Base
  has_many :comments

  # ... other existing code ...
end
```

Similarly, the Comment model, located in app\models\comment.rb, should look like the following:

```
class Comment < ActiveRecord::Base
  belongs_to :article
end
```

Starting with Rails 2.2 belongs_to *is automatically populated for you when scaffolding. In earlier versions it had to be manually specified.*

The highlighted lines employ methods to define associations between models that in turn represent relationships between the respective tables in the database. In this case, you defined a one-to-many relationship between Article and Comment.

As you can see, the syntax of these associated methods is very straightforward. Each of them receives a symbol that indicates the associated object (plus optional arguments). They end up reading like common speech: an article "has many comments" and a comment "belongs to an article."

Notice how the symbol passed to the has_many method is plural, whereas the argument for belongs_to is singular. Other association methods are has_one (for one-to-one relationships) and has_and_belongs_to_many (for many-to-many relationships).

Including that single line for each model automatically adds a series of methods that allow you to effortlessly work with the related tables. For example, you'll be able to use the comments method on any Article object to obtain a list of associated comments. For instance, you'll just issue Article.find(42). comments to obtain an array of Comment objects whose article_id attribute is set to 42. Likewise, you can now use the method article to obtain the Article object that a comment "belongs to."

Having added these associations, the Comment model now has an instance method article so you can reload the page http://localhost:3000/comments/new without seeing any errors, as shown in Figure 6-4.

By the way, errors like the one shown in Figure 6-3 are for troubleshooting purposes and are not displayed when Rails is running in production mode.

While you are at it, you can also add validation for the Comment model. Its code becomes:

```
class Comment < ActiveRecord::Base
  belongs_to :article
```

```
  validates_presence_of :name, :email, :body
  validates_format_of :email, :with => /\A([\w\.\-\+]+)@((?:[-a-z0-9]+\.)+[a-z]
{2,})\Z/i
end
```

You require name, email, and body for each comment. Then you use `validates_format_of` to verify that the email address inserted by the end user is valid. That scary looking thing is a regular expression literal. The `i` after the slash indicates that it should not be case sensitive. Despite its size, this is used to perform only a basic validation of the conformity of email addresses. Regular expressions, which are compliant with RFC 822, are even larger.

You can take a look at a slow implementation here: `http://www.ex-parrot.com/~pdw/Mail-RFC822-Address.html`. *In general it is not a good idea to try to come up with your own very strict regular expression for validating emails. For a discussion on the topic, check out this post:* `http://www.rorsecurity.info/2007/04/16/ruby-regular-expression-fun`, *which the preceding regular expression comes from, and* `http://www.regular-expressions.info/email.html`. *Using a library like the one pointed out by the* `rorsecurity.info` *site may be a good idea.*

New comment

Article

Name

Email

Body

Figure 6-4

Notice in Figure 6-4 that you don't have a convenient drop-down list of possible articles to choose from. `Scaffold` gives you a text field, where you can enter the `article_id`, but that's it. Even if it provided us with a list to choose from, this would still be far from what you want in a blog.

In your blog you'll need to make the following three adjustments:

1. If you run `rake routes`, you'll see a bunch of `/comments` paths due to the fact that `scaffold` added `map.resources :comments` to the project's routes file. You don't really want people to be able reach `http://localhost:3000/comments/new`, because a comment is always associated with a given article. Instead, it would be nice to have nested routes, so as to reflect this logical hierarchy in the URL as well (for example, `http://localhost:3000/articles/42/comments/new`).

2. You shouldn't see a field for `article_id`, but rather the new form should appear beneath an article and be automatically associated with it.

3. A look and feel that is consistent with what you have for the articles. Ideally, you should be able to embed comments in that same layout.

Nested Resources

What you'll need to address all these points is the ability to nest the two resources. Edit your `config\routes.rb` file to replace the following two lines (non-adjacent in your routes file):

```
map.resources :comments
map.resources :articles, :collection => { :unpublished => :get }
```

with:

```
map.resources :articles, :has_many => :comments, :collection => { :unpublished =>
:get }
```

Alternatively, when you need more control, you can use this equivalent block-based syntax:

```
map.resources :articles, :collection => {:unpublished => :get} do |article|
  article.resources :comments
end
```

Once you've added the highlighted line to the routes file, run `rake routes` again and you'll see that all the `/comments` are gone, replaced by `/articles/:article_id/comments`. Awesome!

On top of that, you'll have `_path` and `_url` helpers, as you're accustomed to, for comments as well. Given that the routes are nested, the stem for these methods will be different, as shown in the output of the `routes` task you just ran. For example, `article_comments_url` will accept an article as an argument and return the URL to access a list of all its comments. If you hadn't nested the resources, that helper would have been `comments_url`, and it wouldn't have accepted any arguments.

You changed the routes file, so go ahead and restart Mongrel. The bad news is that if you try to load `http://localhost:3000/articles/1/comments/new` in your browser, you will get a nasty error like this one:

```
undefined method `comments_path' for #<ActionView::Base:0x59bfcf8>
```

The error is pretty obvious if you think about it. The view template generated by `scaffold` in the file `app\views\comments\new.html.erb` uses the default helper methods, such as `comments_path`. Because you changed the routes file to define nested routes, you now need to ensure that any helpers in the controller and the view layers are changed to reflect this new arrangement.

Let's do that right away.

Adapting the Controller

The scaffold generator created a standard controller for the comment resource. However, you changed the routes file so that comments are logically tied to an existing article. For this reason you'll need to adapt the Comments controller.

Let's start by instructing the Comments controller to use the same layout you used for the articles. You do this by invoking the layout method in its definition:

```
layout "articles"
```

This indicates to the Comments controller that it should render the articles.html.erb layout for all the actions it defines. So go ahead and delete the comments.html.erb layout generated by scaffold.

> *The layout method also accepts the* :except *and* :only *conditions whenever you need to define a specific layout only for certain actions. Specifying* layout nil *is one way to indicate that no layouts should be rendered.*

In the index action you have:

```
@comments = Comment.find(:all)
```

This index action will need to list all the comments for a certain article. Assuming that this article is stored in @article, you can access all of its comments with @article.comments. This returns an array of Comment objects. If you need to refine the comment search with some condition, you can do so by chaining a finder method to @article.comments just like you would with a named scope or a regular ActiveRecord::Base object (for example, @article.comments is equivalent to @article.comments.find(:all)).

Replace the preceding line in the index action with the following:

```
@comments = @article.comments
```

Now, change the show, edit, update, and destroy actions. Replace the following assignment in all of them:

```
@comment = Comment.find(params[:id])
```

with:

```
@comment = @article.comments.find(params[:id])
```

Replace this line in the new action:

```
@comment = Comment.new
```

with this:

```
@comment = @article.comments.new
```

This will create a new, unsaved `Comment` object whose `article_id` already references the `id` in `@article`.

Finally, in the `create` action replace:

```
@comment = Comment.new(params[:comment])
```

with:

```
@comment = @article.comments.build(params[:comment])
```

You are almost done with the controller. You just have to replace the redirects so that they'll work with the nested resources. After creating a comment, you want to redirect back to the article that lists all the comments as well (for HTML requests). To do so, change the existing `format.html { redirect_to(@comment) }` in the `create` action with:

```
format.html { redirect_to(@article) }
```

On the other hand, when you update a comment, an operation that the blog's owner might do, you are okay with redirecting back to the `show` action for the comment in question, thus verifying that the comment looks good. To do so you can't simply use `redirect_to(@comment)` because comments are now a resource that is nested into articles. Therefore you'll need to use `redirect_to([@article, @comment])`. This is a succinct notation to express that you want to redirect to the `show` action for the object `@comment`, which "belongs to" the `@article` object. It's equivalent to using `redirect_to(article_comment_url(@article, @comment))`.

Go ahead and replace the following line from the `update` action:

```
format.html { redirect_to(@comment) }
```

with:

```
format.html { redirect_to([@article, @comment]) }
```

Note also that the `destroy` action performs a redirect with `redirect_to(comments_url)` in an attempt to redirect to the list of comments after deleting the comment (well, at least for HTML requests). With your new routes file in place, you'll have to modify this and replace it with `redirect_to(article_comments_url(@article))`.

> When you are confused as to what stem of the helper to use, always remember to use `rake routes`. After a while you'll become accustomed to them and will no longer need to look them up.

The last thing left to do is to ensure that before each action the `@article` variable is set to the article indicated by the `article_id` parameter in the request. You do this in two steps. You first define a private method called `get_article` in the `Comments` controller:

```
private

def get_article
  @article = Article.find(params[:article_id])
end
```

This is private because it's just an auxiliary method in the controller, and it doesn't need to be exposed to the end user as an action. The next step is instructing the controller to invoke this method before any action is executed. You do this by using the `before_filter` method:

```
before_filter :get_article
```

In this way when, for example, in the index action you have `@comments = @article.comments`, the variable `@article` will exist, and already be set to the object whose `id` is the `article_id` parameter in the request. For instance, when you send a GET request for `http://localhost:3000/articles/3/comments` this invokes the `get_article` method, finds and assigns the record with `id` 3 to the `@article` variable, and then invokes the `index` action, which retrieves all the comments for that record with `@comments = @article.comments`.

The resulting code of the controller is shown in Listing 6-1.

In production mode, a 404 status code is returned when a record cannot be found.

Listing 6-1: The comments_controller.rb File Adjusted for Nested Resources

```ruby
class CommentsController < ApplicationController
  layout "articles"

  before_filter :get_article

  # GET /comments
  # GET /comments.xml
  def index
    @comments = @article.comments

    respond_to do |format|
      format.html # index.html.erb
      format.xml  { render :xml => @comments }
    end
  end

  # GET /comments/1
  # GET /comments/1.xml
  def show
    @comment = @article.comments.find(params[:id])

    respond_to do |format|
      format.html # show.html.erb
      format.xml  { render :xml => @comment }
    end
  end

  # GET /comments/new
  # GET /comments/new.xml
  def new
    @comment = @article.comments.new

    respond_to do |format|
```

Continued

```ruby
        format.html # new.html.erb
        format.xml  { render :xml => @comment }
    end
  end

  # GET /comments/1/edit
  def edit
    @comment = @article.comments.find(params[:id])
  end

  # POST /comments
  # POST /comments.xml
  def create
    @comment = @article.comments.build(params[:comment])

    respond_to do |format|
      if @comment.save
        flash[:notice] = 'Comment was successfully created.'
        format.html { redirect_to(@article) }
        format.xml  { render :xml => @comment, :status => :created, :location => @
comment }
      else
        format.html { render :action => "new" }
        format.xml  { render :xml => @comment.errors, :status => :unprocessable_
entity }
      end
    end
  end

  # PUT /comments/1
  # PUT /comments/1.xml
  def update
    @comment = @article.comments.find(params[:id])

    respond_to do |format|
      if @comment.update_attributes(params[:comment])
        flash[:notice] = 'Comment was successfully updated.'
        format.html { redirect_to([@article, @comment]) }
        format.xml  { head :ok }
      else
        format.html { render :action => "edit" }
        format.xml  { render :xml => @comment.errors, :status => :unprocessable_
entity }
      end
    end
  end

  # DELETE /comments/1
  # DELETE /comments/1.xml
  def destroy
    @comment = @article.comments.find(params[:id])
    @comment.destroy
```

Listing 6-1: The comments_controller.rb File Adjusted for Nested Resources

```ruby
    respond_to do |format|
      format.html { redirect_to(comments_url) }
      format.xml  { head :ok }
    end
  end

  private

  def get_article
    @article = Article.find(params[:article_id])
  end
end
```

Adapting the View Layer

The following is the automatically generated code for app\views\comments\new.html.erb:

```erb
<h1>New comment</h1>

<% form_for(@comment) do |f| %>
  <%= f.error_messages %>

  <p>
    <%= f.label :article %><br />
    <%= f.text_field :article %>
  </p>
  <p>
    <%= f.label :name %><br />
    <%= f.text_field :name %>
  </p>
  <p>
    <%= f.label :email %><br />
    <%= f.text_field :email %>
  </p>
  <p>
    <%= f.label :body %><br />
    <%= f.text_area :body %>
  </p>
  <p>
    <%= f.submit "Create" %>
  </p>
<% end %>

<%= link_to 'Back', comments_path %>
```

The highlighted lines are problematic. The first highlighted one doesn't work because you are generating a RESTful form for @comment, but comments are now nested into articles, so the form will need to be aware of the article for which you are generating the form as well. Then you have a text field, and its label, for the article object. These two lines will get scrapped, because you don't want to see an input box prompting you to insert the article_id manually. Finally, due to the nested routes you defined, comments_path is no longer an existing helper, so you'll also need to change this.

You need to modify this code and while you are at it, you should place it into a partial template (as you did for the articles in the previous chapter) given that both the new and edit actions of the Comments controller share almost identical code. Create a _form.html.erb partial and place it in app\views\ comments.

Now add the code shown in Listing 6-2 (downloadable as listing0602.html.erb).

Listing 6-2: The app\views\comments_form.html.erb Partial Template

```
<% form_for [article, comment] do |f| %>
  <%= f.error_messages %>

  <% field_set_tag do %>

    <div class="field">
      <%= f.label :name %>
      <%= f.text_field :name %>
    </div>

    <div class="field">
      <%= f.label :email %>
      <%= f.text_field :email %>
    </div>

    <div class="field">
      <%= f.label :body %>
      <%= f.text_area :body %>
    </div>

  <% end %>

  <% field_set_tag do %>
    <%= f.submit button_value, :class => "button" %>
  <% end %>
<% end %>
```

The first highlighted line uses the array [article, comment]. The form_for method is smart enough to figure out that it should create a comment form for the article specified in article. As usual, if comment is a new unsaved object, the form will be empty (new action) or pre-filled with the existing values if not (edit action).

The second highlighted line is just the usual trick of defining a local button_value variable so that the partial can be rendered from both new.html.erb and edit.html.erb with the button having the names "Create Comment" and "Save Changes," respectively.

Another difference between the scaffold code and the partial is that we added the fieldset tags (through the field_set_tag helper) and the CSS classes to customize the appearance.

Fixing new.html.erb and edit.html.erb

Now you need to modify app\views\comments\new.html.erb and app\views\comments\edit .html.erb to render the partial and fix the links by using helpers for the nested routes.

Replace all the code within `app\views\comments\new.html.erb` with the following:

```
<h1>New comment</h1>
```

```
<%= render :partial => "form", :locals => {:article => @article,
                                           :comment => @comment,
                                           :button_value => "Create Comment"} %>
```

```
<%= link_to 'Back', article_comments_path(@article) %>
```

The highlighted line will assign the `@article` and `@comment` instance variables (defined in the Comments controller) to the local variables `article` and `comment` in the partial `_form.html.erb`. It will also assign the value "Create Comment" to the `button_value` local variable.

You then change the last line to use the helper `article_comments_path(@article)` to obtain a link that sends a GET request for `/articles/:article_id/comments` (where `:article_id` is the actual value of the id of the `Article` object assigned to `@article`). This will allow you to return to the list of comments for the article.

Now replace the content of `app\views\comments\edit.html.erb` with the following:

```
<h1>Editing comment</h1>

<%= render :partial => "form", :locals => {:article => @article,
                                           :comment => @comment,
                                           :button_value => "Save Changes"}
%>

<%= link_to 'Show', [@article, @comment] %> |
<%= link_to 'Back', article_comments_path(@article) %>
```

The code for rendering the partial is identical, except for the `button_value` variable being set to "Save Changes" instead of "Create Comment." At the bottom of the template there is also an extra link to show the comment. This uses `[@article, @comment]` to generate a link that sends a GET request to the server, for the path `/articles/:article_id/comments/:id`, where `:article_id` and `:id` are the actual values of the `id` attribute of the model objects `@article` and `@comment`, respectively. For example, `/articles/1/comments/4` shows the comment with id `4` that was made for the article with id `1`.

Fixing index.html.erb and show.html.erb

You now need to modify the other two templates: `app\views\comments\index.html.erb` and `app\views\comments\show.html.erb`. You are not really too concerned about their appearance, because you'll embed comments into the article template so these templates will only be seen by the blog author.

In other words, they act as your quick admin interface for performing CRUD operations on the comments.

Simply replace the helpers placed in there by `scaffold` with their equivalent nested route helper.

In `app\views\comments\index.html.erb` replace:

```
<td><%= link_to 'Show', comment %></td>
<td><%= link_to 'Edit', edit_comment_path(comment) %></td>
```

```
<td><%= link_to 'Destroy', comment, :confirm => 'Are you sure?', :method =>
:delete %></td>
```

with:

```
<td>
  <%= link_to 'Show', [@article, comment] %> &middot;
  <%= link_to 'Edit', [:edit, @article, comment] %> &middot;
  <%= link_to 'Destroy', [@article, comment], :confirm => 'Are you sure?',
:method => :delete %>
</td>
```

The `&middot;` *is there just to visualize the link in a more compact manner.*

[:edit, @article, comment] is a convenient notation that is equivalent to using edit_article_comment_path(@article, comment).

Also replace the following:

```
<%= link_to 'New comment', new_comment_path %>
```

with:

```
<%= link_to 'New comment', new_article_comment_path(@article) %> |
<%= link_to 'Back to the article', @article %>
```

Now, in `app\views\comments\show.html.erb` replace the following couple of lines:

```
<%= link_to 'Edit', edit_comment_path(@comment) %> |
<%= link_to 'Back', comments_path %>
```

with:

```
<%= link_to 'Edit', [:edit, @article, @comment] %> |
<%= link_to 'Back', article_comments_path(@article) %>
```

All four templates will now be compatible with the nested resources you defined. Try to visit `http://localhost:3000/articles/4/comments` and `http://localhost:3000/articles/4/comments/new`. Assuming that you have an article with id 4, you should now see a (empty) list of comments and the form for creating a new comment, respectively. If you do, all the changes were applied correctly.

We made a lot of chances to the initial scaffolding code. If you see errors instead of nice forms, you can go through the steps presented here again, in order to spot any differences between this text and your code.

The remaining problem is that if you visit `http://localhost:3000` or `http://localhost:3000/articles/4`, nowhere will you see references to comments or a way to create new ones. This is because you haven't touched the article templates yet. Let's do that.

Embedding Comments in Articles

Before you begin modifying the templates, think for a moment about how you want to embed comments. It is safe to assume that the user is accustomed to the following two conventions:

1. On the front page there should be a link to the comments for each article. In your case there is only one article on the front page, but the code should still work if you change your pagination policy.

2. When showing an article, all the comments should be listed below the main text and a form for adding a new one should be present as well.

The first is just a link that needs to be added in the "About this article" section. So go ahead and add the following highlighted line to the `app\views\articles\_article.html.erb` partial:

```
<h3>About this article</h3>
<%= publication_status(article) %><br />
<%= link_to pluralize(article.comments.size, 'comment'), article %>
```

The link uses the `pluralize` helper provided by ActiveSupport, to obtain "1 comment" when there is only one comment or the pluralized version when there are more comments (for example, "23 comments"). The front page with this new link is shown in Figure 6-5. This link leads to the `show` action of the `Articles` controller, which will display the article and (at the bottom) all the existing comments.

Alternatively you could link directly to the comments section through an HTML anchor.

Figure 6-5

The future tense in the previous sentence is necessary because the show action of the Articles controller does not know anything about comments yet. You'll need to perform a few changes in order to be able to display all the comments and a new form at the bottom.

Listing the Comments and the New Form

Currently, the show action of the Articles controller takes care of displaying one article. You'd like to be able to display a list of associated comments and a form to create a new one as well though. To do this, add a @comments and a @comment variable to the show action. In app\controllers\articles_controller.rb add the highlighted lines:

```
@article = Article.find(params[:id])
@comments = @article.comments
@comment = @article.comments.new
```

Now the action will retrieve the article first, and then all of its comments, assigning them to @comments. It will also prepare a new Comment object and assign it to @comment. In the view, let's modify app\views\articles\show.html.erb to take advantage of this. Listing 6-3 shows the updated code.

Listing 6-3: The app\views\articles\show.html.erb Template with Embedded Comments

```erb
<%= render :partial => @article %>

<div class="clear">
  <div class="column span-6">
    <% unless @comments.empty? %>
      <div id="comments">
        <h2 id="comments_count"><%= pluralize(@comments.size, 'Comment') %></h2>
        <ul>
          <%= render :partial => "comment", :collection => @comments %>
        </ul>
      <!-- /comments -->
      </div>
    <% end %>

    <div id="add-comment">
      <h2>Add a comment</h2>
      <%= render :partial => "comments/form",
                 :locals => {:article => @article,
                             :comment => @comment,
                             :button_value => "Create Comment"} %>
    <!-- /add-comment -->
    </div>
  <!-- /column -->
  </div>
<!-- /clear -->
</div>
```

Aside from a few tags and CSS ids and classes to give it a proper look and feel, the juicy parts that you are going to analyze in detail are highlighted.

You first want to display all the comments. Initially you verify if there are any comments so far with `unless @comments.empty?`. Notice that you can't simply say `unless @comments`, because `[]` is still considered as `true` in Ruby.

Then you add an `h2` tag that displays the number of existing comments. Again, `pluralize` is used to ensure that you don't get "1 comments" in order not to irritate the most obsessive-compulsive readers.

You then proceed to render a partial:

```
<%= render :partial => "comment", :collection => @comments %>
```

The partial will contain the code for displaying a comment. The `:collection` option is used so that the partial is rendered for each comment in `@comments`. The name of the partial that's indicated is `comment` and you are going to create it in the `articles` folder in a moment.

Note that you can't use `render :partial => @comments`, *because otherwise ActionView would attempt to render a nonexisting* `comments/_comment.html.erb` *partial. Using* `:partial =>"comment"` *indicates that you want to render the* `_comment.html.erb` *partial defined within the same folder (that is,* `articles`*) as the template invoking* `render` *(that is,* `app\views\articles\show.html.erb`*).*

Go ahead and create `app\views\articles\_comment.html.erb` and add the following code to it:

```
<li>
    <b><%=h comment.name %></b> wrote:
    <div class="entry">
        <%= sanitize comment.body, :tags => %w{strong b em i a p br} %>
    </div>
</li>
```

For each comment, you display its author name (escaped for security reasons) and its body. You don't want angry readers, so their email address is not displayed. Notice that you sanitize the comment by allowing only the `strong`, `b`, `em`, `i`, `a`, `p`, and `br` tags. All other tags will be stripped from their attributes and HTML encoded.

The `:attributes` *option exists as well to specify allowed attributes. If the sanitizing rules are consistent across the application, you can define them in the configuration of the application. Consult the documentation for* `sanitize` *for examples of this.*

Back in Listing 6-3, the last highlighted bit is:

```
<%= render :partial => "comments/form",
           :locals => {:article => @article,
                       :comment => @comment,
                       :button_value => "Create Comment"} %>
```

With this you tell Rails to render the `_form.html.erb` partial defined in the `comments` folder and pass to it `@article`, `@comment`, as well as the label for the button. You are essentially using the partial that you defined before, in the same way as you rendered it in `app\views\comments\new.html.erb`. The only difference is that before you could simply say `:partial => "form"` because the partial was located in the same folder.

If you direct your browser to `http://localhost:3000/articles/4` (or use an id for an article that you actually have), you will see a form at the bottom for adding new comments, as shown in Figure 6-6.

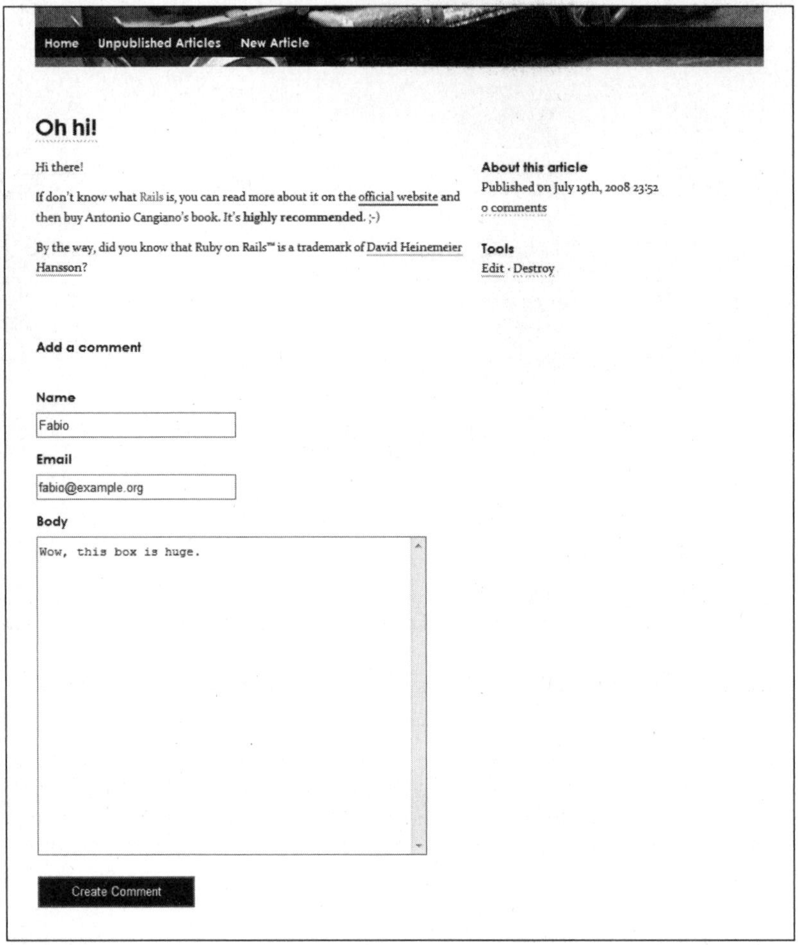

Figure 6-6

This form may be excessively large for comments. Let's make it smaller by modifying the existing form in `app\views\comments\_form.html.erb` to include a `:rows` option for `text_area`:

```
<%= f.text_area :body, :rows => 10 %>
```

`:column`, `:size`, *and* `:disabled` *are also supported options. As usual, check the online documentation for examples.*

Save, reload the page, and you should see a smaller box. Now go ahead and create one or two comments. In doing so, you'll see that these are displayed as well, as shown in Figure 6-7.

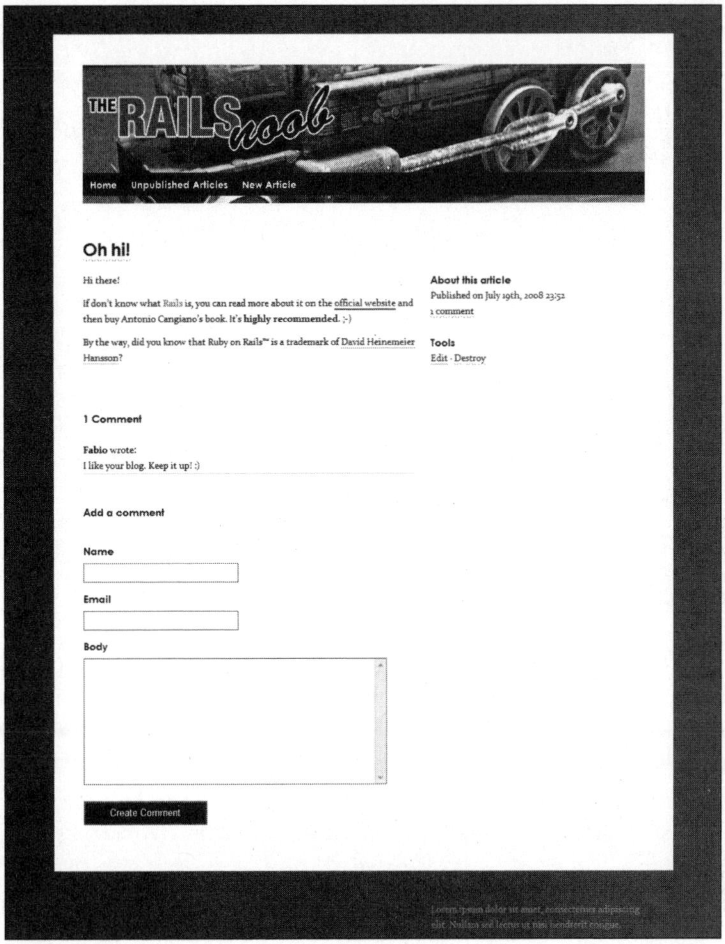

Figure 6-7

Let's also add a link to the "scaffold admin" at the bottom, as shown in Figure 6-8. This way the blog owner will be able to edit and destroy comments. Edit `app\views\articles\show.html.erb` and add the highlighted line:

```
<!-- /add-comment -->
  </div>
<%= link_to "Edit comments", article_comments_path(@article) %>
<!-- /column -->
```

> Notice that for sake of simplicity, we kept the scaffold interface as it is. In the real world, you'd probably want to create a more elaborate small admin interface or ditch the scaffold UI entirely, and change the code to present an Edit and Delete link next to a comment, when the blog author is logged in.

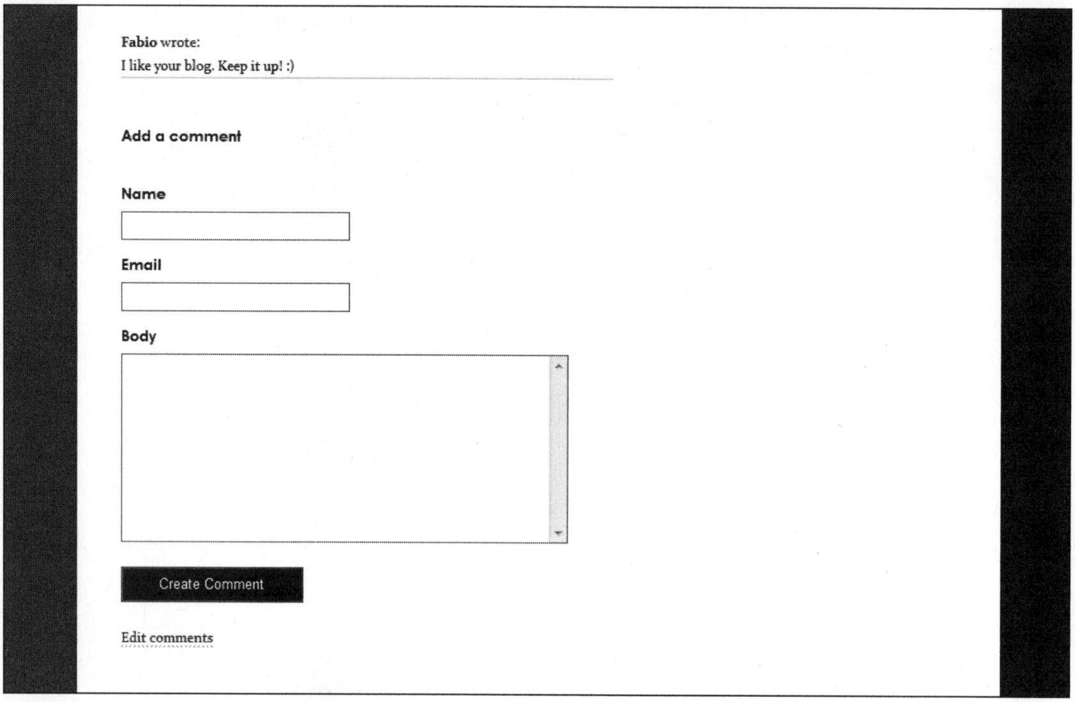
Fabio wrote:
I like your blog. Keep it up! :)
Add a comment
Name
Email
Body
Create Comment
Edit comments

Figure 6-8

When you click that "Edit comments" link, you are redirected to `http://localhost:3000/articles/4/comments` where you will see the scaffold interface for the comments, as shown in Figure 6-9.

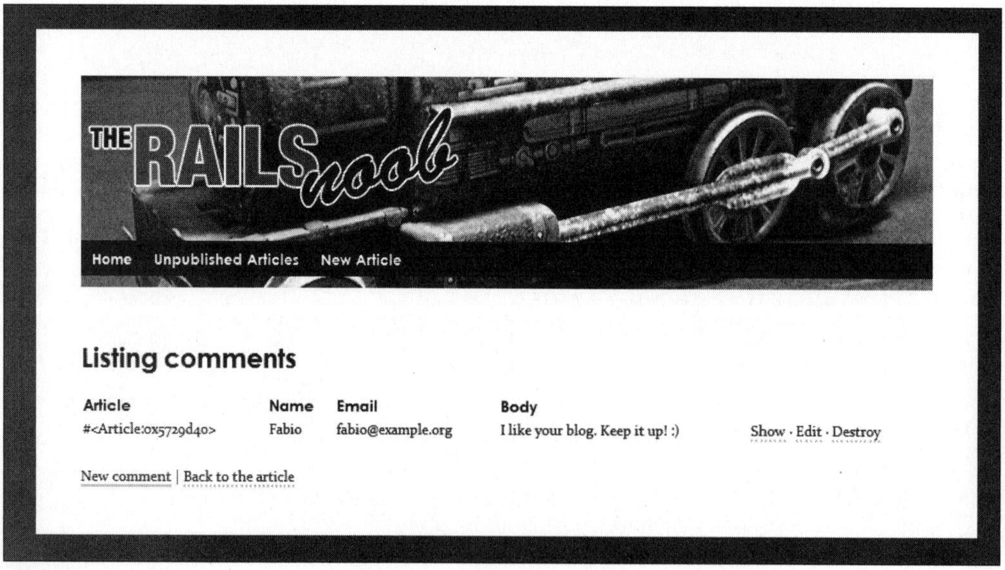
THE RAILS noob
Home
Unpublished Articles
New Article
Listing comments
Article
Name
Email
Body
#<Article:0x5729d40>
Fabio
fabio@example.org
I like your blog. Keep it up! :)
Show · Edit · Destroy
New comment | Back to the article

Figure 6-9

Feel free to click "Back to the article" and add further comments in the page that shows the article, to see how these are displayed between the article and the new comment form.

Having arrived at this point, you can safely take a break from the sample blog application to have a closer look at a few other aspects of the Rails framework.

Runtime Environments

By default, Rails applications have three environments: development, test, and production. As you saw earlier, development is the default environment. These three modes are configured to act differently and in accordance with their purpose. The easiest way to understand the differences among them is to look at their configuration files located in `config\environments`.

Development

This is the code from `config\environments\development.rb`:

```
# Settings specified here will take precedence over those in config/environment.rb

# In the development environment your application's code is reloaded on
# every request.  This slows down response time but is perfect for development
# since you don't have to restart the webserver when you make code changes.
config.cache_classes = false

# Log error messages when you accidentally call methods on nil.
config.whiny_nils = true

# Show full error reports and disable caching
config.action_controller.consider_all_requests_local = true
config.action_view.debug_rjs                          = true
config.action_controller.perform_caching              = false

# Don't care if the mailer can't send
config.action_mailer.raise_delivery_errors = false
```

The comments and code are pretty much self-explanatory.

In development mode the classes are not cached. This is done so that the application's code is reloaded at every request, providing an immediate feedback loop for the developer, who therefore does not need to restart the Web server for code changes (the exception being code within the `config` folder).

If you accidentally call methods on the `nil` object, these are logged. The errors and their backtraces are shown in the browser, because every request is considered local. Caching is not enabled, in order to make it easier to troubleshoot problems. And finally, Rails also ignores delivery error messages when using ActionMailer to send emails.

Not surprisingly, it's an environment tailored for development, where the programmer gets immediate feedback for any possible errors that might arise (mail delivery excluded).

Test

The code for config\environments\test.rb is as follows :

```
# Settings specified here will take precedence over those in config/environment.rb

# The test environment is used exclusively to run your application's
# test suite.  You never need to work with it otherwise.  Remember that
# your test database is "scratch space" for the test suite and is wiped
# and recreated between test runs.  Don't rely on the data there!
config.cache_classes = true

# Log error messages when you accidentally call methods on nil.
config.whiny_nils = true

# Show full error reports and disable caching
config.action_controller.consider_all_requests_local = true
config.action_controller.perform_caching           = false

# Disable request forgery protection in test environment
config.action_controller.allow_forgery_protection   = false

# Tell Action Mailer not to deliver emails to the real world.
# The :test delivery method accumulates sent emails in the
# ActionMailer::Base.deliveries array.
config.action_mailer.delivery_method = :test
```

This is a special environment because you'd like to test the application as if it was in production mode, but you also need to be able to catch errors, as you do in development mode. It's also peculiar because, like the first comment explains, the test environment is used exclusively to run the application's test suite. As such, you can cache classes, but you still need to log errors for methods that are accidentally invoked on nil, and be able to get full error reports. Furthermore, caching can be disabled, just as forgery protection can be. Emails are not actually delivered but placed in the ActionMailer::Base.deliveries array to facilitate their testing.

Production

In production mode you don't want to reveal details of the errors to the end user, and you'd like to cache anything that can be cached. This is accomplished with the following default code:

```
# Settings specified here will take precedence over those in config/environment.rb

# The production environment is meant for finished, "live" apps.
# Code is not reloaded between requests
config.cache_classes = true

# Enable threaded mode
# config.threadsafe!

# Use a different logger for distributed setups
# config.logger = SyslogLogger.new
```

```
    # Full error reports are disabled and caching is turned on
    config.action_controller.consider_all_requests_local = false
    config.action_controller.perform_caching              = true

    # Use a different cache store in production
    # config.cache_store = :mem_cache_store

    # Enable serving of images, stylesheets, and javascripts from an asset server
    # config.action_controller.asset_host                 = "http://assets.example.
    com"

    # Disable delivery errors, bad email addresses will be ignored
    # config.action_mailer.raise_delivery_errors = false
```

Notice that the environment already offers commented-out code for defining a different logger, cache store, the enablement of an asset server, and the ability to decide whether delivering to bad addresses should be ignored.

In Rails 2.2 you can now write (or uncomment):

```
    config.threadsafe!
```

That single line enables multithreaded dispatching of your application and thread safety. This improves performance and reduces the amount of memory required to run a given load. As such it's a highly recommended option in production mode.

Your Own Environment

Occasionally you may wish to define your own environment mode. You can easily accomplish this by creating a Ruby file in config\environments. You can then copy over the code of one of the three default environments and customize it as you wish. In config\database.yml you will need to provide the connection details for this new environment as well.

This means that you'll be able to define environments for troubleshooting unforeseen issues with a live production application, directly from your machine, or define environments for different configurations as needed.

Logging

Both this and the previous chapter mentioned that you could see the executed queries, errors, and other details about the requests in a log file. Depending on the environment you are in, Rails will log a certain amount of information in log\development.log, log\test.log, or log\production.log. The log folder will also contain a server.log file for the Web server (for example, Mongrel).

When you look at the development.log file after having visited the front page of the blog, you see an entry similar to the following:

```
Processing ArticlesController#index (for 127.0.0.1 at 2009-01-28 11:28:11) [GET]
  [4;36;1mArticle Load (0.0ms)[0m   [0;1mSELECT * FROM "articles" WHERE (published
= 't' AND published_at <= '2009-01-28 16:28:11') ORDER BY published_at DESC LIMIT 1
OFFSET 0[0m
```

```
   [4;35;1mSQL (0.0ms)[0m    [0mSELECT count(*) AS count_all FROM "articles" WHERE
(published = 't' AND published_at <= '2009-01-28 16:28:11') [0m
Rendering template within layouts/articles
Rendering articles/index
   [4;36;1mSQL (0.0ms)[0m    [0;1mSELECT count(*) AS count_all FROM "comments" WHERE
("comments".article_id = 2) [0m
Rendered articles/_article (10.0ms)
Completed in 29ms (View: 18, DB: 0) | 200 OK [http://localhost/]
```

This tells you a whole lot of information: the type of request received, the IP it came from and the time-stamp, which controller and action executed your request, the rendered templates, and the queries that were executed behind the scenes. It also tells you the time that it took to execute each of these, and how much time was spent processing the view, versus database access. For example, in the preceding output, the request took 0.029 seconds with no significant time spent querying the database. Finally, you have the HTTP response code and the URL that were sent back to the client.

Analyzing the log files can be an extremely useful way to perform preliminary troubleshooting, spot performance problems, and identify unexpected behavior.

> *Developers operating on non-Microsoft operating systems often use the following command to display the last lines of their current development log:* `tail -f log/development.log`. *On Windows simply use the output of* `ruby script/server` *or a POSIX emulation layer like Cygwin.*

As the logs grow, there are times when you might want to clear all of your `.log` files in `log`. Rather than doing this manually, you can use a provided Rake task:

```
rake log:clear
```

Using Logger

Though Rails logs a good deal of information for you (particularly when in development and test mode), it is incredibly beneficial to be able to log your own messages.

Rails 2.x takes advantage of the `ActiveSupport::BufferedLogger` class to log messages and it provides you with the identifier `logger`, which references the Rails logger instance. In contexts where this is not defined, you can directly reference `RAILS_DEFAULT_LOGGER`, which is a constant that's globally available.

To verify all this, try running the following session:

```
C:\projects\blog> ruby script/console
Loading development environment (Rails 2.2.2)
>> logger
NameError: undefined local variable or method `logger' for #<Object:0x27bf9ec>
        from (irb):1
>> Rails.logger
=> #<ActiveSupport::BufferedLogger:0x51dade4 @no_block=false, @level=0, @log=#<F
ile:C:/projects/blog/log/development.log>, @auto_flushing=1, @buffer=[]>
>> RAILS_DEFAULT_LOGGER
=> #<ActiveSupport::BufferedLogger:0x51dade4 @no_block=false, @level=0, @log=#<F
ile:C:/projects/blog/log/development.log>, @auto_flushing=1, @buffer=[]>
```

Levels of Severity

`logger` exposes several methods that are used to indicate the level of severity of the information being logged. Ordered by severity, these methods/levels are `debug`, `info`, `warn`, `error`, and `fatal`.

Whether you execute `logger.debug "a custom message!"` or `logger.warn "a custom message!"` in your code, the same message gets stored in the log file. Why do you need five methods then?

The existence of these methods representing various levels of severity is justified by the fact that each environment in Rails will only log messages that have been passed to methods above a certain threshold. This threshold for development and testing is `debug`, which means that any logging messages will be added to the log. In production mode, only `info` or more severe methods are logged (that is, `warn`, `error`, and `fatal`). This is how, for example, Rails manages to log all the SQL queries when in development and test mode, but not when in production. This occurs because those SQL queries that you saw before are logged using the `debug` method.

To see the log in production mode, run the following preliminary steps:

```
rake db:migrate RAILS_ENV=production
ruby script/server -e production
```

Once the Web server is running, load the front page of the blog. Within the production log, you should obtain something along the lines of:

```
Processing ArticlesController#index (for 127.0.0.1 at 2009-01-28 12:05:40) [GET]
Rendering template within layouts/articles
Rendering articles/index
Completed in 6ms (View: 2, DB: 1) | 200 OK [http://localhost/]
```

Only messages logged with `info` (or above) are shown, so there are no SQL queries in there.

When you log your own messages, try to stick to this rule of thumb:

- ❑ Use `debug` when the information you want to log is there purely to provide aid in case of troubleshooting at a later stage

- ❑ `info` when the behavior is expected and the information captured is important enough to be published in the production log

- ❑ `warn` when you'd like to keep track of any unexpected behavior that doesn't break your application, but that still needs to be addressed

- ❑ `error` when in the presence of an actual error that breaks a part of the application, but doesn't warrant taking the server offline

- ❑ `fatal` for those occasions when the error is something so serious that the application needs to be manually restarted (and of course, the idea is to fix the cause of the problem as well)

Reducing the Production Log

Writing many messages in production can impact the server performance (I/O is expensive). With this in mind, some people like to increase the level that's required before anything is logged in their production log file. To do this you can add the following line to your `config\environments\production.rb`:

```
config.log_level = :warn
```

In this way, any warning, error, or fatal message is still logged, but simple information isn't. This means that when you go to apply this change and visit the front page again, no entries will be added to the `log\production.log`, unless an error/warning occurred.

> *Similarly, you can define a different file for the log messages that are to be saved, by adding* `config .log_path = 'log/my_log.log'`.

Keep in mind that this can be viewed as a case of premature optimization and it is not recommended that you do it right away. Having knowledge and insight of what your server does is usually much more valuable than trying to squeeze performances from the get-go. Should the need arise though, you know how to do it.

> *You could also modify the way the controller logs errors for common exceptions that do not warrant any changes to the code, by monkey patching the* `log_error` *method. When the issue at hand is the sheer size of the log rather than the row performance impact, setting up log rotation with one of the many tools available for most operating systems can be a good idea.*

Redirecting Logging to the Console

Instead of trying out snippets in the console and then checking out the SQL queries that are executed by looking into the log file, it is convenient in such instances to simply redirect the logging performed by ActiveRecord to the standard output. To do this, first start the console and then run the highlighted lines:

```
C:\projects\blog> ruby script/console
Loading development environment (Rails 2.2.2)
>> ActiveRecord::Base.logger = ActiveSupport::BufferedLogger.new(STDOUT)
=> #<ActiveSupport::BufferedLogger:0x6031d34 @auto_flushing=1, @level=0, @buffer
={}, @log=#<IO:0x44b6af0>, @guard=#<Mutex:0x6031cf8>>>> Article.find(4).comments
  ?[4;36;1mArticle Load (0.001000)?[0m   ?[0;1mSELECT * FROM "articles" WHERE ("
articles"."id" = 4) ?[0m
  ?[4;35;1mComment Load (0.000000)?[0m   ?[0mSELECT * FROM "comments" WHERE ("co
mments".article_id = 4) ?[0m
=> [#<Comment id: 3, article_id: 4, name: "Fabio", email: "fabio@example.org", b
ody: "I like your blog. Keep it up! :)", created_at: "2008-07-27 23:04:53", upda
ted_at: "2008-07-27 23:07:59">]
>>
```

Notice how you create a new instance of `ActiveSupport::BufferedLogger`, indicating that the standard output should be used as the target for the logger. Then when you run `Article.find(4).comments` the queries are printed to the console, before you obtain the actual array of comments (in this case, a single comment).

Filtering Data

Logging is a powerful tool and Rails makes it very easy to use and customize this feature to suit your needs. There are, however, certain pieces of information that you may not want to log. Passwords and credit card numbers come to mind. In production mode the queries are not logged, but this sensitive data may still show up in the log. So how can you log the request parameters without showing certain types of sensitive data, in plain text within your logs?

Once again, Rails really strives to make your life as easy as possible and provides you with a `filter_parameter_logging` method. This method accepts one, or a list, of comma-separated symbols, and instructs the controller not to log any parameters containing that word (or those words). So if you were to uncomment the following line in the `ApplicationController`:

```
filter_parameter_logging :password
```

the logs would show `[FILTERED]` for any parameter matching the regular expression `/password/i` (for example, `:password => [FILTERED]`).

Debugging

Debugging is another important aspect of developing Rails applications. When something goes wrong it's fundamental to be able to understand what exactly is happening, as well as evaluate expressions and easily move around within the code.

As a Microsoft developer, you are probably accustomed to the excellent debugging support offered by Visual Studio and .NET. Having programmed in both environments, I can confirm that the level of support and convenience for debugging offered by .NET was way beyond what the Ruby world had to offer.

Ruby In Steel, covered in Chapter 1, enables you to work with Rails in Visual Studio and provides a fast debugger called Cylon.

Fortunately, there have been many efforts to improve this situation and Rails 2.x really simplifies the process of debugging applications by taking advantage of the fast `ruby-debug` gem. To perform fast debugging in Rails, three things are required:

1. `ruby-debug` needs to be installed.

2. You need to specify a "breakpoint" where you want the debugging session to start.

3. The Web server needs to load the debugger.

Let's start by installing the `ruby-debug` gem. Run the following:

```
gem install ruby-debug
```

Notice that I opted not to add this as a prerequisite in `config\environment.rb` *because it's a gem that's required for development purposes only.*

Having installed `ruby-debug`, you can now place the method `debugger` anywhere you want in the application. Let's temporarily add it to the `index` action of the `Articles` controller before the finder:

```
# GET /articles
# GET /articles.xml
def index
  debugger
  @articles = Article.published.paginate(:page => params[:page], :order =>
"published_at DESC")
```

```
    respond_to do |format|
      format.html # index.html.erb
      format.xml  { render :xml => @articles }
    end
  end
```

You need to load the debugger; so start Mongrel with the −debugger option as shown here:

```
C:\projects\blog> ruby script/server −debugger
=> Booting Mongrel (use 'script/server webrick' to force WEBrick)
=> Rails 2.2.2 application starting on http://0.0.0.0:3000
=> Debugger enabled
=> Call with -d to detach
=> Ctrl-C to shutdown server
** Starting Mongrel listening at 0.0.0.0:3000
** Starting Rails with development environment...
** Rails loaded.
** Loading any Rails specific GemPlugins
** Signals ready.  INT => stop (no restart).
** Mongrel 1.1.5 available at 0.0.0.0:3000
** Use CTRL-C to stop.
```

If you head over to http://localhost:3000 with your browser, the index action of the Articles controller will be invoked. The method debugger will then be executed, starting a debugging session in the command prompt window where you started the server:

```
C:\projects\blog> ruby script/server −debugger
=> Booting Mongrel (use 'script/server webrick' to force WEBrick)
=> Rails 2.2.2 application starting on http://0.0.0.0:3000
=> Debugger enabled
=> Call with -d to detach
=> Ctrl-C to shutdown server
** Starting Mongrel listening at 0.0.0.0:3000
** Starting Rails with development environment...
** Rails loaded.
** Loading any Rails specific GemPlugins
** Signals ready.  INT => stop (no restart).
** Mongrel 1.1.5 available at 0.0.0.0:3000
** Use CTRL-C to stop.
C:/projects/blog/app/controllers/articles_controller.rb:6
@articles = Article.published.paginate(:page => params[:page], :order =>
"published_at DESC")
(rdb:5)
```

The actual output obviously depends on how you formatted your code in the controller (for example, how many lines you use for your finders).

The cursor is positioned on the last (highlighted line); your debug shell (rdb) is ready to receive expressions to evaluate and commands to execute.

You could even step into an irb session, by simply running irb.

Meanwhile the page in the browser is idly waiting, having not yet rendered anything, because everything is frozen in time where you placed the debugger method. The line of code displayed in the debug shell is the current line (which hasn't been executed yet). It's the one immediately below debugger in the index action. The list command shows the code surrounding your current breakpoint:

```
(rdb:5) list
[1, 10] in C:/projects/blog/app/controllers/articles_controller.rb
   1  class ArticlesController < ApplicationController
   2    # GET /articles
   3    # GET /articles.xml
   4    def index
   5      debugger
=> 6      @articles = Article.published.paginate(:page => params[:page], :order
=> "published_at DESC")
   7
   8      respond_to do |format|
   9        format.html # index.html.erb
   10        format.xml  { render :xml => @articles }
```

If you want to evaluate the value of the params[:page] parameter you can do so simply by issuing:

```
(rdb:5) params[:page]
nil
```
Or p params[:page].

In this particular case, it's the front page so no page parameters were passed during the request. If you want to see what parameters do exist, you can evaluate the whole params hash:

```
(rdb:5) params
{"action"=>"index", "controller"=>"articles"}
```

Great! How about moving on to the next line? You do so with the next command:

```
(rdb:5) next


Processing ArticlesController#index (for 127.0.0.1 at 2009-01-28 12:25:39) [GET]

c:/projects/blog/app/controllers/articles_controller.rb:9
respond_to do |format|
(rdb:5) list
[3, 12] in C:/projects/blog/app/controllers/articles_controller.rb
   3    # GET /articles.xml
   4    def index
   5      debugger
   6      @articles = Article.published.paginate(:page => params[:page], :order
=> "published_at DESC")
   7
=> 8      respond_to do |format|
   9        format.html # index.html.erb
   10        format.xml  { render :xml => @articles }
   11      end
   12    end
(rdb:5)
```

With next you executed lines 6/7, and moved onto line 8 (which has yet to be interpreted). list showed you once again where you are. You can now try to evaluate @articles:

```
(rdb:5) @articles
[#<Article id: 4, title: "Oh hi!", body: "Hi there!\r\n\r\nIf don't know what %{
color:red}Rails% ...", published: true, published_at: "2008-07-20 03:52:00", cre
ated_at: "2008-07-16 22:56:33", updated_at: "2008-07-17 16:21:48">]
```

Again, the actual line numbers depend on your code formatting but you get the idea. Other important commands aside from list and next are step, up, and cont. step and up are roughly the equivalent of F11 and Shift+F11 in Visual Studio. You can exit rdb with exit. It's definitely a different approach from what you're used to, but it works quite well and you'll probably learn to appreciate its simplicity and flexibility.

Remember to remove the debugger line after you've experimented with it.

A complete list of commands and their meanings is available online at http://blog.nanorails.com/articles/2006/07/14/a-better-rails-debugger-ruby-debug.

Debugging from the Console

The two-fold process you are using is a bit tedious. You have to start the Web server, visit the page, and only then can you step into the debug shell. The process can be sped up simply by loading the debugger from within the console. Once you've started the console, you'll need to require 'ruby-debug.' At that point, you can send requests such as app.get '/articles/4' and be taken directly to the debugging session.

Rails Directory Structure

Before moving to the next chapter, let's try to recap what folders you've interacted with so far. They were app, config, db, log, public, and script (it contains the scripts you've used so far). The main directory of any Rails application contains more folders though. The following briefly explains their roles:

- ❑ **doc:** This is the directory used to store the documentation that's auto-generated by the rdoc tool. If you have other documentation that you have created, like "a getting started" PDF, this is a good place to put it.

- ❑ **lib:** You can place your own libraries in this folder. If the code is substantial and reusable for other projects, you may consider creating a plugin instead.

- ❑ **test:** The folder that contains all the tests for your application.

- ❑ **tmp:** A folder used by Rails to hold temporary files.

- ❑ **vendor:** A special directory for third-party code. This is where non-gem plugins get installed and where the required gems (plugins or not) and Rails gems are copied whenever you decide to deploy them with the application, as opposed to expecting the deployment server to already have them installed. This is discussed in the chapter dedicated to deployment.

Summary

In this chapter you added a few features to the basic application, and the powerful concept of nested resources was introduced. Also introduced were two fundamental concepts: logging and debugging, which will serve you well as your journey toward learning Rails progresses.

The next three chapters cover the ActiveRecord framework, ActionController, and ActionView. You'll do a bit more incremental development on *The Rails Noob* blog here and there, but the main focus will be on introducing new concepts and reinforcing the existing ones, as opposed to performing major changes to the sample application that you have created so far.

Object-Relational Mapping with ActiveRecord

Before Ruby on Rails, web programming required a lot of verbiage, steps and time. Now, web designers and software engineers can develop a website much faster and more simply, enabling them to be more productive and effective in their work.

— Bruce Perens, Open Source Luminary

ActiveRecord is a Ruby implementation of the Active Record pattern described by Martin Fowler in his classic *Patterns of Enterprise Application Architecture* (Addison-Wesley 2002). The abstraction layer provided by ActiveRecord enables the Ruby developer to ignore many of the low level, database-specific details of the source logic, and focus instead on the domain logic that defines the application. Among the benefits of this approach is a concise and readable syntax (Ruby in place of SQL) that makes programming database-driven applications faster and easier. In the past two chapters, for example, you employed the ActiveRecord framework to create a basic blog application without having to write any SQL code.

ActiveRecord is a key component of the Rails stack, whose presence has no doubt substantially contributed to Rails' popularity and ability to provide developers with a productive environment that enables them to write better code. This chapter introduces the framework by taking a closer look at the essential concepts you'll need to learn in order to work with databases through Rails. As such, this is a fundamental chapter, just as an ADO.NET chapter would be crucial to an ASP. NET book. In fact, ActiveRecord implements the M component of the MVC acronym. Your models are ActiveRecord objects.

Supported Databases

If you've used the .NET Framework before, you should be familiar with the concept of a Data Provider. The .NET Framework offers several types of this sort of class, each used to access data that's stored in SQL Server, Oracle, and data sources exposed using OLE DB and ODBC. Third-party alternatives are provided as well, so that .NET developers have a few options to choose from.

ActiveRecord is an Object-Relational Mapper and works at a higher level of abstraction than ADO.NET. For a database to be supported by ActiveRecord, two components are required: a driver and an adapter. The driver is typically a Ruby extension written at least partially in C, which exposes an API for storing and retrieving data from a given RDBMS (Relational Database Management System).

The adapter is comprised of Ruby code that's required to inform ActiveRecord about the specifics of the database system at hand. For example, the adapter specifies how to map ActiveRecord data types like string or datetime with their actual SQL representation. ActiveRecord doesn't really know anything about the driver either, so it's the adapter that ultimately calls the driver to execute a certain query.

Due to their nature, drivers are installed by the developers and aren't shipped with ActiveRecord or Rails. This is true for any database system. In Chapter 1, for example, you obtained the SQLite3 driver by installing the sqlite3-ruby gem. When it comes to the adapters though, you're looking at a different story. Four adapters ship with the framework: sqlite (for SQLite versions older than 3), sqlite3, mysql, and postgresql.

> You can verify this by heading over to the official repository at http://github.com/rails/ rails/tree/master/activerecord/lib/active_record/connection_adapters/ or by checking the content of the C:\ruby\lib\ruby\gems\1.8\gems\activerecord-2.2.2\ lib\active_record\connection_adapters folder on your system. This path will vary if you installed Ruby in a different folder or if you're using another version of Rails.

In the past other adapters were shipped with ActiveRecord, but in December 2007 with the release of version 2, the controversial decision of limiting the core to the three main open source databases was made. This has a couple of implications for you if you decide to use a different database: you will need to install the adapter separately on your own, and it won't be directly maintained by the Rails core team.

In all but one instance, the maintainer is one or more community volunteers. In the case of the ibm_db adapter — the one I initially developed — the API team at IBM takes care of maintaining, developing, and supporting the adapter (and the driver).

The following table shows currently supported data sources besides SQLite, MySQL, and PostgreSQL, and which adapters/gems need to be installed in order to use them with ActiveRecord.

Data Source	Adapter's Gem
DB2	ibm_db
DBSlayer	activerecord-dbslayer-adapter
Firebird	activerecord-firebird-adapter

Data Source	Adapter's Gem
FrontBase	`activerecord-frontbase-adapter`
Informix	`ibm_db` or `activerecord-informix-adapter`
Interbase	`activerecord-interbase-adapter`
ODBC	`activerecord-odbc-adapter`
OpenBase	`activerecord-openbase-adapter`
Oracle	`activerecord-oracle-adapter` or `activerecord-oracle_enhanced-adapter`
SQL Server	`activerecord-sqlserver-adapter`
Salesforce	`activerecord-activesalesforce-adapter`
Sybase	`activerecord-sybase-adapter`

It is possible that further ActiveRecord adapters for less common databases are going to be developed in the future.

If you list the remote gems (for example, by running `gem list -r`), you'll also notice gems with names such as `activerecord-jdbcsqlite3-adapter`; you can safely ignore these unless you intend to use JRuby.

ActiveRecord Outside of Rails

Much like ADO.NET, ActiveRecord doesn't have to be used only in Web applications. You can load it in any program or script you are writing. Listing 7-1 shows an example of a small script that employs ActiveRecord.

Listing 7-1: A Sample Script That Uses ActiveRecord

```
require 'rubygems'
require 'active_record'

ActiveRecord::Base.establish_connection(:adapter => "sqlite3",
                                         :database => "blog/db/development.sqlite3",
                                         :timeout => 5000)

class Article < ActiveRecord::Base
end

p Article.find(:all)
```

When you save this file as `listing0701.rb` in `C:\projects` and run it, the array of existing articles in the `articles` table within the `C:\project\blog\db\development.sqlite3` database is printed in the output as follows:

```
[#<Article id: 1, title: "Hello, Rails!", body: "Hi from the body of an article.
:)", published: false, published_at: "2008-07-11 09:24:00", created_at: "2008-07-11
09:32:41", updated_at: "2008-07-17 03:18:28">, #<Article id: 2, title: "Lorem
Ipsum", body: "Lorem ipsum dolor sit amet, consectetuer adipiscing...", published:
 true, published_at: "2008-07-17 06:36:00", created_at: "2008-07-16 14:31:33",
updated_at: "2008-07-20 20:20:30">, #<Article id: 3, title: "More Lorem Ipsum",
body: "Etiam justo justo, ultricies sed, semper ac, hendre...", published: true,
published_at: "2008-07-17 01:50:00", created_at: "2008-07-16 14:35:18", updated_at:
 "2008-07-17 01:53:05">, #<Article id: 4, title: "Oh hi!", body: "Hi
there!\r\n\r\nIf you don't know what %{color:red}Rails% ...", published: true,
 published_at: "2008-07-20 03:52:00", created_at: "2008-07-16 22:56:33",
 updated_at: "2008-07-17 16:21:48">]
```

At the beginning of the script, ActiveRecord is loaded:

```
require 'rubygems'
require 'active_record'
```

The first line loads RubyGems which is a requirement given that you installed ActiveRecord through the `gem` command. This line is not strictly necessary if you set the `RUBYOPT` environment variable to `-rubygems`.

The second line loads ActiveRecord. Notice that you use `'active_record'` despite the gem being `activerecord`, because the file that's being required happens to be called `active_record.rb`.

Subsequently, you establish a connection to the database:

```
ActiveRecord::Base.establish_connection(:adapter => "sqlite3",
                                        :database => "blog/db/development.sqlite3",
                                        :timeout => 5000)
```

If you are working in "standalone" mode, not within a Rails application, you don't have a `config\database.yml` file to rely on; hence, you need to explicitly call the `establish_connection` class method and pass a hash argument to it, containing the information for the connection. `establish_connection` is a method that ends up invoking a connection method in the adapter, which in turn invokes a driver method that actually establishes the connection.

Normally, in a Web application, Rails does this for you by invoking that method and passing a hash that's derived from `config\database.yml`. In fact, if you evaluate `ActiveRecord::Base.configurations` from the Rails console, you'll obtain something along the lines of the following (reformatted for clarity):

```
{"development" => {"adapter" => "sqlite3","pool" => 5,
                   "timeout" => 5000, "database" => "db/development.sqlite3"},
 "production" => {"adapter" => "sqlite3", "pool" => 5,
                  "timeout" => 5000, "database" => "db/production.sqlite3"},
 "test" =>      {"adapter" => "sqlite3", "pool" => 5,
                 "timeout" => 5000, "database" => "db/test.sqlite3"}
}
```

Rails 2.3 will have a `reconnect` *option for MySQL. By default its value will be false. When set to true, it will attempt to reconnect if the connection is lost.*

That's a hash of a hash, so when you're in the (default) development mode, the hash `ActiveRecord::Base.configurations['development']` is used as an argument for the `establish_connection` method.

Within an initializer you can connect to a specific mode by simply referring to it through its symbol. For example, `ActiveRecord::Base.establish_connection :my_mode`*.*

Finally, the script defines an `Article` model, which maps to the `articles` table, and you immediately put it to good use, by obtaining a list of all the records through the `find` method:

```
class Article < ActiveRecord::Base
end

p Article.find(:all)
```

Object-Relational Mapping

.NET developers are used to dealing with Connection, Command, Parameter, DataAdapter, DataReader, DataSet, DataTable, DataView, and so on. Most would probably agree that ADO.NET is very powerful, but its architecture veers on the complex side. ActiveRecord, on the other hand, strives to achieve elegance and productivity through simplicity. It all revolves around one concept, the model, which is a class that inherits from the `ActiveRecord::Base` class. As previously stated, that model represents a certain table in the database, and its instances represent the records within that table. It couldn't get much easier than that.

The tradeoff is one that's typical of all highly abstract languages, libraries, or framework: a loss in flexibility, which is usually fully justified by the advantage in productivity and maintainability of the code. For example, a DataTable in .NET can represent an arbitrary table in the database, whereas ActiveRecord has certain, conventional expectations on the nature of the table. Try to create a table lacking an id column and then use the corresponding model, and you'll see what I mean.

The previous chapters employed the `scaffold` generator as a way to get a head start when it comes to building an application that would work with articles and comments. That command generated a whole lot of code for you, including your models. There will be times, though, when you'd like to create a model without the need to generate a whole resource and all the extra files like controllers and view templates. In such instances, you could create the file by hand within the `app\models` directory of your project, but there is a better way. The easiest way to generate a model is to use the `model` generator.

Generating Models

You don't want to disrupt the existing blog application just to try out new things, so let's create a "throw away" Rails application to try out a few tricks with. Go ahead and create the application `chapter7`:

```
C:\projects> rails chapter7
C:\projects> cd chapter7
```

And also create the databases for it:

```
C:\projects\chapter7>rake db:create:all
```

Now you are ready to use the `model` generator. This works in a very similar fashion to the `scaffold` generator you used before. From the `chapter7` directory, try the following:

```
C:\projects\chapter7> ruby script/generate model recipe title:string
instructions:text calories:integer
        exists  app/models/
        exists  test/unit/
        exists  test/fixtures/
        create  app/models/recipe.rb
        create  test/unit/recipe_test.rb
        create  test/fixtures/recipes.yml
        create  db/migrate
        create  db/migrate/20080806011444_create_recipes.rb
```

This command creates the model class `Recipe` in app\models\recipe.rb, a unit test in test\unit\recipe_test.rb, a test fixture in test\fixtures\recipes.yml, and a migration in db\migrate\20080806011444_create_recipes.rb. We discuss testing models at the end of this chapter, but for now consider the code for the model and the migration file:

```
# app\models\recipe.rb
class Recipe < ActiveRecord::Base
end

# db\migrate\20080806011444_create_recipes.rb
class CreateRecipes < ActiveRecord::Migration
  def self.up
    create_table :recipes do |t|
      t.string :title
      t.text :instructions
      t.integer :calories

      t.timestamps
    end
  end

  def self.down
    drop_table :recipes
  end
end
```

Notice that you have to specify attributes only because the table `recipes` didn't exist already in the database, so it's convenient to have a migration file generated for you. If the `recipes` table already existed in the database, you could simply generate your model by running `ruby script/generate model recipe`.

> If you happen to realize that you created a model by mistake and you'd like to automatically delete all the files that have been generated, you can use the `destroy` script in this way: `ruby script/destroy model model_name`. The `destroy` script is the opposite of `generate`, and can be used to neutralize the effects of the `scaffold` generator as well: `ruby script/destroy scaffold resource_name`.

Because you generated a migration file, you can run the db:migrate Rake task to create the table in the database (specified in config\database.yml for the development environment); for example:

```
C:\projects\chapter7> rake db:migrate
(in C:/projects/chapter7)
== CreateRecipes: migrating ======================================
-- create_table(:recipes)
   -> 0.1250s
== CreateRecipes: migrated (0.1250s) =============================
```

Generating Migrations

Besides the scaffold and model generators, migration files also have their own dedicated generator. The migration generator creates a migration class for you within a "timestamped" file in db\migrate.

Say that you realize that you need to add a chef column to the recipes table; you could do so by running ruby script/generate migration add_chef_column (or AddChefColumn) and then modifying the migration class yourself, in order to add the column within the up class method. This would work, but for the common action of adding and removing columns, the migration generator offers an automated way of accomplishing the same results. As long as you name your migration in the format AddAttributesToModel or RemoveAttributesFromModel, you will be able to pass a list of attributes to the generator just like you did with scaffold and model.

In this case, you only need to add one column to your table (that is, chef), so you'll run the following:

```
C:\projects\chapter7> ruby script/generate migration AddChefToRecipe chef:string
        exists  db/migrate
        create  db/migrate/20080806174246_add_chef_to_recipe.rb
```

In a real application, chef would probably be stored in a table of its own, and you would add a foreign key field instead.

The name of the generated file is the snake_case version of the CamelCase string you provided in input, so that reading the generated file name is sufficient to make its purpose obvious. You won't have to wonder what that migration file does.

The migration name can also be passed to the generator in snake_case format.

The class definition contained within is as follows:

```
class AddChefToRecipes < ActiveRecord::Migration
  def self.up
    add_column :recipes, :chef, :string
  end

  def self.down
    remove_column :recipes, :chef
  end
end
```

The highlighted lines show how the add_column and remove_column were added automatically for you. If you have to add multiple columns in the same migration file, you can do so by naming the migration accordingly (for example, `AddCol1Col2ToRecipe`) and then passing to the generator all the attributes in order (for example, `col1:string col2:integer`).

Aside from `create_table`, `drop_table`, `add_column`, and `remove_column`, many other schema alter-ing methods are available. A few common ones are `change_table`, `rename_table`, `change_column`, `change_column_default`, `remove_columns`, `add_index`, and `remove_index`. Consult the documen-tation for the class `ActiveRecord::ConnectionAdapters::SchemaStatements` to obtain a complete list and examples of how to use them.

> *You can find the documentation for this class online at* `http://api.rubyonrails.org/` `classes/ActiveRecord/ConnectionAdapters/SchemaStatements.html`. *Check* `http://api.rubyonrails.org/classes/ActiveRecord/ConnectionAdapters/` `TableDefinition.html#M001150` *for a list of column options.*

Migrations are not only used to modify and add new tables. They can also be used to migrate data. Any valid Ruby code is in fact fair game, as long as your migration affects the database, be it by inserting a bunch of records or by actually modifying its schema.

Customizing Migrations

Real-world projects tend to have rather advanced migration files. Besides the standard aforementioned methods, it isn't uncommon to see custom SQL statements. It isn't hard to imagine a need for this. The first time you want to add some triggers to your database, you'll be faced with the choice of doing it outside of the migration realm or executing the proper SQL statements to create and drop the trigger within your migration file. Arbitrary SQL statements can be executed by the method `execute`.

Experienced developers tend to push this further and create their own methods in addition to the built-in ones, whenever they need to implement custom functionality. These are usually organized in a convenient module that can be "extended"/"mixed in" by the migration class that needs its methods. Let's clarify this with a practical example.

In the previous chapter the tables `articles` and `comments` had a one-to-many relationship but ActiveRecord didn't define a foreign key constraint in the database for you. The reason for this is that many developers in the Rails community prefer to enforce this, and other, constraints at an application level, as opposed to the more conventional database level.

> **Although ActiveRecord doesn't define foreign key constraints in the database, it still provides you with an `add_index` method that can be used to add indexes to the database within a migration class. Indexes are fundamental to obtain reasonable performances.**

If you'd like to define actual foreign key constraints, you may be surprised to learn that there are no methods for adding foreign keys from within migrations. Luckily, you have a couple of options to add custom SQL statements that'll do the trick.

> **The following examples are provided to explain how to customize migrations, but you should not actually add them to the `chapter7` project. This is particularly important because there are a few limitations with SQLite, as explained at the end of this section.**

The first approach is to use the `:options` argument for a column when defining or altering a table definition. For example:

```
create_table :books do |t|
  t.string :title
  t.string :author
  t.string :isbn
  t.text :description
  t.integer :category_id, :null => false, :options => "CONSTRAINT fk_books_
category_id REFERENCES categories(id)"

  t.timestamps
end
```

The `create_table` method accepts a `:force` option that can be used to specify that a table should be dropped and re-created if it already exists in the database (for example, `create_table :books, :force => true`) when running migration tasks.

A more flexible approach is possible thanks to the `execute` method. Say you have the following migration file:

```
class AddCategoryIdToBook < ActiveRecord::Migration
  def self.up
    add_column :books, :category_id, :integer
  end

  def self.down
    remove_column :books, :category_id
  end
end
```

This adds (and removes in the `down` method) the `category_id` column to the hypothetical `books` table. To add a foreign key constraint, you could then transform it into the following:

```
class AddCategoryIdToBook < ActiveRecord::Migration
  def self.up
    add_column :books, :category_id, :integer

    execute %(
      alter table books
      add constraint fk_books_category_id
      foreign key (category_id)
      references categories(id)
    )
  end

  def self.down
    execute %(
      alter table books
      drop foreign key fk_books_category_id
    )

    remove_column :books, :category_id
  end
end
```

The method `execute` accepts a string (and optionally a second one for the logs); in this case the string is defined within `%(` and `)` so as to easily span multiple lines.

This works but it clutters up the two `up` and `down` methods a bit, and it leads you to "repeat yourself" if you were to add more foreign key constraints to the database. You can improve upon this by moving the code into two separate methods (plus one helper method to define the constraint's name) as shown in Listing 7-2.

Listing 7-2: Adding Foreign Keys to Migrations

```ruby
class AddCategoryIdToBook < ActiveRecord::Migration
  def self.up
    add_column :books, :category_id, :integer
    add_foreign_key :books, :category_id, :categories
  end

  def self.down
    drop_foreign_key :books, :category_id
    remove_column :books, :category_id
  end

  def self.add_foreign_key(table, column, referenced_table)
    execute %(
      alter table #{table}
      add constraint #{fk_name(table, column)}
      foreign key (#{column})
      references #{referenced_table}(id)
    )
  end

  def self.drop_foreign_key(table, column)
    execute %(
      alter table #{table}
      drop foreign key #{fk_name(table, column)}
    )
  end

  def self.fk_name(table, column)
    "fk_#{table}_#{column}"
  end
end
```

This is definitely nicer, but it still doesn't solve the problem that these methods will not be available in a different migration file. Embracing the DRY principle, let's improve this approach further. You can move these three methods into a module so that they will be available in any migration file that needs them.

If you were to create a `migration_helpers.rb` file within the `lib` directory in your projects, the code required for the module would be the one shown in Listing 7-3.

Listing 7-3: lib\migration_helpers.rb

```ruby
module MigrationHelpers
  def add_foreign_key(table, column, referenced_table)
    execute %(
      alter table #{table}
      add constraint #{fk_name(table, column)}
      foreign key (#{column})
      references #{referenced_table}(id)
    )
  end

  def drop_foreign_key(table, column)
    execute %(
      alter table #{table}
      drop foreign key #{fk_name(table, column)}
    )
  end

  def fk_name(table, column)
    "fk_#{table}_#{column}"
  end
end
```

And the migration file would simply become Listing 7-4.

Listing 7-4: A Migration Class Taking Advantage of MigrationHelpers

```ruby
class AddCategoryIdToBook < ActiveRecord::Migration
  extend MigrationHelpers

  def self.up
    add_column :books, :category_id, :integer
    add_foreign_key :books, :category_id, :categories
  end

  def self.down
    drop_foreign_key :books, :category_id
    remove_column :books, :category_id
  end
end
```

When this migration is applied, the method `add_foreign_key` will be executed, adding a foreign key constraint to the database. When the migration is rolled back, the `drop_foreign_key` method is executed, dropping the foreign key constraint from the database.

If, at a later stage, a different migration file needs to utilize `add_foreign_key` and `drop_foreign_key`, it will be able to do so as long as you add an `extend MigrationHelpers` statement within the class definition.

Also notice how the methods within the module were not prefixed by `self.` *because* `extend` *takes care of adding these to* `AddCategoryIdToBook` *as class methods.*

A few considerations are in order:

❑   SQLite's support for foreign keys is sketchy at best. The first approach (through :options) would work with SQLite, but the foreign key constraint would not be enforced. A workaround exists, through triggers, as you can read online at http://www.justatheory.com/computers/ databases/sqlite/foreign_key_triggers.html. This is not a huge deal, because few people adopt a file-based database system during production, but if you opt to go this route, you should check out this link.

❑   The second approach that alters the existing table through the execute method in order to add a foreign key constraint will not work with SQLite. If you try this method, you'll obtain an exception pointing out a syntax error near the word "constraint" in the SQL syntax.

❑   The issue with SQLite perfectly illustrates how executing DDL statements directly will often lead you to be database-specific, losing the ability to switch from one database type to another, without altering the existing code. This doesn't usually matter and shouldn't be a big concern. If you really need the application to be compatible with several database systems, you can always use conditional statements to execute one, among several versions of the same query, depending on the adapter in use.

❑   The preceding example served us well as a means of exposing a few techniques that enable you to gain flexibility. Many developers, however, would probably opt in favor of using a plugin such as Foreign Key Migrations, which is available at http://www.redhillonrails.org/ foreign_key_migrations.html.

Finally, it's important to note that migrations are great, but you are not forced to use them. When you create a model Article, the articles table is supposed to be there, but ActiveRecord doesn't care how the table was created, just that it exists in the database. For this reason, some people prefer to approach the database schema creation and evolution the traditional way, opting to skip the migration "framework" in favor of what they are already accustomed to. I recommend that you give migrations a chance though; they are a very useful feature and an integral part of the Rails developer mindset.

ORM Conventions

ActiveRecord endorses the Convention over Configuration principle to its core. While developing the basic blog application in the past two chapters you never had to write XML configuration files. The mapping between the articles and comments tables and their respective models, Article and Comment, was done automatically for you by convention. Naming conventions represent such a fundamental part of being able to work with ActiveRecord that it's worth exploring them further.

Mapping Tables to Models

A model is a subclass of ActiveRecord::Base. For each model that exists in your application, ActiveRecord expects a corresponding table represented by that model (unless you specify otherwise, as you'll see later on). As repeated ad nauseam by now, if the model class is Article, then the table that you expect to find in the database would be articles. But what about irregular plurals or other languages? An Italian developer may decide to call his model Articolo, Italian for article; would ActiveRecord look for the table articoli, the correct Italian plural, or append an s as is the norm in English, and expect a table articolos (which would be okay for Spanish, but not for Italian)?

Besides the fact that choosing a different language other than English for identifiers can be considered a poor development practice, answering the preceding questions will shed some light on how the mapping convention really works.

> The Rails team put forth a great deal of effort to develop an internationalization (I18n) framework for those who need to internationalize their applications. You can read all about it in the *The Rails Internationalization (I18n) API* guide, which is available online at http://guides.rails.info/i18n.html or in the doc folder of your Rails project after running rake doc:guides, which generates the Rails guides locally.

ActiveRecord determines the table name starting from the model name by ultimately taking advantage of the pluralize method of a class called Inflector (defined by ActiveSupport).

The fact that Inflector is defined by the ActiveSupport library implies that you can use it in your own programs, outside of Rails, by simply requiring the gem activesupport.

Let's take it for a spin. Start the Rails console from the chapter7 directory:

```
C:\projects\chapter7> ruby script/console
```

From within the console, you can find the table name for model names that are regular nouns in the English language:

```
>> "article".pluralize
=> "articles"
>> "comment".pluralize
=> "comments"
```

Plural nouns are usually left untouched:

```
>> "money".pluralize
=> "money"
>> "accounts".pluralize
=> "accounts"
```

Irregular words tend to be pluralized correctly as well:

```
>> "mouse".pluralize
=> "mice"
>> "datum".pluralize
=> "data"
>> "cow".pluralize
=> "kine"
>> "person".pluralize
=> "people"
```

By the way, it's the archaic kine and not cows, all thanks to this ticket http://dev.rubyonrails.org/ticket/4929. *Consider it to be an inside joke of sorts.*

Inflector Isn't Perfect

To be exact, ActiveRecord doesn't directly use the pluralize method to determine the table name, but rather the tableize method, which takes advantage of pluralize. Unlike this, tableize takes care of lowercasing the model name and properly pluralizing the last word of a composite model name as shown in the following example:

```
>> "Bank".tableize
=> "banks"
>> "BankAccount".tableize
=> "bank_accounts"
```

Notice how model names should be in CamelCase, whereas tables are supposed to adopt the snake_case convention.

The opposite of `tableize` *is* `classify`, *which turns a table name into its model name. This in turn uses the* `singularize` *method. Good Ruby code uses snake_case for methods and variables; because of this point, it's important to adopt snake_case for the name of the columns in the table, so that the corresponding attributes will do the same thing as well. For example, use* `interest_rate` *not* `interestRate` *as a column name.*

Unfortunately, the `Inflector` class is not as reliable as you might expect it to be. For example, the following irregular nouns are handled incorrectly:

```
>> "nucleus".pluralize
=> "nucleus"
>> "Phenomenon".tableize
=> "phenomenons"
>> "Curriculum".tableize
=> "curriculums"
>> "business".classify
=> "Busines"
```

In the last line we intentionally tricked the `Inflector` *by invoking the* `classify` *method on a singular noun ending in s. Notice how* `classify` *returns a string. Use* `"my_table".classify` `.constantize` *when you need to get the actual class.*

"Bug! Let's report it!" you may be exclaiming. Well, not so fast. The reality is that the `Inflector` tries to pluralize and singularize most nouns correctly, but it's accepted that it won't do so for all of the irregular ones. The developers decided to freeze its code a while ago, primarily as a means of maintaining backward compatibility. Whenever you're in doubt, use the console and the methods mentioned previously to verify model and table name mapping.

The easiest way to actually know what tables a given model is mapping to is to use the `table_name` *method (for example,* `MyModel.table_name`*).*

The pluralization offered by the `Inflector` is more or less as accurate as that of a young child. But that's okay, because you can change the rules and add exceptions to the `Inflector`.

Another issue with the `Inflector`, at least for some, is the fact that it only pluralizes and singularizes English words:

```
>> "articolo".pluralize
=> "articolos"
>> "conto".pluralize
=> "contos"
```

Adding New Inflection Rules

Any Rails application has a `config\initializers\inflections.rb` file generated by default. This file contains the following commented out lines:

```
# Be sure to restart your server when you modify this file.

# Add new inflection rules using the following format
# (all these examples are active by default):
# Inflector.inflections do |inflect|
#   inflect.plural /^(ox)$/i, '\1en'
#   inflect.singular /^(ox)en/i, '\1'
#   inflect.irregular 'person', 'people'
#   inflect.uncountable %w( fish sheep )
# end
```

If you need to add new rules, this is the file that you need to modify. The `plural`, `singular`, `irregular`, and `uncountable` methods provide you with an easy-to-use DSL to customize the inflections. For example, go ahead and add the following to that file within the `chapter7` project:

```
Inflector.inflections do |inflect|
   inflect.irregular 'curriculum', 'curricula'
end
```

Save the file, exit from the console (using `exit`) if you haven't already done so, and then start it again.

Get Familiar with the Console

Whenever you modify your models, you can use the `reload!` command instead of manually restarting the console. In this case, you had to restart it because you modified an initializer.

Remember also that by default the console uses the development environment; if you'd like to specify a different one, just pass its name as an argument to the command. For example, use `ruby script/console production` for the production console.

You should now be able to see that the old rules still apply, as well as the new inflection you defined:

```
C:\projects\chapter7> ruby script/console
Loading development environment (Rails 2.2.2)
>> "curriculum".pluralize
=> "curricula"
>> "recipe".pluralize
=> "recipes"
```

If you want to define your own set of rules from scratch, getting rid of the default ones, you can do so by first clearing them with the `clear` method. This would really be helpful only when your database tables consistently follow a precise naming convention that's different than the default one, or when you are creating a set of rules for a specific language. For example, the following snippet would correctly cover most Italian words (only the regular ones), but would lose the ability to pluralize English words:

```
Inflector.inflections do |inflect|
  inflect.clear
```

```
inflect.singular /^(\w]*)i/i, '\1o'
inflect.plural /^([\w]*)o/i, '\1i'
inflect.singular /^([\w]*)e/i, '\1a'
inflect.plural /^([\w]*)a/i, '\1e'
end
```

You can also be more specific than that, and use clear :plurals, clear :singulars, *or* clear :uncountables.

The regular expressions may make it look scary, but it's really rather simple. Words ending in o should be pluralized by replacing the o with an i and vice versa; words ending in i should be singularized with an o. Similarly, strings ending with an a should be pluralized by replacing that final a with an e.

Notice that the occurrence of a string that matches the pattern between the round brackets is "captured" by \1, *which is then used to define the new word (in the second parameter passed to the methods* singular *and* plural). *For example, if the word is "articolo,"* \1 *will capture "articol," to which* i *is then appended (if you are pluralizing).*

Setting a Custom Table Name for a Model

The path of least resistance is available anytime you stick to the convention for table and model naming. There are times, however, when this is not possible or convenient due to restrictions that are beyond the developer's control. In such instances, overwriting the convention is possible.

Though you could simply modify the inflection rules to influence the mapping as needed, this is not always a clean solution. For example, convincing the Inflector that the plural of recipe is my_cookbook has all the characteristics of a so called "code smell." Luckily for you, ActiveRecord allows you to set the table name for a model explicitly.

As mentioned earlier, at any time you can verify the table represented by a model by using the class method table_name. From the same console for the chapter7 project, try to use this as follows:

```
>> Recipe.table_name
=> "recipes"
```

The table represented by Recipe is recipes, as expected; but let's modify your model to map it with a custom table named my_cookbook, from the preceding example:

```
class Recipe < ActiveRecord::Base
  self.table_name = "my_cookbook"
end
```

Similarly, you can also use the (macro style) method set_table_name:

```
class Recipe < ActiveRecord::Base
  set_table_name :my_cookbook
end
```

Having changed one or more models, you'll need to impart the reload! command in the console. Once you've done that, you'll see that the table associated with the model is now my_cookbook:

```
>> reload!
Reloading...
```

```
=> true
>> Recipe.table_name
=> "my_cookbook"
```

Notice that this will work whether or not that table exists. However, to do anything useful with such a model, the table obviously needs to exist in the database.

Specifying a Prefix or Suffix

Along with setting a custom table name, it's also possible to let all the `Inflector` rules be applied as usual, except for a custom prefix or suffix. For example, say that the table you'd like `Recipe` to represent is `w7c_recipes`, where `w7c` is a department code. You can then set the `table_name_prefix` as follows:

```
class Recipe < ActiveRecord::Base
  self.table_name_prefix = "w7c_"
end
```

Similarly, you can set the `table_name_suffix`.

Setting a prefix or suffix for a single model in this way is not a more concise option than simply using `set_table_name`. Imagine for a moment, though, that all the tables in your application need a `w7c_` prefix. In this sort of scenario you could leverage the setter not for a particular model, but for the `ActiveRecord::Base` class, and all the models in the application would automatically inherit from it. An easy way to do this is to place the following code within an initializer of the application (for example, in a Ruby file within `config\initializers`):

```
class ActiveRecord::Base
    self.table_name_prefix  = "w7c_"
end
```

Using a Different Primary Key

Conventionally ActiveRecord expects tables to have an `id` primary key that's an auto-incrementing integer field.

By the same convention, foreign key columns are supposed to be named by appending `id` *to the singular name of the referenced table (for example,* `article_id`*).*

This convention too can be easily overwritten, even though it's not recommended to do so unless you really have to. ActiveRecord's productivity comes from sticking to its conventions whenever possible. The method used for this task is `set_primary_key`.

If you want to inform the model that the primary key column is `guid`, not `id`, you can do so as follows (in this case, the model is generically named `MyModel`):

```
class MyModel < ActiveRecord::Base
  set_primary_key "guid"
end
```

You can also opt for `self.primary_key = "guid"`.

The method also accepts a block, if the first parameter (in this case `"guid"`) is missing or evaluates to false. In such cases, the returning value of the block will be assigned as the value for the primary key column.

By convention, migrations will generate tables with an `id` primary key column. This too can effortlessly be overwritten, so that it matches the primary key you set in the model:

```
create_table(:my_models, :primary_key => 'guid') do |t|
  # ... some column definitions
end
```

ActiveRecord doesn't support composite primary keys; if you need them in order to support a legacy schema, you might want to check out the Composite Primary Keys plugin at `http://compositekeys` `.rubyforge.org`*.*

Migrations also allow you to specify that no primary key should be defined. This is usually important when creating an intermediary table for a many-to-many relationship that has no corresponding model. The documentation for the `create_table` method offers this example:

```
create_table(:categories_suppliers, :id => false) do |t|
  t.column :category_id, :integer
  t.column :supplier_id, :integer
end
```

The ability to overwrite the conventions described previously should be enough to allow you to use most legacy schemas. There is also a plugin that takes the opposite approach and automatically creates models from an existing database; it's called Magic Models and is available at `http://magicmodels` `.rubyforge.org`.

For further details and tips for working with legacy databases, pop by the wiki page `http://wiki` `.rubyonrails.com/rails/pages/HowToUseLegacySchemas`. Rails' wiki is admittedly in need of a clean up, so you may find the information presented to be disorganized and in some instances obsolete. That said, if you dig through it, you'll certainly find valuable suggestions.

CRUD Operations

One thing should be clear by now. ActiveRecord really shines when it comes to simplifying the basic operations for creating, reading, updating, and deleting data. Let's systematically review the methods that are available when you want to perform CRUD (create, read, update, delete) operations.

Create

Because a table is represented by a model class, and its rows by instances of that class, inserting new records is as easy as creating a new model object and then saving it.

Assume that you have a model that was generated by the following command:

```
ruby script/generate model Book title:string author:string publisher:string
pages:integer isbn:string description:text
```

> This is a long chapter with a lot of reference-like content, so you don't have to follow along and type all code, except when explicitly asked to do so. If you do wish to type along throughout, remember that a model generation must always be followed by running migrations (`rake db:migrate`), so that it can actually create the table in the database.

When you create an empty object, all of its attributes that represent columns will be set to `nil`:

```
C:\projects\chapter7> ruby script/generate model Book title:string author:string
publisher:string pages:integer isbn:string description:text
>> my_book = Book.new
=> #<Book id: nil, title: nil, author: nil, publisher: nil, pages: nil, isbn: nil,
description: nil, created_at: nil, updated_at: nil>
```

As a reminder, the >> and => tokens respectively represent the input and output within a Rails console, starting with `ruby script/console`.

You can use attribute writers to assign values to the columns of your record:

```
>> my_book.title = 'Ruby on Rails for Microsoft Developers'
=> "Ruby on Rails for Microsoft Developers"
>> my_book.author = 'Antonio Cangiano'
=> "Antonio Cangiano"
>> my_book.publisher = 'Wrox'
=> "Wrox"
>> my_book.pages = 450
=> 450
>> my_book.isbn = '978-0470374955'
=> "978-0470374955"
```

The object will now store those values in the respective attributes:

```
>> my_book
=> #<Book id: nil, title: "Ruby on Rails for Microsoft Developers", author:
 "Antonio Cangiano", publisher: "Wrox", pages: 450, isbn: "978-0470374955",
 description: nil, created_at: nil, updated_at: nil>
```

You can also obtain a list of attributes using the `attributes` method (also available as the writer method `attributes=`):

```
>> my_book.attributes
=> {"isbn"=>"978-0470374955", "updated_at"=>nil, "title"=>"Ruby on Rails for
 Microsoft Developers", "author"=>"Antonio Cangiano", "publisher"=>"Wrox",
 "description"=>nil, "pages"=>450, "created_at"=>nil}
```

You'll notice that no `id`, `created_at`, or `updated_at` values have been assigned yet. At this stage, the object contains all the data you want, but the record has yet to be saved in the database.

You can confirm this using the `new_record?` method:

```
>> my_book.new_record?
=> true
```

To actually create the record you'll need to save your object:

```
>> my_book.save
=> true
```

Saving returns a `true` value, which confirms that the procedure of storing a record in the database was successful. If you evaluate the object after you've saved it, you'll now obtain an id and the creation/update date times as well.

```
>> my_book
=> #<Book id: 1, title: "Ruby on Rails for Microsoft Developers", author: "Antonio
Cangiano", publisher: "Wrox", pages: 450, isbn: "978-0470374955", description:
nil, created_at: "2009-01-31 17:24:15", updated_at: "2009-01-31 17:24:15">
```

ActiveRecord offers a few alternatives to creating a variable (and manually assigning values to its attributes). The first enables you to skip the repetition of variable names by employing a block:

```
Book.new do |b|
    b.title = 'Professional Ruby on Rails'
    b.author = 'Noel Rappin'
    b.publisher = 'Wrox'
    b.pages = 457
    b.isbn = '978-0470223888'
    b.save
end
```

More importantly, ActiveRecord allows for the creation of new records by passing a hash, containing the attribute values, to the constructor. This is particularly handy when trying to create a record from a form submitted by a user. For example, imagine that `params[:book]` is the following hash:

```
{ "isbn" => "978-0470189481", "title" => "The Art of Rails", "author" => "Edward
Benson", "publisher" => "Wrox", "pages" => 309 }
```

At this point you can create a new record as follows:

```
book = Book.new(params[:book])
book.save
```

Or more conveniently, by instantiating the object and saving it in one step through the `create` method:

```
Book.create(params[:book])
```

Read

In the previous chapters you saw how finders are used to retrieve data. The simplest possible example you can come up with is the `find` method, to which an id is passed.

```
book = Book.find(3)
```

Finding by Id(s)

The most common scenario for this is to retrieve a record using the id provided by the user:

```
book = Book.find(params[:id])
```

When the id can't be found in the table, an `ActiveRecord::RecordNotFound` exception is raised. In a production environment, this translates into a 404, which is a sensible default. And because `find` accepts a list or an array of ids as well, if any of the ids is missing, the same exception will be raised. Otherwise, an array of instances is returned:

```
>> Book.find(1,3)
=> [#<Book id: 1, title: "Ruby on Rails for Microsoft Developers", author: "Antonio
   Cangiano", publisher: "Wrox", pages: 450, isbn: "978-0470374955", description:
   nil, created_at: "2009-01-31 17:24:15", updated_at: "2009-01-31 17:24:15">, #<Book
   id: 3, title: "The Art of Rails", author: "Edward Benson", publisher: "Wrox",
   pages: 309, isbn: "978-0470189481", description: nil, created_at: "2009-01-31
   17:28:34", updated_at: "2009-01-31 17:28:34">]
```

:first, :last, and :all

`find(:all)` returns an array, and as such you can chain the method with `Enumerable` methods and perform nice tricks:

```
>> Book.find(:all).collect(&:isbn)
=> ["978-0470374955", "978-0470223888", "978-0470189481"]
>> Book.find(:all).sum(&:pages)
=> 1216
```

Incidentally, all three Rails books combined fail to reach the same number of pages as the most popular ASP.NET title.

> `Book.find(:all).collect(&:isbn)` **is a more concise form of** `Book.find(:all)` `.collect {|book| book[:isbn] }`, **which should be familiar to you. Unfortunately in Ruby 1.8.x this "symbol to proc" shortcut is much slower than the regular block form, and as such you should think twice before using it in production.**

Two common symbols found in any Rails application are `:first` and `:all`. Not surprisingly, the first symbol tells the finder to return only the first record in the result set as an instance of the model, and the second symbol, all the records as an array of instances:

```
>> Book.find(:first)
=> #<Book id: 1, title: "Ruby on Rails for Microsoft Developers", author: "Antonio
   Cangiano", publisher: "Wrox", pages: 450, isbn: "978-0470374955", description:
   nil, created_at: "2009-01-31 17:24:15", updated_at: "2009-01-31 17:24:15">
>> Book.find(:all)
=> [#<Book id: 1, title: "Ruby on Rails for Microsoft Developers", author: "Anto
   nio Cangiano", publisher: "Wrox", pages: 450, isbn: "978-0470374955", descriptio
   n: nil, created_at: "2009-01-31 17:24:15", updated_at: "2009-01-31 17:24:15">, #
   <Book id: 2, title: "Professional Ruby on Rails", author: "Noel Rappin", publish
   er: "Wrox", pages: 457, isbn: "978-0470223888", description: nil, created_at: "2
   009-01-31 17:26:37", updated_at: "2009-01-31 17:26:37">, #<Book id: 3, title: "T
```

```
he Art of Rails", author: "Edward Benson", publisher: "Wrox", pages: 309, isbn:
"978-0470189481", description: nil, created_at: "2009-01-31 17:28:34", updated_a
t: "2009-01-31 17:28:34">]
```

A third, perhaps less common symbol, exists as well and it's :last. These three can be used in conjunction with other options as well, but starting with Rails 2.1, three handy methods have been added as shortcuts for them:

```
Book.first # Book.find(:first)
Book.last  # Book.find(:first, :order => "id DESC") or Book.find(:last)
Book.all   # Book.find(:all)
```

These three methods accept other arguments just as find does. In this chapter, they've been used interchangeably.

Finders are extremely flexible in terms of the arguments that they accept, as you can see by reading the online documentation for the methods.

:order and :group

You already encountered the :order attribute, used to specify an SQL fragment to order the results in the query. Invoking the following:

```
Book.find(:all, :order => "created_at DESC")
```

would lead to the execution of the SQL query:

```
SELECT * FROM "books" ORDER BY created_at DESC
```

Similarly, another attribute/option that's available is :group, which translates into a GROUP BY clause:

```
# This becomes SELECT * FROM "books" WHERE (pages > 430) GROUP BY publisher
Book.find(:all, :conditions => ["pages > ?", 430], :group => "publisher")
```

Adding Conditions

You can also add conditions to the finder (as you've seen before, as well):

```
# Equivalent to Book.all(:conditions => "pages > 430", :order => "created_at DESC")
Book.find(:all, :conditions => "pages > 430", :order => "created_at DESC")
```

This becomes:

```
SELECT * FROM "books" WHERE (pages > 430) ORDER BY created_at DESC
```

You don't have to reach for the logs to see the SQL queries generated by the commands you entered into the console. From the console simply run ActiveRecord::Base.logger = Logger.new(STDOUT) *(as long as you aren't in production mode). You can also use the* ActiveSupport::BufferedLogger, *used by Rails and mentioned before in this book.*

Conditions can be specified in several ways. The preceding example uses a string, but other common ways of specifying conditions are hashes and arrays.

A hash can be used as follows:

```
Book.find(:first, :conditions => { :author => "Antonio Cangiano", :pages => 450 })
```

This yields (at least on SQLite3):

```
SELECT * FROM "books" WHERE ("books"."author" = 'Antonio Cangiano' AND
"books"."pages" = 450) LIMIT 1
```

Arrays are used to substitute parameters with their values in an SQL fragment:

```
Book.find(:all, :conditions => ["pages > ?", 430])
Book.find(:all, :conditions => ["pages > :pages", {:pages => 430}])
```

If you had several parameters, the values that need to be substituted would be added to the array in the order that they appear:

```
Book.find(:all, :conditions => ["pages > ? AND author = ?", 430, "Antonio
Cangiano"])
```

Note that the substitution of the parameters with their values happens during the formulation of the query; therefore, the database will execute a normal SQL query and not, say, a parameterized query. You may wonder, then, what is the point of using parameters. Can't you just embed the variables in the SQL fragment as follows?

```
# Don't do this
Book.find(:all, :conditions => "pages > #{params[:pages]}")
```

The problem with this approach is that it poses a considerable security risk. Remember, you can't trust the user's input, and embedding the value in an SQL fragment like the preceding one would make you susceptible to SQL injection attacks. When you use the hash or the more flexible array approach, ActiveRecord takes care of escaping malicious inputs for you.

For example, imagine that a malicious user passed the value `300'; DROP TABLE books;` as a parameter. If you use the correct approach:

```
Book.all(:conditions => ["pages > ?", params[:pages]])
```

you have nothing to fear:

```
SELECT * FROM "books" WHERE (pages > '300''; DROP TABLE books;')
```

The single quote after 300, which would indicate the termination of the string/value, has been properly escaped with a second one, transforming it into a regular character. The topic of security is investigated further in Chapter 11.

> **When the finder's condition is determined by a value provided by the user, always use the array or hash form for** `:conditions`.

:limit and :offset

:limit and :offset are used to specify, respectively, the number of records that should be fetched, and how many records should be skipped. For example:

```
Book.find(:all, :limit => 10, :offset => 5)
```

This will return, if they exist, 10 rows, skipping the first 5 rows. The generated SQL is truly database-specific, and will be different for SQL Server, DB2, or Oracle, but for SQLite, it would be:

```
SELECT * FROM "books" LIMIT 10 OFFSET 5
```

If you were to follow along throughout the chapter, you'd find yourself with three records, so an empty array would be returned by the preceding Ruby instruction.

> *In many circumstances it makes sense to use* :limit *along with* :offset, *but* :limit *can also be used on its own. If, on the other hand, you specify an offset but no limit, this will have no effect on the resulting query. Please note, though, that if you try to specify an offset with no limit, yet you've passed a* :first *or* :last *symbol to the finder, then the* :offset *attribute will have an effect on the query because* :first *and* :last *both implicitly set a* :limit => 1.

:select and :from

You should have noticed by now that all the queries generated by these finders start with SELECT *. If you want to limit the columns returned to just a few, you can use the :select option:

```
>> Book.first(:select => "title")
=> #<Book title: "Ruby on Rails for Microsoft Developers">
```

The resulting query is what you'd expect it to be:

```
SELECT title FROM "books" LIMIT 1
```

When you need more than one column, you can assign a comma-separated list as the string value for the :select key:

```
>> Book.first(:select => "title, author")
=> #<Book title: "Ruby on Rails for Microsoft Developers", author: "Antonio Cang
iano">
```

Not surprisingly, this executes:

```
SELECT title, author FROM "books" LIMIT 1
```

The :select option is particularly useful whenever you want to exclude the joined columns in a join, to avoid duplicates (for example, :select => "DISTINCT books.*"), or improve performances.

The :from option is less common, but it allows you to specify a different table name or database view for the query:

```
# Both execute SELECT * FROM wrox_book_catalog
Book.all(:from => "wrox_book_catalog")
Book.find(:all, :from => "wrox_book_catalog")
```

:include and :joins

:include is a very important option when working with associations. It enables you to perform eager loading and prevent the shudder-inducing 1+N problem, where fetching N records requires the execution of 1+N queries.

Just in case you're not familiar with this issue, and in order to show the usefulness of :include, let's see an illustrative example. Imagine that you have the following schema in the database:

```
create_table :books do |t|
  t.string   :title
  t.string   :publisher
  t.integer  :pages
  t.string   :isbn
  t.datetime :created_at
  t.datetime :updated_at
  t.integer  :author_id
end

create_table :authors do |t|
  t.string   :name
  t.text     :bio
  t.datetime :created_at
  t.datetime :updated_at
end

create_table :reviews do |t|
  t.string   :title
  t.text     :body
  t.string   :reviewer
  t.boolean  :published
  t.datetime :created_at
  t.datetime :updated_at
  t.integer  :book_id
end
```

> The books table declared here clearly has nothing to do with the table defined earlier in the chapter. This is a standalone example provided to illustrate the 1+N problem, but you don't have to type it out.

You can assume that the Book model would have the following definition:

```
class Book < ActiveRecord::Base
  belongs_to :author
  has_many :reviews
end
```

Now imagine that you'd like to print the book title, its author, its publisher, and the title of the latest review that it received within a Ruby script (not necessarily in a Rails application). A first, perhaps naive, approach would be this:

```
Book.all.each do |book|
  puts "Title: #{book.title}"
```

```
    puts "Author: #{book.author.name}"
    puts "Publisher: #{book.publisher}"
    puts "Latest review: #{book.reviews.last.title}"
end
```

The code, as it's written, would raise an exception if a book happened to have no reviews, because it would attempt to run nil.title. *But this is just an example to illustrate the 1+N problem.*

Book.all is equivalent to Book.find(:all) so it will only execute the query once:

```
SELECT * FROM "books"
```

Within the block, book.author.name and book.reviews.last.title will execute two queries that look like the following (the values for id and book_id can change depending on the records at hand):

```
SELECT * FROM "authors" WHERE ("authors"."id" = 1)
SELECT * FROM "reviews" WHERE ("reviews".book_id = 1) ORDER BY reviews.id DESC
LIMIT 1
```

For each iteration, two queries are executed. So if you had 100 records in the books table, in total that snippet would execute 201 queries. What's more, 100 of them would look virtually identical save for the id, which changes, and another 100 would be virtually identical except for their book_id value. This is known as the 1+N problem, and as you can imagine it's a big strike against database performances.

Technically, in this case, you have 2N+1 queries because two queries that involved associations in the loop/block were used.

How can you improve this? Thanks to :include, you can drastically better the situation. Consider the following:

```
Book.all(:include => :author).each do |book|
    puts "Title: #{book.title}"
    puts "Author: #{book.author.name}"
    puts "Publisher: #{book.publisher}"
    puts "Latest review: #{book.reviews.last.title}"
end
```

This executes two queries before you execute a statement within the block:

```
SELECT * FROM "books"
SELECT * FROM "authors" WHERE ("authors".id IN ('1', '2', '3',...))
```

The query is shortened for sake of brevity. Any id for an author that has written a book would be listed between brackets.

Within the loop, because you've included author, but not reviews, you would execute the following query 100 times:

```
SELECT * FROM "reviews" WHERE ("reviews".book_id = 1) ORDER BY reviews.id DESC
LIMIT
```

As things stand, you cut the number of queries from 201 to 102. Not bad. But `:include` allows you to do even better, because you're not limited to eager loading a single field. As a matter of fact, the proper way to handle this hypothetical scenario is to include both `author` and `reviews` as follows:

```ruby
Book.all(:include => [:author, :reviews]).each do |book|
  puts "Title: #{book.title}"
  puts "Author: #{book.author.name}"
  puts "Publisher: #{book.publisher}"
  puts "Latest review: #{book.reviews.last.title}"
end
```

This way you'll execute three queries no matter how many records you have in the `books` table. All the data that you need is "eagerloaded" before you even enter the block.

```sql
SELECT * FROM "books"
SELECT * FROM "authors" WHERE ("authors".id IN ('1', '2', '3',...))
SELECT "reviews".* FROM "reviews" WHERE ("reviews".book_id IN (1,2,3,4,5,...))
```

Again, the last two queries have been shortened for the sake of brevity. Any id for an author that has written a book would be listed between brackets and any id for a book that has reviews would be listed as well.

This demonstrates the importance of eager loading associations, but you should always pay attention to SQL queries that are hidden by the abstraction layer that's provided by ActiveRecord. For example, you need to be very careful when adding `:include` and `:conditions` options at the same time. Consider the following straightforward looking line of code:

```ruby
Book.find(:all, :include => [:author, :reviews],
          :conditions => ['reviews.published = ?', true])
```

It will generate the following SQL (SQlite3 version) for you:

```sql
SELECT "books"."id" AS t0_r0, "books"."title" AS t0_r1, "books"."publisher" AS
t0_r2, "books"."pages" AS t0_r3, "books"."isbn" AS t0_r4, "books"."created_at" AS
t0_r5, "books"."updated_at" AS t0_r6, "books"."author_id" AS t0_r7, "authors"."id"
AS t1_r0, "authors"."name" AS t1_r1, "authors"."bio" AS t1_r2,
"authors"."created_at" AS t1_r3, "authors"."updated_at" AS t1_r4, "reviews"."id" AS
t2_r0, "reviews"."book_id" AS t2_r1, "reviews"."title" AS t2_r2, "reviews"."body"
AS t2_r3, "reviews"."created_at" AS t2_r4, "reviews"."updated_at" AS t2_r5,
"reviews"."reviewer" AS t2_r6 FROM "books"  LEFT OUTER JOIN "authors" ON
"authors".id = "books".author_id  LEFT OUTER JOIN "reviews" ON reviews.book_id =
books.id WHERE (reviews.published = 't')
```

Notice how that = 't' is strongly dependent on the way the adapter defines Boolean values. It's not uncommon for them to be implemented as 1 for true, and 0 for false.

On top of being a bit scary looking when compared to what you've seen so far, this query fails to return books that lack published reviews, because the condition `reviews.published = 't'` applies to the whole SQL statement. This outcome may or may not be what you wanted.

When this approach doesn't match the desired outcome, it is sensible to attack the problem from a different angle. For example, it is common to eager load an association that has conditions defined on it. At this stage don't worry about this somewhat advanced technique. You'll see an example of it later on in this chapter.

:include can also be used to include a hierarchy of associations. ActiveRecord's documentation provides an example of this:

```
Post.find(:all, :include => [:author, {:comments => {:author => :gravatar }}])
```

This will need to generate a single query that's able to load all the posts, their authors, all the comments, their authors, and gravatar pictures. Again, this is a powerful feature and it's okay to include a hierarchy of associations, which isn't too deep. And as a result, performances can improve by choosing this route. But be careful; if you try to add :conditions to something like that, you'll be facing database chocking SQL monsters in no time.

> **Always double-check the queries that ActiveRecord produces to identify bottlenecks and performance issues.**

There are times where :include alone won't cut it and you may need to customize the resulting query by specifying an SQL fragment for additional join clauses. In such instances, you can use the :joins option/attribute.

:readonly and :lock

The :readonly option allows you to specify that the returned records are read-only, so that they can't be altered. Check out this console session (with the error output truncated):

```
>> book = Book.find(:first, :readonly => true)
=> #<Book id: 1, title: "Ruby on Rails for Microsoft Developers", author: "Antonio
   Cangiano", publisher: "Wrox", pages: 450, isbn: "978-0470374955", description:
   nil, created_at: "2009-01-31 17:24:15", updated_at: "2009-01-31 17:24:15">
>> book.title = "A different title"
=> "A different title"
>> book.save
ActiveRecord::ReadOnlyRecord: ActiveRecord::ReadOnlyRecord
```

The :lock option allows you to specify pessimistic locking. This is useful when dealing with concurrent transactions. For example, if a few end users attempt to increase a sales field concurrently, it is possible that you'll find yourself with an incorrect number. Using :lock => true you can lock the row, thus granting access to only one transaction at a time, while the other(s) wait for the first to be completed. This is a sample snippet:

```
Book.transaction do
  book = Book.find(22, :lock => true)
  book.sales += 1
  book.save!
end
```

The books table defined before didn't have a sales column. Consider this example to be a hypothetical scenario.

The contents of the block are wrapped in a transaction. Transactions in ActiveRecord can be instantiated by simply calling the method transaction on a model and wrapping the content of the transaction in the associated block. The book record is returned with :lock set to true when you try to add 1 to the sales field and then save the record.

The `save!` *method is similar to* `save`, *but it raises a* `RecordNotSaved` *exception instead of returning* `false`.

The finder `:lock` option provides a convenient way to perform row-level locking without having to explicitly call the `lock!` method on the object or the `reload(:lock => true)` method.

Optimistic Locking

Unlike pessimistic locking, optimistic locking allows concurrent access to the same record for editing purposes, under the "optimistic" assumption that any conflicts will be minimal. The consistency of the data is achieved by adding a `lock_version` column (that must be defaulted to 0 and can be overwritten with `set_locking_column`) to the table, whose stored value for a given record is automatically incremented at each update.

ActiveRecord will check that value to determine if the record has been changed since you first read it from the database, and if that's the case it won't allow a second update but rather raise `ActiveRecord::StaleObjectError`. At this point, it will be up to the programmer to rescue the exception and decide how to resolve the conflict. Unlike pessimistic locking, which works at the database level by appending a `FOR UPDATE` (or its equivalent) to the query that's generated by the finder, optimistic locking works at the application level. Please consult the documentation for the module `ActiveReco rd::Locking::Optimistic` for further details.

Other options for finder methods exist. Consult the online documentation to learn about each of them. Also remember regardless of the options passed to a finder, it's always possible to pass an `:options` hash as the last parameter, to specify fragments of SQL that should be appended to the query.

Dynamic Finders

By taking advantage of Ruby's powerful metaprogramming features — `method_missing` in particular — ActiveRecord allows you to use dynamic finders. These methods are not defined until the moment you invoke them. They are quite handy and improve the readability of one's code.

This method invocation:

```
Book.find(:first, :conditions => ["title = ?", title])
```

can also be written as:

```
Book.find_by_title(title)
```

Rails 2.2 introduced a similar dynamic finder to retrieve the last result. Instead of writing:

```
Book.find(:last, :conditions => ["title = ?", title])
```

you can now write:

```
Book.find_last_by_title(title)
```

Similarly, consider the following:

```
Book.find(:all, :conditions => ["publisher = ?", publisher])
```

This is equivalent to:

```
Book.find_all_by_publisher(publisher)
```

Nice and concise, isn't it? But it gets even better because you can concatenate a few attributes. For example:

```
Book.find_all_by_title_and_publisher(title, publisher)
```

This is equivalent to the much more verbose:

```
Book.find(:all, :conditions => ["title = ? AND publisher = ?", title, publisher])
```

Despite being defined on the fly during the moment of their invocation, these methods are subsequently cached by Ruby and normally have a negligible amount of impact on performance.

When the Record Can't Be Found

I mentioned that `Book.find(params[:id])` and `Book.find(params[:list_of_ids])` would raise an exception when the record(s) can't be found. This is a sensible choice in the context of Rails, because by default you access the detail page of a record by passing the id, which is handled by the `show` action. If you visit `books/show/5` and the record with id 5 doesn't exist, you'd probably expect a 404 page, which is exactly what Rails does in production.

With that in mind, this behavior is not what you'd generally want when, say, performing a search in your application. For this reason, the `find` method, with the exception of those two cases mentioned previously, will not raise an exception when a record can't be found. If you are retrieving a single record, `nil` will be returned.

If this is not what you want, Rails 2.2 introduced dynamic finders in the form of `find_by_<attribute>!`; these raise an error when a record can't be found.

When retrieving a collection of records through the `:all` symbol, the `all` finder, or through a `find_all_by_<attribute>` dynamic finder, an empty array (that is, `[]`) is returned when no records can be found. It is not uncommon to use a dynamic finder to find a record if it exists and create one if this doesn't exist. For example, `Book.find_or_create_by_title("On the Road")` will return the model object if the book already exists, and if not, it will create one (by actually performing the insert operation in the database) and return the object so that you can, for example, add further details and assign values to its attributes, then invoke its `save` or `save!` method.

Specifying Custom SQL Queries

The finder methods and their many options are definitely nice to work with. They make code easy to write and maintain, and don't require that you provide SQL queries by hand for most reading operations. If you are a .NET developer though, when it comes to executing SQL statements you might be used to thinking in terms of `ExecuteReader`, `ExecuteNonQuery`, and `ExecuteScalar` provided by, among others, the `OleDbCommand` and `SqlCommand` classes.

An initial important difference is that ActiveRecord, being opinionated software, entirely ignores the concept of stored procedures or parameterized queries.

You can work with stored procedures, and with parameterized queries, as long as you are willing to do all the work yourself, by using the database driver directly.

Despite this, perhaps discouraging bit of information, ActiveRecord still allows you to execute arbitrary SQL statements. Your weapon of choice here is find_by_sql. This method is used whenever the many options that are available for regular finders just don't cut it and you'd like to pass a full SQL statement that you've defined to the finder:

```
Book.find_by_sql(sql)
```

Being a generic method, this will return an array of model instances even if you limit the result set to a single record (for example, with LIMIT 1 for certain database engines).

The same considerations that were made in the migration section of this chapter apply here. Whenever you provide your own SQL statements, you lose the ability to be independent from the database server that's being used. Sticking to the SQL standard can help, but there's no guarantee that the application will work out of the box if you switch it from, say, MySQL to SQL Server.

Technically it's always possible to work at an even lower level of abstraction, by using the driver directly or by employing the various methods that are available through the connection *object (for example,* Book.connection.execute *or* Book.connection.insert*).*

Calculations

ActiveRecord provides several calculation methods such as count, sum, average, minimum, maximum, and calculate. The first five are just common shortcuts for the last one.

Consider count:

```
>> Book.count
=> 100
```

This returns the number of records within the table books. The following is the executed SQL query:

```
SELECT count(*) AS count_all FROM "books"
```

It can also be used to return the number of records whose column (passed to the method) has a value:

```
>> Book.count(:isbn)
=> 76
```

This translates into:

```
SELECT count("books".isbn) AS count_isbn FROM "books"
```

This method is often used in its simplest form, but it accepts many options including :conditions, :joins, :include, :order, :having (for example, :having => 'min(pages) > 200' to exclude short books), :group, :select, :distinct (to turn this into a distinct calculation), and of course the ever present :options for appending custom SQL fragments. Please consult the online documentation for details and further examples.

Earlier on you saw this one-liner:

```
Book.find(:all).sum(&:pages)
```

This executes SELECT * FROM books and then uses Ruby's ability to work with Enumerable to calculate the sum. That's not the most efficient way of doing it, especially if there are many records in the table that wouldn't have to be retrieved anyway. Perhaps more worrisome, if a row doesn't have a value in the pages column, this would be seen as nil by Ruby, which in turn would raise a TypeError: nil can't be coerced into Fixnum error when it tries to sum things up.

There is a better way that solves both problems; use the sum method instead:

```
>> Book.sum(:pages)
=> 43870
```

This is the actual query generated by that call:

```
SELECT sum("books".pages) AS sum_pages FROM "books"
```

As a reminder, when I mentioned that a given method translates into a certain query, I offered the SQLite3 version for illustrative purposes. This is often common among several database engines, but each adapter may end up translating queries slightly differently. For example, the :limit option is translated in a LIMIT clause in SQLite, but it's a TOP clause in SQL Server.

Unlike count, and like average, minimum, and maximum, sum requires a column name and accepts only the :options option.

Here is an example that showcases average, minimum, and maximum:

```
>> Book.average(:pages)
=> 438.7
>> Book.minimum(:pages)
=> 189
>> Book.maximum(:pages)
=> 1680
```

These three will execute the following queries:

```
SELECT avg("books".pages) AS avg_pages FROM "books"
SELECT min("books".pages) AS min_pages FROM "books"
SELECT max("books".pages) AS max_pages FROM "books"
```

calculate is a more generic method. For example, Book.count can also be written as:

```
Book.calculate(:count, :all)
```

If you were using SQL Server, you could, for instance, use it to perform calculations such as:

```
Book.calculate(:stdev, :pages)
Book.calculate(:var, :pages)
```

And this would generate SQL queries that take advantage of the STDEV and VAR functions that are available in SQL Server.

Update

You have several ways to update a record with ActiveRecord. The first one is to assign new values to the attributes that need to be changed:

```
book = Book.find_by_title("A sample book")
book.pages = 435
book.publisher = "Penguin"
book.save
```

This is the SQL query that's generated:

```
UPDATE "books" SET "pages" = 435, "publisher" = 'Penguin', "updated_at" = '2008-
08-21 23:50:03' WHERE "id" = 34
```

This assumes that 34 is the id of the "A sample book" book.

If there are associations, this technique can be employed as well, but you need to be careful:

```
book = Book.first
book.author.name = "John Doe"
book.save # Don't do this. It won't change the author name
book.author.save # Saves the author name
```

This only showcases how to update an associated record.

Notice how invoking save on a Book object will only execute a query if there is an attribute that's been changed. The author_id value hasn't changed in this case, so book.save will return true but won't really do anything. To update the Author object with the new name, you'll have to invoke save on book.author, yielding the following SQL query:

```
UPDATE "authors" SET "name" = 'John Doe', "updated_at" = '2008-08-21 23:58:36'
WHERE "id" = 1
```

Partial Updates and Dirty Objects

Prior to Rails 2.1, updates to ActiveRecord objects would generate SQL queries where all the columns in a row would be updated. Starting with ActiveRecord 2.1, partial updates were introduced so that only modified attributes ended up in the query (plus updated_at, which is automatically handled). This works thanks to the so-called "dirty objects" (an attribute is "dirty" when it's changed) that track unsaved attribute changes. When you call save or save! ActiveRecord updates these and only these attributes.

This example showcases a few available "dirty object" methods:

```
book = Book.first
book.changed?                      # false
book.title                         # "A title"
book.title = "A different title"
book.changed?                      # true
book.title_changed?                # true
book.title_was                     # "A title"
book.title_change                  # ["A title", "A different title"]
book.publisher                     # "Penguin"
book.publisher = "Wiley"
book.changed                       # ["title", "publisher"]
book.changes
# {"title"=>["A title", "A different title"], "publisher"=>["Penguin", "Wiley"]}
book.save                          # true
```

changed?, changed, and changes are regular methods, whereas title_changed?, title_was, and title_change are dynamic methods that are defined when invoked with the usual method_missing trick. As such, they can be adapted to the name of the attribute that you want to track (for example, publisher_change).

The query executed by book.save then becomes:

```
UPDATE "books" SET "title" = 'A different title', "publisher" = 'Wiley', "updated_
at" = '2008-08-22 00:34:30' WHERE "id" = 1
```

> There is an important gotcha that you must be aware of. Dirty attribute tracking only works when the values of an attribute are altered through direct assignment. If the values have been changed in a different way, ActiveRecord won't be aware of the changes!

Observe this session:

```
book = Book.first
book.title.upcase!
book.publisher << "-Blackwell"
book.changes # {}
book.save     # true, but no actual changes were made
```

You'd probably expect the title and publisher attributes for the record to be updated. In reality, the changes to the object have not been saved in the corresponding table. No queries whatsoever have been executed upon issuing book.save.

To solve this issue, use the *_will_change! method for attributes that are going to change through means different than a simple assignment:

```
>> book.title_will_change!
=> "A different title"
>> book.title.upcase!
=> "A DIFFERENT TITLE"
```

```
>> book.publisher_will_change!
=> "Wiley"
>> book.publisher << "-Blackwell"
=> "Wiley-Blackwell"
>> book.changes
=> {"title"=>["A different title", "A DIFFERENT TITLE"], "publisher"=>["Wiley",
"Wiley-Blackwell"]}
>> book.save
=> true
```

This time, the record is properly updated through the following query:

```
UPDATE "books" SET "title" = 'A DIFFERENT TITLE', "publisher" = 'Wiley-Blackwell',
"updated_at" = '2008-08-22 01:28:15' WHERE "id" = 1
```

As a reminder, dates and times will obviously be different on your machine. Actually, within this chapter you will find some dates from 2008 and others from 2009 depending on whether the reported output was from the first draft of the chapter, or from its revision. Of course, the dates and times in the output are entirely irrelevant.

update_attribute and update_attributes

Updating an attribute value can also be achieved through the update_attribute method:

```
>> book.update_attribute(:title, "Yet another title")
=> true
```

Just as you'd expect, the SQL statement issued by this is:

```
UPDATE "books" SET "title" = 'Yet another title', "updated_at" = '2008-08-22
01:33:02' WHERE "id" = 1
```

Similarly, and this is much more useful, you have the update_attributes method. You encountered this method before while analyzing the code produced by the scaffold generator.

```
>> book.update_attributes(:title => "A newer title", :publisher => "Wrox")
=> true
```

The reason why this is particularly useful is that it allows you to update a record directly from the hash that's received as a parameter from an input form:

```
>> book.update_attributes(params[:book])
=> true
```

Updating Multiple Records

ActiveRecord provides you with yet another two methods to update records: update and update_all.

This is the signature for the method update:

```
update(id, attributes)
```

where id is a single id or a list of ids of objects that need to be updated; attributes is a hash of attributes to be assigned to a single object, or an array of hashes to update multiple records.

Update a single record as follows:

```
Book.update(3, { :title => "Ruby on Rails for Microsoft Developers", :publisher =>
  "Wrox", :isbn => "978-0470374955" })
```

This translates into:

```
UPDATE "books" SET "isbn" = '978-0470374955', "title" = 'Ruby on Rails for
Microsoft Developers', "publisher" = 'Wrox', "updated_at" = '2008-09-01 20:09:11'
  WHERE "id" = 3
```

If you need to update multiple records, you can do so at the same time as follows:

```
books = { "1" => { :publisher => "Wiley" }, "2" => { :title => "The Art of
Rails", :publisher => "Wrox" } }
Book.update(books.keys, books.values)
```

This translates correctly into the following two queries:

```
UPDATE "books" SET "publisher" = 'Wiley', "updated_at" = '2008-09-01 20:20:14'
WHERE "id" = 1

UPDATE "books" SET "title" = 'The Art of Rails', "publisher" = 'Wrox', "updated_at"
= '2008-09-01 20:20:15' WHERE "id" = 2
```

The update method is not very flexible. Sure, it's going to be useful at times, but imagine that you need to update all the records in the table, or those that meet a certain condition. update will require an array of ids, as well as an array of hashes, whose cardinality depends on the number of records affected. Fear not; there is a better way without having to resort to issuing custom SQL statements: the update_all method.

This method has the following signature:

```
update_all(updates, conditions = nil, options = {})
```

where updates is a string containing a comma-separated list of column/value pairs to be set for any row that meets the conditions specified by conditions.

The following line would affect all the records in a books table:

```
Book.update_all("publisher = 'Wrox', returned = 0")
```

Again, this is not the table that we defined much earlier on in the chapter, because it didn't contain a returned field, but rather it's just an example.

Or just books that contain the word Rails:

```
Book.update_all("publisher = 'Wrox', returned = 0", "title LIKE '%Rails%'")
```

This translates into the following SQL:

```
UPDATE "books" SET publisher = 'Wrox', returned = 0 WHERE (title LIKE '%Rails%')
```

update_all returns a number indicating how many records were affected by the update.

Delete

Deleting a row can be accomplished through the delete class method or the destroy method (available as a class and as an instance method). delete can be used to delete both a single row or a list of rows based on their ids:

```
Book.delete(5)
Book.delete([3, 7, 12])
```

The usual returning value (it's defined by the adapter) is the number of rows that were deleted. Just like update and update_all, delete has a variant called delete_all:

```
Book.delete_all(["sales < ?", min_sales])
```

destroy is available as a class method and is used just like delete:

```
Book.destroy(5)
Book.destroy([3, 7, 12])
```

Unlike delete, destroy returns the affected record. If the record can't be located, delete returns 0, whereas destroy would have raised an ActiveRecord::RecordNotFound error.

destroy can also be invoked as an instance method:

```
book = Book.last
book.destroy
```

After deleting a row in the table, the book object is frozen to prevent accidental assignments to its attributes.

destroy_all can be used just like delete_all:

```
Book.destroy_all("title IS ?", nil])
```

destroy_all returns an empty array if no records are found to meet the condition, or an array of affected model objects otherwise. If no condition is passed to destroy_all, all the records will be destroyed.

The main difference between the two types of methods is that delete bypasses business rules defined through validations and callbacks, and directly executes a DELETE statement in the database. destroy plays by the rules, instantiating the object (if used as a class method) and respecting any callbacks or validations you may have in place. Because of this, destroy is usually a safer bet when you want to delete a single record while still enforcing any business rules you may have defined.

On the other hand, `delete_all` is often favored over `destroy_all` because it will delete all the records with a single query. `destroy_all` will find the records, instantiate them, and then invoke the instance method `destroy` on each of them. The end result is two queries for each record, and as such it's really not the way to go for larger sized tables.

ActiveRecord Associations

Associations are highly readable class methods used to define relationships between models, allowing you to easily work with associated objects. The convenience of `Book.find_by_title("On the Road").author.name` is only possible thanks to the fact that you established a relationship between the `Book` and `Author` class models through a pair of association methods. By employing them (`has_many` and `belongs_to`), and respecting the foreign key naming convention by adding an `author_id` column to the `books` table, you automatically obtained several methods that are added to instances of both models, including `author`, which returns the `Author` object for any given `Book` object.

The association methods are:

❑   `belongs_to`

❑   `has_one`

❑   `has_many`

❑   `has_and_belongs_to_many`

These ActiveRecord associations are used to define three types of relationships between models: one-to-one, one-to-many, and many-to-many. These are covered in the next few sections.

One-to-one Relationships

One-to-one relationships are relationships in which one row in a certain table references one row (at most) of the related table; so it could also reference no rows. A one-to-one relationship between models can be established by employing the `has_one` and `belongs_to` association methods. It is common for newcomers to confuse which model should have which of the two methods in their definition. The rule is rather clear though: use `belongs_to` in the definition of the model whose corresponding table has the foreign key.

The following example establishes a one-to-one relationship between an `Account` model and an `Employee` model:

```
class Account < ActiveRecord::Base
  belongs_to :employee  # foreign key: employee_id
end

class Employee < ActiveRecord::Base
  has_one :account
end
```

Note that following the ActiveRecord convention for foreign key fields, as the rule described earlier stated, the table `accounts` needs to have an `employee_id` foreign key that references the primary key of the `employees` table.

One-to-many Relationships

One-to-many relationships are relationships in which one row in a certain table references an arbitrary number of rows in the related table. One-to-many relationships between models are established through the `has_many` and `belongs_to` methods. Imagine that you have two models, `Product` and `Company`. It's reasonable to assume that "a company has many products, and a product belongs to a company," right? Let's translate this into code:

```
class Company < ActiveRecord::Base
  has_many :products
end
```

```
class Product < ActiveRecord::Base
  belongs_to :company  # foreign key: company_id
end
```

That was rather effortless, and is pretty much what you did in the previous chapter with articles and comments. Notice that you passed a symbol to the `has_many` method (that is, `:products`), which represents a collection, and as such, the plural form was employed. As usual, the model whose definition contains the `belongs_to` call is the one whose corresponding table has the foreign key. In this case, this is `company_id` in the table `products`.

Many-to-many Relationships

Many-to-many relationships are relationships in which an arbitrary number of rows in a table reference an arbitrary number of rows in another table. This type of relationship between models can be established in two different ways.

Using a Join Table

The first approach requires a join table that's been named according to the convention, which is going to contain two foreign keys, one for each of the referenced tables. This table is not supposed to have an `id`, because the foreign key pair uniquely identifies each record.

This join table doesn't have a model that represents it, and its name should be created by joining the two table names in alphabetical order, separating them with an underscore. When this approach is taken, the verbose method `has_and_belongs_to_many` (aka, *habtm*) is used in both models to specify the many-to-many relationship.

If you take into consideration a `Post` and a `Category` model, it isn't unreasonable to state that "a post has and belongs to many categories" and of course, vice versa, "a category has and belongs to many posts." This translates directly into this code:

```
class Post < ActiveRecord::Base
  has_and_belongs_to_many :categories
end

class Category < ActiveRecord::Base
  has_and_belongs_to_many :posts
end
```

Note that in a real project, a model may have several types of relationships with other models. Because of this, it's common to see several association methods within the definition of a model.

Once again, the principle of Convention over Configuration makes our life easy. The join table will need to be called `categories_posts`, unless you specify otherwise, and will only contain a `category_id` and `post_id` foreign key column. No foreign keys for this relationship should be included in either the `categories` or `posts` tables.

The join table doesn't have a representing model, but you may still want to create it through migrations. The peculiarity of this table is that it has no id, so the code within the migration will need to look like this:

```
create_table :categories_posts, :id => false do |t|
    t.integer :category_id
    t.integer :post_id
end
```

You can add an optional `:null => false` parameter to each column when you want to prevent categories that don't reference any posts, and posts that don't reference any categories.

Specifying `:id => false` as the second argument of the `create_table` method is enough to prevent the table from having the default `id` primary key. Also note that join tables are notorious for quickly growing large in size; for this reason it's highly recommended that you add a couple of indexes to the migration, which will also help to maintain acceptable performances:

```
add_index(:categories_posts, [:category_id, :post_id], :unique => true)
add_index(:categories_posts, :post_id, :unique => false)
```

The first composite index speeds up searches on the foreign key pair and (usually) for looking up `category_id` as well. The second index speeds up lookups for `post_id`. You pass `:unique => true` to the first `add_index` call because each pair containing `category_id` and `post_id` is unique.

Using a Join Model

The second approach when it comes to building many-to-many relationships employs an intermediary model. This will act as your join table, and unlike the preceding approach, the corresponding table can contain other columns for fields you'd like to track.

Imagine wanting to create a many-to-many relationship between the model `Actor` and the model `Movie`. An actor "has" many movies, and a movie has many actors. Instead of proceeding as you did before with a join table, you'll introduce a third "join" model, `Appearance`. The corresponding table `appearances` will contain the foreign key columns to reference actors and movies, as well as other fields that you are interested in. For example, you may wish to store and retrieve the fictional character (for example, Austin Powers), the role (for example, Protagonist), and whether the actor/actress received an Oscar for their performance (a Boolean will do). The migration file for such a table might look like this:

```
create_table :appearances, :id => false do |t|
    t.integer :actor_id
    t.integer :movie_id
    t.string :character
```

```
    t.string :role
    t.boolean :oscar
end
```

The models will then be:

```
class Appearance < ActiveRecord::Base
  belongs_to :actor
  belongs_to :movie
end

class Actor < ActiveRecord::Base
  has_many :appearances
  has_many :movies, :through => :appearances
end

class Movie < ActiveRecord::Base
  has_many :appearances
  has_many :actors, :through => :appearances
end
```

appearances is the table with the foreign keys, so the belongs_to method is found in the corresponding Appearance model. Also, both actors and movies have many appearances, so you need to specify that point with has_many :appearances in both the Actor and Movie model.

The key point, and the new element here, is the :through parameter. That parameter allows you to specify a collection, a plural form of the join model (that is, Appearance) that enables the relationship to exist. In other words, you need to specify that "a movie has many actors through appearances" and that "an actor has many movies through appearances."

Auto-generated Methods

Declaring associations is important because it greatly simplifies the process of working with tables that are related. Instead of providing custom queries or requiring multiple steps to retrieve the information you need from a related table, associations allow you to work with linked objects by automatically adding new methods to the model class.

Every time you add has_one, belongs_to, has_many, or has_and_belongs_to_many to a model, you are also automatically adding a series of instance methods to that model, so that you can easily retrieve, create, update, and delete related/linked objects. You already saw this in the previous chapter, when you were able to retrieve a list of comments for a given article by simply invoking the method comments, but dig a little deeper to see how useful associations really are.

Consider the one-to-many example shown earlier. Imagine that you have found a certain product based on the id that the user specified:

```
product = Product.find(params[:id])
```

If associations didn't exist, and you wanted to retrieve the name of the company that produced a particular product, you'd have to specify your own SQL query or do something like this:

```
company_id = product.company_id
company_name = Company.find(company_id).name
```

Thanks to `belongs_to :company` within the model definition, the instance method `company` was added for you, so you can do this in one straightforward step:

```
company_name = product.company.name
```

Similarly, if you wanted to retrieve a list of products for a given company, you could use the `products` method added by `has_many :products`:

```
Company.find(551).products
```

> Because the instance methods added to the model are based on the name of the association, it's important that you don't create associations with the same name as any pre-existing `ActiveRecord::Base` instance methods. If you do, the generated methods will overwrite the existing ones, thus breaking your application. The official API documentation warns against names such as `attributes` and `connection`, but don't be afraid to double-check the existing instance methods in the documentation and read over this — somewhat in need of a cleanup — Wiki page: `http://wiki.rubyonrails.org/rails/pages/ReservedWords`.

Depending on the macro-like method employed, different instance methods are automatically defined for you. Let's check them out.

belongs_to

The `belongs_to` method adds a series of methods to deal with a single associated object. The names of the generated methods are determined by the symbol that's passed as the first parameter to the method. To keep things generic enough we'll use — just as the documentation does — the generic term `association` to identify the name of the associated object:

❑   `association(force_reload = false)`: Returns the associated object if it exists. If it doesn't, `nil` is returned. The result is cached, so pass `true` if you'd like to force the method to actually hit the database.

❑   `association=(associate)`: Assigns an associate object by assigning the primary key of `associate` to the foreign key (for example, `associate_id`) of the receiver.

❑   `association.nil?`: Answers the question, "Are there no associated objects?"

❑   `build_association(attributes = {})`: Returns a new associated object that's instantiated with the attributes that were passed to the method. The object is instantiated but hasn't been saved in the database yet.

❑   `create_association(attributes = {})`: Does the same thing as `build_association`, but it actually saves the associated object (assuming that the existing validations are passed).

Let's see what this means in practice. In the relationships described before, the following models employed the `belongs_to` method:

1.   `Account`: in a one-to-one relationship with `Employee` (that is, `belongs_to :employee`).

2.   `Product`: in a one-to-many relationship with `Company` (that is, `belongs_to :company`).

3. Appearance: join model in a many-to-many relationship between `Movie` and `Actor` (that is, `belongs_to :movie` and `belongs_to :actor`).

`Account` objects will have these new methods: `employee`, `employee=`, `employee.nil?`, `build_employee`, and `create_employee`.

Likewise, `Product` objects will have these methods added: `company`, `company=`, `company.nil?`, `build_company`, and `create_company`.

Not surprisingly, `Appearance` objects will be able to access the linked `Movie` and `Actor` objects with the following methods: `movie`, `movie=`, `movie.nil?`, `build_movie`, `create_movie`, and `actor`, `actor=`, `actor.nil?`, `build_actor`, and `create_actor`.

To illustrate the usage of these methods, let's consider `Product` and `Company` (assuming that you started with a database without any records in it):

```
>> Product.all
=> []
```

You can create a new product as usual through the `create` method:

```
>> product = Product.create(:name => "Time-travel machine", :copies => 3)
=> #<Product id: 1, name: "Time-travel machine", copies: 3, company_id: nil, cre
ated_at: "2008-08-25 22:41:33", updated_at: "2008-08-25 22:41:33">
```

Let's put the `company` and `company.nil?` methods we talked about to good use:

```
>> product.company
=> nil
>> product.company.nil?
=> true
```

`product` is just a variable that contains a reference to the `Product` object. It could be named arbitrarily.

The company is `nil` because the `company_id` attribute for `product` is `nil`. Had `company_id` stored the value of the primary key of an existing company, `product.company` would have returned that company object and `product.company.nil?` would have been `false`.

You can change this by linking the product to a company. In our hypothetical scenario, you don't have a company yet, so you'll have to create one. The easiest way to do that is to use the `create_company` method:

```
>> product.create_company(:name => "Back to the future Inc.")
=> #<Company id: 1, name: "Back to the future Inc.", address: nil, city: nil,
 country: nil, postal_code: nil, phone: nil, created_at: "2008-08-25 22:57:11",
 updated_at: "2008-08-25 22:57:11">
```

Not all the attributes for the company were assigned a value, because I only specified the name. This is okay, as long as those fields are nullable.

This has created a new company (with id 1) and automatically linked this object to the product object. You can verify this by running:

```
>> product.company
=> #<Company id: 1, name: "Back to the future Inc.", address: nil, city: nil,
country: nil, postal_code: nil, phone: nil, created_at: "2008-08-25 22:57:11",
updated_at: "2008-08-25 22:57:11">
```

Now you can conveniently access the company that a product belongs to. Because the `company` method returns a `Company` instance, you can access its attributes as well:

```
>> product.company.name
=> "Back to the future Inc."
```

The link between the product and the company object is created through `create_company`, by assigning the `id` of the company object to the `company_id` attribute of the product object. You can verify this by running:

```
>> product.company_id
=> 1
```

Notice that if you want to assign an existing company to a given product, you can easily do so through the `company=` writer method:

```
product.company = another_company
product.save
```

`product.save` is required to actually store this change in the database.

Assuming that `another_company` *is a* `Company` *object.*

---

product.build_company

You could have used `product.build_company` instead of `product.create_company`. It's important to understand the differences though.

Using `build_company` would have instantiated a new company object and linked it to the product object. However, the company object would not have been saved in the database yet.

Furthermore, it's true that `product.company` would return this new object, but the `id` of this new company would be `nil` because the object hasn't been saved yet. As a direct consequence of this, the product's attribute, `company_id`, would not have been changed either.

A `save` call is required to save the new company in the database. Invoking `product.company.save` would save the company object in the database, but fail to update the foreign key `company_id` in the product, with the newly generated company id. To save the company in the database and permanently assign it to the product, just like `create_company` automatically did for you, you'd have to use `product.save`. This would store the new company in the table and set its id as the value of the product's `company_id` attribute.

`belongs_to` accepts several options. `:class_name` is used to specify a class name that is different from the name of the association. For example, `belongs_to :perfomer, :class_name => "Actor"` will create a `performer` association that uses the `Actor` model.

By convention, ActiveRecord assumes that the foreign key will be the name of the association, plus `_id`, `:foreign_key` can be used to specify a foreign key with a different name.

> `:class_name` *and* `:foreign_key` *are often employed when defining self-referential relationships. These are relationships in which rows of a table can refer to rows of that same table through a foreign key column.*

`:conditions`, `:select`, `:include`, and `:readonly` are also available, and they are essentially the usual options you've seen before when describing finders.

> **When using** `:select` **to define an association, always include the primary key and the foreign keys or you'll run into trouble.**

If you check the online documentation you'll notice that there are three extra options `:polymorphic`, `:counter_cache`, and `:dependent`. The first is used for polymorphic associations, a concept that's explained later on in the chapter, and `:counter_cache` is used for counter cache columns, a subject you'll deal with in Chapter 11, when covering performances and optimization.

The third one, `:dependent`, allows you to specify a business rule when it comes to associated objects. If `:dependent` is not specified, when you drop an object you won't automatically drop the associated object. The `:dependent` option can accept `:destroy` as a value to specify that the associated object (for example, an `employee`) should be destroyed when you invoke `destroy` on the object (for example, an `account`). This key can also be set to `:delete`, in which case the associated object is deleted without invoking the `destroy` method (do you remember the difference between `delete` and `destroy`?).

For example, you can modify the definition of `Account` in the scenario indicated in the one-to-one relationship section to include `:dependent`:

```
class Account < ActiveRecord::Base
  belongs_to :employee, :dependent => :destroy
end
```

If you now destroy an `Account` object, the associated `Employee` object is also destroyed. The `:dependent` option allows you to enforce referential integrity directly from your application code.

It's important to be careful with this option. For example, if you drop a product, what will happen to the associated company? Should you drop it as well? The answer is simply, no, because a company may have many other products. You don't want to have "orphan" products whose parent company has just been destroyed. For this reason, never specify the `:dependent` option for a `belongs_to` when this is used in conjunction with `has_many` to establish a relationship.

For all intents and purposes, this option is only used when establishing a relationship where a `has_one` has been used in the associated class. In such a one-to-one relationship, like the employee/account example above, it's reasonable to assume that there are times when the `:dependent => :destroy` option may be required. When you destroy an order, you may want to destroy the associated invoice; when you destroy a user, you may want to destroy the associated profile, and so on.

has_one

`belongs_to` added several methods to operate on what can be considered the "parent" object. `has_one` sits at the opposite side of a one-to-one relationship, and as such adds a series of methods to operate on the "child" object.

> *The terms "parent object" and "child object" are loosely used to indicate an object that represents a row in the parent table and in the child table. In this context, parent/child has nothing to do with class inheritance.*

As a matter of fact, the methods you saw before still apply: `association`, `association=`, `association .nil?`, `build_association`, and `create_association` (again, replace association with the real name of the association at hand). Sticking to the `Employee` and `Account` example, an employee object automatically has the following methods added to it: `account`, `account=`, `account.nil?`, `build_account`, and `create_account`.

At this point, you may wonder why you need a different macro-like method to obtain the same methods in the end. The reality is that there are a few important differences between them, including but not limited to, the many other parameter options available for `has_one`.

Unlike `belongs_to`, with `has_one`, assigning an associated object automatically saves that object and the object that is being replaced (if it exists), unless the parent/receiver object is a new record (verifiable through `new_record?`). For example, consider the following:

```
employee.account = an_unsaved_account
```

Unless `employee` is a new record, this will save the newly created object `an_unsaved_account`, assigning the `id` of `employee` to the attribute `employee_id` of `an_unsaved_account`. It will also save the existing `employee.account` unless it was `nil`, so that its `employee_id` can be updated to `nil`, therefore breaking the link with the `employee` object and making it an "orphan."

> *As a reminder, when an attribute is assigned a* `nil` *value, and then the record is saved, the value that's actually stored in the row is* `NULL`.

Among the additional options are `:order` to specify the order in which the associated object will be picked through an SQL fragment string; `:as` for polymorphic associations, and `:through`, `:source`, and `:source_type` to work with a join model.

> *For details and examples of the many options available, always check the up-to-date online documentation. For these methods, check the documentation for module* `ActiveRecord::Associations::Cl assMethods`.

The `:dependent` option for `has_one` indicates to ActiveRecord what it's supposed to do when you destroy a parent object. `:destroy` or `true` destroys the corresponding row in the child table, whereas `:nullify` turns it into an orphan by assigning `NULL` to the foreign key, and `:false` or `nil` tells ActiveRecord not to update the child object or row.

has_many and habtm

The `has_many` and `has_and_belongs_to_many` methods both add a series of methods that are used to operate on a collection of associated objects. Using the generic name `collection`, the methods automatically added to the model instances are:

- ❏ `collection(force_reload = false)`: Returns an array of all the associated objects or an empty array if none are found. Pass `true` to bypass caching and force the method to query the database.

- ❏ `collection<<(object, ...)`: Adds one or more objects to the collection, assigning their foreign key to the primary key of the parent object. Unless the parent is a new record, adding objects to a collection automatically saves them in the database.

- ❏ `collection.delete(object, ...)`: Removes one or more objects from the collection by assigning their foreign key to NULL. In a one-to-many relationship (where an object's model defines a `belongs_to`, referring to the parent's model), the objects will also be destroyed if so indicated through a `:dependent` option. However, this is not the case if the association was created with a `:through` option.

- ❏ `collection=objects`: Removes the existing objects and adds any new ones that are being assigned to the collection.

- ❏ `collection_singular_ids`: Returns an array of ids for the associated objects in the collection.

- ❏ `collection_singular_ids=ids`: Similar to `collection=`, it replaces the collection by identifying the new objects that are to be assigned through their ids.

- ❏ `collection.clear`: By default this method removes all the objects from the collection by assigning the value NULL to their foreign key. When a `:dependent => :destroy` has been specified though, it destroys the records. Likewise, `:dependent => :delete_all` deletes them directly from the database without invoking `destroy`.

- ❏ `collection.empty?`: Returns true if there are no associated objects, and false if at least one object belongs to the collection.

- ❏ `collection.size`: Returns the number of associated objects.

- ❏ `collection.find(*args)`: Finds an associated object by following the same rules of the `ActiveRecord::Base.find` method.

- ❏ `collection.build(attributes = {}, ...)`: Returns one or more new objects of the collection type, instantiated with the attributes passed to the method. Each object is linked to the parent but it has yet to be saved.

- ❏ `collection.create(attributes = {})`: Similar to `build`, but it actually saves the objects.

ActiveRecord's development, which spanned several years, implied that there were, and still are, other similar methods available, each with slight differences from the ones mentioned here. For example, there is size, but also length and count. There is clear, but also delete_all and destroy_all. Knowing the handful of methods described here should be more than enough to master most situations. The official documentation is a great place to check which methods are available, as well as the subtle differences between them.

> *The generated method here (generically called* `collection`*) is an array, so other regular Ruby methods will be available to work with it as well.*

Taking into consideration the one-to-many relationship between the `Company` and `Product` models, `has_many` adds all the methods mentioned previously to `Company` objects: `products`, `products<<`, `products.delete`, `products=`, `products_singular_ids`, `products_singular_ids=`, `products.empty?`, `products.size`, `products.find`, `products.build`, and `products.create`.

In the many-to-many example, where the `:through` option has been employed, both `Movie` and `Actor` objects have methods that access each other's collections, as well as the `appearances`' rows. So you may invoke `a_movie.actors`, `an_actor.movies`, or even `a_movie.appearances` and `an_actor.appearances`.

Many options are available for the `has_many` method: `:class_name`, `:conditions`, `:order`, `:foreign_key`, `:include`, `:group`, `:limit`, `:offset`, `:select`, `:as`, `:through`, `:source`, `:source_type`, `:uniq` (to omit duplicates), `:readonly`, `:dependent`, `:finder_sql` (to specify a full SQL statement), `:counter_sql` (to specify a full SQL statement to retrieve the size of the collection), and `:extend`.

`:dependent` admits `:destroy`, which destroys all the associated objects by calling their `destroy` method; `:delete_all`, which deletes all the rows from the table without calling the `destroy` method; and `:nullify`, which sets the foreign key to `NULL` for all the associated objects without calling their `save` callbacks. You'll dig deeper into the issue of callbacks later on in this chapter.

> **As an exercise, feel free to go ahead and modify the `Article` model in the blog application you defined in Chapters 5 and 6, so that when an article is destroyed, all of its comments are deleted (for example, use `:dependent => :delete_all`).**

`:extend` is used to specify a named model that extends the proxy. The whole concept is covered in the next section.

The method `has_and_belongs_to_many` doesn't have a `:dependent` option, and as such, `collection.clear` doesn't destroy any objects from the join table. Options are also available that are specific to habtm: `:join_table` (to specify a custom table name), `:association_foreign_key`, `:delete_sql`, and `:insert_sql`. Please check the online documentation for details and examples.

Association Extensions

When you define an association, you can pass a block to it, in which it's possible to define methods that are only available from the association.

For example, you can define the method `best_sellers` for the `products` association collection:

```ruby
class Company < ActiveRecord::Base
  has_many :products do
    def best_sellers(limit)
      find(:all, :limit => limit, :order => "sales DESC")
    end
  end
end
```

Eager Loading Associations

Earlier in the chapter I mentioned how it's dangerous to use conditions in conjunction with a hierarchy of :include due to the resulting complex (and slow) SQL. I mentioned that "it is common to eager load an association that has conditions defined on it." That sentence was rather cryptic at the time, but now that you have gained knowledge of associations and their options, I can provide you with an example (from the official documentation).

Rather than doing this:

```
Post.find(:all, :include => [ :author, :comments ],
:conditions =>
['comments.approved = ?', true])
```

You can define an association with a condition:

```
class Post < ActiveRecord::Base
  has_many :approved_comments, :class_name => 'Comment',
:conditions =>
  ['approved = ?', true]
end
```

And then eager load the association, which contains only your approved comments, with :include:

```
Post.find(:all, :include => :approved_comments)
```

You can then use it as a regular method of the collection:

```
Company.find(5).products.best_sellers(10)
```

Associations can also be extended by adding all the methods you want to define into a module, and then using the :extend option to add them to the association as class methods:

```
class Company < ActiveRecord::Base
  has_many :products, :extend => SalesFinder
end
```

Assign an array of modules to :extend *, if you need to include the methods from several modules.*

ActiveRecord Validations

Validations are a feature that enables you to specify certain rules before a record is created or updated in the database. Several high-level helpers are provided for the most common tasks, but it's good to know the three generic validation methods that allow you to perform validations based on a method that you've defined. These are validate, validate_on_create, and validate_on_update.

When you define a validation rule with validate, ActiveRecord applies that rule to determine whether or not the object should be saved. If the object fails the validation, it's not saved and an error message is added to it so that, in the context of Rails, the view can display it to the user again, who can correct the error by changing the data in the form and trying to resubmit it.

validate_on_create is similar to validate, but it's triggered only when a new record is being created, not when this is being updated. Vice versa, validate_on_update validates attempts to update a record, but not the creation of new ones. The method valid? can also be used to trigger all the existing validations defined for a model object.

Because the method save is used for both the creation and the update of a record, how does ActiveRecord know which of the two operations it needs to perform? The answer is that it uses the new_record? method, which returns true if it's a new record (wherein an INSERT is performed), or false, in which case an UPDATE statement is issued,

> *You'll also notice that when you create a new record, it doesn't have an id, because the primary key is auto-generated. If it's an existing record, its id will not be nil.*

When using any of these three generic validation methods, error messages for a specific attribute are added with the method errors.add(:column_name, message), whereas errors for the whole object are added through errors.add_to_base(message). The error for a specific attribute can be retrieved through the method errors.on(:attribute_name) (and its alias errors[:attribute_name]). Clearing the error messages for an object can be accomplished by using the method errors.clear.

Let's see a practical example of how you can use these methods to define validation rules:

```ruby
class Book < ActiveRecord::Base
  validate :valid_page_count?
  validate_on_creation :unique_book?

  private

  def valid_page_count?
    unless pages && pages > 48
      errors.add(:pages, "is missing or less than 49")
    end
  end

  def unique_book?
    if Book.find_by_isbn(isbn)
      errors.add(:isbn, "exists already")
    end
  end
end
```

By passing the symbol :valid_page_count? to validate, you instructed ActiveRecord to execute the private method valid_page_count? before allowing any insert or update. The method adds an error message for the attribute pages, if it has been assigned a value that's less than 49 (or if no value was assigned).

Likewise, by passing :unique_book? to validate_on_creation, the private method unique_book? is invoked upon an attempt to create a record for a new book. This method tries to find the book through its ISBN among the existing ones and, if it can, it adds an error for the attribute that indicates that the book already exists in the database.

> *These two methods are private because you most likely don't want Book objects to be able to invoke them directly. These methods can also be used in their block form.*

If `Book` didn't have an `isbn` attribute, the finder probably should have searched for a book with the same title, author, and publisher. In such instances, where multiple attributes are involved, `errors.add_to_base("The book exists already")` would be used to add an error for the whole object.

Validation Helpers

While building the basic blog application you didn't use `validate` (or its variants), but rather high-level helpers such as `validate_presence_of` and `validates_uniqueness_of`. The creators of ActiveRecord tried to simplify our lives by providing a series of helpers for common validation purposes as follows:

❑ `validates_acceptance_of`: Handy when trying to validate the acceptance of an agreement.

❑ `validates_associated`: Validates any kind of associated object.

❑ `validates_confirmation_of`: Used to validate a confirmation for a field like email address or password.

❑ `validates_each`: Used to validate multiple attributes against a block.

❑ `validates_exclusion_of`: Validates that the value of the specified attribute is not within an enumerable object provided.

❑ `validates_format_of`: Validates the value of the specified attribute against a provided regular expression.

❑ `validates_inclusion_of`: Validates that the value of the specified attribute is an element of an enumerable object provided. It's the opposite of `validates_exclusion_of`.

❑ `validates_length_of`: Validates the length of a specified attribute value against provided restrictions. It has an alias called `validates_size_of`.

❑ `validates_numericality_of`: Validates whether a specified attribute value is numeric.

❑ `validates_presence_of`: Validates that the specified attribute value exists by employing the method `blank?`. Because of this, the object won't pass the validation if the attribute value is `nil` or, for example, an empty string.

❑ `validates_uniqueness_of`: Validates whether the value of the specified attribute is unique or whether it already exists in the table. For example, to verify that a book is unique (as you did before), you can just use `validates_uniqueness_of :isbn`. An index is often added to the column represented by the specified attribute, as means of further guaranteeing uniqueness, even when dealing with concurrent transactions.

> **Do not use** `validates_presence_of` **to validate Booleans because** `false.blank?` **evaluates to** `true`. **Use** `validates_inclusion_of :attribute_name, :in => [false, true]` **instead.**

All of them have a default message (that used to be defined in `ActiveRecord::Errors.default_error_messages`), which can be overwritten with the `:message` option. Conversely, you can have conditional validations by using the options `:if` or `:unless`, which accept a symbol (for a method that defines the condition), a string (evaluated by `eval`), or a `Proc` object.

> `ActiveRecord::Errors.default_error_messages` **has been deprecated in Rails 2.2.2, and replaced by** `I18n.translate 'activerecord.errors.messages'`.

All three of them should return `true` or `false`, and both the method and the `Proc` object receive the current model instance as an argument:

```
class Book < ActiveRecord::Base
  validates_presence_of :title, :author, :publisher
  validates_uniqueness_of :isbn, :message => "must be unique"
  validates_length_of :pages, :in => 49..3000, :allow_nil => false
  validates_presence_of :sales, :if => Proc.new { |book| book.published == true })
end
```

`validate` had the `validate_on_creation` and `validate_on_update` variants. These additional versions are not necessary for the preceding helper methods, because the `:on` option is used instead. This accepts the values `:save`, `:create`, and `:update`:

```
validates_format_of :email, :with => /\A([^@\s]+)@((?:[-a-z0-9]+\.)+[a-z]{2,})
\Z/i, :on => :create
```

Please consult the online documentation for these methods — defined in the module `ActiveRecord::Validations::ClassMethods` — to see examples and the exact options available for each.

When none of the validation helpers is sufficient for the rule that you want to enforce, you'll always able to fall back on `validate`, `validate_on_creation`, and `validate_on_update`.

Advanced ActiveRecord

Having covered most of what makes ActiveRecord an excellent ORM, you can move onto the next level, with more advanced topics; the knowledge of which will certainly come in handy more than a few times.

Single Table Inheritance

Relational databases work under the assumption that tables can be related through associations, as you have seen so far in this chapter. Object-oriented programming tends to use, where appropriate, inheritance, a concept that is foreign to the world of RDBMS. To bridge this gap, ActiveRecord allows you to easily implement single table inheritance.

Imagine that you want to represent photos, videos, and songs in your application. The traditional approach would be to use three tables (and three corresponding models):

```
create_table :songs do |t|
  t.string :name
  t.string :file_path
  t.integer :user_id
end
```

```
create_table :videos do |t|
  t.string :name
  t.string :file_path
  t.integer :user_id
end

create_table :photos do |t|
  t.string :name
  t.string :file_path
  t.integer :user_id
end
```

The problem with this approach is that it forces you to use three structurally identical tables to represent what are essentially just media files. Single table inheritance allows you to use a single common table for all three of them, whose corresponding model is the superclass of the three (Song, Video, and Photo) models.

The single table will be media_files:

```
create_table :media_files do |t|
  t.string :name
  t.string :file_path
  t.string :type
  t.integer :user_id
end
```

t.references *or* t.belongs_to *instead of* t.integer *would work as well.*

Notice that this has a special string column called type. This is used by ActiveRecord to distinguish a media file that happens to be a video from one that happens to be a photo or a song.

At this point, you'll have one parent model corresponding to that table and three subclasses:

```
class MediaFiles < ActiveRecord::Base
  belongs_to :user
end
```

```
class Song < MediaFiles
  # Some Song specific methods
end
```

```
class Video < MediaFiles
  # Some Video specific methods
end
```

```
class Photo < MediaFiles
  # Some Photo specific methods
end
```

This is very well organized from an object-oriented perspective and it uses a single table for all our media files. If you want to determine the class of a retrieved record, you can do so through the class method:

```
media_file = MediaFiles.find_by_name("Darkest Dreaming")
media_file.class # Song
```

Three important caveats apply:

1. Don't try to access the `type` attribute directly, because `type` is also the name of a deprecated Ruby method. The far safer choice is to check the class through the `class` method and to automatically assign `type` a value by using a subclass of the main model (for example, `Photo.create`). If you really have to change the underlying value for an already defined object, use the hash notation. For example: `media_file[:type] = Video`.

2. The superclass model can contain attributes that are defined only for certain subclasses. For instance, you could add a column called `duration` to the table `media_files`, which keeps track of the length of a song or a video. This attribute wouldn't apply to `Photo` though, so it would be important that such a column was defined as nullable.

3. Unless you are using a table for single table inheritance, never add a column called `type` to it, because this will mislead ActiveRecord and result in all sorts of problems.

Polymorphic Associations

Polymorphic associations are a second option to simplify and improve the code quality when working with multiple models. They are very straightforward but tend to confuse newcomers. The prerequisite to avoid confusion is to understand the reason why you need them. Imagine that you have a one-to-many relationship between `Post` and `Comment`; the `comments` table will be akin to the following:

```
create_table :comments do |t|
  t.text :body
  t.string :author
  t.references :post_id
end
```

```
add_index :comments, :post_id
```

Notice that you need a foreign key to reference `posts`, and ideally, an index for it. Now, imagine that as you develop the application, you realize that you'd like to have the ability to add comments about companies, milestones, projects, and tasks. The `comments` table would have to include foreign keys for these as well:

```
create_table :comments do |t|
  t.text :body
  t.string :author
  t.references :post_id
  t.references :company_id
  t.references :milestone_id
  t.references :project_id
  t.references :task_id
end
```

```
add_index :comments, :post_id
add_index :comments, :company_id
add_index :comments, :milestone_id
add_index :comments, :project_id
add_index :comments, :task_id
```

Pretty ugly isn't it? What's worse is that in the database, you'll have records that look like the ones shown in the following table (which presents values in the comments table without polymorphic associations):

id	body	author	post_id	company_id	milestone_id	project_id	task_id
1	"…"	"Stan"	NULL	13	NULL	NULL	NULL
2	"…"	"Kyle"	27	NULL	NULL	NULL	NULL
3	"…"	"Eric"	NULL	NULL	NULL	3	NULL
4	"…"	"Kenny"	NULL	NULL	NULL	NULL	42
5	"…"	"Randy"	NULL	NULL	5	NULL	NULL
6	"…"	"Chef"	27	NULL	NULL	NULL	NULL

This results in a table with many foreign keys, yet only one of them is actually used per record. When Kyle and Chef commented on a post, none of the foreign keys except for `post_id` were used to store integer values. When Stan commented on the company with `id` 13, the foreign keys `post_id`, `milestone_id`, `project_id`, and `task_id` were NULL. And so on for the remaining records.

The model `Comment` would have to be the following:

```
class Comment < ActiveRecord::Base
  belongs_to :post
  belongs_to :company
  belongs_to :milestone
  belongs_to :project
  belongs_to :task
end
```

Not really nice either!

Polymorphic associations allow you to DRY both the table definition and the resulting model by defining a common foreign key of choice, and a common type column that's named accordingly. The `comments` table would become:

```
create_table :comments do |t|
  t.text :body
  t.string :author
  t.integer :commentable_id
  t.integer :commentable_type
end

add_index :comments, [:commentable_id, :commentable_type]
```

> **Always add an index for polymorphic tables. They tend to get large rather quickly and their performance can be severely impacted if indexes have not been defined.**

Now the Comment model simply becomes:

```
class Comment < ActiveRecord::Base
  belongs_to :commentable, :polymorphic => true
end
```

You define a commentable association and specify that it's a polymorphic one through the :polymorphic option, so that ActiveRecord knows how to automatically handle commentable_id and commentable_type.

This will enable you to access the associated object through the method commentable. For example:

```
c = Comment.first
c.author                  # "Kenny"
c.commentable.class.to_s  # "Task"
c.commentable.name        # "Great job with the migrations, Sean!"
```

The other five models will be able to access the comments for each of their objects, as long as they include has_many :comments, :as => commentable:

```
class Post < ActiveRecord::Base
  # ... some other associations ...
  has_many :comments, :as => commentable
end

class Company < ActiveRecord::Base
  # ... some other associations ...
  has_many :comments, :as => commentable
end

class Milestone < ActiveRecord::Base
  # ... some other associations ...
  has_many :comments, :as => commentable
end

class Project < ActiveRecord::Base
  # ... some other associations ...
  has_many :comments, :as => commentable
end

class Task < ActiveRecord::Base
  # ... some other associations ...
  has_many :comments, :as => commentable
end
```

That :as => commentable *is required to specify a polymorphic interface.*

For example:

```
Company.find_by_name("IBM").comments.each do |c|
  puts "Comment by #{c.author}: #{c.body}"
end
```

Behind the scenes, the second `SELECT` query (the one that retrieves the comments) issued ends with `WHERE (comments.commentable_id = 22 AND comments.commentable_type = 'Company')`, assuming that 22 is the id of the company IBM.

The table `comments` will also look slimmer and more compact as shown in the following table:

id	body	author	commentable_id	commentable_type
1	"..."	"Stan"	13	"Company"
2	"..."	"Kyle"	27	"Post"
3	"..."	"Eric"	3	"Project"
4	"..."	"Kenny"	42	"Task"
5	"..."	"Randy"	5	"Milestone"
6	"..."	"Chef"	27	"Post"

ActiveRecord automatically converts between the class and the corresponding string that's actually stored in the database.

Serializing

Generally speaking, it's possible to instruct ActiveRecord to store a Ruby object in a given column. The conversions from, and to, the database data type will be handled automatically then. To achieve this, you simply need to use the `serialize :attribute_name` method in the model definition. This is handier and safer than performing manual serialization, by converting an object into YAML format before an `INSERT` (with the `to_yaml` method), and then converting it back manually when you need to retrieve the object (for example, with `YAML::load`).

Notice that `commentable` is an arbitrarily chosen word and could be replaced with any non-reserved word of your choice. You just have to be consistent in using it for the foreign key, for the `*_type` column, and in the model definitions.

The example I've used here lends itself to explain why polymorphic associations are a very useful feature. That said, to implement comments the polymorphic way in your projects, you can probably save some time and code by employing the `acts_as_commentable` plugin instead.

Callbacks

Though ActiveRecord is happy to handle the life cycle of objects on its own, it also provides you with a series of special methods, called callbacks, that allow you to intervene and decide that certain actions should be taken before or after an object is created, updated, destroyed, and so on.

Callback methods for validations are:

- ❏ before_validation
- ❏ before_validation_on_create
- ❏ before_validation_on_update
- ❏ after_validation
- ❏ after_validation_on_update
- ❏ after_validation_on_create

Their names are quite self-explanatory. The before_* callbacks are triggered before a validation, and the after_* callbacks are used to execute code afterwards. The *_on_update and *_on_create callbacks are only triggered by validations for update and create operations, respectively. before_validation and after_validation apply to both updates and creations.

Callbacks specific to the creation of an object are:

- ❏ before_create
- ❏ after_create

Likewise, callbacks triggered by the update of a record only are:

- ❏ before_update
- ❏ after_update

The following two callbacks are executed for both updates and inserts:

- ❏ before_save
- ❏ after_save

Callbacks specific to destroy are:

- ❏ before_destroy
- ❏ after_destroy

There are then two after_* callbacks, without a before version:

- ❏ after_find
- ❏ after_initialize

Note that for each call to save, create, or destroy, there is an ordered chain of callbacks that allows you to intervene with the execution of your custom code in the exact spot that you desire. For example, for the creation of a new record the callback order is as follows:

1. before_validation
2. before_validation_on_create

3. `after_validation`

4. `after_validation_on_create`

5. `before_save`

6. `before_create`

7. `after_create`

8. `after_save`

Between 2 and 3, the validation occurs, and between 6 and 7, the actual `INSERT` is issued.

To execute code during a callback, you'll need to use any of these methods in the model definition. Three options are available.

You can define the callback method within the model:

```
class User < ActiveRecord::Base
  # ...

  def before_save
    # Some code to encrypt the password
    # ...
  end
end
```

Or, in a nicer way, you can pass a symbol representing the handler method:

```
class User < ActiveRecord::Base
  # ...
  before_save :encrypt_password

  private

  def encrypt_password
    # Some code to encrypt the password
    # ...
  end
end
```

The method `encrypt_password` will be always executed before a user is created or updated.

You could even create a class that defines several callback methods so that they can be shared among several models. To do so, you'll just need to pass an object to the callback method within the model required (for example, `before_save MyClass.new`, but first `require "myclass"` in the model's file).

The third way to define code that's to be executed during a callback is to use a block:

```
class User < ActiveRecord::Base
  # ...
  before_save do |user|
    # Some code to encrypt the password
```

```
        # user is the instance that will be saved
    end
  end
```

Association Callbacks

Regular callbacks allow you to hook into the life cycle of an ActiveRecord object, but what about an association collection? It turns out that ActiveRecord allows you to execute custom code before and after an object is added or removed from an association collection. The callback options are :before_add, :after_add, :before_remove, and :after_remove. For example:

```
class Company < ActiveRecord::Base
  has_many :employees, :after_add => :enable_badge, :after_remove => :disable_badge

  def enable_badge(employee)
    # ...
  end

  def disable_badge(employee)
    # ...
  end
end
```

> **Just as with regular callbacks, if an exception is raised during the execution of a** :before_add **callback, the object will not be added to the collection. Likewise, if an exception is raised during the execution of the handler for the** :before_remove **callback, the object will not be removed from the collection.**

Observers

As previously mentioned, it's possible to share the callbacks that are defined within a class with several models. To do this you first define a class with a few callbacks:

```
class MyCallbackObject

  def initialize(list_of_attributes)
    # ... initialize here...
  end
  def before_save
    # ... your logic here ...
  end

  def after_save
    # ... your logic here ...
  end
end
```

And then, include them in each model that requires those callbacks:

```
class MyModel < ActiveRecord::Base
```

```
  cb = MyCallbackObject.new([:attr1, :attr2, :attr3])

  before_save cb
  after_save cb
end
```

Obviously replace all the generic names with the ones that apply. For example, instead of `attr1`, *use the name of the real attribute that is required by the callback object. Check the online documentation for* `ActiveRecord::Callbacks` *for more examples and details.*

> **At the time of this writing, when you define an** `after_find` **or** `after_initialize` **within a callback object, these will need to appear in the model as empty methods as well, because otherwise ActiveRecord won't execute them.**

The main downside of using callback objects is that they clutter the model, often with a series of functionalities, like logging, which are not really the model's responsibility. That clutter is then repeated over and over for each model that requires the callbacks that have been defined by the callback object.

The Single Responsibility Principle has led ActiveRecord's developers to include a powerful and elegant feature that solves this problem: observers. `Observer` classes are used to access the model's life cycle in a trigger-like fashion without altering the code of the model that's being observed.

Observers are subclasses of `ActiveRecord::Observer` are by convention named after the class they observe, to which the `Observer` token is appended:

```
class UserObserver < ActiveRecord::Observer
  def after_save(user)
    user.logger.info("User created: #{user.inspect}")
  end
end
```

Conventionally, observers are stored in `app\models` *just like models or callback objects.*

The problem with this convention is that observers are often used to "observe" many models, so it's usually necessary to overwrite the convention through the `observe` method:

```
class Auditor < ActiveRecord::Observer
  observe User, Account

  def after_save(model)
    model.logger.info("#{model.class} created: #{model.inspect}")
  end
end
```

Without having to touch the code of `User` or `Account`, the preceding code will log the creation of both users and accounts, as long as you enable the observer in your Rails application. But first you'll need to add the following line in your `config\environment.rb` file, where a commented, similar line already exists:

```
config.active_record.observers = :auditor
```

If you've created more than one observer, you can assign a comma-separated list of symbols to `observers`.

If, on the other hand, you are not using Rails, you can load observers through their `instance` *method:* `ModelObserver.instance`.

Testing Models

Testing is an integral part of developing in Rails. The subject matter is quite large and this book isn't even going to begin to do it enough justice. Nevertheless, it would do you a great disservice to close a chapter on ActiveRecord without at least scratching the bare surface of unit testing.

It is called unit testing, because individual units of code (for example, models) are tested to verify that they work correctly.

The Rails community embraces Test-Driven Development (TDD) and many developers even go as far as to write tests first, so that they act as a well-defined spec, and only then write code to pass those tests (a practice commonly known as Test-First Development).

Lately many developers have been embracing BDD (Behavior-Driven Development), often by employing the excellent RSpec. I recommend that, with the help of Google, you check out this alternative testing framework.

Many people dislike testing because they tend to prefer to spend their time writing "real code." But the reality is that, aside from being a staple of the XP methodology, testing improves the quality of your application. Testing cannot guarantee a complete lack of bugs in your Web application, but with good testing coverage you can ensure that many basic cases/functionalities are properly handled.

More importantly, it gives you confidence when it comes time to make changes and develop the application further, without having to worry that a change may break a related piece of code somewhere else in the code repository. With a good set of tests, you'll be able to spot "what broke what," in many cases.

Other secondary, positive side-effects include the fact that tests provide a form of documentation for how your application is supposed to work; they can force programmers to think more thoroughly about the code they are about to write, and they can also be a warning sign for problematic code. In fact, it's been my experience that code that is hard to test is often code that could be refactored and better thought through.

Testing has a bit of a learning curve to it, but the payoff far outweighs the initial time investment. And if you are used to the NUnit framework with .NET, it will all be rather familiar, while at the same time you'll be able to appreciate how much nicer it is to work with Ruby's unit testing library. In fact, ActiveRecord essentially relies on Ruby's `Test::Unit` framework, which ships as part of the Standard Library.

You are going to operate on the sample blog application again.

The first thing that you'll do is run the unit tests. From the main folder of the project, run the following task:

```
rake test:units
```

The output of the command should be similar to the following:

```
(in C:/projects/blog)
c:/ruby/bin/ruby -Ilib;test "c:/ruby/lib/ruby/gems/1.8/gems/rake-0.8.3/lib/rake/
rake_test_loader.rb" "test/unit/article_test.rb" "test/unit/comment_test.rb"
Loaded suite c:/ruby/lib/ruby/gems/1.8/gems/rake-0.8.3/lib/rake/rake_test_loader
Started
..
Finished in 0.593 seconds.

2 tests, 2 assertions, 0 failures, 0 errors
```

For each test that passes, a dot is displayed beneath the word `Started`. At the end of the report, a line summarizes the outcome after you've run the test suite. In this case, it informs you that there were two tests, two assertions, and no failures or errors.

Tests are public methods (defined in a test case) that contain one or more assertions, whereas assertions are comparisons between an expected value and the value of an expression. These either pass or fail, depending on whether the assertion is actually true or false during the execution of the test suite. If a test causes an unrescued exception, this outcome is reported as an error, as opposed to a failure.

The aim is to have zero failures and errors. When all the tests have passed successfully, you can go ahead and change the application or add a new feature (and add new tests for it). If upon running the tests again the application fails this time around, you'll know for sure that your change or new feature was problematic. When there are failed assertions, the value expected by the assertion and the actual value are both shown. If there are errors, the error message and stacktrace are displayed in the output as well.

Let's take a look at the two tests and assertions that you've just passed, by opening the files `article_test.rb` and `comment_test.rb` in the project's `test\unit` directory:

```
# test\unit\article_test.rb
require 'test_helper'

class ArticleTest < ActiveSupport::TestCase
  # Replace this with your real tests.
  test "the truth" do
    assert true
  end
end# test\unit\comment_test.rb
require 'test_helper'

class CommentTest < ActiveSupport::TestCase
  # Replace this with your real tests.
  test "the truth" do
    assert true
  end
end
```

The test case is a subclass of `ActiveSupport::TestCase` and the method `test` is passed a string literal that acts as a label for the test. With the method's block there is just a placeholder with a single assertion: `assert true`. `assert` is a method that defines an assertion that always passes except when the argument is `false`, `nil`, or raises an error. If you change `article_test.rb` so that the test body is `assert false` and run the tests again, you would obtain one failure, an F instead of a dot, and the message `<false> is not true`. Changing it to `assert 3/0` would give you one error, an E instead of a dot, and the error message `ZeroDivisionError: divided by 0` (as well as the stacktrace).

> `assert false` *is equivalent to the method* `flunk`, *which always fails.*

This is the general structure of a test case file in a Rails setting:

```ruby
require 'test_helper'

class NameTest < ActiveSupport::TestCase
  fixtures :models

  # Run before each test method
  def setup
    # ...
  end

  test "a functionality" do
    # assertions
    # ...
  end

  # Run after each test method
  def teardown
    # ...
  end
end
```

The code within the optional method `setup` will be executed before each test method, whereas `teardown` is invoked after each test. Because you are testing models, and doing assertions is all about comparing the evaluated expressions against known values, you'll need a way to store all the well-known records that are not subject to change in the test database. The perfect answer to this can be found in fixtures, which are loaded through the `fixtures` method.

If you take a look at the `test\fixtures` directory within the project, you'll notice that two fixture files were generated by the `scaffold` generator: `articles.yml` and `comments.yml`. These are YAML files that can contain several records that you'd like to load into the database before running the tests. These records have a name, and besides being available to you when reading the test database, they can also be accessed through a hash. This is important when you want to verify the correctness of the data obtained through a model.

This is what `articles.yml` looks like (as you can see it respects the table structure of `articles`):

```yaml
# Read about fixtures at http://ar.rubyonrails.org/classes/Fixtures.html


one:
  title: MyString
  body: MyText
  published: false
  published_at: 2008-07-10 22:46:42
```

```
two:
  title: MyString
  body: MyText
  published: false
  published_at: 2008-07-10 22:46:42
```

Notice that the indentation is arbitrary, as long as it's consistent. It's still good idea to indent by two spaces as per usual in Ruby.

The two records, `one` and `two`, are statically defined, but YAML fixtures allow you to embed ERb code with the usual `<% %>` and `<%= %>` pairs. Therefore, it's possible to dynamically define more records or define their values programmatically. CSV fixtures are also permitted, in which case the record names are auto-generated. However, YAML is the default and generally favored format.

Let's change the `articles` fixtures into something less repetitive and specify the `id` while you're at it (because this would be random otherwise):

```
hello:
  id: 1
  title: Hello, World!
  body: puts "Hello, world!"
  published: true
  published_at: 2008-09-08 05:30:22

fall:
  id: 2
  title: Fall is coming
  body: Some interesting text
  published: false
  published_at: 2008-09-08 07:48:12
```

Now load these fixtures by adding `fixtures :article` to the `ArticleTest` test case.

As you can imagine, the single test that you have right now is pretty useless, so you'll get rid of it and instead write a couple of tests that are more meaningful, using a few of the many assertion methods available.

Consult the Ruby documentation for `Test::Unit` for a list of available assertions. A few common ones are `assert`, `assert_nil`, `assert_equal`, `assert_raise`, and `assert_not_raised`. All the assertion methods accept an optional argument to specify a custom message.

To get started you can test that the validations are working as follows:

```
test "article validations" do
  no_title_or_body = Article.new(:published => true, :published_at => Time.now)

  no_title = Article.find(1)
  no_title.title = nil

  duplicate_body = Article.find(2)
  duplicate_body.body = articles(:hello).body
```

```
      assert_equal false, no_title_or_body.save

      assert_raise ActiveRecord::RecordInvalid do
        no_title.save!
      end

      assert_raise ActiveRecord::RecordInvalid do
        duplicate_body.save!
      end
    end
```

Notice how you can access the named records defined in the fixtures file by passing their symbol to the name of the fixtures (for example, `articles(:hello)`*).*

The `Article` model defines validations that prevent objects from being saved when they're missing a body or title, or if the body already exists. The test instantiates a record without a body and title, so it's fair to expect that invoking `save` will lead to `false` being returned. You assert this with:

```
      assert_equal false, no_title_or_body.save
```

It then retrieves an existing record and assigns `nil` to its title. Again, this is in direct violation of the validation you defined in the model so invoking `save!` should lead to an `ActiveRecord::RecordInvalid` error being raised. You assert this with `assert_raise`, which accepts the error class and a block that is supposed to raise that error type:

```
      assert_raise ActiveRecord::RecordInvalid do
        no_title.save!
      end
```

Note that `save` *would not raise any errors, but rather quietly return* `false`*.*

Finally, the test retrieves another record and assigns the value of the first record to its body attribute. Because you can't have two records with the same body, you'll assert that you expect the call to `save!` to raise an `ActiveRecord::RecordInvalid` error:

```
      assert_raise ActiveRecord::RecordInvalid do
        duplicate_body.save!
      end
```

`ActiveRecordError` *is the generic exception class. All the error classes defined by ActiveRecord inherit from it, which in turn inherits from Ruby's* `StandardError`*.*

Now you can add a test for the `published` and `unpublished` named scopes:

```
    test "article status" do
      published_article = Article.find_by_published(true)
      unpublished_article = Article.find_by_published(false)
      scheduled_article = Article.create(:title => "A post in the future",
                                         :body => "... some text ...",
                                         :published => true,
                                         :published_at => 2.hours.from_now)
```

```
    assert Article.published.include?(published_article)
    assert Article.unpublished.include?(unpublished_article)
    assert Article.unpublished.include?(scheduled_article)
    assert_equal false, Article.published.include?(unpublished_article)
    assert_equal false, Article.published.include?(scheduled_article)
    assert_equal false, Article.unpublished.include?(published_article)
  end
```

The test first retrieves two records, respectively: a published and an unpublished one, and then creates a new scheduled one (published with a future publication date). Then you assert that the published one should be included in the array returned by the `published` named scope, and the unpublished and scheduled ones should be included in the array returned by the `unpublished` named scope. And for good measure, you'll also make sure it checks that neither of the named scopes include an inappropriate record (for example, you don't want a scheduled post to appear in the published list).

The resulting test case is shown in Listing 7-5.

Listing 7-5: The ArticleTest Test Case with a Couple of Tests

```ruby
require 'test_helper'

class ArticleTest < ActiveSupport::TestCase
  fixtures :articles

  test "article validations" do
    no_title_or_body = Article.new(:published => true, :published_at => Time.now)

    no_title = Article.find(1)
    no_title.title = nil

    duplicate_body = Article.find(2)
    duplicate_body.body = articles(:hello).body

    assert_equal false, no_title_or_body.save

    assert_raise ActiveRecord::RecordInvalid do
      no_title.save!
    end

    assert_raise ActiveRecord::RecordInvalid do
      duplicate_body.save!
    end
  end

  test "article status" do
    published_article = Article.find_by_published(true)
    unpublished_article = Article.find_by_published(false)
    scheduled_article = Article.create(:title => "A post in the future",
                                       :body => "... some text ...",
                                       :published => true,
                                       :published_at => 2.hours.from_now)
```

Continued

Listing 7-5: The ArticleTest Test Case with a Couple of Tests *(continued)*

```
      assert Article.published.include?(published_article)
      assert Article.unpublished.include?(unpublished_article)
      assert Article.unpublished.include?(scheduled_article)
      assert_equal false, Article.published.include?(unpublished_article)
      assert_equal false, Article.published.include?(scheduled_article)
      assert_equal false, Article.unpublished.include?(published_article)
   end
end
```

When the setup logic is common among a few tests, it's better to refactor the test case so that the setup logic is moved to the setup *method, which is invoked before the execution of each test case.*

Running the tests you now obtain:

```
C:\projects\blog> rake test:units
(in C:/projects/blog)
c:/ruby/bin/ruby -Ilib;test "c:/ruby/lib/ruby/gems/1.8/gems/rake-0.8.3/lib/rake/
rake_test_loader.rb" "test/unit/article_test.rb" "test/unit/comment_test.rb"
Loaded suite c:/ruby/lib/ruby/gems/1.8/gems/rake-0.8.3/lib/rake/rake_test_loader

Started
...
Finished in 0.354 seconds.

3 tests, 10 assertions, 0 failures, 0 errors
```

Great! Keep in mind that this is not by any means a complete set of tests, and you'd probably want more records in your fixtures to play around with. But the example should be enough to get you started.

You can check some interesting stats about your application, including the code-to-test ratio, by running the rake task stats.

Unit Testing and Transactions

By default the execution of each test is wrapped in a transaction that is rolled back upon completion. This has two positive consequences. The first is related to performance. This approach doesn't require you to reload the fixture data after each test, which speeds up the execution of the whole test suite considerably. Second, and perhaps more importantly, each test will start with the same data in the database, therefore eliminating the risk of creating dependencies between different tests, where one test changes the data and the other needs to be aware of it in order to work. That'd be a very bad approach to testing and a route that you definitely don't want to go down.

As a final exercise, try to create additional tests for `Article` and perhaps move onto the `Comment` model's tests as well. You'll notice that the fixtures within `comments.yml` have an article `article` key. You can assign the name of an article fixture (for example, `hello`) to that column as follows:

```
   article: hello
```

You'll get back to the subject of testing in the next chapter, which discusses functional and integration tests.

Summary

ActiveRecord has changed the way many developers write Web applications. This chapter has provided you with a wide spectrum of topics that are considered fundamental for any Rails programmer. Integrating this knowledge with the official API documentation should enable you to write all sorts of database-driven Web applications.

The next chapter deals with the fundamentals of working with controllers, the C component of the MCV triad. Chapter 9 completes it, by introducing a few fundamental notions concerning the view layer.

8

Handling Requests with ActionController

*Rails is the most well thought-out web development framework I've ever used.
And that's in a decade of doing web applications for a living. I've built my own
frameworks, helped develop the Servlet API, and have created more than a
few web servers from scratch. Nobody has done it like this before.*

— James Duncan Davidson, Creator of Tomcat and Ant

ActionController is a key module used by Rails to handle incoming requests by mapping
them with, and handing over control to, specific public instance methods known as *actions*.
ActionController works closely with ActionView to formulate a proper response for each request,
and together they form a powerful framework known as ActionPack.

The process of going from an incoming request to a complete response that's sent back to the
user's browser can be divided into three logical steps: routing the request to determine which
action should handle it; executing the code of the action; and finally rendering a template in the
view layer. The first two steps are managed by ActionController and, together with testing, are
the main subject of this chapter.

When a request comes in, ActionController uses a routing component that looks up the routes
defined for the project to determine which controller and action should handle the incoming
request. As soon as the controller has been identified, its class is instantiated. The details of the
incoming request and a new response object are then passed to its `process` method (defined
by `ActionController::Base`). This method takes care of extracting the action name from
the request parameters, executing the action's code and ultimately disposing of the controller
instance when the request-response cycle is complete.

> ## ASP.NET Routing and Rails Routing
>
> When ASP.NET MVC introduced a routing system inspired by Rails, it was immediately clear that the namespace System.Web.Routing was going to be beneficial for regular ASP.NET developers outside of the MVC context. For this reason, Microsoft decided to include it with its .NET 3.5 Service Pack 1 release.
>
> If you've had the chance to experiment with ASP.NET Routing, you'll find the concepts and ideas illustrated in this chapter somewhat familiar, or at least not overly foreign. Sure, the syntax, data structures, and the specific method calls will be different, but knowing ASP.NET Routing will help give you a good head start. On the other hand, if you haven't tried it, Rails' routing shouldn't be too confusing either, as long as you focus on the big picture.

ActionController::Base defines two process methods: a class method and an instance one. The class method acts as a factory that instantiates the controller through the new method, and then invokes the instance method process on it. The instance method is the one that, among other things, actually extracts the action name, executes the action's code, and eventually discards the controller object when a response has been formulated.

All this is possible because you tell ActionController what rules should be used to find the right controller and action. In Rails applications this is typically done in a config\routes.rb file. For the blog application, routes.rb was defined as follows (stripped of its many comments):

```
ActionController::Routing::Routes.draw do |map|
  map.root :controller => "articles"
  map.resources :articles, :has_many => :comments,
                           :collection => { :unpublished => :get }

  map.connect ':controller/:action/:id'
  map.connect ':controller/:action/:id.:format'
end
```

Any mapping happens within the block passed to ActionController::Routing::Routes.draw. The naming makes sense if you think of it as the process of drawing routes.

Within the block, you employ two types of routings: a RESTful one, which is based on the concept of resource and defined through the method resources, and conventional pattern-matching routing, which is obtained through connect.

resources creates HTTP-verb aware named routes for a collection resource (for example, articles) . resources was also the method that provided all the handy *_url and *_path helpers that are based on the named routes. connect, on the other hand, creates an unnamed route only, and this is based solely on two things: the pattern passed as the first parameter (for example, ':controller/:action/:id') and an optional hash of options.

Rails offer maximum flexibility thanks to the fact that within your routes.rb file, you can use one style or the other, or a mix of both. Let's take a speedy look at both routing styles.

Defining Routes with map.connect

When you create a new application, Rails generates a `config\routes.rb` file that defines two default (unnamed or anonymous) routes:

```
map.connect ':controller/:action/:id'
map.connect ':controller/:action/:id.:format'
```

The routing subsystem will try to find a match between the defined patterns and the URL of the incoming request.

For example, take the first route into consideration:

```
map.connect ':controller/:action/:id'
```

This tells Rails that the route recognizes only paths that include an arbitrarily named controller, action, and id. Hence, `'/library/borrow/25189'` matches this route, and instructs Rails to map the first token in the URL (that is, `library`) to the `:controller` parameter, the second token (for example, `borrow`) to the `:action` parameter, and the third token to the `:id` parameter, which has a value of `"25189."` The `params` object will then look like this:

```
params = { :controller => "library", :action => "borrow", :id => "25189" }
```

Rails will therefore be able to process the request, by instantiating the library controller and executing the `borrow` action defined within it. As a developer, you'll be able to retrieve the `:id` parameter from within the controller through `params[:id]`.

Default Parameters

`/library/borrow/25189` results in the parameters `{ :controller => "library", :action=> "borrow", :id => "25189" }`, but not all three parameters are strictly required.

You could omit an id, issuing perhaps a request for the path `/library/catalog` instead. The parameters would then be the following:

```
params = { :controller => "library", :action => "catalog" }
```

Such a match is possible, despite the missing third parameter, because `connect` defines a default for :id. Unless a value is specified in the URL, `:id` is nil. And `:id => nil` doesn't appear in the `params` hash-like object, because `nil` parameters that are not specified in the path are not included.

Similarly, `connect` defines a default value when the action is missing. Reasonably so, this default value is `"index"`. `/library` will therefore be mapped to `{ :controller => "library", :action => "index" }`.

Before scaffolding was refactored to become RESTful, the default routes and their default values still enabled beautiful paths such as `/library`, `/library/list`, and `/library/show/12345` to work just as you'd expect them to. To this day, if you have a non-RESTful controller, the presence of these default routes in `routes.rb` will allow you to have paths in the format `/controller_name`, `/controller_name/action_name`, and `/controller_name/action_name/id`.

Customizing Your Routes

This default route is rather generic, because its pattern will be matched by requests whose URLs contain an arbitrary controller name (as long as the controller exists), an arbitrarily named action (whether or not it exists), and an arbitrary id. On top of that, any HTTP verb is fair play for this route. But don't let this mislead you into thinking that it would match any path. On the contrary, /library/borrow/ 43274/something or /library/something/borrow/43274 will not match this route, because they both have four tokens, rather than the three expected.

> *The* :id *parameter can have any value, and it's not limited to numeric values enclosed in a string, although this is often the case because* params[:id] *is usually passed to* ActiveRecord::Base's find *method.*

:controller and :action are specially named parameters because they are used to identify the controller and the action that should process the request, respectively. Any other symbol within the pattern, even :id, will, however, be considered as a regular named parameter and included in the params object. :controller and :action can be used anywhere you need to match a controller or action name; it's also possible to explicitly require a specific controller, and/or action, by passing an option (for example, :controller or :action) to the connect method. For example, consider the following route declaration:

```
map.connect 'library/:action/:isbn', :controller => "library"
```

/library/borrow/9780470189481 will then be mapped as follows:

```
params = { :controller=> "library", :action=> "borrow", :isbn=> "9780470189481" }
```

The route will also match the path /library/archive/9780470189481. In fact, this will yield:

```
params = { :controller=> "library", :action=> "archive", :isbn=> "9780470189481" }
```

> *The method* with_options *can be used to declare several conditions that are common to a series of routes defined within the block passed to the method. Check the online documentation for examples.*

Notice how the action is "variable," and can be arbitrary because you use the :action symbol in the pattern. However, the controller is not variable, so for the route to match, the path requested by the user must begin with /library/ and be followed by an action and an ISBN. :id defaults to nil but your custom named parameter :isbn doesn't. This means that a value must be provided or you won't have a match. Consequently, you can't just have /library/9780470189481 either, because 9780470189481 would be interpreted as the value that's supposed to be assigned to :action and the :isbn value would still be missing in Rails' eyes.

There are times when this is exactly what you want: a mandatory set of parameters that cannot be omitted for a certain route. For example, the previously defined route doesn't work well if you want to map actions like borrow and archive in LibraryController, assuming as you can imagine neither of these actions would be meaningful without access to an :isbn parameter that identifies a certain book.

> *Here* archive *is intended as the action of "returning a book" to the archive, as opposed to listing the catalog, which wouldn't require an* :isbn *parameter.*

It is, however, possible to define your own default values through the `:defaults` option. To make `:isbn` an optional parameter, for example, you could do the following:

```ruby
map.connect 'library/:action/:isbn', :controller => "library",
                                      :defaults => { :isbn => nil }
```

If you omit the ISBN, it will simply not appear in the parameters hash. And because you removed this constraint, you can now also omit an action (for example, `"/library"`) and fall back on `:action`'s default value, which is `"index."`

Route Globbing

Ruby methods can have a variable number of arguments thanks to the splat operator that we encountered in the Ruby section of this book. You might recall that in the method signature, a parameter that's prefixed by a splat operator has to be the last one in the signature.

Within the pattern of a route, you can do something similar in an attempt to catch a variable number of slash-separated tokens provided in the URL. If you place `*path` (or any other name, really) in the pattern, you'll be able to catch a variable quantity of tokens in the URL through `params[:path]` (assuming you used `*path`).

This is known as "route globbing" and unlike regular Ruby methods, the glob doesn't have to be the last parameter in the pattern.

For example, if the pattern is `'library/:action/:isbn/*extra/preview'` and the path requested by the user is `'/library/borrow/9780470189481/3/weeks/preview,'` not only will there be a match between the path and the pattern specified for this route, but you'll also be able to access those additional parameters through `params[:extra]`, which will contain the array `["3", "weeks"]`.

The first parameter passed to `connect` already gives you a great deal of flexibility, especially if you consider that you can have an arbitrary number of defined routes and can therefore fine tune which URLs are handled by which route. Declaring routes is, however, even more customizable thanks to the fact that `connect` accepts a second parameter, a hash of options. Let's review all the accepted keys for that option hash:

❑   `:action`: Used to indicate what action should handle the request when there is a match between the requested URL and the pattern specified by the route declaration. If `:action` is present within the pattern, this has precedence over the `:action` option. This means that passing `:action => "my_action"` to `connect` will only have an effect if no action name has been indicated in the URL. In such a circumstance, `:action` is equivalent to adding an entry for the action to `:defaults`.

❑   `:conditions`: Used to define restrictions on routes, it supports the `:method` condition that specifies which HTTP methods can access the route among `:post`, `:get`, `:put`, `:delete`, and the catch-all `:any`. This is particularly handy when, for example, you want to specify that a different action should handle the requested URL, depending on whether this is a GET or POST request. To handle that situation, you could specify two routes, and pass `:action => "first_action", :conditions => { :method => :get }` to the first route, and `:action => "second_action", :conditions => { :method => :post }` to the second route.

❏ :controller: Similarly to :action, this is used to indicate which controller should be mapped to the route. If the catch-all :controller symbol appears within the pattern specified by the route, the :controller => "example" option will only apply when a controller is not provided in the URL. Just like in the case of :action, you have the option to use :defaults instead, if you'd like.

❏ :defaults: Used to specify default values for one or more named parameters included in the pattern passed to connect. For instance, consider the following route declaration:

```
map.connect 'library/:action/:isbn', :controller => 'library',
                                      :defaults => { :action => 'info',
                                                     :isbn => nil }
```

This will map the path '/library' as requested by an end user, with the controller library and the action info (an :isbn key will not be added to params, because the :isbn named parameter was defaulted to nil).

❏ :<parameter_name>: This option can be used for two different tasks depending on the assigned value. When a regular expression is assigned, this sets a requirement for the named parameter (for example, :quantity => /\d+/). If the condition is not satisfied (for example, :quantity exists in the URL but its value is not composed entirely of digits), the route will not match the request. The second way of using this is to assign a regular value so that the parameter is added to the params object. Note that, unlike entries in the :defaults hash, parameters added in this way are not required to be named parameters within the pattern. In practice, this means that you can use :my_parameter => "my_value" anytime you need to associate a parameter with a certain request. The params object will enable you to retrieve that value from within the action (for example, with params[:my_parameter]).

❏ :requirements: Used to specify constraints on the format of one or more parameters that appear in the URL. If any of the parameters specified in the request fail to satisfy the condition defined within the :requirements hash, the route will not apply. This is entirely equivalent to using multiple :<parameter_name> options whose assigned values are regular expressions. A typical example to illustrate the usefulness of :requirements is the permalink of blog engines. If the pattern used for the route is 'example/:year/:month/:day,' you'll be able to retrieve the three named parameters from within the controller through params[:year], params[:month] and params[:day]. However, this doesn't guarantee that the three values you received were properly formatted. It would be better to show a 404 page for requests whose URLs are meaningless, like '/example/1492/10/12' (unless you're transcribing Columbus' diary) or '/example/2008/03/50.' In that case, it will be sufficient to pass :requirements => { :year => /20\d\d/, :month => /(0?[1-9]|1[012])/, :day => /(0?[1-9]|[12]\d|3[01])/ } to connect. If any of the three named parameters don't meet the specified conditions, a match between the incoming request and this route will not appear.

Note that the regular expressions in this case are just an aid to exclude the majority of incorrect dates and values. However, this doesn't take into account leap years or the fact that certain months don't have 31 days.

Each route that you define will typically have a pattern with a few named parameters in it (for example, :isbn), and a few options that are different from the ones we encountered earlier (for example, :defaults), in a manner that enables the developer to define with surgical precision how URLs should be recognized and mapped.

Route Priority

The block passed to `ActionController::Routing::Routes.draw` in `route.rb` can contain multiple routes, and it's also possible to have more than one route that matches the incoming request URL and HTTP verb. Yet, each request needs to be mapped with only one route, so that Rails unequivocally knows which controller, and action, should handle the request, and what parameters should be available to them.

Thankfully, routing solves this problem for you by giving a different priority to each route you define. Starting from the top and moving toward the bottom, the pattern-matching algorithm will check each route's pattern, conditions, and requirements against the request until it finds a match. When a matching route is located, no further routes are checked for that request. This implies that the routes within the block are presented in order of their priority. The first route will have the highest priority and the last route the lowest.

This is an important notion because you don't want the intended route for a given request to be obscured by another matching route that happens to have greater priority. This is why the default routes are placed toward the end of the block, rather than at the beginning. The default routes are so generic that they can be considered as "catch-all" routes (to a certain extent), when more specific routes do not apply. If no routes match the incoming request (not even the default ones), an `ActionController::RoutingError` exception is raised.

Take into consideration the `routes.rb` file defined for the simple blog application. If you were to change the order of the routes, and place the default routes on top, you'd have the following:

```
# Don't do this
ActionController::Routing::Routes.draw do |map|
  map.connect ':controller/:action/:id'
  map.connect ':controller/:action/:id.:format'


  map.root :controller => "articles"
  map.resources :articles, :has_many => :comments,
                           :collection => { :unpublished => :get }
end
```

When a RESTful request comes in, in trying to visualize an article at `/articles/3/show`, routing would try to match that with the first route. The pattern in the first route is now `':controller/:action/:id.'` Do you have a match? Indeed, because the default route is so generic that it requires only three tokens in the URL and accepts any HTTP verb.

The end result would be that the request is mapped to the `articles` controller (correct), the action 3 (wrong), and the id `show` (wrong again).

It is in fact advisable to comment out the default routes altogether if they are not needed within a RESTful application. It is also a matter of preventing the existence of default routes that can be used to create or delete objects with simple GET requests. So please go ahead and delete or comment them out in the blog application you created, so that the `routes.rb` file appears as follows:

```
ActionController::Routing::Routes.draw do |map|
  map.root :controller => "articles"
  map.resources :articles, :has_many => :comments,
                           :collection => { :unpublished => :get }
end
```

> The order in which routes appear matters. Always place the most generic routes at the bottom. If yours is a RESTful application, it is advisable to comment out the default routes.

Routes from the Console

The console was an indispensible tool when dealing with ActiveRecord, and not surprisingly, it can be highly useful when working with controllers as well. Things are, however, less straightforward, so let's explore how you can work with routes from the console.

When working with routes, you're interested in two tasks. The first is to determine which route matches a given URL, so that you see which controller, action, and parameters result from the request. The second is the exact opposite: you have a controller, action, and parameters and you need to obtain a URL.

All the routes that you define in `routes.rb` are added to `Routes`, which is a `RouteSet` object. Both the class and the object are defined in `ActionController::Routing`. You use `Routes` and its methods to both recognize a given path and generate URLs. Let's investigate the former first.

You need to start the console and assign `ActionController::Routing::Routes` to a local variable for the sake of convenience:

```
>> routes = ActionController::Routing::Routes
```

The output generated will be quite large because a lot of information is stored in this object.

Now that you have a handle to play with, you can use the `recognize_path` method.

Notice that for this to work, the controller needs to be defined in the application. If you are testing the routing for controllers you haven't defined yet, you can place their names in an array, and pass that array to `use_controllers!`:

```
>> ActionController::Routing::use_controllers! ["main", "library"]
```

As well, you should reload the routing file for good measure (that is, `load 'config/routes.rb'`).

You can now recognize paths as follows:

```
>> routes.recognize_path '/main/show/3'
=> {:action => "show", :controller => "main", :id => "3"}
```

On the flip side, generating URLs can be accomplished through the `generate` method:

```
>> routes.generate :controller => 'main', :coupon => 1920321
=> "/main?coupon=1920321"
```

These are just examples, of course; the output depends entirely on the routes you define.

:coupon is a parameter that was not specified in the pattern for the route that applies, and as such it's appended to the URL.

Normally you'd use the method url_for in the controller (and the link_to helper in the view) to generate a URL for a certain controller, action, and its required parameters. For anonymous routes, a link in the controller might look like this:

```
@borrow_link = url_for(:controller => 'library', :action => 'borrow',
                                                  :isbn => @book.isbn)
```

Controllers can be defined within modules, and in such cases the specified controller is assumed to be local to the module that contains the controller that issues the request. Use /example to indicate that it's an absolute "path" to the controller.

This will assign a string like 'http://localhost:3000/library/borrow/9780307237699' to @borrow_link. The actual string will of course depend on the hostname, port (typically 80 in production), and :isbn parameter, and assumes that the default route was specified in the routes.rb file.

The url_for method is quite flexible; check the online documentation for a complete list and description of accepted options.

Note that you can't use url_for directly from the console, but that you have to resort to the analogous generate method. A similar method called url_for is available through the special object app, which is an instance of ActionController::Integration::Session, but it doesn't behave exactly like the url_for method in a controller does. For example, if it lacks an associated request, the generated URL will use www.example.com as the hostname.

Named Routes

The connect method generates unnamed routes, but ActionController provides the ability to define labels for your routes, known simply as named routes. An initial example of this was shown when you defined the following line in the routes.rb file that you've been playing with so far:

```
map.root :controller => "articles"
```

By using root rather than connect, this created a named route root. As you saw before, this route will easily be accessible through the methods generated by appending _url and _path to its name, namely root_url (for example, http://localhost:3000/) and root_path (for example, /).

This method is special, in the sense that it also serves the purpose of informing routing about which controller (for example, articles) and action (for example, by default index) should be invoked whenever the root of the application is requested (that is, /). Remember, the public\index.html file needs to be removed in order for this to work; otherwise the static file will have precedence over the index action you defined.

Named routes are handy because you can use helper methods to refer to them, rather than having to specify the controller, action, default values, and so on every time, to methods like url_for, redirect_to, or link_to. Evidence of the advantages of named routes is admittedly weak when you consider the example of root, which could just as easily be accessed by using /.

The real power behind named routes becomes self-evident upon introducing the notion that `connect` and `root` are not the only available method names. In fact, you can pick an arbitrary name that you'd like to use for your route by simply using it instead of `connect`. For example, consider the following route declaration:

```
map.catalog "library/", :controller => "library", :action => "list"
```

This generates a named route called `catalog`, which can be referenced through `catalog_url` and `catalog_path` (which excludes the hostname and port number). For instance, to redirect to the controller library's list action, you could use the following:

```
redirect_to(catalog_url)
```

Short and sweet, and because you chose the name of the route, it's also meaningful and readable.

Compare this with what's needed for an analogous anonymous route (created by using `connect`):

```
redirect_to(:controller => "library", :action => "list")
```

That's not too bad, but it's not as concise or nice either. Let's consider a second route, this time with a named parameter:

```
map.borrow_book "library/borrow/:isbn",
                :controller => "library",
                :action => "borrow"
```

Obtaining the URL for this route will be as easy as employing `borrow_book_url` and passing the ISBN to the method:

```
borrow_book_url("9780307237699")
```

Or alternatively:

```
borrow_book_url(:isbn => "9780307237699")
```

If more named parameters are present within the pattern, they'll be passed to the helper in the order that they appeared, or in the conventional hash notation (as in the preceding line of code).

RESTful Routes

REST (REpresentational State Transfer) was already introduced earlier in the book when you developed the basic blog application. This section briefly recaps how this new paradigm affects Rails' routing.

RESTful routing is considered to be the new standard for Rails applications and, whenever possible, it should be favored over the traditional style described so far. In short, RESTful routing doesn't simply match a URL to code within the controller, but rather maps resource identifiers (think URLs) and HTTP verbs to seven predefined actions. These actions normally perform CRUD operations in the database as well, through the model layer.

map.resources

RESTful routes can be defined through the `resources` method. Consider this route:

```
map.resources :books
```

Whenever you need to declare more than one resource, you can do so on a single line by passing a list of symbols (for example, `map.resources :books, :catalogs, :users`) to `resources`.

This manages to pull off a fair bit of magic, by abstracting and hiding many of REST's implementation details, as well as providing you with named routes and easy-to-use helpers to work with. A single concise line creates seven RESTful routes, as shown in the following table.

Route Name	HTTP Method	URL	Action in BooksController
books	GET	/books	index
formatted_books	POST	/books	create
new_book	GET	/books/new	new
book	GET	/books/:id	show
edit_book	GET	/books/:id/edit	edit
formatted_book	PUT	/books/:id	update
formatted_book	DELETE	/books/:id	destroy

Each named route will also be accessible when needed through the `_url` and `_path` helpers (four pairs are generated excluding the ones starting with `formatted_`).

> **Formatted routes are going to be removed from Rails 2.3 because they are rarely used and have an impact on the memory footprint. As such, the formatted helpers will disappear as well; they will be replaced by a `:format` parameter passed to regular route helpers (for example, `books_path(:format => "xml")`).**

Keep in mind that in reality the number of routes generated is more than seven because a counterpart that includes a `:format` parameter exists for all of the routes listed in the preceding table. The whole REST paradigm is founded on the idea that for a given resource there can be several "Representations." This means that in addition to the ones already listed, you also have the routes shown in the following table.

Route Name	HTTP Method	URL	Action in BooksController
formatted_books	GET	/books.:format	index
formatted_books	POST	/books.:format	create
formatted_new_book	GET	/books/new.:format	new

Continued

(continued)

Route Name	HTTP Method	URL	Action in BooksController
`formatted_book`	GET	/books/:id.:format	
`formatted_edit_` `book`	GET	/books/:id/ edit:format	edit
`formatted_book`	PUT	/books/:id.format	update
`formatted_book`	DELETE	/books/:id.:format	destroy

The value of the id will of course be accessible through `params[:id]` (as it is with any other route), and `params[:format]` will do the trick for the `format`. However, as you've seen before, the `respond_to` method spares you from having to worry about retrieving the format through the `params` hash-like object.

The request `GET /books` will be handled by the `index` action, but `POST /books` will be mapped with the `create` action. Similarly, `GET /books.xml` will still be handled by the `index` action, but the format of the request will be XML, and the action should handle this accordingly, by providing an XML response.

Because the HTTP verb is meaningful and used by the routing subsystem, to destroy a resource it won't be enough to simply reach a URL. You have to explicitly send a `DELETE` request. In practice this means that you'll be provided with further protection from accidental, potentially damaging operations. To illustrate this point, think of Web crawlers. They follow links — smart ones may even dynamically come up with requests — but they definitely do not send `DELETE` requests to your Web application.

> **If you don't require all of the seven actions, you can save memory resources by indicating that only some routes need to be generated or excluded. The options for this are** `:only` **and** `:except` **(for example,** `map.resources :books, :only =>` `[:index, :show]`**).**

map.resource

Defining a series of routes through `resources` assumes that an `index` action is going to show a list of resources, while other actions allow you to show, edit, create, and destroy a single resource. The `resource` method exists for times when you need to work with a singular resource (known as singleton resource), as opposed to a collection of resources. The symbol passed to the method needs to be singular as well, whereas the corresponding controller is by default pluralized:

```
map.resource :catalog
```

The generated routes are slightly different and all singular as shown by running `rake routes`:

```
            POST   /catalog            {:controller=>"catalogs", :action=>"create"}
            POST   /catalog.:format    {:controller=>"catalogs", :action=>"create"}
new_catalog
            GET    /catalog/new        {:controller=>"catalogs", :action=>"new"}
formatted_new_catalog
```

```
        GET    /catalog/new.:format   {:controller=>"catalogs", :action=>"new"}
edit_catalog
        GET    /catalog/edit          {:controller=>"catalogs", :action=>"edit"}
formatted_edit_catalog
        GET    /catalog/edit.:format   {:controller=>"catalogs", :action=>"edit"}
catalog
        GET    /catalog                {:controller=>"catalogs", :action=>"show"}
formatted_catalog
        GET    /catalog.:format        {:controller=>"catalogs", :action=>"show"}
        PUT    /catalog                {:controller=>"catalogs", :action=>"update"}
        PUT    /catalog.:format        {:controller=>"catalogs", :action=>"update"}
        DELETE /catalog                {:controller=>"catalogs", :action=>"destroy"}
        DELETE /catalog.:format        {:controller=>"catalogs", :action=>"destroy"}
```

Visualizing routes through the console is admittedly lame. For projects with complex routes, consider installing the Vasco plugin, which is a route explorer available at `http://github.com/relevance/vasco`.

`GET /catalog` will show the singleton resource (that doesn't have to be identified by an id, being the only one globally identified) and no `index` action is mapped by any of the routes either, because there is only one catalog and hence you don't need a list.

Customizing RESTful Routes

The routes defined by `resources` can be customized by passing a hash of additional parameters to the method. Many of these can be used with `resource` as well. Aside from `:only` and `:except`, as mentioned earlier (introduced in Rails 2.2), these are as follows.

:as

The `:as` option specifies a different name to be used for the path of each generated route. Consider the following:

```
map.resources :books, :as => "titles"
```

This will generate the routes shown in the previous tables, but with the path being `titles` not `books`. Therefore `GET /titles/42` will be mapped with the action `show` of the `BooksController`. This option is often used when the resource name contains an underscore, but you'd like the URLs to contain a dash instead. It's important to notice that the `*_url` and `*_path` helpers generated are still based on the name of the resource; so, for example, you still have `new_book_url` and `new_book_path` and not `new_title_url` and `new_title_path`.

:collection, :member, and :new

These three options are used when you need to add routes to map to any action other than the seven default ones. `:collection` specifies one or more named routes for actions that work on a collection resource:

```
map.resources :books, :collection => { :search => :get }
```

This will recognize GET /books/search requests and even generate the search_books_url and search_books_path helpers (as well as the two corresponding helpers obtained by appending formatted). The acceptable values for the HTTP method are :get, :post, :put, :delete, and :any. When the HTTP verb of the request doesn't matter, you can use :any.

:member is very similar, but is reserved for actions that operate on a single member of the collection:

```
map.resources :books, :member => { :borrow => :post }
```

This will generate the route helpers to access the borrow_book named route. Finally, :new is used to define routes for creating a new resource:

```
map.resources :books, :new => { :register => :post }
```

Requests such as POST /books/new/register will be recognized and handled by the register action of the BooksController. The named routes generated will be register_new_books and formatted_register_new_books. Note that if you'd like to alter the accepted verbs mapping to the existing new method, you can do so through the :new parameter as well by, for example, binding the new action to the :any symbol representing any verb:

```
map.resources :books, :new => { :new => :any, :register => :post }
```

:conditions

The :conditions parameter was introduced first in this chapter as an option for the method connect. Because this defines HTTP verb restrictions on single routes, it's hardly needed in a RESTful context.

:controller

The :controller option is used to specify a different controller for the generated routes. For example, consider the following:

```
map.resources :books, :controller => "titles"
```

When a request for GET /books comes in, Rails knows that the index action of the TitlesController should handle the request. The named routes, and therefore the helpers, generated are going to be based on the name of the resource, and will therefore not be affected.

:has_one and :has_many

:has_one and :has_many are two options used as a shorthand to declare basic nested resources. The difference between the two is that :has_one maps singleton resources rather than plural ones.

Consider this:

```
map.resources :books, :has_one => :author, :has_many => [:reviews, :categories]
```
Notice how multiple resources are assigned through an array of symbols.

This is equivalent to declaring the nested routes as follows:

```
map.resources :books do |book|
  book.resource :author
```

```
      book.resources :reviews
      book.resources :categories
  end
```

This second, more explicit, notation enables you to create resources that are nested within resources, which in turn are nested within resources and so on to create a hierarchy that's as deep as you want it to be. But don't be tempted to fall in this trap. A deeply nested resource will be accessible through very long URLs and helpers that are no longer easy to remember or type. The consensus within the Rails community is that one level of nested routes, as demonstrated in Chapter 6 for the comments resource, is an acceptable compromise.

Technically, there is also a :shallow => true option that can be passed to resources before the block, to indicate that the routes/helpers declared within the block can be used without prefixing the name of the resource that contains them (or any :name_prefix or :path_prefix specified) when accessing an individual resource through its id.

To learn more about this and other options, check the online documentation and consider reading the official guide "Rails Routing from the Outside In," available at http://guides.rails.info/routing/routing_outside_in.html. Most of the material is covered in this chapter, but you may find a few extra bits of specialized information there.

Generating Rails Guides

Rails guides are available online, but you can also generate all of Rails' official guides by running rake doc:guides from within your Rails project. This task will place the guides within the doc\guides folder. Upon launching index.html within your browser, you will be able to select the guide that interests you among the ones shown (as you can see in Figure 8-1).

Currently these are "Getting Started with Rails," "Rails Database Migrations," "Active Record Associations," "Active Record Finders," "Layouts and Rendering in Rails," "Action View Form Helpers," "Rails Routing from the Outside In," "Basics of Action Controller," "Rails Caching," "Testing Rails Applications," "Securing Rails Applications," "Debugging Rails Applications," "Benchmarking and Profiling Rails Applications," and "The Basics of Creating Rails Plugins." New guides are likely to be published in the future.

Reading these guides will solidify, integrate, and augment the concepts presented within this book.

Other Options

If all the options mentioned so far are not enough for what you need to do, a few further options are available. :name_prefix and :path_prefix, respectively, are used to add a string prefix (for example, "book_") and for adding a prefix that includes variables in the same format as the pattern passed to connect (for example, "/publisher/:publisher_id") to the generated routes.

:singular (not available for resource) and :plural are used to specify the correct singularization and pluralization of the resource name. Two other options, already discussed for connect, are :requirements and arbitrarily named parameters (previously indicated with the generic name :<parameter_name>).

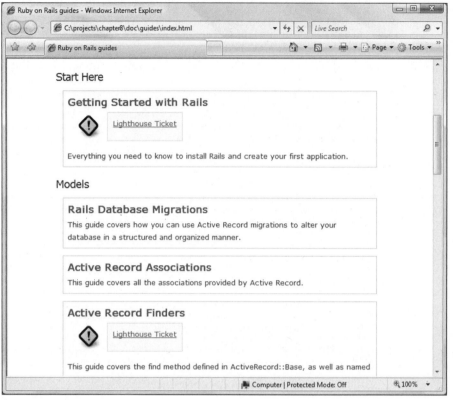

Figure 8-1

Namespaced Resources

Rails supports the so-called namespaced resources. These are resources that are consistently prefixed by a given string. ActionController defines the method namespace that automatically prefixes the generated routes for you. For example, consider the following:

```
map.namespace(:admin) do |admin|
   admin.resources :books
end
```

There are quite a few implications to this:

❑   Each book-related route will now expect the incoming URL to be prefixed by admin. For instance, to access the list of books, you'll need a GET /admin/books request.

❑   The controller is now expected to be located within the app\controllers\admin folder and therefore have its name prefixed by Admin::. In this case, the controller name needs to be changed to Admin::BooksController.

❑ If you generate the `BooksController` by scaffolding, you will be surprised to see that the application no longer works. This is because now all the helpers used by the application to access book-related routes are going to be prefixed by admin (for example, `admin_books_url`).

Despite the adjustments that are required, it's often a good idea to group a few controllers within a common namespace. The most usual scenario is indeed grouping a series of controllers that belong to an administration section.

The same results can be accomplished by carefully combining `:name_prefix` *and* `:path_prefix`, *but there is really no reason to do so if namespaced routes fit the bill.*

Helpers and RESTful Routes

Besides being able to generate routes in a concise manner, RESTful routes also have an advantage when it comes to working with helpers. Consider the following method calls, taken from the blog application:

```
redirect_to(@article)
redirect_to([@article, @comment])
redirect_to(article_comments_url(@article))
<%= link_to 'Edit', edit_article_path(article) %>
<%= link_to 'Show', [@article, @comment] %>
```

Notice how these methods are able to understand the URL that needs to be generated, by simply passing objects to them. This magic is possible thanks to the usual Convention over Configuration principle. Helpers are "smart" and understand that passing an object (for example, `@article`) means that you want to display that resource, and therefore the URL should be generated by using the corresponding controller name and the id of that object (for example, a GET request for `/articles/12`).

The same helpers are also aware of nested routes, and `[@article, @comment]` are automatically mapped, in this specific case, to paths like `/articles/12/comments/3`. That array is essentially telling the method it's passed to (for example, `redirect_to` or `link_to`) that you want to show that comment (for example, with id 3); keep in mind the fact that it's nested within an article resource (for example, with id 12).

You can consider this notation to be a shorthand version of some of the more verbose `*_url` and `*_path` helpers.

Working with Controllers

Routing is just the first part of the equation, with the second one being the actual code defined within controllers. If you are familiar with ASP.NET, this is conceptually similar to the Code Behind model, and a vital component of every Rails application. The final aim is to have separation of concerns and place just enough logic in the controller to orchestrate the application, while the heavy lifting is performed by the model layer and the presentation is delegated to the view.

Generating Controllers

In the examples presented so far, the controller was never created directly, but rather was generated as a consequence of running the scaffold generator. Controllers are contained within textual files so you could create a file in the right directory and define the code by hand. A more convenient and practical approach, though, is passing the controller argument to the generate script, as shown in the following example:

All controllers inherit from the ApplicationController *class defined in* application.rb. *In Rails 2.3, this file is renamed as* application_controller.rb *to be more consistent with the naming convention of every other controller.*

```
C:\projects\> rails chapter8
C:\projects\> cd chapter8
C:\projects\chapter8> ruby script/generate controller Account
      exists  app/controllers/
      exists  app/helpers/
      create  app/views/account
      exists  test/functional/
      create  app/controllers/account_controller.rb
      create  test/functional/account_controller_test.rb
      create  app/helpers/account_helper.rb
```

This generates the controller file (for example, account_controller.rb), a helper to define helper methods that are specific to this controller (for example, account_helper.rb), and a functional test case (for example, account_controller_test.rb).

Use app\helpers\application_helper.rb *to define helpers that can be reused by every controller in the application.*

The generated controller will then be:

```
class AccountController < ApplicationController
end
```

> Notice that controllers defined in such a way are not RESTful by default. To make them so, you have to use methods like map.resources in routes.rb, as well as add the corresponding default seven actions. For this reason, when you need to create a RESTful controller, it is usually more convenient to rely on the scaffold generator that does this specific task for you.

The controller generator also accepts a list of actions/views:

```
C:\projects\chapter8> ruby script/generate controller BankAccount deposit withdraw
      exists  app/controllers/
      exists  app/helpers/
      create  app/views/bank_account
      create  test/functional/
      create  app/controllers/bank_account_controller.rb
      create  test/functional/bank_account_controller_test.rb
```

```
create   app/helpers/bank_account_helper.rb
create   app/views/bank_account/deposit.html.erb
create   app/views/bank_account/withdraw.html.erb
```

This generates the usual controller files as well as the default XHTML code for the views indicated in the given arguments. The generated controller will contain the corresponding actions:

```
class BankAccountController < ApplicationController
  def deposit
  end

  def withdraw
  end

end
```

Use `ruby script/destroy controller ControllerName` to destroy an existing controller and all the associated files that were generated for it.

You can use either CamelCase (like the class name) or snake_case (like the file name) strings to indicate the name of the controller that needs to be generated or destroyed.

Action Processing

Routing directs Rails as to which controller class should be instantiated and which method name (the action) should be invoked. But what happens if the method name is not there? To understand how things work, it is necessary to learn about the algorithm used by Rails for action processing.

Imagine that the incoming request requires the execution of the action `deposit`. The steps taken are straightforward. Rails will:

1. Search for a public method `deposit` in the controller. If the method is found, this is executed.

2. If the method cannot be found, Rails looks for a `method_missing` method within the controller. If this exists, it's executed. From within `method_missing` it's possible to access the action name because this is passed as a parameter.

3. If `method_missing` is (fittingly) missing, Rails searches for a corresponding template. If the controller is `AccountController` and the action requested through a Web browser is `deposit`, the template `desposit.html.erb` is searched for in `app\views\account`.

4. Finally, if none of the above could be found, an "Unknown action" exception appears.

These four steps have a few implications for the developer. The first step is usually the desired outcome, so it's important that your actions are defined as public methods (Ruby's default). If you define them as protected or private, these methods will be available from within the controller, but won't be accessible to the end user as actions.

If you need to hide a method that absolutely must be public, you can also use the method `hide_` *`action`. Usually this is not necessary though and almost always symptomatic of code that could use some redesigning.*

The `method_missing` method can be used to implement a metaprogramming trick to dynamically determine the code that will be executed for the incoming request:

```
def method_missing(method)

  #... code ...

end
```

This can be useful in very specific cases where there's a concrete need for such a feature, but be wary of abusing this option for sake of coolness.

Finally, the third step implies that you can define "static" pages by simply defining a template. The template will still take advantage of the layout defined for the controller at hand, and will still be able to use ERb, but in the controller there will be no corresponding action for it.

Many still find it useful to keep track of all the actions, by defining empty/stub actions in the controller for these templates, even if they are not strictly necessary. Searching Google for "Rails static pages" (without quotes) will lead to a series of articles and blog entries on the topic, and will give you a lot of insight about more elaborate approaches that are taken to serve static content in a highly dynamic Rails application.

Rendering

An action's main goal is to enable the formulation of a response for each user request. To be exact, that's one response per request. An action typically sets up one or more instance variables and renders a template that uses these variables to present them in a meaningful way. This is not always the case though; when appropriate, a request can send only headers back and not the actual body of the content. This is fairly common for some Ajax requests.

> **Because only one response is sent back to the client, at most an action should invoke the rendering of one template.**

Whether a template is involved or you're sending a string of text or just headers back to the template, the method of choice is the fittingly named `render`.

render

Invoked without parameters, `render` will render the default template for the given action. For example, the following snippet renders the `hello.html.erb` template back to the client:

```
def hello
  render
end
```

Notice that this is the default behavior, and the explicit `render` is not required. As mentioned in the previous section, for such a basic case, not even the action needs to be declared because Rails automatically looks for the template.

If you are working with a legacy Rails application, the template that is rendered could be called `hello.rhtml`. *This is the old-fashioned extension for HTML ERb templates in Rails.*

By passing a `:text` argument, you can render a string back to the browser thus bypassing any template rendering:

```
def hello
  render(:text => "Hello, Rails!")
end
```

Even though the parentheses are recommended in general, in many code bases this is found without parentheses.

Passing `:action` allows you to render the default template for another action:

```
def hello
  render(:action => "index")
end
```

The `index.html.erb` template is rendered, but the code of the `index` action is not. For this reason, if that template expects to use instance variables that have been set up by `index`, these have to be set up in `hello` as well. But if that's the case, chances are that you should use `redirect_to` (as explained further later on in this chapter).

> `render :action` **doesn't execute the code within the specified action; only its default template is rendered.**

A template name can be rendered through the `:template` option:

```
def hello
  render(:template => "example/my_template")
end
```

Notice that both a controller and a template name must be specified.

If a `:locals` hash is passed to the method as well, the values assigned to its key will be available as local variables within the template.

Likewise, a template can be specified as an absolute file path through the option `:file`. Aside from `:locals`, in this case `render` also accepts a `:user_full_path` Boolean option, to switch to a relative path.

It's also possible to provide the source for a template inline as a parameter. Use `:inline` and assign a string representing the template to it. Within this string you can embed variable evaluations (for example, `#{my_var}`) as well as accessing values passed within the `:locals` hash. The template engine defaults to ERb, but you can specify differently through the `:type` key. This accepts `"erb"`, `"builder"`, and `"rjs."`

Other common options are `render(:nothing => true)` to send an empty body back to the client, `:partial` to render a partial template, and `:xml` and `:json` for rendering XML and JSON data and to set the content type appropriately (for example, `application/xml`). Finally, an `:update` option is available if you want to pass the current page object to a block of RJS code.

Consult the more than extensive online documentation for the `ActionController::Base#render` method, to see further examples and details about the many extra options (for example, `:layout`) available for each of these rendering types.

Running the API Documentation Locally

Rails has become a fairly large and flexible framework. For each method or concept that's introduced, many more options are available to customize its behavior to your liking. Due to the limited size of the book you are holding, it's neither possible nor wise to reproduce the whole API documentation, which already exists online. You should become well acquainted with it, because it's going to become your main tool when working with Rails.

Aside from accessing the documentation online, you can also download a local copy from sites like `http://www.railsbrain.com`. Another option, perhaps less fancy in terms of presentation, is to run a documentation server locally. This makes the documentation available not just for Rails, but for all of the gems for which RDoc documentation has been installed on your system. To do so run: `gem server` from anywhere in your system. The documentation for this is available at `http://localhost:8808`.

Aside from a more Spartan presentation, the downside to this is losing both the Ajax search facility and the insightful comments and notes that you can find on sites like `http://apidock.com/rails`.

---

send_data and send_file

So far you saw that it's possible to send "nothing" (well, just the headers), a string, or a template-based response. But what about files or more "generally arbitrary" data streams? Rails provides two methods for this: `send_data` and `send_file`.

The following is a fictitious example, inspired by the awesome movie *Office Space*, of how to send a PDF report in response through `send_data`:

```
def report
  tps_report = QualityAssurance.generate_report(Date.today, :format => :pdf)
  send_data(tps_report, :type => "application/pdf", :filename => "tps_report.pdf"
end
```

Notice how it is passing three arguments to the method: the data that constitutes the document, image, or binary file; an HTTP content type (which defaults to `application/octet-stream`); and the file name suggested to the browser. Two other two available options are `:disposition` and `:status`. `:disposition` defaults to `"attachment"` (save and download) but can also be set to `"inline"` (often used for images). `:status` is used to indicate an HTTP status code (defaults to `"200 OK"` of course).

For working with reports, I highly recommend the Ruby gem Ruport. You can read more about it on its official website at `http://rubyreports.org`.

Similarly, it's possible to send a file that's available on the server, to the client. The following example shows how to use send_file to do just that:

```
def download
  send_file '/path/to/ebook.zip'
end
```

This method also accepts several options, including :filename, :disposition, :type, and :status, as seen with send_data. Other available options are :stream, :buffer_size, :url_based_file-name, and x_send_file:

❑   :stream determines if the file should be sent to the user agent as soon as it's read (if set to true, which is the default behavior if the option is omitted) or if it should only be sent after the entire file has been read (if set to false).

❑   :buffer_size specifies the buffer size in bytes for streaming (defaults to 4096 bytes).

❑   :url_based_filename can be set to true if you want the browser to determine the file name based on the URL. This is necessary for i18n file names on certain browsers. Specifying a file name overrides this option.

❑   :x_send_file is an option that, when set to true, enables support for the X-Sendfile HTTP header in the Apache Web server. The file will be served directly from the disk and not by streaming through a Rails process. The end result is a faster, less memory-intensive operation. This option was incorporated into Rails 2.1 (previously it was available as a plugin), but not all Web servers support it.

NGINX and x_send_file => :true

Nginx — an excellent Russian Web server that's popular within the Rails community — can take advantage of the x_send_file feature as long as you set the header to X-Accel-Redirect (which is similar to the X-Sendfile of Apache). To do so, add the following line to your environment.rb or to an initializer:

```
ActionController::Streaming::X_SENDFILE_HEADER = 'X-Accel-Redirect'
```

---

redirect_to

When the code generated through scaffolding was analyzed, it contained several redirect_to methods. This method allows an action to hand control over to another action. This is very useful and it's a technique that's used in pretty much all Rails applications. Think about the destroy action in your RESTful articles controller:

```
def destroy
  @article = Article.find(params[:id])
  @article.destroy

  respond_to do |format|
    format.html { redirect_to(:back) }
    format.xml  { head :ok }
  end
end
```

This action destroys an article and then, if the requested format is in HTML, it redirects to the articles_url (or the unpublished page, whichever triggered the deletion), which will be handled by the same controller's index action (or again, unpublished). This shows a list of articles to the user, who will see that the article was just deleted.

> As mentioned before for render, **only one** redirect_to **should be ever executed within an action.**

Aside from providing :back or a path, it's also possible to redirect directly to an action:

```
redirect_to(:action => :thanks)
```

The options provided (for example, :action, :controller, :id, and so on) will be passed to url_ to generate the actual URL that Rails needs to redirect to. This means that all the nice options discussed in the routing section are available to redirect_to as well.

By default these redirects are performed as "302 Found," but it's possible to specify otherwise through the :status option by setting it to, for example, :301 (or the equivalent :moved_permanently):

```
redirect_to(articles_url, :status => :301)
```

Less elegantly, it's also possible to set the Status key (in the headers hash) within the action before performing a redirect:

```
headers["Status"] = "301 Moved Permanently"
redirect_to(articles_url)
```

Finally, remember that redirect_to(:back) is just a syntax sugar for redirecting back to the page that issued the request, without the need to write your own logic (that is, redirect_to(request .env["HTTP_REFERER"])).

Accessing the Request and Response Environment

The last couple of examples do something very interesting: the first alters the HTTP headers for the response that is about to be sent, and the second accesses the HTTP REFERER of the request. This is neat, but Rails offers much more when it comes to accessing request and response information.

The following is a list of special identifiers that you can use from within your controller: action_name, cookies, headers, logger, params, request, and response.

Their names are self-descriptive: action_name is a method that returns the name of the current action; cookies represents the cookies for the request; headers is a hash of HTTP headers for the response; logger is a ActiveSupport::BufferedLogger object that's available throughout the application as discussed before; and params is the parameters hash.

request and response are objects that represent the request being processed and the response that is about to be sent, respectively.

You rarely have to modify the response object directly, because Rails takes care of formulating a proper response on its own. However, in the few circumstances where you need to alter the object before it's sent to the client, you can do so easily by accessing one or more of its attributes. Among these, the two that will most likely be used to alter the response object are body and headers.

request, on the other hand, is slightly more complex, and is used frequently enough to warrant further explanation.

To learn more about these two objects, check the documentation for the abstract classes ActionController::AbstractRequest *and* ActionController::AbstractResponse.

The request Object

The environment of a request is captured in the read-only attribute env. From within a debugging session for a simple request, I obtained the following output for request.env:

```
(rdb:5) request.env
{"SERVER_NAME"=>"localhost", "PATH_INFO"=>"/main",
"HTTP_ACCEPT_ENCODING"=>"gzip,deflate,bzip2", "HTTP_USER_AGENT"=>"Moz
illa/5.0 (Windows; U; Windows NT 6.0; en-US) AppleWebKit/525.13 (KHTML, like Gecko)
 Chrome/0.2.149.30 Safari/525.13", "S
CRIPT_NAME"=>"/", "SERVER_PROTOCOL"=>"HTTP/1.1", "HTTP_HOST"=>"localhost:3000",
"HTTP_ACCEPT_LANGUAGE"=>"en-US,en", "REM
OTE_ADDR"=>"127.0.0.1", "SERVER_SOFTWARE"=>"Mongrel 1.1.5",
"REQUEST_PATH"=>"/main", "HTTP_ACCEPT_CHARSET"=>"ISO-8859-1,
*,utf-8", "HTTP_VERSION"=>"HTTP/1.1", "REQUEST_URI"=>"/main",
 "SERVER_PORT"=>"3000", "GATEWAY_INTERFACE"=>"CGI/1.2", "HT
TP_ACCEPT"=>"text/xml,application/xml,application/xhtml+xml,text/html;q=0.9,text/pl
ain;q=0.8,image/png,*/*;q=0.5", "HTTP
_CONNECTION"=>"Keep-Alive", "REQUEST_METHOD"=>"GET"}
```

That's a lot of information that can be used to obtain details about the client and the request. For example, request.env["HTTP_USER_AGENT"] retrieves the user agent for the browser that's being used (in this case Google Chrome).

env is the only attribute for request, but many methods are defined by this object.

Purposely, many of these methods are there to facilitate access to the same information that's available in the env *hash-like object.*

headers returns a hash of HTTP headers:

```
(rdb:5) request.headers
{"SERVER_NAME"=>"localhost", "HTTP_USER_AGENT"=>"Mozilla/5.0 (Windows; U; Windows
NT 6.0; en-US) AppleWebKit/525.13 (KHT
ML, like Gecko) Chrome/0.2.149.30 Safari/525.13",
"HTTP_ACCEPT_ENCODING"=>"gzip,deflate,bzip2", "PATH_INFO"=>"/main", "H
TTP_ACCEPT_LANGUAGE"=>"en-US,en", "HTTP_HOST"=>"localhost:3000",
```

```
"SERVER_PROTOCOL"=>"HTTP/1.1", "SCRIPT_NAME"=>"/", "REQ
UEST_PATH"=>"/main", "SERVER_SOFTWARE"=>"Mongrel 1.1.5",
"REMOTE_ADDR"=>"127.0.0.1", "HTTP_VERSION"=>"HTTP/1.1", "HTTP_A
CCEPT_CHARSET"=>"ISO-8859-1,*,utf-8", "REQUEST_URI"=>"/main",
"SERVER_PORT"=>"3000", "GATEWAY_INTERFACE"=>"CGI/1.2", "HT
TP_ACCEPT"=>"text/xml,application/xml,application/xhtml+xml,text/html;q=0.9,text/pl
ain;q=0.8,image/png,*/*;q=0.5", "REQU
EST_METHOD"=>"GET", "HTTP_CONNECTION"=>"Keep-Alive"}
```

Similarly, `body`, `content_type`, and `content_length` return the request's body as an IO stream, the MIME type (for example, `Mime::XML`), and the length of the body in bytes. `accepts` and `format`, respectively, return the accepted MIME types and the format (as a MIME type as well) used in the request. If no format is available, the first of the accepted types will be used (for browsers this is usually `Mime::HTML`).

> *When you are using the `respond_to` method introduced in Chapter 5, there is usually no need to invoke these "low-level" mime methods directly. The logic that needs to be implemented for each format in the request (among the registered ones, known to Rails) will be defined within the block passed to the method `respond_to`.*

`host`, `domain`, `port`, `port_string`, `host_with_port`, `protocol`, `request_uri`, `url`, and `parameters` all work as you'd probably expect them to:

```
(rdb:5) request.host
"localhost"
(rdb:5) request.domain
"localhost"
(rdb:5) request.port
3000
(rdb:5) request.port_string
":3000"
(rdb:5) request.host_with_port
"localhost:3000"
(rdb:5) request.protocol
"http://"
(rdb:5) request.request_uri
"/main"
(rdb:5) request.url
"http://localhost:3000/main"
(rdb:5) request.parameters
{"action"=>"index", "controller"=>"main"}
```

`remote_ip` is used to retrieve the IP address that issued the request. This method returns a string containing a single IP, or more IPs if one or more proxies are involved.

The `request` object also has the two methods `method` and `request_method`. These return the HTTP method used for the request as a symbol:

```
(rdb:5) request.method
:get
(rdb:5) request.request_method
:get
```

The difference between the two is that method will return :get when a :head request is issued. The reason for this is that from an application standpoint there is usually no need to distinguish between a :get and a :head request.

There is a series of methods that return Boolean values. These methods follow Ruby's convention of ending with a question mark. Among the most common are get?, post?, put?, delete?, head?, ssl?, xhr?, and xml_http_request?.

The first five, corresponding to their five respective verbs, will return true only if the request was issued using the proper HTTP method. request.post?, for example, will return true for POST requests and false for any other type of request verb.

It is common to see an if request.get? or if request.post? statement within an action. This is usually present whenever an action acts differently based on whether the incoming request was a GET or a POST request. In a RESTful controller, if an action is accessible only by a GET or only by a POST request, there is no need to use these methods to check the verb.

Dangerous GET requests

The golden rule of Web development is that any request that retrieves information should be a GET request, and any request that affects the data stored on the server should use the POST HTTP method.

This rule is constantly violated and it's not rare to see publicly accessible links that issue GET requests and have the ability to delete or modify data on the server side. You should avoid this at all costs. Using buttons to submit forms rather than links is a sufficient countermeasure. Another is to use intermediary pages that confirm the requested action.

In the world of REST, you are not limited to GET and POST. You can (and should) use DELETE to destroy resources, POST to create them, PUT to update them, and GET to retrieve them. So PUT and DELETE can affect the state of the server as well, whereas GET shouldn't, whether or not you are in a RESTful context.

Also keep in mind that at this point in time most browsers don't support PUT and DELETE, so these are emulated through POST requests.

---

ssl? is used to determine whether this was an SSL request, and finally, xml_http_request? (and its alias xhr?) are used to check if the incoming request is an Ajax request. This is done by verifying that the value "XMLHttpRequest" was assigned to the request's X-Requested-With header.

This method is fundamental to Ajax applications, because a response will typically vary depending on whether or not the request was an Ajax one. Ajax requests will normally require a response that updates only certain elements of the page, whereas a regular HTML request requires rendering the whole page.

Maintaining the State

It is fair to state that each request-response pair is a world unto itself. For example, an instance variable set within the index action is not going to be available in the view when serving a second request for the edit action.

> By the way, go easy on the number of instance variables that you define in each action. These are expensive and introducing an excessive number of instance variables is considered to be faux pas. If a variable within a controller is not going to be used by the view, declare it as a local variable (that is, don't prefix it with a @ sign).

The stateless nature of the Web poses the challenging question of how to maintain the state. This could be something as simple as carrying a message over from an action to another when a redirect is required, or a more elaborate solution to keep track of which users are currently logged in, without prompting them to re-enter their username and password at each new request for a protected page.

In Rails, the first scenario is resolved through a `flash` object, and the second by employing sessions.

Flash

As mentioned previously, instance variables defined within an action are not available to requests that are serving a different action. The reason for this is that with each request, a brand new instance of the controller is generated. This implies that instance variables cannot be used as a means to pass messages between actions whenever you are performing a redirect (which is, for all practical purposes, a new request). For example, the following snippet will not work because `@message` will be `nil` within the confirm action:

```ruby
# Don't do this
def create
  @email = Email.new(params[:email])
  if @email.save
    @message = 'Your email has been subscribed to our newsletter'
    redirect_to(:action => "confirm")
  else
    render(:action => "new")
  end
end

def confirm
  render :text => @message
end
```

Flash is a hash-like object that has the peculiar characteristic of making its content available until the next request has been processed. Because of this, it's possible to store informative and error messages that you intend to display in the action that you are redirecting to. For example, this is the code for the `create` method in the `ArticlesController` of the blog application:

```ruby
def create
  @article = Article.new(params[:article])

  respond_to do |format|
    if @article.save
      flash[:notice] = 'Article was successfully created.'
      format.html { redirect_to(@article) }
      format.xml  { render :xml => @article, :status => :created,
                                              :location => @article }
```

```
      else
        format.html { render :action => "new" }
        format.xml  { render :xml => @article.errors,
                             :status => :unprocessable_entity }
      end
    end
  end
```

When serving a regular request that comes from a browser, the `:notice` "key" of the hash-like flash object is assigned a confirmation message before redirecting to the `show` action for the article that was just created. That message is then retrieved by the view, while processing the next action (`show`). In fact, in this case (and by default when scaffolding), you render the value of `flash[:notice]` in green within the `articles.html.erb` layout:

```
...
<div id="main" class="container">
    <p style="color: green" id="notice"><%= flash[:notice] %></p>
    <%= yield %>
</div>
...
```

The evaluation of this value could have been placed in any view (for example, `show.html.erb`), but it's usually convenient to make it available for all the actions of a controller, by positioning it within the layout just before the `yield` method.

When the `show` action is finally processed and the message has been displayed, flash will automatically clear its content. You can choose any key (for example, `flash[:confirmation]`), but the most common ones in Rails projects are:`notice`, `:warning`, and `:error`.

The object offers a few methods to alter the default behavior. `discard` enables you to mark the flash to be swiped at the end of the current action. You can either discard the whole object or just one entry:

```
flash.discard         # Discard all
flash.discard(:error) # Discard :error only
```

`now` sets the flash so that it's available for the current action only. You can use it as follows:

```
flash.now[:notice] = "You're still in the current action!"
```

Having used `now` doesn't affect the way the flash entries are retrieved in the view (for example, `flash[:notice]`).

Finally, the method `keep` allows you to extend the lifespan of the flash entries for one more action. Just like `discard`, you can scope the method to a single entry:

```
flash.keep         # Keep all the entries
flash.keep(:notice) # Keep the :notice entry only
```

Behind the scenes, both `discard` and `keep` use the same method, namely `use`, which is a private method that allows them to mark flash entries as already having been used (for `discard`) or as unused (for `keep`).

Any serializable object can be stored in the flash, but it's highly recommended that you keep it simple, and limit the contents to messages (strings) or parameter passing (to the next action).

The flash is stored in the session data, and as such it requires that the sessions are enabled (which they are by default) to work properly. The flash mechanism could easily be emulated by saving the message in the session directly. Unlike saving the messages in a key within the session though, flash is handy because it automatically clears itself after a response has been provided for the next request, whereas objects in the session stick around until the session data has been explicitly removed or the session has expired.

Sessions

Because HTTP is a stateless protocol, Rails sessions are used to persist the state across several actions/requests. If you've done Web development before, this concept should not be new to you. For example, if you are familiar with the ASP.NET session state, you know that session variables are stored in a `SessionStateItemCollection` object, which in turn is exposed within a WebForms page as its `Session` property.

Setting session variables in ASP.NET is fairly straightforward thanks to `Session`:

Visual Basic (.NET)

```
Dim firstName As String = "Antonio"
Dim lastName As String = "Cangiano"
Session("FirstName") = firstName
Session("LastName") = lastName
```

C#

```
string firstName = "Antonio";
string lastName = "Cangiano";
Session["FirstName"] = firstName;
Session["LastName"] = lastName;
```

And so is retrieving them:

Visual Basic (.NET)

```
Dim firstName as String = CType(Session.Item("FirstName"), String)
Dim lastName as String = CType(Session.Item("LastName"), String)
```

C#

```
string firstName = (string)(Session["FirstName"]);
string lastName = (string)(Session["LastName"]);
```

In the Rails world, session data is stored in a collection-like object too (or hash-like in Ruby speak), which is accessible through the `session` (lowercase) attribute of each controller. Setting the same values outlined previously in Rails is done as follows:

```
session[:first_name] = "Antonio"
session[:last_name] = "Cangiano"
```

And retrieving values set elsewhere is just as easy, like if you were dealing with a regular hash:

```
first_name = session[:first_name]
last_name = session[:last_name]
```

session's keys can be strings, but it's idiomatically preferred to use symbols. The distinction between strings and symbols is explained in Chapter 3.

What to Store in the Session?

Though sessions can store any serializable object (those that can be marshaled and unmarshaled through Ruby's `Marshal.dump` and `Marshal.load` methods), it is a good idea to try to keep your session data's size to a minimum. Instead of storing a whole ActiveRecord object (which is a very bad practice to get in the habit of), just store its id. Don't store too much data (as you will see, the cookie-based sessions are limited to 4Kb) and try to avoid storing important information within the session before it has been safely persisted in the database.

Like the ASP.NET session state, Rails sessions are identified by a unique id known as the session id. This is randomly generated as a 32-hexadecimal characters long value, and just like the `SessionID` property in ASP.NET, this too is stored in a cookie by default, ready to be retrieved at each request to identify which session data belongs to which request.

The cookies generated by Rails are crypto-signed, to ensure that their content is valid and that they haven't been tampered with by a malicious user (even though their content is not encrypted and is therefore visible in clear text). Furthermore, Rails 2.2 increases the security of your projects by setting by the default option `:session_http_only` to `true`. This disables JavaScript from having access to the cookies.

The fact that the `session_id` key is assigned 32 hexadecimal characters implies that a Rails application is able to uniquely identify up to 340282366920938463463374607431768211456 different active sessions (that's 16 to the 32nd power).

When dealing with sessions, the most important question to ask is where to store the session data.

Session Storage Options

Rails offers several session storage options, each of which has its own pros and cons, depending on your application type, traffic, and deployment arrangements.

ActiveRecordStore

With the `ActiveRecordStore` session data is marshaled in Base64 format and stored in a `data` column within a `sessions` table in the database by default. That table has a `session_id` text field and, by convention, the usual `id` primary key. As usual, these defaults can be overwritten if need be. By default the table is defined with the automatically handled `updated_at` and `created_at` attributes, which makes implementing session expiration fairly easy.

Run `rake db:sessions:create` to create a migration file for the `sessions` table. The generated file will then be defined as follows:

```
class CreateSessions < ActiveRecord::Migration
  def self.up
    create_table :sessions do |t|
      t.string :session_id, :null => false
```

```
      t.text :data
      t.timestamps
    end

    add_index :sessions, :session_id
    add_index :sessions, :updated_at
  end

  def self.down
    drop_table :sessions
  end
end
```

Notice how `session_id` *is not nullable, a default* `id` *column is generated, and indexes are defined for both* `session_id` *and* `updated_at` *to improve performance.*

At this point, all you have to do is migrate (`rake db:migrate`) and set `active_record_store` as the session storage for the application in `config\environment.rb`. There is a commented out line for this particular option already, so all you have to do it is uncomment it:

```
config.action_controller.session_store = :active_record_store
```

That symbol corresponds to the class `CGI::Session::ActiveRecordStore`. Like the other options you'll see in a moment, the symbol used for setting the session store is always the snake_case version of the class name.

When you develop, at times you may need to clear all the sessions. To do so quickly and easily, use the handy `rake db:sessions:clear`.

CookieStore

`CookieStore` is Rails' default session storage. Unlike `ActiveRecordStore`, where the session data is stored server side in the database, `CookieStore` stores the data client-side in cookies.

We can only assume that this would be his favorite session storage option if Cookie Monster were to ever entertain the idea of programming in Rails.

The session data stored in cookies is limited to 4096 bytes. The user cannot modify the content of a cookie, though (for example, altering a `user_id` variable to access other people's session data). In fact, each cookie includes a message digest and the integrity of the cookie is checked through the SHA1 algorithm. This can be changed to other digests supported by OpenSSL (for example, SHA256, MD5, and so on).

> In `environment.rb` you'll find a `:secret` option set for verifying cookie-based sessions. This is randomly generated for you and needs to be at least 30 characters long. Don't replace it with common words, or it will be vulnerable to dictionary attacks. If you are porting a legacy application to Rails 2.2, you can use `rake secret` to have a cryptographically secure key generated for you.

Because this is Rails' default option, it usually isn't required that this is set explicitly; but if you were to do so, it would be set as follows:

```
config.action_controller.session_store = :cookie_store
```

Rails provides you with a cookies *attribute as well, which enables you to work directly with cookies should you need to. This wraps the process of reading and writing cookies into an abstraction layer that works similarly to a hash.*

The CookieStore is a sensible default, given that it's very easy on the server and there is nothing to set up. It is in fact a good choice for applications that expect a lot of traffic. But there are two important caveats: CookieStore is only suitable if the data that's being stored doesn't exceed 4 Kb (it's always a good idea to keep your sessions light) or isn't sensitive/confidential, given that the end user can read the marshaled content.

CookieStore *is "easy on the server" because all of the session data is stored client side. All the server has to do is serialize the data and write it in a cookie at the end of the request processing, and conversely read the data from the cookie, verify its integrity, and unmarshal its content for the controller to use.*

DrbStore

DRb stands for Distributed Ruby and it's a library that's used to share objects via TCP/IP. When adopting DrbStore, the marshaled session data is stored on a DRb server. This server doesn't belong to the application, and as an external entity is not handled by Rails either.

Rails provides you with a DRb server, but it's very primitive and is essentially a hash that's enabled for DRb access. You can find it in C:\ruby\lib\ruby\gems\1.8\gems\actionpack-2.2.2\ lib\action_controller\session\drb_server.rb *(your actual location may vary depending on where you installed Ruby and whether you installed Rails as a gem).*

To use this option, specify:

```
config.action_controller.session_store = :drb_store
```

This is theoretically a highly scalable solution for session management, because the distributed nature of DRb would enable scaling out with multiple processes on several servers serving many requests that need to access the same session object. The caveat to this is that an efficient DRb server, with the ability to expire sessions as well, is required (for example, you may have to develop one).

MemCacheStore

memcached is a high-performance, distributed memory object caching system that was originally developed for LiveJournal, but now it's used by many of the largest websites on the net, including YouTube, Wikipedia, Slashdot, Flickr, Digg, and Twitter. The basic idea behind this open-source program (released under the BSD license) is to alleviate the database load by reducing the amount of access to the database that's required to retrieve data. Data and objects are in fact cached in memory, often in a distributed fashion across multiple machines. The database is only accessed if the data has not been stored in the in-memory cache. If this is the case, memcached falls back on the database.

This option is set by including the following line in config\environment.rb (or config\environ-ments\production.rb if you only need it for production):

```
config.action_controller.session_store = :mem_cache_store
```

There are quite a few options that you can specify and the MemCacheStore's configuration and setup are beyond the scope of this book. Just keep in mind that should your high-traffic site adopt memcached to ease the database server load, then taking advantage of memcached for the sessions as well, through the MemCacheStore, is a good idea. As an added benefit, you get the ability to set the expiration time in the configuration, and you no longer have to worry about routinely expiring/cleaning up the session data:

```
config.action_controller.session_options[:expires] = 1200
```

PStore

When you use this option, ActionController stores sessions within files (in PStore format, keeping the data in marshaled form) on the server. It can be set as follows:

```
config.action_controller.session_store = :mem_cache_store
```

Assigning strings to session_options's keys is possible if you want to define a prefix for the files (with :prefix), as well as their location (with :tmpdir). By default the generated files are stored in the tmp\sessions folder of your application and can be tidied up as you develop with the rake task tmp:sessions:clear.

In production, the same files will typically need to be cleaned up periodically, often executing the file elimination through cron, which is a scheduling service for Unix-like systems.

In theory PStore can work well if you have a fast SAN (Storage Area Network) in place or if you have one server and a limited amount of traffic; but as the number of sessions grow, beyond a certain thresh-old having to create so many files in the file system will inevitably become a bottleneck, which will therefore perform poorly when compared to the other solutions mentioned previously.

Other Storage Options

For the sake of completeness, two other storage options exist: MemoryStore and FileStore. These store the session data in either the memory (fast but not scalable) or in plain files (which only accept strings and have the same limits of PStore). In practice, no Rails developer worth their salt would be likely to choose either of these options.

If you search for them, you'll also find that other *Store classes have been released by some developers, but these are not part of the Rails core and their quality and stability may vary.

In conclusion, there isn't a clear winner when it comes to choosing how to store your sessions. It depends on too many factors to be able to broadly suggest which one you should take up for your projects. As a very general rule of thumb, I'd say that you might want to start with CookieStore if the 4Kb limit works for you and you don't need to store confidential information in the session. Failing that, ActiveRecordStore is a good choice that's relatively fast, easy to maintain, and scalable. Should the success of your Web appli-cation cause you to need to offload some of the database work, then MemCacheStore or DrbStore should do the trick. In any case, I would probably stay away from a file-based solution like PStore.

Enabling and Disabling Sessions

Aside from choosing a proper session storage type, you can use the session method within your controllers to fine tune how sessions should be handled. By default sessions are enabled for all the actions within each controller in your application, but it's possible to be more selective than that.

Sessions in Rails 2.3 are "lazy loaded," meaning that they are not loaded unless you make explicit use of them.

To disable sessions within a controller pass :off to the macro-like session method:

```
class ExampleController < ActionController::Base
  session :off
  #...
end
```

This disables session management for all the actions defined within ExampleController.

To disable session management for all the actions, save for a few, within a controller, use the :except option:

```
session :off, :except => %w(download feed)
```

Conversely, to do the exact opposite and disable sessions for only a few actions, use :only:

```
session :off, :only => %w(download feed)
```

An :if option exists for times when you need to disable (or enable) a session based on a condition. This option expects a Proc object:

```
# Disables session management for all the actions, excluding index,
# if the request was not an HTML or Ajax request.
session :off, :except => :index,
        :if => Proc.new { |req| !(req.format.html? || req.format.js?) }
```

session can be used within ApplicationController, so that its effects are inherited by all the other controllers. For example, the following disables sessions for the whole application:

```
class ApplicationController < ActionController::Base
  session :off
  #...
end
```

If you need to enable sessions for a few controllers and/or a few actions only, you can do so by using session :on. For example, consider the following controllers:

```
class ApplicationController < ActionController::Base
  session :off
  #...
end
```

```
class FirstController < ActionController::Base
  session :on
  #...
end

class SecondController < ActionController::Base
  session :on, :only => :feed
  #...
end
```

This disables session management for all the controllers, but turns it back on for all the actions in the first controller, and for the feed action in the second controller.

The same method can be used to specify a few more options as well. Some common ones are setting a session domain (:session_domain), a default session id (:session_id), the name to be used for the session in cookies (:session_key), the request path for the cookies (:session_path), and whether sessions are enabled over SSL only (:session_secure).

As a matter of fact, Rails automatically sets the session key based on the application's name. For example, your blog application had the following in config\environment.rb:

```
config.action_controller.session = {
  :session_key => '_blog_session',
  :secret      => 'c410dcb43b70ece50b4856a4b2e5d029404338e51d8ae45b642659781...'
}
```

Remember, session options can be specified within a controller or within an environment configuration file (like Rails 2.x does by default).

For a complete list of accepted options check the documentation for the method ActionController::Base.process_cgi.

Session Expiration

One of the problems related to session management is expiring and/or removing old session data. The reason for this is that you typically don't want users to be able to access session data after a certain amount of time has passed. For example, a login system would normally ask you to re-login after 15, 30, or 60 minutes of inactivity. The need to expire users' sessions is coupled with the fact that sessions stored on the server side take up valuable resources, so over time you need to come up with a system that performs regular clean ups.

The expiration logic varies depending on the session storage option you've chosen, but generally speaking, deleting the session data is easier than, and just as effective as, implementing the expiration of a particular session_id stored in a cookie.

As mentioned before, for PStore sessions, a cron job (or equivalent) that deletes the files within tmp\ sessions at regular intervals will do. If you are using ActiveRecordStore, you can do the same thing but execute a DELETE SQL query, taking advantage of the updated_at column. For DrbStore, your server should implement the expiration logic for the shared session data. MemCacheStore sessions can be expired automatically by simply configuring the session_options[:expires] option, as shown in the previous section.

Finally, cookie-based sessions are automatically taken care of when the users close their browser, but there are several possible ways to implement a timeout to limit the validity of a cookie to a set amount of time.

You can find a somewhat disorganized discussion about some of these possibilities and available plugins on the official Rails Wiki at http://wiki.rubyonrails.org/rails/pages/ HowtoChangeSessionOptions. *Some of the information provided is out of date as well, but it's a decent pointer.*

Whenever you need to explicitly clear the session data for a current session, you can do so by calling the method reset_session within your actions. This will typically be used for "sign out" or "clear history" types of links in your application, but can also be used when defining your own expiration logic. For example, you could store the cookie time in the session (for example, in session[:updated_at]), and check whether the expiration time has passed. When that's the case, you can invoke reset_session to clear the session data.

Filters

Filters are a convenient way to wrap actions and execute code before and/or after an action has been, or is being, processed. Before filters are executed before the action processing takes place. If any of the filters in the before filter chain returns false, processing is terminated and no other filters (or the action itself) are executed for that request. Likewise, the code within after filters is executed after the code within the action has been processed.

The main filters are before_filter, after_filter, and around_filter. When any one of them appears within a controller, its effect applies to all the actions within the current controller and its subclasses. As you can probably imagine, placing a filter within ApplicationController adds that filter to the chain of filters for all the actions in the application. All three filters accept the :only and :except options — which you should be familiar with by now — to limit the number of actions for which the filter should be applied.

These methods accept a method name as a symbol:

```
class ExampleController < ActionController::Base
  before_filter :authenticate

  #...

  private

  def authenticate
    #...
  end
end
```

The method authenticate *will be executed before any actions within* ExampleController.

or a block:

```
class ExampleController < ActionController::Base
  after_filter do |controller|
```

```
      # The action name is stored in controller.action_name
      #...
    end

  #...
end
```

In addition, they even accept any class (an object in the case of the around filter) that contains a definition for a method `filter`. That method needs to be a class method (for example, `self.filter(controller,&block)`) for before and after filters, and an instance method (that is, `def filter(controller,&block)`) for the around filter. For example:

```
class ExampleController < ActionController::Base
  before_filter LogFilter, :except => :download
  around_filter BenchmarkFilter.new, :only => :speed_test

  # ...
end
```

Every time `before_filter` or `after_filter` is defined in a controller, the filter that it defines is appended to its respective before or after filter chains. If, for instance, you were to define a before filter in a controller, and a before filter in its superclass, the filter within the controller would be executed only after the filter inherited from the parent class was executed (and only if this didn't return `false`). This may not be what you want in every scenario. To prefix, rather than append, a filter to its filter execution chain, you can use the corresponding methods `prepend_before_filter` and `prepend_after_filter`.

Unlike the other two filters, `around_filter` executes some code before the action is invoked, then the action is processed, and finally more code gets executed within the filter. As the name suggests, around filters wrap around an action. When passing a method name as a symbol, the action is invoked through `yield`:

```
class ExampleController < ActionController::Base
  around_filter :benchmark, :except => :login

  #...

  private

  def benchmark
    start = Time.now
    yield
    exec_time = Time.now - start
    logger.info("Processing #{action_name} took #{exec_time} seconds.")
  end
end
```

And as mentioned before, you also pass a block to the method. In this case, the method will have two block parameters, one for the controller and another for the action as a `Proc` object that's ready to be executed through the `call` method:

```
class ExampleController < ActionController::Base
  around_filter(:except => :login) do |controller, action|
    start = Time.now
```

```
      action.call
      exec_time = Time.now - start
      logger.info("Processing #{controller.action_name} took #{exec_time} seconds."
  end
end
```

An around filter will typically invoke the execution of the action, but this is not necessarily the case. If `yield` (when passing a symbol to the filter declaration) or `action.call` (when passing to it a block) is not invoked, the action will not be executed.

> **These examples are just a sample of how** `around_filter` **can be used; you shouldn't time your actions, because this information is already available in your logs.**

When there are multiple declarations for `around_filter`, they're chained together by merging them, so that all the code before the execution of the action is executed in the order it appears, and all the code after the action is invoked will be executed after the action processing in the order that appears as well.

To clarify this further with an example, consider the following code that has three filters defined, in the order `first_filter`, `second_filter`, and then an unnamed filter that uses a block:

```
def ExampleController < ActionController::Base
  around_filter :first_filter, :second_filter

  around_filter do |controller, action|
    logger.info("In the block before the action")
    action.call
    logger.info("In the block after the action")
  end

  def index
    logger.info("In the index action")
  end

  private

  def first_filter
    logger.info("In the first filter before the action")
    yield
    logger.info("In the first filter after the action")
  end

  def second_filter
    logger.info("In the second filter before the action")
    yield
    logger.info("In the second filter after the action")
  end
end
```

When `/my/index` is invoked, the following result is yielded in the logs:

```
In the first filter before the action
In the second filter before the action
```

```
In the block before the action
In the index action
Rendering m/index
In the block after the action
In the second filter after the action
In the first filter after the action
```

It's also possible to skip the filters defined in a parent class from within children classes by invoking the methods `skip_before_filter`, `skip_after_filter`, and `skip_filter` (which skips any filter, including around filters). Declarations using these three methods accept only a method name as a symbol, and therefore can only skip filters defined through a symbol (and not those defined through a block or a class/object).

Just like filters, these declarations also accept `:only` *and* `:except`.

Filters are just regular code that's defined within the controller and as such they can access all the attributes and objects available to normal actions, including the ability to redirect and render content back to the user. For this reason, before filters are often used for authentication purposes and after filters are frequently delegated to the task of altering the response object in some way (for example, to compress the output when the user's browser supports it).

Verification

A higher abstraction layer based on filters is provided by Rails through the `verify` method. This method enables you to verify certain conditions before an action is executed. In practice, this is a fancier `before_filter` that's able to guard an action against the possibility of being invoked if certain conditions are not met. These conditions can verify the existence of a particular parameter key, flash key, session key, HTTP method, and whether it was an Ajax request (by passing `:xhr`).

Consult the documentation for examples and reference points for the method `Action Controller::Verification::ClassMethods.verify`.

Using Filters for HTTP Basic Authentication

Having introduced the concept of filters, it is now easy to show how HTTP basic authentication can be added to the blog app. Rails provides a lengthy method called `authenticate_or_request_with_http_basic`, which enables you to log in through HTTP Basic Authentication, without the need to design an ad-hoc form. This is probably not something you'd want to expose your users to (usually), but as a blogger who needs to access a reserved area, you won't likely mind this. It's functional and extremely easy to implement. Moreover, it's a good example of how filters can aid in the design of Rails applications.

Open the `ArticlesController` and add the following:

```
class ArticlesController < ApplicationController
  before_filter :authenticate, :except => %w(index show)

  #... All the existing actions ...
```

```
    private

    def authenticate
      authenticate_or_request_with_http_basic('Administration') do |username,
password|
        username == 'admin' && password == 'secret'
      end
    end
end
```

Whenever an action on an article is requested, with the exception of `index` and `show`, which should be visible to the public, the application will try to authenticate the user. For example, try to click the Unpublished Articles link in the menu and you should be prompted for a username and a password as shown in Figure 8-2. Enter `admin` and `secret`, and you'll be able to log in and see the page. Clicking the Cancel button will produce an HTTP Basic: Access denied message (but you could just as easily create a redirect to a public page). When the user has already been authenticated, the login dialog will no longer be shown. However, unless the Remember Password check box has been marked off, or the browser remembers the credentials automatically for you, when you close your browser you are essentially "logging off" and will be prompted for credentials the next time you visit a protected link.

Figure 8-2

Notice that you get a warning about a basic authentication without a secure connection. The username and password will in fact be sent in clear text, so it's a very good idea to adopt SSL in production mode.

Now you need to protect a few actions in the `CommentsController` as well, because you don't want to allow your users to destroy or edit comments. Change it to look like this:

```ruby
class CommentsController < ApplicationController
  layout "articles"

  before_filter :get_article
  before_filter :authenticate, :only => %w(edit update destroy)

  #... All the existing actions ...

  private

  def get_article
    @article = Article.find(params[:article_id])
  end

  def authenticate
    authenticate_or_request_with_http_basic('Administration') do |username, password|
      username == 'admin' && password == 'secret'
    end
  end
end
```

When you visit `/articles/1/comments/1/edit` now you are prompted for a username and password.

> Rails 2.3 adds a more secure form of HTTP Basic Authentication, known as HTTP Digest Authentication. This makes use of the `authenticate_or_request_with_http_digest` method.

Ideas for Improving the Authentication System

That `username == 'admin' && password == 'secret'` is extremely simplistic and that password in clear text might make you cringe. But the principle behind using `before_filter` along with HTTP Basic Authentication stands. You could, for example, replace that line of code with a `User.authenticate(username, password)` of sorts, and then implement `authenticate` as a class method in the model. Perhaps something like this:

```ruby
def self.authenticate(username, password)
  user = self.find_by_username(username)
  user && user.valid_password?(password)
end
```

Where `valid_password?` *is a method defined in the model, so that* `User` *instances are able to compare the password provided with the encrypted version stored in a field of the table.*

As long as the method returns `true` when the user can be authenticated and `false` when the user cannot, `authenticate_or_request_with_http_basic` will be pleased and this basic logging system will work.

There is no User model in the sandbox/basic application, but many projects will have one.

Also note that the simplicity of the implementation shown in this example has a big downside: you show "admin" links to regular unauthenticated users. In some applications this might be okay, but for a blog this is not the case. To solve this problem, you could set an instance variable `@is_authenticated` within the `authenticate` method:

```
@is_authenticated = authenticate_or_request_with_http_basic('Administration') do
|username, password|
  username == 'admin' && password == 'secret'
end
```

And then you could check in the `articles.html.erb` layout `if @is_authenticated`, before visualizing admin links. You could even define a helper method within the `ApplicationController`:

```
class ApplicationController < ActionController::Base
  helper :all # include all helpers, all the time
  helper_method :logged_in? # Make logged_in? available in the view

  def logged_in?
    @is_authenticated
  end

  #...
end
```

With this in place, in the view it's possible to show a link only if the user is logged in, in this way:

```
<li><a href="/">Home</a></li>
<% if logged_in? -%>
  <li><%= link_to 'Unpublished Articles', unpublished_articles_path %></li>
  <li><%= link_to 'New Article', new_article_path %></li>
<% end -%>
```

The process will have to be repeated for every link that isn't supposed to appear to the unauthenticated user. Of course, if you were to do so, you'd be left with no link with which to trigger the login system when you, the blogger, aren't authenticated yet. In that case, you could either leave a single generic Admin link that points to a protected link, or simply bookmark a URL that triggers an action affected by the `before_filter` (for example, the path `/articles/unpublished`).

If you are experimenting with this, remember to assign the result of the authentication method to the `@is_authenticated` instance variable in the `CommentsController` as well, and hide links in the templates in `app\views\comments` too.

You may notice that having similar code in both controllers (articles and comments) is a minor infraction of the DRY principle. But nothing that can't be resolved with a bit of refactoring, for example, by placing the `before_filter` declaration and authentication method within an `AdminController`, subclass of `ApplicationController`, and having all the administrative controllers inherit from it. Or perhaps in a simpler manner, by defining the `authenticate` method within `ApplicationController` so that is accessible to both controllers.

It's also worth pointing out that with the namespaces provided by routing, it may be worth separating the publicly available actions from the administrative ones; for example, having `index` and `show` within `ArticlesController` and moving the other five actions to `Admin::ArticlesController`. The URLs would change, the helpers for the actions defined within the administrative articles controller would be prefixed by admin, and therefore it would be easy to distinguish between the two controllers. Keep in mind, though, that this would require quite a bit of renaming in both the controller layer and in the view layer. For a larger project, this method of separation would be recommended.

Feel free to experiment with these and other ideas that you might have, because making mistakes and figuring out how to solve them is an important part of the process of learning.

Finally, for real applications, consider using the restful_authentication plugin instead. This is the plugin used by most Rails sites out there and it has many useful features, including secure password handling and the ability to send validation emails before activating accounts. You could write your own user authentication and authorization system, but the restful_authentication plugin is usually a good starting point. Checking its code is also an excellent way to learn more about "best practices"; for example, how to encrypt passwords in the database (with a cryptographic salt for added security). You can find its code online on GitHub:

```
http://github.com/technoweenie/restful-authentication/tree/master
```

There is also a fork that's aimed at being internationalization-friendly, called restful-authentication-i18n. This too is available on GitHub, which is now the most popular repository site for Ruby and Rails code, outside of RubyForge.

Testing Controllers

Testing is an important component of performing Agile Web development. In fact, as stressed multiple times before, one of the fundamental principles of the Agile methodologies is the ability to change the software code base to respond to changes in requirements.

It's easy enough to verify that routing and controllers are working as expected by firing up your favorite browser and trying out paths within the application. But this approach is not systematic and won't provide you with any level of confidence, as you continue to change and evolve your application. Furthermore, working on a code base that doesn't have good test coverage is risky and tends to require much more time and effort while debugging.

As a reminder, at any time you can check your test coverage and other interesting statistics about your project by running rake stats.

For these reasons, this chapter concludes with a brief tour of what Rails bakes-in for testing routes and controllers.

Testing Routes

Route testing consists of writing unit tests that verify that the mapping between paths and the controllers' code works as expected.

Your routing tests can be stored in `test\unit\routing_test.rb`, which is just going to be a regular test case (within the context of Rails):

```
require 'test_helper'

class RoutingTest < ActiveSupport::TestCase

  #... Your routing tests...

end
```

This file is not generated automatically by Rails and must be manually created by developers who intend to test routes.

Routing consists of two parts: generating paths from amidst a bunch of options (like `:controller` and `:action`), and obtaining these same options by recognizing paths. Not surprisingly then, Rails provides us with three assert methods related to routes: `assert_generates`, `assert_recognizes`, and `assert_routing`, which unites the two previous ones.

These are defined in `ActionController::Assertions::RoutingAssertions` and their signatures are as follow:

```
assert_generates(expected_path, options, defaults={}, extras = {}, message=nil)
assert_recognizes(expected_options, path, extras={}, message=nil)
assert_routing(path, options, defaults={}, extras={}, message=nil)
```

`extras` *is used to store query string parameters.* `extras` *and* `options` *need to use symbols for keys and strings for their values, or assertions will fail. Ignore the* `defaults` *parameter that's currently unused. As usual, the* `message` *parameter is used to provide a custom error message upon failure.*

If you consider the blog application, you could use `assert_generates` to write the following assertion:

```
assert_generates("/articles/unpublished", :controller => "articles",
                                          :action => "unpublished")
```

This verifies the assertion that the hash of options { `:controller => "articles"`, `:action => "unpublished"` } generates the path `/articles/unpublished`.

The opposite of that assertion would be:

```
assert_recognizes({ :controller => "articles", :action => "unpublished" },
                  "/articles/unpublished")
```

This verifies that the path `/articles/unpublished` is correctly recognized in the hash of options { `:controller => "articles"`, `:action => "unpublished"` }.

Finally, both of them can be tested at the same time through `assert_routing`. For example, in the following very simple test case, I tested for both recognition and generation of the path:

```
require 'test_helper'

class RoutingTest < ActiveSupport::TestCase
```

```
load "config/routes.rb"

test "generating and recognizing /articles/unpublished" do
  assert_routing("/articles/unpublished", :controller => "articles",
                                          :action => "unpublished")
end
end
```

Notice that the `routes.rb` *file needs to be loaded explicitly.*

By the way, the descriptive string for test cases is a feature that has been long available through third-party code (typically in BDD frameworks like RSpec and Shoulda) but that has now been integrated into the core. The old syntax (for example, `def test_unpublished`) is still supported for backwards compatibility.

You can run routing tests by executing `rake test:units`. If your source code is stored in an SVN or, starting with Rails 2.2, in a Git repository, you can use the command `rake test:uncommitted` to speed up testing, by limiting the test run to the tests whose files have not been committed yet (for example, they have been changed locally).

Using autotest -rails

Many professional Rails developers like to use `autotest`, which continuously monitors the files you change so that the associated tests are run. The advantage of this is that you don't have to sit there and wait for your entire test suite to run, because they'll run continuously and will alert you when any test fails or goes into error. This promotes Test-Driven development, reduces the context switch between writing code, using the command line to run tests, and opening up the browser. You can install it with `gem install ZenTest` (prepend `sudo` if you are not running Windows) and then run it as `autotest -rails` in your Rails project. You can read an enthusiastic blog post about it and watch a quick screencast online at `http://nubyonrails.com/articles/autotest-rails`.

Functional Testing

Functional testing is the process of testing actions within a single controller. If you inspect the `test\functional` folder for the blog application, you'll notice that the `scaffold` generator has created `articles_controller_test.rb` and `comments_controller_test.rb` for you. In fact, anytime a controller gets generated a functional test case for it is created as well. When you generate a controller through the `controller` generator, the functional test case is just a stub; however, `scaffold` does one better than that. In fact, the following is the automatically generated code for `articles_controller_test.rb`:

```
require 'test_helper'

class ArticlesControllerTest < ActionController::TestCase
  test "should get index" do
    get :index
    assert_response :success
```

```
    assert_not_nil assigns(:articles)
  end

  test "should get new" do
    get :new
    assert_response :success
  end

  test "should create article" do
    assert_difference('Article.count') do
      post :create, :article => { }
    end

    assert_redirected_to article_path(assigns(:article))
  end

  test "should show article" do
    get :show, :id => articles(:one).id
    assert_response :success
  end

  test "should get edit" do
    get :edit, :id => articles(:one).id
    assert_response :success
  end

  test "should update article" do
    put :update, :id => articles(:one).id, :article => { }
    assert_redirected_to article_path(assigns(:article))
  end

  test "should destroy article" do
    assert_difference('Article.count', -1) do
      delete :destroy, :id => articles(:one).id
    end

    assert_redirected_to articles_path
  end
end
```

Spend a few minutes analyzing this code, and you'll notice that it's quite readable and easy to understand. Consider the first test:

```
  test "should get index" do
    get :index
    assert_response :success
    assert_not_nil assigns(:articles)
  end
```

get :index simulates an HTTP GET request for the index action. This method, and others in "its family," expects an action name and three optional hashes for storing parameters, session variables, and flash messages that should be associated with the request.

Remember that if you are passing a hash to the method, skipping any previous hashes in the signature, you'll need to provide an empty hash to indicate to Ruby that your hash is an nth parameter and not the second one (for example, `get :index, {}, { :my_key => "my value" }`*).*

You then expect the response to be successful (200 OK), so you assert that with `assert_response :success`. Finally `assert_not_nil assigns(:articles)` asserts that an `@articles` instance variable was set by the `index` action.

Let's consider a slightly more complex test, among the auto-generated ones:

```ruby
test "should destroy article" do
  assert_difference('Article.count', -1) do
    delete :destroy, :id => articles(:one).id
  end

  assert_redirected_to articles_path
end
```

`assert_difference` takes two arguments, and indicates that you expect `Article.count` to be smaller by one, after the code within its associated block has been executed. In fact, within its block here I destroyed an article by simulating an HTTP DELETE request for the `destroy` action, and passing it an `:id` parameter. `articles(:one).id` is just the id of the first of the two records within your fixture.

These two records are automatically loaded in the test database from the default fixture file (`arti-cles.yml`*) in* `test\fixtures`*.*

The test then goes on asserting that after an article has been deleted, it should be redirected to `articles_path` (once again, these helpers make your life easier).

You can run this test case by executing `rake test:functionals`, but it's also possible to run a single test case as follows:

```
ruby -I test test/functional/articles_controller_test.rb
```

For improved reporting of test errors and failures, you may want to consider the TURN library, available at `http://codeforpeople.rubyforge.org/turn`*.*

Scaffolding has also generated a similar test case, which you can always augment, for the comments controller. If you run `rake test:functionals` you'll notice though that things don't quite work out of the box. And the reason for this is that you changed the default behavior of these controllers by nesting them, and defined your own logic for redirecting so that the blog appears to be laid out logically (well most of it, at least) to its user and visitors. You also changed the fixtures within Chapter 7, as I introduced the subject of testing models, so the current functional test, for example, expects a "one" fixture that doesn't exist.

Consider this as the perfect opportunity to experiment with working with tests. It would be a very beneficial exercise if you were to attempt to correct the default test cases so that they work for your application. You could also add more tests and assertions, and perhaps even change the code of the application, as you discover odd or unwanted behaviors. The keyword here is experiment. Try things out to get acquainted with these concepts; even if you make mistakes, `rake test:functionals` will tell you when you get it right.

> **It is recommended that you read the functional tests section of the official Rails guide dedicated to the subject of testing, which you can find online at** `http://guides.rubyonrails.org/testing_rails_applications.html`.

It's important to notice that the request type methods available are `get`, `post`, `put`, `head`, and `delete` to be able to properly test RESTful controllers. Also, `assigns` is not the only hash available after one of those five methods has been used. In fact, while `assigns` stores all the instance variables that were set in the action (as they are accessible to the view), `cookies` gives you access to the cookies that were set, as `flash` does to the flash object and `session` to the session variables and data.

> *For historical reasons,* `assigns` *is the only object whose keys are accessed through round brackets.* `cookies`, `flash`, *and* `session` *all use the regular square brackets with a symbol or a string as a key.*

After having simulated a request, you also get access to three useful instance variables: `@controller`, `@request`, and `@response`. As their names suggest, these are, respectively, the controller processing your request, the request object, and the response object produced by the controller.

Besides `assert_response` and `assert_redirected_to` many more useful assertions are available. Check the API documentation for the module `ActionController::Assertions`. All the assertions defined by `ActionController` are contained within six classes of that module: `DomAssertions`, `ModelAssertions`, `ResponseAssertions`, `RoutingAssertions`, `SelectorAssertions`, and `TagAssertions`.

Integration Testing

Whereas functional testing pertains to the domain of a single controller, integration testing aims to test the integration of multiple controllers. This isn't very different from testing a single controller, except that there are a few practical implications. The test case needs to inherit from `ActionController::IntegrationTest`, its file is not automatically generated for you when a controller is created (use the `integration_test` generator instead for this), and it needs to be stored in `test\integration`. Fixtures are not automatically loaded, but you need to explicitly include them through the `fixture` method. It also means that a few helpers are provided in support of being able to test the flow of the application. For example, there are methods like `https!` (to emulate a request over HTTPS) and `follow_redirect!`, `open_session`, or `put_via_redirect`, which creates an HTTP PUT request and follows any redirect caused by a controller's response. If you generated the Rails guide in your project, open the file `doc\guides\testing_rails_applications.html#_integration_testing` in your favorite browser to learn more about integration testing and see a few examples of it.

Summary

Routing and controllers are fundamental aspects of every Rails application. This chapter tried to provide an overview of most of the features that are available for you to use.

Parts of this chapter can be viewed as reference-like and are admittedly harder to digest. So don't worry, no one is expecting you walk away remembering every single method or every option in the API. Whenever you need a specialized bit of information, you can always go back to what you read, as well as consult the official API documentation.

In fact, the goal of this chapter, and this book as a whole, is to provide you with a good introduction, show you a few advanced aspects, and give you a good sense of what developing in Rails looks like as well as what the pieces that compose the framework puzzle are, so that you can quickly get started and apply these concepts to your own Rails projects.

Caching and performance testing are covered within Chapter 11, but in the next chapter, you'll finally complete the MVC triad by analyzing the view layer.

Rendering the User Interface with ActionView

*After researching the market, Ruby on Rails stood out as the best choice.
We have been very happy with that decision. We will continue building on
Rails and consider it a key business advantage.*

— Evan Williams, Creator of Blogger, ODEO and Twitter

The previous chapter analyzed the controller's role in a Rails application. For each request that comes in, a proper response is formulated, often by combining the data retrieved from the model layer with a template in the view layer. The functionalities provided by the view are all incorporated in the ActionView framework which, along with ActionController, forms ActionPack.

Working with Templates

At a certain point, the controller hands over control to the view so that it can build the body of the response based on the appropriate layout, view templates, and partials. This can happen implicitly, when you let Rails process the default template for an action and request format, or explicitly by invoking the `render` method.

Rendering Templates

This section first reviews how default templates are determined and how it's possible to specify a non-default template to be used for the response to a request. It then takes a look at the available template types and standard engines that Rails bakes-in.

Default Templates

The view prominently enters into the picture whenever the response's body depends on a template. As you can imagine, this is the norm for HTML requests because their bodies are typically XHTML documents displayed through a browser. When `render` isn't called, the default template for a given action is rendered. As mentioned several times, the name of the default template that's going to be used is determined based on the action name and the format requested. If the controller is `ExampleController`, the view templates for its actions are conventionally stored in `app\views\example`.

When processing the following action, `index.html.erb` is rendered by default:

```
# index.html.erb will be rendered by default
def index
  @books = Book.all
end
```

If the expected template is missing, a 500 Internal Server Error is raised and a "Template is missing" page is displayed in the browser.

The default template also depends on the format of the request:

```
def show
  @book = Book.find(params[:id])

  respond_to do |format|
    format.html # show.html.erb
    format.xml  { render :xml => @book }
    format.js   # show.js.rjs
  end
end
```

For instance, in the preceding snippet, the two highlighted lines indicate that the view should render the `show.html.erb` template for HTML requests and the `show.js.rjs` for JavaScript requests (for example, an Ajax call). The template engine used for the two is different as well. The first uses ERb to mingle XHTML and Ruby code, whereas the latter uses RJS so as to enable you to be able to write code in a Ruby DSL (Domain-Specific Language), which will be translated and rendered as JavaScript back to the user's browser.

Bypassing Templates with render

In its simplest form, `render` can be used to send a response that does not involve a template. You can render plain text:

```
render(:text => "Confirmed") # Sends the text without rendering the layout
render(:text => "<h1>OK!</h1>"), :layout => true
```

XML, JSON, or JavaScript:

```
render(:xml => @article)
render(:json => @article)
render(:js => "alert('Hello from JavaScript');")
```

*to_xml and *`to_json` *will automatically be invoked for you in the first two lines. Call them explicitly with the* :only, :except, :include, *or* :method *arguments if you need to customize what should be included in the transformation of the object(s) to those two formats.*

Though I've grouped more than one `render` call in each snippet to save space, remember that you should only render one per request.

or leave it blank (for an empty body):

```
render(:nothing)
```

This works if you only need to send headers in the response, but it's preferential to use the head *method instead.*

Rendering a Specific Template

When the `render` method is used explicitly, it can be leveraged to inform ActionView that a non-default template should be used. You can do this by rendering a template that's associated with a different action:

```
render(:action => "show")
```

or, when you need to render a template defined for an action within a different controller, by using the `:template` option:

```
render(:template => "sales/show")
```

or even from a specific file:

```
render(:file => "/path/to/a/shared/view/somewhere/show.html.erb")
```

You could also specify the template markup directly in the controller:

```
# Don't do this
render(:inline => "<% articles.each do |a| %><p><%= a.title %></p><% end %>")
```

And you could even do a `render(:update)` and pass a block of RJS code to it, so as to perform JavaScript-like updates directly in the controller.

> **"Could" is the keyword here. You could, but that doesn't mean that you should. In fact, do not embed template markup or JavaScript-like page updates in your controller. Templates belong to the view layer, and the separation of concerns promoted by the MVC architectural pattern must be preserved.**

Excluding bad practices like inline markup in the controller, a `render :action`, `render :template`, or `render :file` will tell the view to take over and formulate a proper response's body based on the specified template.

Partials

The view does not simply combine instance variables (for example, @article) with a single template (for example, show.html.erb). In fact, as seen in Chapters 5 and 6, the resulting document is usually the product of rendering a layout, which yields the rendering of the template at hand, which in turn can invoke the rendering of other templates and/or one or more partials. Partials, as explained earlier, are fragments of pages that can be used to improve the reusability and DRY adherence of the code.

It is also possible to have layouts that apply to partials. Unlike regular layouts that are scoped for an entire action and in many cases apply to a whole controller, these layouts are aimed at providing common code that wraps fragments of the view (that is, partials). These work in a very similar fashion to regular layouts; they contain a <%= yield %> where the partial should be rendered, and can be applied to a partial when this is called with the :layout option. For example:

```
<%= render :partial => "user", :layout => "admin", :locals =>
{ :admin => @user } %>
```

Partials can also be shared among views that are associated with different controllers. In such cases, it's conventional to place them within app\views\shared. When rendering these shared partials from within a template, you need to include the shared folder in the argument passed to render. Rails will be smart enough to understand that the last, and only the last, token is the name of the partial, while the rest is the path of a folder within app\views:

```
<%= render :partial => "shared/my_partial" %>
```

Check the documentation for ActionView::Partials for further details.

Communication with the Other Layers

Templates are able to access instance variables that have been defined within the controller as well as the flash. This is what the view is expected to do so that it can communicate with the controller. However, it's not limited to this alone. The view layer is capable of accessing a series of attributes you encountered in the previous chapter about controllers.

These attributes are controller, session, request, response, header, params, logger, and the debugger method (which triggers a debugging session). The view is even capable of interacting with the model directly. You could, for example, execute Book.all directly from the view.

As is often the case in the world of programming, the freedom that's provided to the programmer should not be abused. Yes, you could call the model directly from the view, but that would be a major "code smell" as well as a strong violation of the principle of separation of concerns. Likewise, with the exception of debugger, the aforementioned attributes are normally the domain of the controller, which handles them as required.

Never query the model directly from the view. Use the controller instead.

Despite this due warning and premise, the ability to access them can come in handy when troubleshooting. In fact, Rails provides us with a debug helper, which dumps (using the YAML format) the object that is passed in argument. This turns out to be an easy way of inspecting the contents of the attributes mentioned earlier.

Built-in Template Engines

A template enables the view to dynamically generate the response's body by combining dynamic values, like instance variables and the flash object, and static content like HTML tags and text. Throughout this book you've been exposed to ERb templates as a means of generating XHTML documents. Yet ERb is not limited to this task and can be used to generate any other type of document that requires a mix of static and dynamic content (that is, Ruby code).

For the sake of convenience, Rails ships with two other built-in template engines: Builder and RJS. And whereas ERb is normally used for XHTML pages, Builder is particularly handy for XML content and RJS for writing JavaScript responses in Ruby code.

To tell Rails what document type is going to be rendered, and what template engine is going to be used, you add two extensions to each template: myfile.html.erb for XHTML produced through ERb, myfile.xml.builder for XML produced through Builder, and myfile.js.rjs for JavaScript produced through RJS.

Note that for historical reasons, the old extension format is still accepted. If you work with legacy code, you may find the equivalent myfile.rhtml, myfile.rxml, and myfile.rjs. As you upgrade an existing project to Rails 2.2 or a newer version, you can safely rename them.

ERb

ASP.NET developers are used to thinking in terms of controls that are positioned within a page. In ERb templates, the approach is entirely different. In fact, most templates contain regular XHTML code intermingled with Ruby code that gets evaluated at runtime. Expressions evaluated inline are contained between the tags <%= and %>, whereas Ruby code that doesn't need to produce an output is contained between <% and %>. The amount of Ruby code is kept to a minimum, because the view layer is supposed to have as little application logic as possible, and focus on the presentation of the content instead.

> In many code bases you'll often find -%> as the closing tag. As mentioned before, this is used to trim the output from extra newlines so that it results in more compact XHTML code.

This means that a typical ERb template will evaluate instance variables declared in the associated controller, display flash messages, and dynamically control the structure of the page with a few conditional statements and iterations/loops (to display data contained within a collection of objects).

Because there are no "fancy controls" available in Rails, and you don't want business logic in the view, ERb templates rely instead on predefined helpers like the form_for or link_to or user-made helpers.

There is a secondary and very practical reason why ERb templates are supposed to be fairly straightforward: the view templates are often handed over to the designer, who has to be able to understand and modify them to make the page look as he or she would prefer it to. Most of their work will probably be accomplished through CSS files, but keeping the view clean from complex logic can only facilitate their job, and in turn avoid accidental changes that can break your application.

As a general rule of thumb, try to centralize the information within the controller, so that the view is limited to the presentation of the data. For example, consider the following trivial template:

```
<h2>Discount Coupon</h2>
<p>Your coupon <%= @coupon %> is valid until <%= @expiration = 7.days.from_now
%>.</p>

<!-- some more HTML -->

<p>Don't forget to take advantage of your discount before <%= @expiration %>.</p>
```

7.days.from_now *is not standard Ruby. This highly readable expression is possible thanks to the extensions provided by ActiveSupport.*

Notice how you are able to assign a variable (`@expiration`) and then evaluate it a few lines later. This works but it has a problem. Variables are better assigned in a centralized place, and that place is the controller. In fact, tomorrow you might decide that the coupons are going to expire in 14 days instead and you'll be forced to track each view template that hard codes 7.days.from_now to change it. Furthermore, as the application's requirements change, you may require the application of different coupon expiration policies depending on the customer that's currently logged in. Remember the mantra, Don't Repeat Yourself!

An initial quick refactoring leads you to place `@expiration = 7.days.from_now` within the controller's action and replace `<%= @expiration = 7.days.from_now %>` in the template with `<%= @expiration %>`.

To improve it further, you'd probably also want to get rid of that magic number (7), and use a constant to store that value instead.

I discussed this point amply while developing the blog example, but it warrants repeating. There is a big security risk in simply using `<%=` when the evaluated expression is originated by a user. In fact, the expression could contain malicious script code and this would be interpreted nevertheless. For this reason, most Rails users almost have an automatic reflex to place an h after the opening tag (that is, `<%=h`), so that the `html_escape` helper, whose alias is h, is invoked on the expression that's being evaluated. `html_escape` escapes HTML tag characters so that "`<script>`" is rendered in the response as "`&lt;script&gt;`".

> **Always use `<%=h` as the opening tag when you want to evaluate any expression that could potentially be unsafe (for example, comes from the user). If you need to allow certain tags, consider using an alternative helper like `sanitize`.**

Builder

Builder templates are called as such because of the homonymous library they use, the aim of which is to provide a simple way to generate XML. The basic concept is that you can use regular Ruby code and a special `xml` object to generate any XML content. Arbitrarily named methods are translated into tags, the first parameter passed to these methods is translated into the value contained within the pair of tags, and any other parameter passed in a hash form will be an attribute. It's also possible to nest tags by using Ruby blocks.

The following example should clarify this:

```
xml.message do
  xml.time(Time.now)
  xml.from(@sender)
  xml.to(@receiver)
  xml.body("Don't forget the milk", :type => "plain")
end
```

This produces an XML document like the following:

```
<message>
  <time>Tue Nov 5 22:23:00 -0500 2008</time>
  <from>Jessica</from>
  <to>Tony</to>
  <body type="plain">Don't forget the milk</body>
</message>
```

The do after `xml.message` indicates that all the element's content within the block should be contained within the `<message></message>` tags. Also notice how `:type` was passed as a second parameter to add the `type` attribute to the `body` element.

A much more practical example of how to use Builder templates is provided in the section titled "Adding an RSS and Atom Feed," in which an RSS and Atom feed will be added to your blog application.

> *This library is quite flexible and you are welcome to check out further information about its usage online at* http://builder.rubyforge.org.

RJS

RJS templates are used to generate a JavaScript that's executed by the browser in response to an Ajax request. Much like other template types, when an Ajax request is received, Rails looks for the associated `.js.rjs` file within `app\views` and the subfolder named after the current controller.

> *Notice that you may find yourself in situations where you wish to use ERb, as opposed to RJS, as the template engine for your JavaScript. This typically happens when you need to insert JavaScript code in a template. In this case the file would have the extension* `.js.erb`.

RJS templates are usually employed when the page needs to be updated without a refresh, and are particularly useful when grouping a series of changes to the page, which are triggered by a simple action like clicking a link or a button.

Although exploring the vast topic of Ajax programming is beyond the scope of this book, a small example that showcases how to work with RJS templates is shown in the second half of this chapter, in the section "Adding a Sprinkle of Ajax."

Adding an RSS and Atom Feed

Responding to a request for a given resource in XML format is usually done without the need for a Builder template. For example, in the `ArticlesController` you had:

```
respond_to do |format|
  format.html # index.html.erb
  format.xml  { render :xml => @articles }
end
```

The highlighted line will invoke the `to_xml` method and render the collection of `Article` objects in the default XML representation. In this case, `@articles` will contain only one record because you set the pagination to one article per page. Reaching for `/articles.xml` will provide the following (depending on your content, of course):

```
<?xml version="1.0" encoding="UTF-8"?>
<articles type="array">
  <article>
    <body>Hi there!

If you don't know what %{color:red}Rails% is, you can read more about it on the
&quot;official website&quot;:http://rubyonrails.org and then buy Antonio Cangiano's
book. It's *highly recommended*. ;-)

By the way, did you know that Ruby on Rails(TM) is a trademark of &quot;David
Heinemeier Hansson&quot;:http://loudthinking.com?</body>
    <created-at type="datetime">2008-07-16T18:56:33-04:00</created-at>
    <id type="integer">4</id>

    <published type="boolean">true</published>
    <published-at type="datetime">2008-07-19T23:52:00-04:00</published-at>
    <title>Oh hi!</title>
    <updated-at type="datetime">2008-07-17T12:21:48-04:00</updated-at>
  </article>
</articles>
```

A great example of when this approach is not sufficient is the publication of an RSS (from version 2.0 this stands for Really Simple Syndication) or an Atom (to be exact, Atom Syndication Format) feed. Every feed is supposed to be a valid XML document, but their format also differs from the standard representation of the data provided by the method `to_xml`.

What you need for both of these formats is a Builder template that specifies how the final XML data is supposed to be formulated. And to provide you with a couple of concrete examples, you are going to add an RSS and an Atom feed to the "The Rails Noob" blog.

format.rss and format.atom

Modify app\controllers\articles_controller.rb, so that its index action looks like this:

```
def index
  @articles = Article.published.paginate(:page => params[:page],
                                          :order => "published_at DESC")
```

```
@syndicated_articles = Article.published.all(:limit => 10,
                                             :order => "published_at DESC")

    respond_to do |format|
      format.html # index.html.erb
      format.xml  { render :xml => @articles }
      format.rss  { render :rss => @syndicated_articles }
      format.atom { render :atom => @syndicated_articles }
    end
  end
```

When you want to syndicate, say, 10 articles from among the ones you've published and present them in reversed chronological order so that newer articles are at the top, what you need to do is to retrieve those articles with `Article.published.all` and assign them to `@syndicated_articles`. That will be your source of information for the feeds that are independent from the syndication format you'll be using.

In the last two highlighted lines, you added a `format.rss` and `format.atom` within the `respond_to` block, so that the application now knows how to handle `application/atom+xml` and `application/rss+xml` media types (for example, requests for `/articles.rss` and `/articles.atom`).

> As a reminder, Rails already recognizes both formats. If you want to specify a format that Rails doesn't know, you will need to register its MIME type in `config\initializers\mime_types.rb`, before you'll be able to use it within the `respond_to` block.

Within the respective inline blocks, you use `render :rss` and `render :atom` similarly to how you applied `render :xml` to the preceding line, except this time you are passing the `@syndicated_articles` variable instead of `@articles`. The real twist, however, lies in the view. You will in fact prepare two Builder templates: `index.rss.builder` and `index.atom.builder`.

index.rss.builder and index.atom.builder

When a request for `/articles.atom` comes in, Rails executes that last line of code corresponding to the Atom format and makes the `@syndicated_articles`'s content available to the template. Rails expects to find an `index.atom.builder` template much like it would expect an `index.html.erb` for HTML requests. And the same is true for the RSS format as well.

Listing 9-1 is the Builder template for your RSS feed.

Listing 9-1: app\views\articles\index.rss.builder

```
xml.instruct! :xml, :version => "1.0"
xml.rss :version => "2.0" do
  xml.channel do
    xml.title("The Rails Noob")
    xml.description("My latest articles")
    xml.link(formatted_articles_url(:rss))

    for article in @syndicated_articles
      xml.item do
```

Continued

Listing 9-1: app\views\articles\index.rss.builder *(continued)*

```
              xml.title(article.title)
              xml.description(textilize(article.body))
              xml.pubDate(article.published_at.to_s(:rfc822))
              xml.link(formatted_article_url(article, :rss))
              xml.guid(formatted_article_url(article, :rss))
            end
          end
        end
      end
```

The basic idea is that you use the xml object (which was introduced earlier) and with it you define a series of elements that are required by the RSS specification before looping through all the articles that are going to show up in the feed. The :rfc822 symbol that was passed to article.published_ at.to_s ensures that the timestamp appears in the expected format.

Figure 9-1 shows the resulting feed in Internet Explorer.

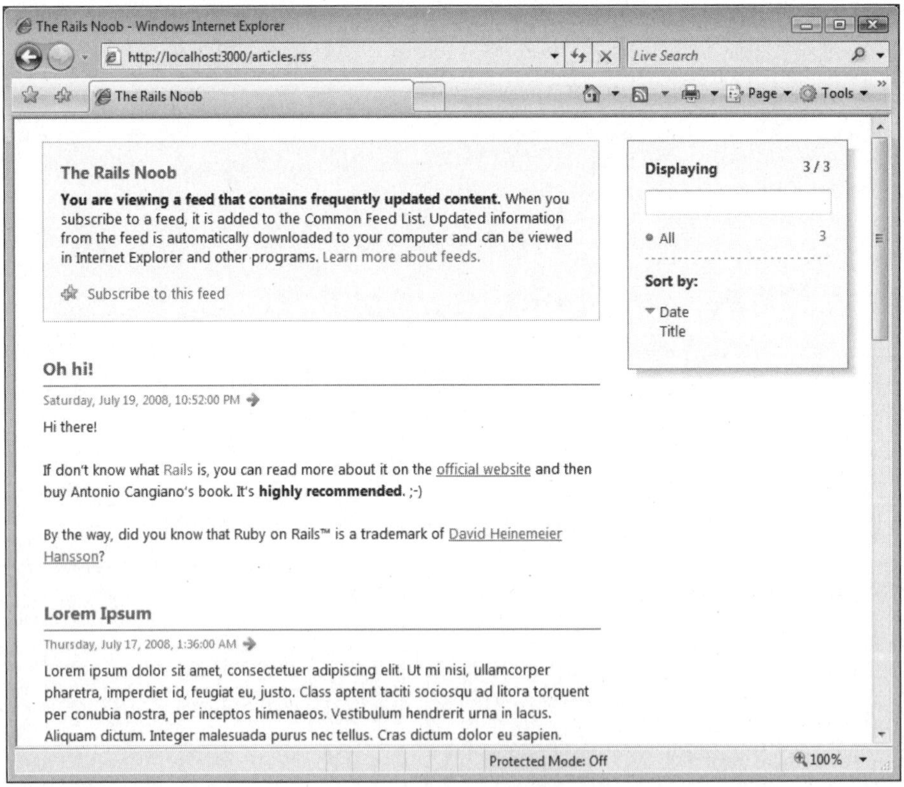

Figure 9-1

In Listing 9-2 you'll find the code for the Atom feed's template.

Listing 9-2: app\views\articles\index.atom.builder

```
atom_feed do |feed|
  feed.title("The Rails Noob")
  last_article = @syndicated_articles.first
  feed.updated(last_article.published_at) if last_article

  for article in @syndicated_articles
    feed.entry(article) do |entry|
      entry.title(article.title)
      entry.content(textilize(article.body), :type => 'html')

      entry.author do |author|
        author.name("Antonio Cangiano")
      end
    end
  end
end
```

Note how the `article.body` *is passed to the helper* `textilize`, *so that the body content is transformed from Textile to HTML.*

Here you wrap all of the code in the block that was passed to the special method `atom_feed`, you define a few required elements like the feed title and the time of your last update, and loop through the collection of articles that are intended for syndication (including their titles, content, and author names). Elements for the publication and updates for each individual entry will be added automatically by `feed.entry`.

Figure 9-2 shows the output in Internet Explorer.

Feed Entry Order

You will notice that the order of the first two posts is different in Figure 9-1 and Figure 9-2. The reason for this is that Internet Explorer uses the `updated` element instead of `published` to determine how to order the entries within the Atom feed. In my particular case, the "Lorem Ipsum" post was published before the "Oh hi" post, but I modified "Lorem Ipsum" last, and therefore its `updated_at` column is more recent in the database.

Upon opening the same feeds in Firefox, the entries will show up in the same order for both the RSS and Atom feeds. Depending on the feed reader used by the subscriber, when clicking "Subscribe to this feed," the entries will be displayed in the order of publication or their respective updates.

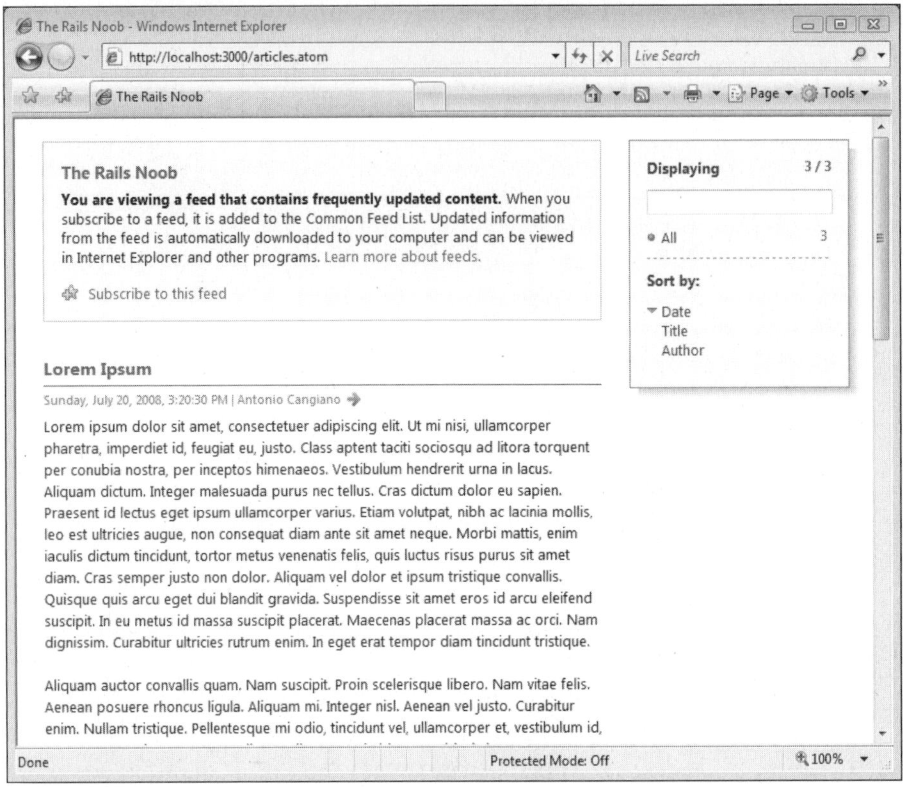

Figure 9-2

The output generated by the template for the RSS feed will be similar (depending on your data, of course) to the following output (truncated for clarity):

```xml
<?xml version="1.0" encoding="UTF-8"?>
<rss version="2.0">
  <channel>
    <title>The Rails Noob</title>
    <description>My latest articles</description>
    <link>http://localhost:3000/articles.rss</link>
    <item>
      <title>Oh hi!</title>
      <description>&lt;p&gt;Hi there!&lt;/p&gt;

&lt;p&gt;If you don&amp;#8217;t know what &lt;span
style=&quot;color:red;&quot;&gt;Rails&lt;/span&gt; is, you can read more about it
on the &lt;a href=&quot;http://rubyonrails.org&quot;&gt;official website&lt;/a&gt;
and then buy Antonio Cangiano&amp;#8217;s book. It&amp;#8217;s &lt;strong&gt;highly
recommended&lt;/strong&gt;. ;-)&lt;/p&gt;

&lt;p&gt;By the way, did you know that Ruby on Rails&amp;#8482; is a trademark of
&lt;a href=&quot;http://loudthinking.com&quot;&gt;David Heinemeier
Hansson&lt;/a&gt;?&lt;/p&gt;</description>
```

```
      <pubDate>Sat, 19 Jul 2008 23:52:00 -0400</pubDate>
      <link>http://localhost:3000/articles/4.rss</link>
      <guid>http://localhost:3000/articles/4.rss</guid>
   </item>

   <item>
      <title>Lorem Ipsum</title>
      <description>&lt;p&gt;Lorem ipsum dolor sit amet, consectetuer adipiscing
elit. Ut mi nisi, ullamcorper pharetra, imperdiet id, feugiat eu, justo. Class
aptent taciti sociosqu ad ...
      ...
      ...
      </description>
      <pubDate>Thu, 17 Jul 2008 02:36:00 -0400</pubDate>
      <link>http://localhost:3000/articles/2.rss</link>
      <guid>http://localhost:3000/articles/2.rss</guid>
   </item>
   ...
   ...
  </channel>
</rss>
```

For the Atom feed you'll have the following:

```
<?xml version="1.0" encoding="UTF-8"?>
<feed xml:lang="en-US" xmlns="http://www.w3.org/2005/Atom">
  <id>tag:localhost,2005:/articles</id>
  <link type="text/html" rel="alternate" href="http://localhost:3000"/>
  <link type="application/atom+xml" rel="self" href="http://localhost:3000/
articles.atom"/>
  <title>The Rails Noob</title>
  <updated>2008-07-19T23:52:00-04:00</updated>
  <entry>
    <id>tag:localhost,2005:Article/4</id>
    <published>2008-07-16T18:56:33-04:00</published>
    <updated>2008-07-17T12:21:48-04:00</updated>
    <link type="text/html" rel="alternate"
href="http://localhost:3000/articles/4"/>
    <title>Oh hi!</title>
    <content type="html">&lt;p&gt;Hi there!&lt;/p&gt;

&lt;p&gt;If you don&amp;#8217;t know what &lt;span style=&quot;color:red;&quot;&gt;
Rails&lt;/span&gt; is, you can read more about it
on the &lt;a href=&quot;http://rubyonrails.org&quot;&gt;official website&lt;/a&gt;
and then buy Antonio Cangiano&amp;#8217;s book. It&amp;#8217;s &lt;strong&gt;highly
recommended&lt;/strong&gt;. ;-)&lt;/p&gt;

&lt;p&gt;By the way, did you know that Ruby on Rails&amp;#8482; is a trademark of
 &lt;a href=&quot;http://loudthinking.com&quot;&gt;David Heinemeier
Hansson&lt;/a&gt;?&lt;/p&gt;</content>
    <author>
      <name>Antonio Cangiano</name>
    </author>
  </entry>
```

```
    <entry>
      <id>tag:localhost,2005:Article/2</id>
      <published>2008-07-16T10:31:33-04:00</published>
      <updated>2008-07-20T16:20:30-04:00</updated>
      <link type="text/html" rel="alternate" href="http://localhost:3000/articles/2"/>
      <title>Lorem Ipsum</title>
      <content type="html">&lt;p&gt;Lorem ipsum dolor sit amet, consectetuer
 adipiscing elit. Ut mi nisi, ullamcorper pharetra, imperdiet id, feugiat eu, justo.
 Class aptent taciti sociosqu ad ...
      ...
      ...
      </content>
      <author>
        <name>Antonio Cangiano</name>
      </author>
    </entry>
   ...
   ...
</feed>
```

Nowadays most developers favor Atom over RSS, but they are both extremely common.

Linking to the Feeds

At this point, all you need to do is provide your users with a link to at least one of your feeds, as well as allow browsers/clients to auto-discover it.

For the links, it's sufficient enough to use the two helpers, `link_to` and `formatted_articles_path`, within the `articles.html.erb` layout:

```
<li><%= link_to 'Feed', formatted_articles_path(:atom) %></li>
```

This translates into:

```
<li><a href="/articles.atom">Feed</a></li>
```

If you want to advertise both versions of the feed, add a second link by passing :rss to the path helper. Alternatively, you may want to include an RSS feed icon to make the presence of a feed more prominent.

> **In Rails 2.3** `formatted_articles_path(:atom)` **will be written as** `articles_path(:format => "atom")`.

To add an auto-discovery link to the layout, use the `auto_discovery_link_tag` helper:

```
<head>
  <meta http-equiv="content-type" content="text/html;charset=UTF-8" />
  <title>The Rails Noob</title>
  <%= auto_discovery_link_tag :atom, formatted_articles_url(:atom) %>
  <%= stylesheet_link_tag 'site' %>
</head>
```

This facilitates the discovery of the feed URL starting from the site onward in feed readers and other automated services. It will also add the standard (typically orange) feed syndication icon to most browsers, as shown in Figure 9-3 and 9-4, respectively, for Internet Explorer and Mozilla Firefox.

You can check the validity of your feeds online at `http://feedvalidator.org`.

Figure 9-3

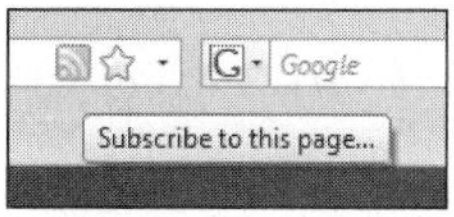

Figure 9-4

> As an exercise, feel free to create a feed for all the most recent comments and/or for the comments associated with a given article.

Helpers

Whereas in ASP.NET you have controls that you can drag and drop to help ease the development process, keep you productive, and maintain relatively lean pages, in Rails you have helpers. These handy methods provide a convenient way to write HTML controls, as well as perform other operations on a given input in order to provide the required output. For example, whereas in ASP.NET you have the following line of code:

```
<asp:TextBox ID="TextBox1" runat="server"></asp:TextBox>
```

in Rails, you would use the `text_field` or `text_field_tag` helper, depending on whether or not the resulting `input` tag needs to be bound to a particular model attribute.

Rails defines many helpers besides form ones. Consider, for instance, the `pluralize` and `excerpt` textual helpers:

```
<%= excerpt(@article, 'sed', 50) %>

<%= pluralize(@people.size, 'person') %>
```

This will display output such as the following:

```
...lis porttitor. Curabitur elementum risus eu eros. Sed elit. Praesent elit
sapien, dictum ac, ornare por...

3 people
```

Helpers offer multiple advantages. In particular, they encourage reuse, simplify the templates, ease development, make testing easier, adhere to the DRY principle, and discourage the inclusion of application logic within the view templates. Their usage is more than encouraged. Two types of helpers exist: those included by ActionView and those defined by the developer.

Predefined Helpers

Helpers defined by Rails are included in the module `ActionView::Helpers`. Consulting the API documentation will reveal a wealth of helpers that are available, as well as examples of their usage. It is, however, important to first understand how these helpers are categorized. `ActionView::Helpers` includes many helper modules itself, which in turn define the actual helper methods. These are the children modules:

- ❑   `ActionView::Helpers::ActiveRecordHelper`
- ❑   `ActionView::Helpers::AssetTagHelper`
- ❑   `ActionView::Helpers::AtomFeedHelper`
- ❑   `ActionView::Helpers::BenchmarkHelper`
- ❑   `ActionView::Helpers::CacheHelper`
- ❑   `ActionView::Helpers::CaptureHelper`
- ❑   `ActionView::Helpers::DateHelper`
- ❑   `ActionView::Helpers::DebugHelper`
- ❑   `ActionView::Helpers::FormHelper`
- ❑   `ActionView::Helpers::FormOptionsHelper`
- ❑   `ActionView::Helpers::FormTagHelper`
- ❑   `ActionView::Helpers::JavaScriptHelper`
- ❑   `ActionView::Helpers::NumberHelper`
- ❑   `ActionView::Helpers::PrototypeHelper`
- ❑   `ActionView::Helpers::RecordIdentificationHelper`
- ❑   `ActionView::Helpers::RecordTagHelper`
- ❑   `ActionView::Helpers::SanitizeHelper`
- ❑   `ActionView::Helpers::ScriptaculousHelper`
- ❑   `ActionView::Helpers::TagHelper`
- ❑   `ActionView::Helpers::TextHelper`
- ❑   `ActionView::Helpers::UrlHelper`

Their names are, in most cases, self-explanatory and you can bask in the knowledge that you will not need to memorize them by heart. As you progress in your journey of learning Ruby on Rails, you'll become accustomed to the most frequent helpers defined by these modules, and the less familiar ones will be at your fingertips in the documentation.

ActiveRecordHelper contains helper methods like form or error_messages_for that simplify working with forms built around ActiveRecord objects. AssetTagHelper simplifies the generation of HTML for linking to assets like images, JavaScript files, CSS files, and so on. The helper auto_discovery_link_tag that you used a few paragraphs ago is defined in this module, and so are, among many others, javascript_include_tag (to include JavaScript libraries), stylesheet_link_tag (to link to a stylesheet), and image_tag.

AtomFeedHelper defines the atom_feed helper you just used in your Builder template, and BenchmarkHelper implements a benchmark helper that's used to measure the execution time of blocks passed to the method. The resulting time is then logged. For example, the following fragment will log (by default at the info level) a message such as "Render chat log (0.602143)":

```
<% benchmark "Render chat log" do %>
  <%= print_chat(@chat_log) %>
<% end %>
```

CacheHelper provides a cache method that can be used to cache fragments of a view template (both static and dynamic content). I talk more about caching, performances, and benchmarking in Chapter 11.

CaptureHelper implements two useful methods for code reuse: capture and content_for. capture is used to easily assign fragments of a template to an instance variable. That instance variable will then be available throughout the view layer. content_for allows you to mark a given fragment of view that was passed to the helper as a block, so that it can be reused elsewhere. You could, for example, identify a section as your footer:

```
<% content_for :footer do %>
 <! - some footer content -> 
<% end %>
```

and then render that content elsewhere:

```
<%= yield :footer %>
```

If you define several fragments with the same identifier, they'll be chained in the order that they were processed.

DateHelper is a module you should familiarize yourself with. As the name implies, it implements helpers for working with dates and times. Helpers exist that produce HTML select/options tags, such as select_date, select_datetime, select_day, select_hour, select_minute, select_month, select_second, select_time, select_year, date_select, datetime_select, and time_select, as well as handy methods that work with the date and time provided in input, such as distance_of_time_in_words, distance_of_time_in_words_to_now, and time_ago_in_words. If you wanted to display the time that's elapsed because an article was published in your blog application, rather than its publication date, you could use one of these helpers.

DebugHelper defines the debug method that was mentioned earlier in this chapter. This makes it easy to inspect the content of complex objects as they are rendered on the pages.

FormHelper and FormTagHelper

`FormHelper` and `FormTagHelper` are both modules that relate to form generation, but they differ in the fact that `FormHelper` methods generate code that assumes that the form is for a model object, whereas `FormTagHelper` methods do not. You will use one or the other, depending on whether or not you need to "bind" a form to a particular model object's attribute.

The presence of `tag` in the name of a helper indicates that it will generate HTML code that's not associated with a model object or its attributes.

The methods implemented by `FormHelper` are `check_box`, `fields_for`, `file_field`, `form_for`, `hidden_field`, `label`, `password_field`, `radio_button`, `text_area`, and `text_field`. All but `fields_for` and `form_for` accept a first argument, which indicates the object, and a second one that individuates the attribute that's being represented. Alternatively, when invoked on the block variable, these methods do not require the object (because it's provided by the receiver):

```erb
<% form_for(@article) do |f| %>
  <%= f.error_messages %>
    <% field_set_tag do %>
      <div class="field">
          <%= f.label :title %>
          <%= f.text_field :title %>
      </div>

      <div class="field">
          <%= f.label :body %>
          <%= f.text_area :body %>
      </div>

      <div class="field">
          <%= f.label :published_at %>
          <%= f.datetime_select :published_at %>
      </div>

      <div class="field">
          <%= f.check_box :published %>
          <%= f.label :published %>
      </div>
    <% end %>

    <% field_set_tag do %>
        <%= f.submit button_value, :class => "button" %>
    <% end %>

<% end %>
```

`form_for` creates the form for a model instance, which is something that it can do in a resource-oriented way (REST style), by receiving the instance in argument and automatically configuring the form. For example, in a "new" form, the code will be equivalent to:

```erb
<% form_for :article, Article.new, :url => articles_path, :html => { :class =>
"new_article", :id => "new_article" } do |f| %>
  <!- ... -->
<% end %>
```

However, in an "edit" form, the same code becomes (depending on the id attribute of the object):

```
<% form_for :article, @article, :url => article_path(@article), :html => { :method
=> :put, :class => "edit_article", :id => "edit_article_3" } do |f| %>
  <!- ... ->
<% end %>
```

How does the helper know whether you intend the form to be used for the creation of new records or to edit them by populating the existing attribute values in the form? The model instance passed to form_ *for is used to verify if it is a new record (for example, using the method* new_record?*) or if it's an existing one, and the form is then rendered accordingly.*

This is the preferred way to operate with form_for in Rails, but it is still possible to manually configure all the form parameters, as shown in the preceding output, as needed.

fields_for is an important helper because it allows you to create a scope around a particular model instance, without creating a form tag in the HTML. What this means in practice is that you can use fields_for any time you need a form that represents more than one model. You cannot have more than one form HTML tag, so using form_for twice in the same template is out of the question, but by using fields_for to wrap the controls for a second model instance, you can have multiple model forms with relative ease.

> **Rails 2.3 simplifies the process of creating complex forms through the so-called Nested Object Forms. You can read more about this online at** http://ryandaigle .com/articles/2009/2/1/what-s-new-in-edge-rails-nested-attributes

---

File Uploads

file_field is a helper that generates a file upload input tag that's associated with the model instance attribute. That said, dealing with attachments is a notoriously error prone, and somewhat annoying, problem.

For this reason, when dealing with attachments, many Rails developers prefer more refined solutions, such as those that are made available through plugins. Two popular choices are attachment_fu and Paperclip.

These facilitate handling uploads in Rails and add further features like the ability to thumbnail images, resize them, or store the uploaded file on Amazon S3's storage service.

You can find them online at http://svn.techno-weenie.net/projects/plugins/ attachment_fu and http://github.com/thoughtbot/paperclip, respectively

FormTagHelper includes the following methods: check_box_tag, field_set_tag, file_field_tag, form_tag, hidden_field_tag, image_submit_tag, label_ tag, password_field_tag, radio_button_tag, select_tag, submit_tag, text_area_tag, and text_field_tag. Again, these are meant to be used when the form does not have a corresponding model object.

FormOptionsHelper

FormOptionsHelper offers a quick way to convert collections into select/options tags. The methods implemented by this module are collection_select, option_groups_from_collection_for_select, options_for_select, options_from_collection_for_select, select, time_zone_options_for_select, and time_zone_select.

Consider the following usage of the select helper:

```
select("article", "category_id", Category.all.collect {|c| c.name, c.id },
{ :include_blank => 'None' })
```

This would generate the following:

```
<select name="article[category_id]">
  <option value="1">Python</option>
  <option value="2" selected="selected">Ruby</option>
  <option value="3">C#</option>
  <option value="4">Visual Basic</option>
  <option value="5">Delphi</option>
</select>
```

This assumes that the helper was placed within a form that was being displayed so as to edit an article, and as such you can imagine that the value "Ruby" was already selected because the article's category_id *attribute is 2.*

Consult the official API documentation to learn more about the other methods in the module and their usage.

---

country_select

In September 2008, before Rails 2.2 was released, the Rails team decided to remove the country_select and country_options_for_select helpers. The main reason for this decision was the lack of agreement on a definitive list of countries to be included and the culturally sensitive issue that this provoked. If you are curious, you can read about the controversy on the blog of a Rails Core team member at http://www.koziarski .net/archives/2008/9/24/countries-and-controversies.

Listing countries is still a recurring feature in many registration and shipping forms, though, so once again you can rely on plugins to help you out with this feature.

Currently a good choice for this purpose is the localized_country_select plugin, because it also leverages Rails' i18n features in order to provide a list of countries that are localized to the language of the application. You can find this plugin on GitHub: http://github.com/karmi/localized_country_select.

JavaScriptHelper, PrototypeHelper, and ScriptaculousHelper

These three modules are there to facilitate working with JavaScript and Ajax in your views (RJS templates or not). `JavaScriptHelper` implements several useful methods including the following:

❑ `button_to_function`: Generates a button that triggers a JavaScript function. For example, `button_to_function "Hello", "alert('Hello!')"` translates into `<input onclick="alert('Hello!');" type="button" value="Hello" />`.

❑ `link_to_function`: Equivalent to `button_to` but generates a link instead: `<a href="#" onclick="alert('Hello!'); return false;">Hello</a>`.

❑ `define_javascript_functions`: Used to include all the JavaScript libraries that ship with ActionPack within a single `<script>` tag.

❑ `escape_javascript`: Escapes carrier returns and both single and double quotes for JavaScript (that is, prefixing them with a backslash).

❑ `javascript_tag`: Generates a JavaScript `<script>` tag that wraps the content passed as an argument or a block. For example, `<%= javascript_tag "alert('Hello!')" %>` returns:

```
<script type="text/javascript">
//<![CDATA[
alert('Hello!')
//]]>
</script>
```

CDATA sections are used to allow modern browsers to interpret the content as a script, while being safely ignored by XML parsers (which would otherwise interpret it as XML).

Prototype is one of the most popular JavaScript frameworks; it simplifies working with the DOM (Document Object Model), Ajax, and object-orientation in JavaScript. Rails ships with this library and provides you with the `PrototypeHelper` to access its functionalities from Ruby.

Prototype ships with Rails, but it must be included in your application in order to be able to use it, as you'll see later on.

This module implements several helpers that conveniently wrap the Prototype API. Many of these contain the word `remote` to distinguish them from the regular helpers that are used in non-Ajax forms. For example, you have `remote_form_for` and its alias `form_remote_tag` in place of `form_for` and `form_tag`, and you have `link_to_remote` instead of `link_to`, or again `submit_to_remote`. When a `remote_form_for` or its alias `form_remote_for` is used, the form will be submitted in the background using `XMLHttpRequest`, instead of sending (by default) the `POST` request and reloading the page. For instance, consider the following:

```
<% remote_form_for(@article) do |f| %>
  <!- ... ->
<% end %>
```

This would translate into a `<form>` tag along the lines of the following:

```
<form action="/articles/3" class="edit_article" id="edit_article_3" method="post"
onsubmit="new Ajax.Request('/articles/3', {asynchronous:true, evalScripts:true,
parameters:Form.serialize(this)}); return false;">
```

When the form is submitted, a new asynchronous `Ajax.Request` is instantiated. In fact, as fancy as it sounds, Ajax is all about being able to send an `XMLHttpRequest` from the browser to Rails, so that a background request for a given action is initiated without having to completely reload the page. Rails will then be able to process the action and update the page accordingly. The helper `update_page` yields a `JavaScriptGenerator`, which can be used to update multiple elements on the same page, for a single request as it's received. I highly recommend that you read the extensive API reference for the `PrototypeHelper` and for `PrototypeHelper::JavaScriptGenerator::GeneratorMethods` so as to gain familiarity with working with Prototype in Rails.

Firebug and the Web Developer Toolbar

Most Web developers, including myself, use Mozilla Firefox as their browser of choice. Though testing for Internet Explorer compatibility is still done, it is rare to see a Rails developer who consciously chooses to use Internet Explorer over other open-source browsers that are available. The main reason for this is not purely ideological, but finds its roots in the advantages and far smaller number of quirks that Firefox provides. In fact, many Web applications end up requiring special arrangements to guarantee compatibility with the latest versions of Internet Explorer.

Two killer Firefox add-ons that are must-haves for any Web developer are Firebug and the Web Developer toolbar. Firebug in particular is essential for any developer who intends to work with Ajax applications. This Firefox extension provides a console, a DOM inspector, HTTP traffic analysis, and many other fundamental features that are necessary to be able to debug the client side. If you haven't already done so, be sure to install Firefox, and get Firebug and Web Developer. I cannot stress enough how much these three will improve your development workflow.

No matter how good Firefox is, it's important to test your application with multiple browsers, particularly with Internet Explorer; and because it is with this browser that most compatibility quirks arise, it makes sense to have similar tools for Internet Explorer as well. Though not as refined as their Firefox counterparts, two equivalent tools for IE have been released: the IE Developer Toolbar and DebugBar. I highly encourage you to get and install them as well.

Other browsers have similar projects underway to provide comparable functionalities. For example, Opera is developing a Firebug equivalent known as Dragonfly.

- ❏ **Firebug:** `http://getfirebug.com`
- ❏ **Web Developer:** `https://addons.mozilla.org/en-US/firefox/addon/60`
- ❏ **IE Developer Toolbar and DebugBar:** `http://tinyurl.com/ie-tools`
- ❏ **Opera Dragonfly:** `http://www.opera.com/products/dragonfly/`

---

script.aculo.us is a JavaScript library that's built on top of Prototype and its main aim is to provide visual effects and nice-looking Ajax controls. ActionPack ships this library as well, and just like Prototype, it needs to be included explicitly in your application before you're able to use it. Prototype is also required because script.aculo.us builds on top of it. Luckily, Rails provides a convenient way to include them both in your layouts via the `include_javascript_tag` helper, as you'll see later on in a practical Ajax example.

`ScriptaculousHelper` defines four highly configurable helpers: `draggable_element`, `drop_receiving_element`, `sortable_element`, and `visual_effect`. This last method is often used in conjunction with other Ajax helpers to give them nice visual effects once the background request has been completed. This can be done inline:

```
<%= link_to_remote "Load Results",
                 :update => "results",
                 :url => { :action => "results" },
                 :complete => visual_effect(:highlight, "results", :duration => 0.7) %>
```

or it can be used more elegantly in an RJS template. In Appendix A, I've provided you with resources and a bibliography to help you explore the topic of Ajax further. You will also see a quick, concrete example in the section titled "Adding a Sprinkle of Ajax."

Many more Ajax functionalities are available through plugins. Browse `http://agilewebdevelopment.com/plugins/list` *and* `http://www.railslodge.com/plugins` *for an extensive list of available plugins.*

Other Helpers

`NumberHelper` provides helpers that convert numbers into strings. The exposed methods are `number_to_currency`, `number_to_human_size`, `number_to_percentage`, `number_to_phone`, `number_with_delimiter`, and `number_with_precision`. They are useful at times, but admittedly not revolutionary at all.

`SanitizeHelper` and `TextHelper`, respectively, offer methods that sanitize potentially unsafe user input and work with text. `TextHelper` in particular has many interesting methods including `auto_link`, which automatically recognizes and transforms text into links; `pluralize` and `excerpt`, which were mentioned before; `truncate`, `word_wrap` (which forces the wrapping of long lines of text), and `highlight` (for highlighting certain words in the input text); `simple_format` to apply simple transformation rules to the input text like adding a `<br />` tag after a single newline; and the familiar `textilize` and `markdown`.

`UrlHelper` is a module that contains many of the methods used in previous chapters. Besides `link_to`, `button_to`, and `url_for`, this also implements the `link_to_if`, `link_to_unless`, `link_to_unless_current`, `current_page?`, and `mail_to` helpers. The first three are conditional links, each of which has a tag that is generated only when a given condition is satisfied. `link_to_unless_current` is particularly handy when creating navigation menus where you do not want the current page to be linked. When visiting the Archive page, the following will render links for the Home and About pages only:

```
<ul id="menubar">
  <li><%= link_to_unless_current("Home", { :action => "index" }) %></li>
  <li><%= link_to_unless_current("Archive", { :action => "archive" }) %></li>
  <li><%= link_to_unless_current("About", { :action => "about" }) %></li>
</ul>
```

current_page? verifies that the current URI was generated by the options passed in argument to the helpers, and mail_to generates a link to a mailto:, which triggers the user's default mail client to send emails client-side.

The three remaining, not particularly common helper modules are TagHelper, RecordTagHelper, and RecordIdentificationHelper.

TagHelper allows you to define tags programmatically (check out the tag and content_tag helpers) and RecordTagHelper exposes methods that create HTML elements whose id and class parameters are tied to a specified ActiveRecord object. Finally, RecordIdentificationHelper exposes three delegate helpers used by the view to identify conventional names for markup code from ActiveRecord and ActiveResource objects.

Creating Helpers

Predefined helpers will take you a long way when it comes to Rails applications, but helpers would be very limiting if it wasn't for the ability to define your own.

To define a helper all you have to do is declare a method in a helper module. By default, application-wide helpers defined by the user are contained within ApplicationHelper in app\helpers\application_helper.rb, whereas controller-specific helpers are defined in their own module/file. For example, if the controller is ExampleController, the associated helper will conventionally be in ExampleHelper, which in turn is defined in app\helpers\example_helper.rb.

---

helper and helper_method

The helper method is used to indicate which helper module should be made available for templates that correspond to a particular controller. Because helper :all is present within ApplicationController, all the helpers within the folder app\helpers will be available as well.

It's important to understand that helpers are available to the view layer (including other helper modules) only, and not to controllers. If you tried to use the method time_ago_in_words in a controller, for example, you'd get an error because the method is not defined in that scope.

In the rare instances where a user-defined helper needs to be available to both the controller and the view, you can define a method in the controller and then use helper_method to declare it as a helper (for example, helper_method :my_helper). As usual, don't abuse this facility, because it's important not to mix presentation and business logic, and to respect the Separation of Concerns principle.

Custom-defined helpers are regular methods that accept an input (usually a few options) and spit out an output that's normally used in the rendering of a page. For example, consider the following trivial helper:

```
module ApplicationHelper
  def three_times
    3.times { yield }
  end
end
```

Once defined, this would allow you to insert the following in any ERb template:

```
<% three_times do -%>
  <p>Lorem Ipsum...</p>
<% end -%>
```

and obtain:

```
<p>Lorem Ipsum...</p>
<p>Lorem Ipsum...</p>
<p>Lorem Ipsum...</p>
```

In all fairness, this helper is not terribly useful, but it shows the flexibility of this approach. This is particularly true when you consider that any predefined Rails helper is available within helper modules, and as such, it is possible to create helpers that build on ones that already exist.

Adding a Sprinkle of Ajax

To add a sprinkle of Ajax to the blog example, you are going to allow your users to comment without reloading the page. The first thing that you need to do is to include the default JavaScript libraries that ship with Rails. Do this by modifying the `articles.html.erb` layout within the `<head>` tag as shown here:

```
<head>
  <meta http-equiv="content-type" content="text/html;charset=UTF-8" />
  <title>The Rails Noob</title>
  <%= auto_discovery_link_tag :atom, formatted_articles_url(:atom) %>
  <%= stylesheet_link_tag 'site' %>
  <%= javascript_include_tag :defaults %>
</head>
```

The `javascript_include_tag` is a helper used to include JavaScript libraries. When used in a layout, it makes these libraries available to all of the view templates for which the layout applies. You can pass it the names (with or without extension) of JavaScript files located in `public\javascripts` and these will be included on each page for which the layout was rendered. In the highlighted line I used the `:defaults` symbol, which tells Rails to include both Prototype and script.aculo.us, as well as `application.js` in `public\javascripts`, if it exists. Passing `:all` will include all the JavaScript files in that directory and its subdirectories. In production, it is usually a good idea to cache all the JavaScript files into a single `all.js` file. This is done automatically for you by passing the `:cache => true` option to the helper, and will work as long as `ActionController::Base.perform_caching` is set to `true` (which is by default the case for production and not for development).

In the blog application, `<%= javascript_include_tag :defaults %>` generates code such as the following:

```
<script src="/javascripts/prototype.js?1215726390" type="text/javascript"></script>
<script src="/javascripts/effects.js?1215726390" type="text/javascript"></script>
<script src="/javascripts/dragdrop.js?1215726391" type="text/javascript"></script>
<script src="/javascripts/controls.js?1215726391" type="text/javascript"></script>
<script src="/javascripts/application.js?1215726391" type="text/javascript"></script>
```

The next step is to transform the form used to create comments, from a regular form to an Ajax one. Go ahead and edit the app\views\comments_form.html.erb partial so that it uses form_remote_for as shown in Listing 9-3.

Listing 9-3: app\views\comments_form.html.erb

```erb
<% form_remote_for [article, comment] do |f| %>
    <%= f.error_messages %>

    <% field_set_tag do %>

        <div class="field">
            <%= f.label :name %>
            <%= f.text_field :name %>
        </div>

        <div class="field">
            <%= f.label :email %>
            <%= f.text_field :email %>
        </div>

        <div class="field">
            <%= f.label :body %>
            <%= f.text_area :body, :rows => 10 %>
        </div>

    <% end %>

    <% field_set_tag do %>
        <%= f.submit button_value, :class => "button" %>
    <% end %>
<% end %>
```

This simple change is sufficient because it modifies the way the form is handled upon submission.

The third step is to modify the CommentsController's create action so that it's able to respond to JavaScript requests. Change it by adding the highlighted line:

```ruby
# POST /comments
# POST /comments.xml
def create
  @comment = @article.comments.build(params[:comment])

  respond_to do |format|
    if @comment.save
      flash[:notice] = 'Comment was successfully created.'
      format.html { redirect_to(@article) }
      format.xml  { render :xml => @comment, :status => :created,
                                             :location => @comment }
      format.js
    else
      format.html { render :action => "new" }
```

```
        format.xml  { ender :xml => @comment.errors, :status =>
:unprocessable_entity }
      end
    end
  end
```

This tells ActionPack that a `create.js.rjs` template should be used to formulate a response, when the incoming request is an Ajax one.

You might have noticed that if the comment fails to save, nothing happens to the existing form. This may or may not be the desired outcome, depending on the application. In some instances, you may want to handle the failed attempt by informing the user about the problem that prevented the object from being saved; for example, by placing a `format.js { render :template => "shared/error .js.rjs" }` *in the* `else` *branch and implementing an* `error.js.rjs` *template.*

The fourth and last step (I didn't say that it would be hard, now did I?), is therefore to create an RJS template. Go ahead and create `app\views\comments\create.js.rjs`, then copy the code from Listing 9-4.

Listing 9-4: app\views\comments\create.js.rjs

```
page.insert_html :bottom, :comments, :partial => "articles/comment", :object => @
comment
page.replace_html :comments_count, pluralize(@article.comments.size, 'Comment')
page[:new_comment].reset
page.replace_html :notice, flash[:notice]
flash.discard
```

If you require nice visual effects when an object is created, destroyed, or a change is made, use the method `page.visual_effect`.

Before delving into the analysis of this snippet, start the Web server and try to add a new comment to an existing post. You should see that the comment is immediately added without reloading the page, the comment counter before the comments section was updated, and the reassuring green, flash message "Comment was successfully created." should be displayed. Congratulations, you just added a simple Ajax feature to your first Rails application.

The RJS template in Listing 9-4 is easy to understand. `page` is a `JavaScriptGenerator` object that represents the page that issued the request, so that it can be easily manipulated from Ruby code. In the first line, you append, at the bottom of the DOM element with id `comments`, the partial `articles\_comment.html.erb`, which displays the comment you've just created:

```
page.insert_html :bottom, :comments, :partial => "articles/comment",
                                      :object => @comment
```

`insert_html` is a helper that's defined in the class `ActionView::Helpers::PrototypeHelper ::JavaScriptGenerator::GeneratorMethods`. Similar helpers defined by the same class are `replace_html`, `hide`, `show`, and `toggle`, which switches between hiding and showing a given element.

WATIR and Selenium

Aside from regular functional and unit testing, many Rails developers opt to further test their applications by using software that is able to automate the browser interaction with the application, and compare the expected results with what was actually obtained.

This sort of black-box testing, before the release of an application, is a form of automated *Acceptance Testing* and can be very beneficial when it comes to improving the Q&A of a Web application. And because the browser is automatically operated, as opposed to performing some sort of emulation, Rich Internet Applications are not a problem. No matter how much Ajax your application uses, these types of tests will be able to interact with the application and capture the produced output.

In the Rails world, two tools are very popular: Watir (Web Application Testing in Ruby, pronounced "water") and Selenium. Watir works through OLE to automate Internet Explorer, whereas Selenium is multi-platform and can be used with a variety of modern Web browsers. There is also a project, FireWatir, which is working to bring Watir to Mozilla Firefox. An effort to merge these two is currently underway. I highly encourage you to check out Watir and Selenium and try to give them a spin.

- ❑ **Watir:** `http://wtr.rubyforge.org`

- ❑ **Selenium:** `http://selenium.seleniumhq.org`

- ❑ **FireWatir:** `http://code.google.com/p/firewatir`

In the second line of Listing 9-4, you replaced the DOM element with id `comments_count` (with the updated number of comments):

```
page.replace_html :comments_count, pluralize(@article.comments.size, 'Comment')
```

You now need to clean up the form that was filled in to create the form. You do this by using the method `reset` on the page element with id `new_comment` (your form):

```
page[:new_comment].reset
```

You then need to replace the empty flash notice in the page with your success message. You do this as usual with `replace_html`:

```
page.replace_html :notice, flash[:notice]
```

And finally, you invoke `flash.discard` to discard the flash message. You need this final step to clear the flash for the next page reload. If you left out this line of code, the flash would still be on hand for the next request.

As demonstrated by this small example, Rails really simplifies the process of working with Ajax and JavaScript. Professional Web developers will inevitably end up writing JavaScript code as well, but Rails tries to keep everything as simple as possible by providing you with a Ruby DSL.

> **A Bug and an Exercise for the Reader**
>
> If you pay close attention, you will notice that the RJS template updates several elements in the page, but it doesn't update the number of comments in the right sidebar, just below the "Published on" date and time. So you will have a page that reads "4 comments" in the right sidebar, and above the comment section "5 comments." Solving this bug, which was intentionally left in, will be your exercise. All you'll have to do is add an id to the element in the sidebar, and then add a line to the RJS template so that its content is replaced as well when the request is completed.

Alternatives

Rails is opinionated software, and as such ships with a set of sensible defaults. As you have seen throughout this chapter, Rails assumes that you'll be using ERb, Builder, and RJS templates, and that you're going to employ Prototype and script.aculo.us. But it's important to understand that you are not limited to these options. Should you prefer a different template engine, you are free to adopt one instead of ERb. Common choices are Haml (`http://haml.hamptoncatlin.com`) and Liquid (`http://www.liquidmarkup.org`). If you'd like to simplify writing CSS, you can also check Haml's sister project, Saas.

Regarding Ajax, more than 200 frameworks are out there. Prototype is one of the best and most popular, but should you feel inclined to work with a different framework, you can copy it over in `public\javascripts`, include it with `javascript_include_tag`, and then it will be ready for you to use whenever you like. Of course, you'd be using JavaScript, as opposed to comfortable Ruby wrappers, but you can always define your own Ruby helpers and perhaps share and distribute them with others as a plugin. In fact, many plugins for alternative JavaScript libraries exist or are under development at the moment.

One JavaScript library in particular has been gaining a lot of momentum: jQuery. It's very light, fast, powerful, and well written, and it's been able to catch the interest of many Rails developers. If you are among the legions of jQuery fans, you should use the jRails plugin (`http://ennerchi.com/projects/jrails`), which provides a drop-in jQuery replacement for Prototype and script.aculo.us.

There is then the matter of alternatives to Ajax. Quite a few people were able to successfully interface Adobe Flex and Rails, skipping Ajax altogether. Similarly, as IronRuby matures, it will be interesting to be able to deploy Silverlight (or its open source counterpart Moonlight) and Ruby on Rails in production mode, an effort that's already underway thanks to experimental plugins like Silverline (`http://www.schementi.com/silverline`).

> **Sending Emails**
>
> Ruby on Rails enables developers to send emails thanks to ActionMailer. In order for your application to be able to send emails, you'll mainly need to define a model that inherits from `ActionMailer::Base` and a mailer view that is a regular ERb template that represents the body of your email.
>
> I highly recommend that you read the official Rails guide "Action Mailer Basics" to learn more about how to configure and use ActionMailer to send emails in your Rails applications. You can find it locally in `doc` (as discussed before) or online at `http://guides.rubyonrails.org/action_mailer_basics.html`.

Summary

Whether you have the luxury of a dedicated Web designer to help you out or you are in charge of both back-end and front-end, having a solid understanding of how the view layer works is fundamental, and this chapter should have helped you to get started.

It also concludes the broad panoramic of the MVC architectural pattern as implemented by Rails. It has been a somewhat lengthy journey, but it was a necessary undertaking to grasp the essential principles behind how the framework functions.

Moving on, the last two chapters in this book will be specialist ones, respectively dedicated to the topic of Web Services and then a whirlwind tour of performance and optimization, security, a few enterprise considerations, as well as deployment.

10

ActiveResource
and Web Services

*Your paradigm is so intrinsic to your mental process that you are hardly aware of its
existence, until you try to communicate with someone with a different paradigm.*

— *Donella Meadows, Environmental Scientist*

Web Services are systems used to allow machines to interact over a network. Within the context
of Web development, the network is the Internet itself, and the interaction is between at least one
computer that exposes a Web API and other machines that use this API to require services.

The previous chapters analyzed how you can define resources through `ActionController::
Resources` and hence easily define a RESTful service that exposes an API. When the format
requested was XML, Rails would formulate a response in XML that was suitable for other computers
to understand.

> *Historically XML has been the lingua franca for communicating among machines. Another
> younger contender is JSON (JavaScript Object Notation).*

What you did not explore yet, and what will be the main subject of this chapter, is how to consume REST Web Services that are defined through Rails. Enter the world of ActiveResource (also
known as ARes).

ActiveResource

Because requesting `GET /articles.xml` in your blog example produces XML data, you could interact with the REST service in this manner, without any wrapper and with "low-level" requests. But
just like interacting with databases via low-level queries is more time consuming and error prone
than using ActiveRecord, so is working with Web Services by sending handmade HTTP requests.

The idea behind ActiveResource is then very simple. ActiveRecord simplifies the process of interacting with databases, by providing object-relational mapping between relational data and business objects. ActiveResource does the same, only mapping REST resources. Both ActiveRecord and ActiveResource rely on a series of conventions and assumptions to be able to provide a wrapper to map structures containing the data (relational tables and resources, respectively) to model objects.

A script, desktop application, or Web application, can take advantage of ActiveResource, by simply defining a model for a given remote REST resource. When this prerequisite has been fulfilled, it will be possible to use that model through an API similar to ActiveRecord's one. Unlike ActiveRecord, which operates on database records and sends queries to the database, ActiveResource operates on remote HTTP resources by sending XML requests to the remote Web Service. Any XML received in response will then be opportunely serialized, so that you can continue to work with Ruby objects, as opposed to raw data.

Under the hood, the HTTP methods GET, POST, PUT, and DELETE are used to send the request, depending on the operation intended on the resource. For example, GET will be used to retrieve resources, POST to create new resources, PUT to update them, and finally, DELETE to, not surprisingly, delete resources.

Notice my use of the word "resource" as opposed to "record." In fact, though a resource will often represent actual database records, in which case ActiveResource indirectly provides an API to perform CRUD operations on a remote database, this doesn't have to be the case. There can be resources that do not represent database data.

Creating ActiveResource Models

The process of creating ActiveResource models is very similar to that for ActiveRecord models. When the client consuming a REST Web Service is another Rails application, an ActiveResource model is located in app\models. The class is conventionally named after the name of the remote resource and inherits from ActiveResource::Base.

First start the blog sample application as usual with ruby script/server, so that your Web Service will be up and running.

> *Please use the blog application without authentication. If you've already added authentication to your blog app, you can use the blog version provided with Chapter 6 in the code download at wrox.com.*

Next, create a new Rails application that will use it:

```
C:\projects> rails blog_consumer
C:\projects> cd blog_consumer
```

Proceed by creating an Article model. Create an article.rb file in app\models with the following content:

```
class Article < ActiveResource::Base
    self.site = "http://localhost:3000/"
end
```

The highlighted line sets a class variable site, so that ActiveResource knows where to find the remote REST Web Service that needs to be invoked. In this particular case, you are running the blog application on localhost, so the model will be mapped to `http://localhost:3000/articles`, but the assigned value could be any valid URI.

Another useful class variable is `timeout` (for example, `self.timeout = 4`), which is used to express the timeout in seconds. When a request times out, the error `ActiveResource::TimeoutError` is raised. You can rescue it and decide how to proceed after each timeout. Generally speaking it's recommended that you keep the timeout value to a rather small number, to respect the Fail-fast principle (you can read more about it online at `http://en.wikipedia.org/wiki/Fail-fast`). The default value for timeout depends on the Ruby implementation that is running Rails, but it's usually 60 seconds.

Avoiding Duplicates

In this scenario you have an `Article` ActiveRecord model on a server, and an `Article` ActiveResource model on the client, so there is no conflict whatsoever. However, what happens if your Rails application that acts as a client for the Web Service exposed by another Rails application already has an existing `article.rb` file for ActiveRecord in `app\models`?

When this happens, you can avoid duplication by simply setting the `element_name` for the ActiveResource model:

```
class ArticleResource < ActiveResource::Base
  self.site = "http://localhost:3000/"
  self.element_name = "article"
end
```

CRUD Operations

To experiment with this new model, you will work from the console. Open it by running:

```
C:\projects\blog_consumer> ruby script/console
```

Once inside the console, you'll proceed by performing a few CRUD operations. The whole process should appear familiar, because it's analogous to what you did with ActiveRecord, but don't forget that you are not interrogating a database but a remote REST service.

Again, for simplicity, I'm assuming you are using the blog application without authentication enabled, as per the code attached with Chapter 6.

If your Web Service has HTTP authentication in place, you can assign the credentials in the URL (for example, `self.site = http://myuser:secret@mydomain.com/`).

Alternatively, you can also use the class methods `user=` and `password=`, which are the only option when the username is an email address and as such cannot be included in the URL:

```
self.site = "https://mydomain.com/"
self.user = "myuser@mydomain.com"
self.password = "secret"
```

It is recommended that in production you use SSL to encrypt the communication between the Web Service consumer and the server, so that the password will not be sent in clear text (for example, `self.site = https://myuser:secret@mydomain.com/`*).*

Read

Let's try to retrieve a resource by its id:

```
>> article = Article.find(1)
=> #<Article:0x61322c4 @prefix_options={}, @attributes={"updated_at"=>Thu Jul 17
03:18:28 UTC 2008, "body"=>"Hi from the
 body of an article. :)", "title"=>"Hello, Rails!", "published"=>false, "id"=>1,
"published_at"=>Fri Jul 11 09:24:00 UTC
 2008, "created_at"=>Fri Jul 11 09:32:41 UTC 2008}>
```

Assuming that the resource whose XML element id is 1 exists, ActiveResource will retrieve the XML document and instantiate an `Article` object for you. All the entries defined within `@attributes` will be available as attributes of the object:

```
>> article.published
=> false
>> article.title
=> "Hello, Rails!"
```

If an XML element contains other XML elements, this will be mapped as its own object (for example, `article.complex_object.sub_element`*).*

If the record doesn't exist, an `ActiveResource::ResourceNotFound` exception is raised:

```
>> Article.find(100)
ActiveResource::ResourceNotFound: Failed with 404 Not Found
        from d:/Ruby/lib/ruby/gems/1.8/gems/activeresource-2.2.2/lib/active_
resource/connection.rb:170:in `handle_respon
se'
        from d:/Ruby/lib/ruby/gems/1.8/gems/activeresource-
2.2.2/lib/active_resource/connection.rb:151:in `request'
        from d:/Ruby/lib/ruby/gems/1.8/gems/activeresource-
2.2.2/lib/active_resource/connection.rb:116:in `get'
        from d:/Ruby/lib/ruby/gems/1.8/gems/activeresource-
2.2.2/lib/active_resource/base.rb:593:in `find_single'
        from d:/Ruby/lib/ruby/gems/1.8/gems/activeresource-
2.2.2/lib/active_resource/base.rb:521:in `find'
        from (irb):31
```

Note that although you can retrieve a collection of resources through `find(:all)`, the alias methods `all` (as well as `first` and `last`) are not available for ActiveResource models.

Whenever the `find` method is invoked on your `Article` model, a GET request (for the XML format) is sent. For example, `Article.find(1)` generates a request on the server running the REST Web Service with the following parameters:

```
{ "format" => "xml", "action" => "show", "id" => "1", "controller" => "articles" }
```

Using JSON Rather Than XML

The default ActiveResource format is XML. If you'd like to set JSON as the format for your ARes models, add `self.format = :json`. Doing so changes the value of the parameter format from `"xml"` to `"json."` The Web Service will need to be able to deal with JSON requests or you'll get an `ActiveResource::ClientError` with a `406 Not Acceptable` status code.

Create

Creating new resource instances is just as easy thanks to methods like `save` and `create`. These are the ActiveResource equivalents of the familiar methods you used for ActiveRecord.

Consider this example, which also employs the `new?` method to verify that an article resource hasn't been saved yet:

```
>> article = Article.new(:title => "Hi from ActiveResource", :body => "...some
text...")
=> #<Article:0x611d018 @prefix_options={}, @attributes={"body"=>"...some text...",
"title"=>"Hi from ActiveResource"}>
>> article.new?
=> true
>> article.save
=> true
>> article.id
=> 6
```

Instead of `new` and `save`, you can also use the `create` method to reduce the creation process to a single method.

When `article.save` is executed, a POST request for `http://localhost:3000/articles.xml` is sent by the client. Notice that the resource `id` doesn't exist until you invoke `article.save`. When a new resource request is sent, the Web Service will try to create a new record (in our case) and if successful will return a 201 HTTP status code (Created), with a `Location` header like `http://localhost:3000/articles/6`. This is a RESTful URI that indicates the location of the resource you just created. Out of this URI the `id` is parsed and assigned to the receiver (for example, the object referenced by `article`).

Please note that server-side validations apply. If a validation fails, `article.save` will fail and return `false`. You can check the validity of a resource through the method `valid?` and read a list of errors by calling `errors.full_messages` on the object you tried to save.

You can define validations in your ActiveResource models to perform validations client side, in a similar manner to how ActiveRecord validations work server side. Check the documentation of `ActiveResource::Validations` for further information.

Update

To update a resource, you can modify its attributes and then invoke the `save` method:

```
>> article = Article.find(1)
=> #<Article:0x60d3f80 @prefix_options={}, @attributes={"updated_at"=>Thu Jul 17
```

```
03:18:28 UTC 2008, "body"=>"Hi from the
 body of an article. :)", "title"=>"Hello, Rails!", "published"=>false, "id"=>1,
 "published_at"=>Fri Jul 11 09:24:00 UTC
 2008, "created_at"=>Fri Jul 11 09:32:41 UTC 2008}>
>> article.title = "Hello!"
=> "Hello!"
>> article.save
=> true
```

Updating a resource sends a PUT request, in this case, for http://localhost:3000/articles/1.xml. Unlike creating a resource, successfully updating a resource returns an empty response with a 204 HTTP status code (No Content).

Delete

Deleting remote resources can be accomplished through the instance method destroy, or with the class method delete (by passing an id). These send a DELETE request for the resource location (including .xml which specifies the format) and returns an empty response with HTTP status code of 200 (OK).

The existence of a resource can be verified with the method exists?.

> **Don't let the uncanny similarity between the basic CRUD methods defined by ActiveRecord and ActiveResource fool you. You won't be able to use many methods defined by ActiveRecord, including dynamic finders like find_by_title, with ActiveResource models, unless you define them yourself.**

Beyond CRUD

The four basic CRUD operations and a few extra methods to verify the status of a model instance will fall short when trying to consume certain APIs. For this reason, ActiveResource enables you to use your own custom REST methods, through get, post, put, and delete.

For example, consider the following:

```
>> Article.get(:unpublished)
=> [{"updated_at"=>Sun Nov 30 19:25:43 UTC 2008, "title"=>"Hello!", "body"=>"Hi
from the body of an article. :)", "published"=>false, "id"=>1, "published_at"=>Fri
Jul 11 09:24:00 UTC 2008, "created_at"=>Fri Jul 11 09:32:41 UTC 2008}]
```

This translates to GET /articles/unpublished.xml request. Because you defined an unpublished REST method, you obtain the expected result.

The same is true for the other verbs as well. For example, the following by default will translate in a POST request for /books/new/add.xml, under the assumption that the Web Service has defined a custom REST method add:

```
Book.new(:title => "Advanced Calculus").post(:add)
```

Any extra argument passed to any of these methods will be interpreted as a parameter. For instance:

```
Book.find(1).put(:deposit, :overdue => true)
```

will issue a PUT /books/1/deposit.xml?overdue=true request.

Of course, you can go further and define add or deposit class methods within the ARes model, by taking advantage of post and put, respectively.

Note that the last two book examples are generic; I'm not referencing other book examples I made in Chapter 7.

Nested Resources

I mentioned that despite the similarity between the ActiveRecord and ActiveResource APIs, only selected methods are available for the latter. This also means that, while tempting, reaching for the methods that provide access to a collection of objects associated with a given object like you'd do in ActiveRecord is not going to work in ActiveResource.

ActiveResource, in fact, knows nothing about databases, tables, and records. The fact that a one-to-many relationship between the articles table and the comments table exists is absolutely irrelevant to ActiveResource. What ActiveResource minds is resources and their relationships. Because you specified that comments are nested within articles in config\routes.rb, you are now able to work with nested resources from an ActiveResource client as well.

The comment.rb model in app\models needs to look like this:

```
class Comment < ActiveResource::Base
  self.site = "http://localhost:3000/articles/:article_id"
end
```

Notice how you need to provide the suffix articles/:article_id because comments are nested within articles, so an article_id is always necessary in order to access comments.

With this model definition, you can then access a list of comments for a given article as follows:

```
Comment.find(:all, :params => {:article_id => 1})
```

You can also retrieve a particular comment resource, modify its attributes, and then request an update:

```
c = Comment.find(:last, :params => { :article_id => 1 })
c.name = "A different commenter"
c.save #=> true
```

Specifying the article_id through params is fundamental, otherwise the URI generated for a request like Comment.find(:last) will be the malformed /articles//comments.xml.

To help you determine the URI generated you can use the helper methods `element_path` and `collection_path`. Take a look at the following two examples of their usage:

```
>> Comment.element_path(3, { :article_id => 1 })
=> "/articles/1/comments/3.xml"
>> Comment.collection_path(:article_id => 2)
=> "/articles/2/comments.xml"
```

`element_path` is therefore used for retrieving the path for a single resource, whereas `collection_path` is for retrieving the path to a list of resource objects, like the list of comments for a particular article.

Please notice that `element_path` *and* `collection_path` *do not accept a* `:params` *key.*

Consuming and Publishing REST Web Services from .NET

REST is a relatively new technology, but it's gaining momentum with an increasing number of websites exposing RESTful APIs. Truth to be told, not all of the APIs called "RESTful" actually are, but those sites that genuinely provide a REST Web Service can be "consumed" client side by ActiveResource, whether the Web Service has been implemented in Ruby on Rails or in a different language/framework.

This is great news when you need to use these services from within Ruby. Whether you are writing a Rails application or a regular Ruby program, you can use ActiveResource to interact with the Web Service.

You may, however, find yourself in a different position. Perhaps you just created a nice RESTful Rails application and would now like to be able to consume the REST Web Service it exposes from your existing .NET infrastructure.

This is not such a farfetched scenario, given that it's one of the easiest ways to start introducing Rails into a company that is mainly .NET-based. The other way is consuming through ARes a REST Web Service implemented in .NET.

Because your client will be written in .NET code, you cannot use ActiveResource (short of tinkering with IronRuby), so face the challenge of consuming a REST Web Service.

The REST architecture is based on the HTTP protocol and there is very little voodoo about it. It is so straightforward that you could decide to formulate requests and parse the XML content retrieved on your own. You could, for example, use `XmlDocument` or the `XElement` class defined by `System.Linq.XML` for your `GET` requests, and use it along with the `HttpWebRequest` class when you need to specify a different HTTP verb.

If the Web Service returns JSON, rather than XML, you can use the class `JavaScriptSerializer`.

Finally, should you require to publish RESTful Web Services using .NET, you can take advantage of the Windows Communication Foundation (WCF) REST Starter Kit, which includes samples, code, templates, screencasts, and a wealth of information about working with REST in .NET. You can find it on MSDN at `http://msdn.microsoft.com/wcf/rest`.

SOAP, XML-RPC, and ActionWebService

In the previous chapters you learned about creating RESTful Rails applications, which effortlessly allow you to expose a Web Service as well. In this chapter, you learned about how to consume these Web Services from Ruby, through ActiveResource. It's fair to state that as far as REST is concerned, Rails gets you covered from both the publishing and the consuming ends.

The bad news is that REST is not the most popular type of architectural style for Web Services, yet. In fact, a good part of the Enterprise world is still using and adopting "Big Web Services" or SOA (Service-Oriented Architecture) Web Services. In fact, REST Web Services are not currently very popular among .NET and Java development teams. Though this is bound to change, at the present, you may be forced at times to step outside of the REST boundaries, where things are less smooth and simple.

Thankfully both Ruby and Rails provide tools to interoperate with these other types of Web Services. When you need to publish a SOAP-based or XML-RPC Web Service from Rails, you can use the ActionWebService plugin, available as the `actionwebservice` gem (online at `http://rubyforge.org/projects/aws`). ActionWebService used to be part of the Rails core, before REST found its way to the heart of the framework and the community.

AWS tries to simplify the process of publishing APIs via WSDL (Web Service Definition Language), based on the SOAP or XML-RPC protocols.

> *A fairly complete manual used to be available online at* `http://manuals.rubyonrails.com/read/book/10` *but at the time of writing, this is only available through the Google Cache. Checking the "raw" documentation may be the best bet at this stage.*

Please note that AWS does not implement the full W3C specification, but it's limited to the basic functionalities required to interoperate with Java and .NET.

If you need to consume a SOAP-based Web Service written in .NET or Java from Ruby/Rails, you can either still use the abstractions provided by ActionWebService or, perhaps more simply, use Ruby's `SOAP` library. You can find an example of this online in this blog post: `http://webgambit.com/blog/calling-a-net-web-service-from-rails-original`.

> *If you have an interest in Web Services, you should definitely check out the Atom Publishing Protocol (APP) as well. You can start from* `http://www.atomenabled.org`.

Summary

In the past few years, Web Services have assumed an increasingly important role in the world of computing. Think about all the cloud services and the APIs published by so-called Web 2.0 applications.

Ruby on Rails marries the most modern architectural style for Web Services, making it dead easy to publish RESTful Web Services and, thanks to ActiveResource, just as easy to consume them, whether these were published by another Rails application or an entirely different stack.

In its simplicity, ActiveResource does a lot for you. It transforms ActiveRecord-like methods into requests, composed by an HTTP verb, a RESTful URI, and an XML (or JSON) body. And when a response is received, this is handled and processed so that its details are available to the developer through model objects and their attributes.

REST is definitely the way to go when developing in Rails, but I hope to have you reassured that alternatives exist, albeit less straightforward.

The next chapter touches on the subjects of deployment, security, and optimization.

11

Going Into Production

Phusion Passenger, aka mod_rails, has been on a tour de force lately and rightfully so. It makes Rails deployment so much simpler and, combined with REE, faster and with less memory overhead. So I'm really happy to see that lots of the hosting companies in the Rails world are adopting it and making it available to their customers.

— *David Heinemeier Hansson*

Ruby on Rails is notorious for its ability to provide developers with a quick and relatively easy way to prototype Web applications. Yet building an application is only the first in a series of steps that are required before you're able to see your creation live.

This chapter supplies you with a few important considerations about security, performance and optimization, and deployment. Because entire books have been written on each of these topics, my aim with this final chapter is merely to provide you with a few essential notions and considerations before you advance on your own journey of further improving your Ruby on Rails skills. We'll start with the fundamental topic of securing your Web application.

Security Considerations

It would be nice to be able to publish Web applications and sites without worrying about them being hacked, but it is not realistic. It's a jungle out there on the Internet, and unless you take serious precautions, your site is bound to become compromised sooner or later.

To make things more challenging, the security of an application is like a chain: it's only as strong as its weakest link. Covering the subject of securing a Web server is well beyond the scope of this book. If you are not familiar with the process, hosting companies and plans are available that will take care of this for you. What they cannot do, though, is guarantee that your application is secure as well. As a developer, application-level security is your responsibility, and this section should help you make more conscious choices in this regard.

Cross-Site Scripting (XSS)

Cross-site scripting (XSS) attacks take advantage of vulnerabilities in a Web application to inject malicious code that will be executed when other users view the page.

To better understand how XSS attacks work, let's take a look at one possible scenario. Assume that you have a blog application that allows comments. If that comment form is vulnerable to XSS attacks, a malicious user could publish a comment that includes JavaScript code. Once the comment is published on the site, every visitor who comes across that page executes the malicious JavaScript code (assuming JavaScript was enabled in their browsers).

This is dangerous because the vulnerable form enables a malicious user to publish arbitrary code that would be executed by other users. The malicious user could, for example, inject JavaScript code that would grab the cookie of a legitimate user and send it over to a server where it would be collected and processed. If the genuine user was logged in to the application, the malicious user would then be able to use the stolen cookie to gain access to the application as if he were the authenticated, genuine user. And that genuine user, who visited the compromised page on the application, could be the administrator of the site, granting the malicious user full control of the application and its data.

It's important to understand that this attack relies on vulnerable pages that publish unsafe values without properly escaping them first. While you're developing Web applications, you need to be ruthless when it comes to any value that could originate from a malicious user.

For example, the following is vulnerable to XSS attacks, because it displays the content coming from the user as it is:

```
<%= params[:body] %>
```

If `params[:body]` contains a `<script>` tag, it will be published and executed by any future visitors to that page.

html_escape

In Rails, the easiest way is to escape any HTML tags is with the already amply discussed h helper (alias for `html_escape`). This helper will transform < and > occurrences within the argument into `&lt;` and `&gt;`. The correct way to display the previous example is as follows:

```
<%= h(params[:body]) %>
```

or as it will often appear in many code bases:

```
<%=h params[:body] %>
```

With this in place, all tags will be displayed instead of being interpreted/executed. Any `<script>` in input becomes an innocuous `&lt;script&gt;`, which is rendered as the string `<script>` by any browser.

sanitize

Escaping HTML tags with h is good practice from a security standpoint, but it's also very limiting when you need to allow certain tags to be displayed. These occasions warrant the use of `sanitize`, which takes a whitelist approach, by allowing only a specific set of tags and attributes.

Everything else is escaped (tags) or stripped (attributes). This process of sanitizing the input also strips dangerous protocols (for example, `javascript:`), preventing them from being used as values for `href` and `src` attributes. Finally, `sanitize` tries to combat any tricks that black-hat hackers may have up their sleeve, and their attempts to bypass the JavaScript filters with special characters (for example, hexadecimals).

Without optional arguments, `sanitize` is used as follows:

```
<%= sanitize(@comment.body) %>
```

You may be wondering what tags, attributes, and protocols are allowed by default. To verify which ones are, you need to dig into Rails' code in `actionpack/lib/action_controller/vendor/html-scanner/html/sanitizer.rb`, to discover the following snippet:

```
# A regular expression of the valid characters used to separate protocols like
# the ':' in 'http://foo.com'
self.protocol_separator    = /:|(&#0*58)|(&#x70)|(%|&#37;)3A/

# Specifies a Set of HTML attributes that can have URIs.
self.uri_attributes        = Set.new(%w(href src cite action longdesc xlink:href
  lowsrc))

# Specifies a Set of 'bad' tags that the #sanitize helper will remove completely,
as opposed
# to just escaping harmless tags like &lt;font&gt;
self.bad_tags              = Set.new(%w(script))

# Specifies the default Set of tags that the #sanitize helper will allow unscathed.
self.allowed_tags          = Set.new(%w(strong em b i p code pre tt samp kbd var
sub sup dfn cite big small address hr br div span h1 h2 h3 h4 h5 h6 ul ol li dt dd
abbr acronym a img blockquote del ins))

# Specifies the default Set of html attributes that the #sanitize helper will leave
# in the allowed tag.
self.allowed_attributes    = Set.new(%w(href src width height alt cite datetime
title class name xml:lang abbr))

# Specifies the default Set of acceptable css properties that #sanitize and
#sanitize_css will accept.
self.allowed_protocols     = Set.new(%w(ed2k ftp http https irc mailto news gopher
nntp telnet webcal xmpp callto feed svn urn aim rsync tag ssh sftp rtsp afs))
```

The `:tags` and `:attributes` options are used to specify additional tags and attributes that can be permitted. For example:

```
<%= sanitize(@comment.body, :tags => %w{table tr td}, :attributes => %w{id class}) %>
```

These can also be specified globally for the application within an initializer (that is, in `config\environment.rb` or in a file within `config\initializers`):

```
Rails::Initializer.run do |config|
  config.action_view.sanitized_allowed_tags = 'table', 'tr', 'td'
  config.action_view.sanitized_allowed_attributes = 'id', 'class'
end
```

You can also disallow some of the existing tags or attributes by deleting them from the default list:

```
Rails::Initializer.run do |config|
  config.after_initialize do
    ActionView::Base.sanitized_allowed_tags.delete('img')
  end
end
```

Alternatively, for a whitelist approach that removes all tags by default, consider the Sanitize gem. You can find more information about it online at `http://wonko.com/post/sanitize`.

XSS vulnerabilities are not limited to regular forms. Allowing users to upload files that become available to other users can also be dangerous. In fact, a malicious user could misrepresent the file's content type and try to let other users execute the file's content as opposed to simply downloading the file. Another risk is attempting to pass a relative path to the server to make sensitive files that are located on the server (for example, `../../config/database.yml`) available for download. Using the Rails plugin Paperclip (`http://www.thoughtbot.com/projects/paperclip`) and its validations eases the process of working securely with attachments.

Cookie Security

In the scenario described in the previous section, the malicious user was able to log in as a different user thanks to both a vulnerable form and the application's reliance on the session data stored in the cookie to identify a user.

Along with escaping/stripping/validating the user input, a (admittedly less effective) step is attempting to render the stolen cookie useless. In the pursuit of this aim, a common countermeasure is to store the IP address of the legitimate user in the session data. This way when a malicious user tries to use the cookie from a different IP, the IP address won't match up and the controller will be able to invalidate the session data, preventing the attacker from getting through. This does not offer 100% protection, because the attacker could have the same IP (if for example, both legitimate and malicious users are behind the same NAT or Web Proxy). Furthermore, it's an inconvenience for those users whose dynamic IP addresses change regularly.

Because of the possibility of inconveniencing many users, a developer should think carefully about the pros and cons of adopting this countermeasure.

This is also a possible countermeasure against Session Fixation Attacks. In these kinds of attacks, the malicious user manages to assign a session id to a user through vulnerabilities, such as XSS, and then waits for the user to log in with that session id, allowing the malicious user to impersonate a legitimate user. Storing the IP address of the user in the session data within the cookie, reduces — but doesn't eliminate — the risk of this type of attack.

Another common technique that is very effective against Session Fixation Attacks is to issue new session data whenever a user logs in. This way, the attacker who's waiting for the "victim" to log in with the "fixed" session id will be disarmed, because the legitimate user will log in but doing so with a new session id that was assigned by the Rails application.

The session ids (SIDs) are larger in size and randomly generated by Rails on purpose, so as not to be simply guessed at.

SQL Injection

XSS attacks can be very dangerous, but when it comes to application-level security risks, SQL injection attacks take the cake. As the name implies, these attacks consist of injecting fragments of SQL containing meta-characters into legitimate queries, so as to gain access to the database and execute arbitrary queries.

It's important to understand that these attacks are not Rails-specific. Independently from the language and/or framework that's been employed, any application can be vulnerable to these types of attacks if the developer doesn't pay close enough attention and provide valid countermeasures. Conversely, these countermeasures are framework-specific.

Imagine for a moment that you created a login form without properly escaping the user input. A malicious user could provide the following input:

```
Login: admin
Password: anything' or 'a'='a
```

And with these simple strings the attacker would suddenly gain access to your application as an administrator. Let's see how this works and what you can do to prevent it from happening.

> SQL injection attacks are database-specific and each RDBMS allows different SQL syntaxes, which means that attackers will try several variants of this exploit.

A developer would be expecting the database to execute queries as follows:

```
SELECT * FROM users WHERE username = 'someuser' AND password = 'somepwd';
```

When the previous malicious input is provided, the executed query becomes:

```
SELECT * FROM users WHERE username = 'admin' AND password = 'anything' or 'a'='a';
```

As you can see, the condition to the right of AND is always true, and therefore the attacker manages to log in as an administrator (provided the admin username was admin).

Thankfully this can easily be avoided by using Rails' built-in finders correctly. Whenever you retrieve a record based on its id, escaping of special characters like ' and " is done automatically for you. For example, look at the following SQL injection attempt:

```
User.find(params[:id]) # params[:id] is ' or 1—
```

It generates the harmless query:

```
SELECT * FROM "users" WHERE ("users"."id" = 0)
```

Similarly, using dynamic finders without manually adding SQL conditions is a safe move as well:

```
Book.find_by_title(params[:title])
```

Problems begin to arise when you adopt options in your finders that allow you to specify custom fragments of SQL. For example, one typical mistake is to evaluate expressions directly within a string that's been assigned to the key :conditions. The following line is vulnerable to SQL injection attacks:

```
# Don't do this
Account.find(:all, :conditions => "name LIKE '%#{params[:name]}%' AND active =
'#{params[:active]'")
```

You should never embed tainted expressions (ones that are coming from the user) in SQL fragments, because these strings are not escaped and are able to be exploited. You can pass an array to :conditions instead. The first element is a string with question marks in place of the actual values, and the remaining elements of the array are values in order of how they should be substituted:

```
Account.find(:first, :conditions => ["name LIKE ? AND active = ?",
"%#{params[:name]}%", params[:active])
```

This will automatically escape dangerous characters that could be used to hijack your queries. Likewise, you can opt for the hash form as well:

```
Account.find(:first, :conditions => { :username => params[:username],
                                       :password => params[:password] })
```

It is worth noticing that in the industry, parametric queries are often used as a means of optimizing performances and securing databases against SQL injection attacks. The current version of ActiveRecord does not make use of these however.

Check out the official documentation for santize* methods that you can use whenever you're defining your own model's methods (that involve potentially unsafe SQL strings).

Little Bobby Table

xkcd is an online webcomic that's very popular among developers. In what is now a famous comic strip called "Exploits of a Mom," a school runs into big trouble due to a student named Robert'; DROP TABLE Students; —, or "Little Bobby Table" as he's nicknamed at home. In the last frame of this hilarious strip, the school informs the mother that they've lost this year's student records because of his name. And the mother tells the school: "And I hope you've learned to sanitize your database inputs." Indeed, SQL injection is a serious threat and as Web developers it is our responsibility to carefully sanitize any input. You can find the strip online at http://xkcd.com/327/ and I also recommend that you check out the wealth of other xkcd comics that are available there, if you're into geeky humor.

Protecting Your Records

Another important security risk is leaving your records' attributes unprotected. Imagine that you have a User model with the following attributes: name, email, password, is_admin, and photo. For regular users, the form for editing one's profile will probably contain all of these fields but it will leave out the field is_admin. Unless you protect your records, by default the users will be able to save the page on their hard drive, modify it to add a checkbox for the is_admin boolean field, mark off that checkbox, and then click submit to grant themselves admin access to the application.

Alternatively, a malicious user could opt to manipulate the URL instead.

In fact, in your code you'd probably update the user like this:

```
current_user.update_attributes(params[:user])
```

Note that this will perform a mass-assignment for all the available model attributes that are contained within `params[:user]`. That's problematic because users can alter all the fields they want as well as the associated objects if associations between models were defined.

Mass-assignments are possible through methods such as `update_attributes`, `new`, *and* `attributes=`.

Rails provides two macro-like methods to prevent this risky default behavior. The first is `attr_protected` and the second is `attr_accessible`. The former adopts a blacklist approach, in which you specify attributes that should be protected from mass-assignments. The latter uses a whitelist approach, allowing you to specify which attributes can be modified through mass-assignment, and blocking all the rest.

In the previous example, you can protect the `is_admin` field when performing mass-assignments as follows:

```
class User < ActiveRecord::Base
  attr_protected :is_admin
end
```

Likewise, you could have specified a list of allowed fields:

```
class User < ActiveRecord::Base
  attr_accessible :name, :email, :password, :photo
end
```

This second approach is more verbose, but it protects all the attributes from mass-assignments by default, hence protecting attributes defined by associations as well. Furthermore, any future attributes added to the model at a later stage will automatically be protected as well.

Other Costly Mistakes

A common mistake made by beginners is to leave all the methods in their controllers as public. When a method defined in a controller, including `ApplicationController`, is public, it becomes an action that can be accessed by visitors to the site. Whenever you have a method used by other actions that shouldn't be accessible to the end user, you need to declare it as private (or protected).

Another typical mistake is to allow access to other users' data by simply accepting the id provided in input. Because the id appears in the URL, it doesn't take a hacker to increment or change it. The easiest way to protect your application from this type of vulnerability (which concerns privacy as well) is to perform your searches based on the id (or other parameters) as well as verify that the current user has the right to access it.

For example, in the `show` action of a `BankAccountController` you should retrieve the bank account through an id as well as the condition that the owner of the account is the current user. So don't run `@account = BankAccount.find(params[:id])` or everyone will have access to the account of everyone else. Instead, add a condition like `:conditions => ["user_id = ?", @user.id]` where `@user` is an instance variable set in a private before filter method.

> **Remember that on its own "security through obscurity" rarely works. Don't rely on hard-to-guess ids as a means of protecting your users' data.**

When `find` (by id) fails to find a record an error is raised. This error could be rescued within a `rescue` clause, in which a redirect to the homepage or another appropriate page is performed.

Ruby on Rails Security Guide

The subject of security is very wide and it's beyond the scope of this book to provide you with a complete set of possible security countermeasures in Rails applications. It would also be a duplication of the excellent work carried out by the Rails community to provide informative online material.

My suggestion to you is to read the official Ruby on Rails Security Guide, which is available online at `http://guides.rails.info/security.html` or through `rake doc:guides`. This guide is extensive and covers all you realistically need to know.

I also recommend checking the Ruby on Rails Security Project at `http://www.rorsecurity.info`. Its blog has plenty of interesting articles related to Rails security and it also provides a short, free e-book that you may want to check out.

Finally, in order to keep your applications secure, I can't stress enough the importance of subscribing to the official Rails blog, Riding Rails, which is available at `http://weblog.rubyonrails.org` as well as keeping an eye on the Rails Security mailing list available at `http://lists.rubyonrails.org/mailman/listinfo/rails-security`. Any vulnerability or security concerns will be publicly announced there, as well as the availability of Rails upgrades.

Performance and Optimization

An important step before releasing your application to the world is to ensure that the application's performances are acceptable. This section briefly provides pointers to do just that.

Measuring Performance

Because it is said that premature optimization is the root of all evils, you first must determine how well your application performs and identify where possible bottlenecks exist. In other words, you need to be able to benchmark and profile your application.

Several tools are available to measure the performance of your applications. The first most obvious approach is to check your production logs.

Remember, applications running in development mode are usually much slower than in production mode. You can run `ruby script/server -e production` or uncomment `ENV['RAILS_ENV'] ||= 'production'` in your `config\environment.rb` file, to ensure that the application will run in production mode.

Reading Logs

Each entry within the logs provides timing information. Prior to Rails 2.2, the logs would report the throughput for the request (the number of requests per seconds as shown here):

```
Processing ArticlesController#index (for 127.0.0.1 at 2009-01-04 03:49:51) [GET]
  Session ID: f88e2cf214faf1ad32c8c3564900828a
  Parameters: {"action"=>"index", "controller"=>"articles"}
Rendering template within layouts/articles
Rendering articles/index
Completed in 0.01900 (52 reqs/sec) | Rendering: 0.00800 (42%) | DB: 0.00100 (5%) |
200 OK [http://localhost/]
```

In Rails 2.2, this has been changed to report the amount of time for each request:

```
Processing ArticlesController#index (for 127.0.0.1 at 2009-01-04 04:01:26) [GET]
Rendering template within layouts/articles
Rendering articles/index
Completed in 62ms (View: 62, DB: 0) | 200 OK [http://localhost/articles]
```

Notice how the rendering time is separated from the database processing time to help you identify which of the two may cause slowdowns.

Though it is tempting to think in terms of requests per second, it's far more effective to consider the actual amount of time per request. For example, imagine that the throughput for a given action is 1000 reqs/s. Bringing this to 2000 reqs/s may seem like a great accomplishment, because you "doubled the performance." In reality, you simply went from 1 millisecond per request to half a millisecond per request. Sure, you'll be able to serve more requests and that's a good thing, but under a regular load no user is going to notice the difference.

In other words, this new approach invites developers to go after real bottlenecks and slow actions as opposed to prematurely trying to optimize what really doesn't need to be optimized.

This becomes self-evident if you use the Firebug extension for Firefox (or equivalent). This add-on has a Net panel that breaks down the amount of time required to load a page. As soon as you start using it, you'll immediately see how milliseconds spent within the Rails stack to respond to a request are only a minimal part of the whole process of loading the page client side (as shown in Figure 11-1). Of course slow queries (or rendering times) need to be fixed, but just remember to pick your battles.

If you want to time and log a specific snippet of code in your model, controller, or view, you can use the benchmark method. This method is available in three flavors, depending on where you intend to use it.

Use benchmark defined in ActionController::Benchmarking::ClassMethods to benchmark blocks within your controllers. For the view, use the helper version defined in ActionView::Helpers::BenchmarkHelper:

```
<% benchmark("Process TPS reports") do %>
  <%= process_reports %>
<% end %>
```

Figure 11-1

This will add something like `"Process TPS reports (1331.2ms)"` to your log. Finally, for models, use the `benchmark` class method defined by `ActiveRecord::Base`.

Other Tools

If you are familiar with the *nix world, you can use tools like `grep` (available on Windows through Cygwin) to data mine your logs, rather than manually reading them.

Even better, you can use a log analyzer. Two common choices are the Production Log Analyzer (available at `http://rails-analyzer.rubyforge.org`) and the Request Log Analyzer (available at `http://github.com/wvanbergen/request-log-analyzer`).

Another set of tools for measuring performance and profiling your Rails applications is RailsBench, available on RubyForge at `http://railsbench.rubyforge.org`. Patching the Ruby interpreter with a patch (available at the same URL) that improves the garbage collector (aka GC) is unfortunately a requirement.

`ruby-prof` is a fast profiler for Ruby that acts as a replacement for the slow built-in one available through the option `-r profile`. It can be installed via `gem install` and provides a series of reporting options (for example, flat, graph, HTML graph, and so on). This is often used to profile Rails applications as well, as described in the helpful documentation at `http://ruby-prof.rubyforge.org`.

You'll also notice that in the `script` folder of your Rails applications there is a `performance` folder containing three scripts: `benchmarker`, `profiler`, and `request`. These are provided for convenience and can be used to quickly benchmark, profile, and simulate a number of requests.

For example, you could run the following to compare two expensive (equivalent) methods and evaluate which one is the fastest (with 100 iterations):

```
ruby script/performance/benchmarker 100 'Article.method1' 'Article.method2'
          user       system      total        real
#1     0.842000    0.031000    0.873000  (  0.881000)
#2     0.874000    0.094000    0.968000  (  0.948000)
```

Likewise, you could run the profiler for a single method. This will automatically use Ruby's built-in profiler or the `ruby-prof` extension mentioned earlier, if installed. The quantity of information outputted by the profiler is admittedly overwhelming, but it's usually enough to focus on the top entries to spot unusually slow calls:

```
ruby script/performance/profiler 'Article.method1' 1000 flat
Loading Rails...
Using the ruby-prof extension.
Thread ID: 33481630
Total: 1.629000

  %self     total      self      wait     child     calls   name
   8.78      0.42      0.14      0.00      0.28      5000   Integer#times-1
(ruby_runtime:0}
   7.00      0.11      0.11      0.00      0.00     28000
<Module::SQLite3::Driver::Native::API>#sqlite3_column_text (ruby_runtime:0}
   6.63      0.18      0.11      0.00      0.08      4000   Hash#each_key
(ruby_runtime:0}
   6.51      0.33      0.11      0.00      0.23        17   Kernel#gem_original_require-1
(ruby_runtime:0}
   4.36      0.07      0.07      0.00      0.00      5000
<Module::SQLite3::Driver::Native::API>#sqlite3_step (ruby_runtime:0}
   3.87      0.06      0.06      0.00      0.00      5023   Array#flatten
(ruby_runtime:0}
   3.50      0.68      0.06      0.00      0.63      5000   SQLite3::ResultSet#next
(d:/Ruby/lib/ruby/gems/1.8/gems/sqlite3-ruby-1.2.3-x86-
mswin32/lib/sqlite3/resultset.rb:89}
   3.31      0.05      0.05      0.00      0.00        98   <Class::Dir>#[]
(ruby_runtime:0}
   2.82      0.15      0.05      0.00      0.11      8090   Array#each (ruby_runtime:0}
```

Finally, the `request` script allows you to benchmark or profile on a per-request basis. This requires the name of a file containing the request script. For example, the simplest script possible would be the following:

```
get '/'
```

And this could be run (for 200 times) as follows:

```
ruby script/performance/request -n 200 home.rb
Warming up once
0.32 sec, 1 requests, 3 req/sec

Profiling 200x
`gem install ruby-prof` to use the profiler
```

> If you install `ruby-prof`, be warned that unless you also patch the garbage collector with the patch mentioned previously, this script will crash the Ruby interpreter on Windows. In fact, some of the features of `ruby-prof` require the GC fix. And building Ruby from source on Windows in order to patch it is a less than straightforward process. My advice is to avoid using this particular script on Windows or simply miss the profiling functionality it provides.
>
> You shouldn't worry about this script that benchmarks and profiles integration tests, because it has become deprecated in Rails 2.3. If you intend to use it in the next version of Rails (2.3), you should install the `request_profiler` plugin, which provides the same functionality.

For further information about benchmarking and profiling, including how to write performance tests, I recommend that you read the official Performance Testing Rails Applications guide available online at `http://guides.rails.info/performance_testing.html`. You may also want to check out the following blog post about how to profile Rails applications: `http://cfis.savagexi.com/2007/07/10/how-to-profile-your-rails-application`.

Should the URL no longer be valid by the time you read this page, simply visit the newly announced portal for Rails guides, available at `http://guides.rails.info`. *There you will find all the new versions of the guides mentioned throughout this book, and new ones that are being written and are already updated to the latest version of Rails. Alternatively, you can always rely on the guides produced for your version of Rails, by generating them with* `rake doc:guides`. *As you probably know by now, they will be placed in the* `doc` *folder of your application.*

Stress Testing

Among the non–Rails-specific tools, `httperf` and `ab` are commonly used to stress test your application and simulate a very high load of browser requests. If these are not an option for you, Microsoft Web Application Stress Tool will do as well. The main idea is to find out how well your Web server configuration handles a large volume of requests before your site is actually hit by real traffic.

Commercial Monitoring

Using some of the tools mentioned in the previous sections, you should be able to resolve performance and scalability issues before your application goes into production. Slow queries, sluggish helpers, and far too complex routes can all be caught early on. Once that job is done and your application has been deployed into production, the second part of the equation becomes monitoring its performance while it's live, up, and running.

You can still use log analyzers of course, but a few companies emerged to tackle the challenge of making it easy to make sense of the overwhelming amount of information available in your logs (and more). Three well established names are New Relic, FiveRuns, and Scout.

FiveRuns has a very interesting blog that features "Rails TakeFive" interviews with prominent Ruby and Rails members of the community. You can find it at `http://blog.fiveruns.com`.

New Relic (`http://newrelic.com`) offers a service called RPM. After installing a plugin and choosing your subscription plan, it automatically monitors your application and provides you with detailed and helpful reports about the performance of your application. Its lite version is free and provides basic reporting.

FiveRuns (`http://fiveruns.com`) offers two products, TuneUp and Manage. The former is free and it's aimed at monitoring the application during development, before it goes into production. The latter, its commercial offering, is similar to New Relic RPM in scope, and aims at monitoring and identifying performance drops in Rails apps running in production.

Finally, Scout (`http://scoutapp.com`) offers a very similar service to New Relic RPM and FiveRuns Manage, and allows you to sign up for your first server for free. Commercial plans allow you to add more servers, longer data retention for the output of the plugin, and more frequent reporting intervals.

All three commercial services have achieved a great deal of interest in the Rails community and are widely used. If you are interested in this type of service, I highly recommend that you try them before you decide which one works best for you.

Performance vs. Scalability

Performance and scalability are two related but distinct concepts. Performance has to do with how fast your application is, whereas scalability indicates the ability to handle an increasingly larger volume of traffic. The two are related, especially because most often performance becomes an issue only when a large number of requests start rolling in, but it's important to understand the difference.

During performance optimization the attention is focused on improving speed and eliminating bottlenecks. Scaling an application, on the other hand, means being able to take advantage of additional hardware resources.

Scaling vertically (aka scaling up) is the ability to take advantage of additional resources, typically additional RAM and CPUs, added to a single server. Conversely, scaling horizontally (aka scaling out) means being able to easily add more nodes/servers to serve your application. Adding extra Web and/or database servers to handle the increasing load is an example of scaling out.

Thankfully, the Rails ecosystem is well equipped with tools to help you scale your application, when the need arises.

Caching

When talking about performance we can't fail to mention caching. Caching is a necessary evil. For instance, it makes your application harder to test and to debug. All things considered, though, caching can grant you a huge performance boost. Instead of repeating slow operations in the back-end, the result of the computation is calculated once and stored in the cache where it will be easily retrieved at the next request.

Taking ActionPack into consideration, three levels of caching are available: page caching, action caching, and fragment caching. In order to use any of these, you'll need to have caching enabled in your environment's configuration files. By default, this is disabled in development and test mode, but enabled in production:

```
# In production mode
config.action_controller.perform_caching = true
```

Page caching caches a whole page within a static file on the server's filesystem. Because this is saved by default as an HTML file in `public`, at the next request for that page, the HTML file will be served bypassing the whole Rails stack de facto. This type of caching has the advantage of being extremely fast, because at each request for the same page, you'll be serving a static file.

Sadly, there are a few disadvantages as well. If a page has dynamic content that changes often, it shouldn't be cached in this way. Likewise, if a page needs to be protected by authentication, page caching cannot be used. Perhaps more importantly, the biggest drawback is that expiring the cache is not automated because the cached files (for example, `public/show.html`) are regular HTML pages and will be happy to stay there forever unless they are removed somehow.

Page caching is performed by using the `caches_page` method in your controllers:

```
caches_pages :index
```

Expiring pages can be achieved by adopting special observers known as Sweepers or strategically using the method `expire_page`:

```
def create
  #...
  expire_pages :action => :index
end
```

Action caching is very similar to page caching, but it doesn't serve the cached file directly. Instead, ActionPack handles the request allowing you to run before filters and other rules to satisfy authentication and other requirements. Its usage is analogous to page caching:

```
# Caches the edit action
caches_action :edit

# ...

# Expires the edit action
expire_action :action => :edit
```

Finally, the third type of cache is fragment caching and it's aimed at allowing you to cache certain parts of the page, whenever caching the whole page is not possible. This is usually the case with highly dynamic pages that have several "moving parts" that cannot all be cached or expired at the same time. Fragment caching is also an easy way to speed up the process of serving more static content, like a navigation menu or regular HTML code.

To perform fragment caching you can use the `cache` helper:

```
<% cache do %>
  <%= render :partial => "sidebar" %>.
<% end %>
```

This helper also accepts an `:action` and an `:action_suffix` that you can use to identify fragments, whenever you want to cache multiple fragments for an action. Expiring them can then be accomplished through the `expire_fragment` helper.

Outside of the realm of ActionPack, the M component of the MVC triad has caching as well. In fact, ActiveRecord has built-in caching capabilities and the results of every SQL query already executed within the lifespan of an action are cached. So if you perform the same query more than once within an action, the database will only be hit once.

For further details about caching, I highly encourage you to read the official guide, "Caching with Rails," available online at `http://guides.rubyonrails.org/caching_with_rails.html`.

> As an exercise, try to add various forms of caching to the sample blog application and benchmark the application to see their effect.

Application-Level Performance Considerations

Before moving on to the "Deploying Rails" section, I'd like to leave you with a few additional bits of advice, in what can be considered an incomplete checklist or a list of common mistakes/pitfalls:

❑ Don't go randomly looking for places where you should optimize your code, but rather put your trust in the profiler (and in running benchmarks).

❑ Caching is not your friend, but a necessary acquaintance. A judicious and conservative use of caching is necessary and can do wonders to improve your application's responsiveness and ability to handle heavy loads.

❑ Most of the code that you write when developing in Rails is Ruby code. Ruby is not the fastest language out there so it's important that the code you write is reasonably efficient.

❑ Rails' routing system can be quite slow. Simplify your routes and avoid complex ones.

❑ Define indexes on large tables for fields that are commonly looked up.

❑ ActiveRecord is a nice abstraction layer, but don't forget that you have a full-blown relational database at your hands – don't be afraid to use it. This means that even if certain features are not available in ActiveRecord, you shouldn't hesitate to use them, because they're able to give you a much needed performance boost. Depending on the database system you are using, your requirements, and the bottlenecks you are experiencing, this could mean using stored procedures, triggers, parametric queries, actual foreign key constraints, hand-tuned SQL queries through `find_by_sql`, and so on.

❑ If you are retrieving a larger record only to use a very small portion of it, you should use the `:select` option to limit the set of returned fields and therefore the resultset size.

❑ Eager load your associations using `:include`. This will also prevent the 1+N problem discussed in Chapter 7.

❑ Avoid combining deeply nested `:includes` with `:conditions` because this leads to the generation of slow and very hefty sized SQL queries.

❑ Don't use `length` to retrieve the size of an associated collection of objects. For example, use `user.comments.size` or `user.comments.count` instead of `user.comments.length`. The reason for this is that the first two formulate a `COUNT(*)` query, whereas `length` will retrieve all the records and then count them with the `Array` instance method `length`. That's extremely inefficient.

❑ Related to the previous point, consider using counter caches. These are fields that can be used to automatically keep track of the associated record's count, without having to query the database every time. In a scenario where `Article` and `Comment` are your models, you could, for example, define a `comments_count` integer column with default 0 in the `articles` table, and have `belongs_to :article, :counter_cache => true` within the `Comment` model. Be aware that `size` and `count` are not aliases when using counter caches. `size` is the only one that will look at the cache value stored in `comments_count` and as such it won't hit the database. `length` and `count`'s behavior is the same as described in the previous point.

❑ When appropriate, group multiple queries within a transaction. Furthermore, if you need to import a great deal of data, consider using the `ar-extensions` gem, which adds an `import` class method to `ActiveRecord::Base`, which is ideal for bulk updates.

❑ Review the performance considerations made in Chapter 7, in regards to the available session stores.

❑ Don't make your user-defined helpers bloated. Try to make them small and efficient, particularly those that will end up being executed multiple times by loops and iterators within your view.

❑ Keep your controllers lean and delegate your data-related heavy lifting to the model layer.

❑ Rails 2.3 will take advantage of a middleware feature codenamed "Metal." Whenever you are creating a service where every millisecond counts and you need raw performance, Metal will be a good fit. This new feature is essentially a wrapper that goes around Rake's middleware. Rake is a thin layer that provides an interface between Ruby-enabled Web servers and Ruby frameworks. As such, Metal lets you be "closer to the metal" and bypasses most of the Rails stack. You can read more about it in the official announcement at http://weblog.rubyonrails .org/2008/12/17/introducing-rails-metal.

❑ Merb is a clone of Rails that's aimed at being very modular, because it allows users to choose what components should form the MVC stack. More relevantly to this chapter, it aims at improving performance by optimizing the implementation of many Rails parts. Luckily for both communities, the two projects have joined forces and merged into what will soon become Rails 3.0. This means that you can expect future versions of Rails to be faster and more modular. Likewise, the community is slowly moving toward Ruby 1.9.1, which is a much faster version of the main Ruby interpreter. Once it becomes widely adopted, Ruby 1.9.1 will no doubt help give your applications a boost in speed.

❑ Install the YSlow extension for Firebug, available at `http://developer.yahoo.com/yslow`. This checks your site against a set of guidelines for improving the performance and responsiveness of your Web pages, as shown in Figure 11-2. Those guidelines are not Rails-specific, but rather best practices for most sites, particularly those with heavy traffic.

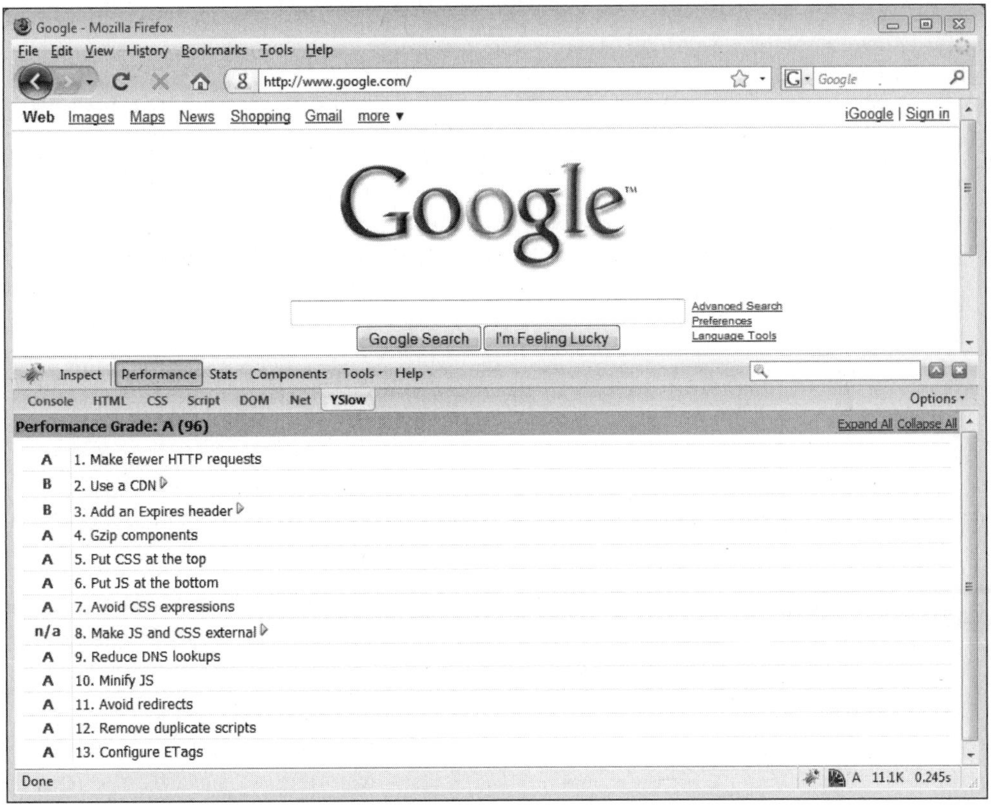

Figure 11-2

Deploying Rails

Deploying a Rails application into production is an exciting moment. After a journey that brought you from requirement gathering to a full implementation of the application, you are finally ready to deploy your application to the world (or to a selected few within an intranet).

This may come as a surprise to you, but historically, this was often the exact moment when troubles started brewing. In fact, the easy-to-use framework that increased your productivity and made you love Web programming was once anything but easy when it came to moving from development to production mode.

A Brief History of Deploying Rails

Deployment has always been Rails' Achilles' heel. While PHP developers had their mod_php module for the Apache Web server, and ASP and ASP.NET developers could count on IIS, Rails developers were left with a bad taste in their mouths due to a series of solutions that didn't really work reliably.

The timeline of recommended deployment configurations and technologies has been a rollercoaster ride and moved just as speedily as one. In the beginning there was WEBrick, but it wasn't really meant for production use, so in 2004 when Rails came out, the recommended configuration for Rails or any other Ruby Web framework was to use Apache with FastCGI. The problem was that FastCGI was, for all intents and purposes, an old and abandoned technology that somehow managed to get the spotlight thanks to the fact that an equivalent module a la PHP didn't exist for Rails. The community at large quickly learned about the instability of this configuration and started looking for something better. Apache + FastCGI was also a very poor solution for shared hosting, because it required far too much maintenance and in some cases users were forced to open tickets with their hosting company just to restart FastCGI whenever it inexplicably stopped working.

Thanks to a more solid implementation of FastCGI, a lightweight and fast Web server called Lighttpd (aka Lighty) managed to become the de facto recommended configuration for deploying applications in 2005. Some users experimented with Lighttpd and SCGI, or Apache and FastCGID, but most people in the Rails community were rolling with Lighty and its implementation of FastCGI.

There were some people who were satisfied by this solution and a few of them are probably still using this configuration to a certain extent, but most experienced Rails developers will confess to the fact that FastCGI was rather problematic. Other alternatives popped up but none of them really hit it big with the mainstream audience.

Until 2006 that is. Two years after Rails' first release, a drastically better solution came along. Zed Shaw created an application server called Mongrel. It was fast and allowed you to run a cluster of Mongrels (a few processes each responding on a different port). Suddenly, a proper deployment solution was available. In fact, it was now possible to use Apache2 to serve static content while proxying the execution of Ruby code to Mongrel (or a cluster of Mongrel processes). Apache2 was very fast at serving static content, and Mongrel did a great job as a Ruby-based application server. Zed Shaw and his oddly named application server saved the day.

In 2007, several people started to show an appreciation for a Russian Web server called Nginx. It was lighter than Apache2, faster according to many, and easy to configure. In 2007, Nginx + Mongrel finally became a widely adopted solution. Engine Yard, one of the most prominent Rails hosting companies out there, embraced the combination and to date is still using it to flawlessly serve millions of page views.

Whether in conjunction with Apache2, Lighttpd, Ngnix, or other load balancing software, proxying HTTP requests to Mongrel or similar application servers (for example, Ebb or Thin) became (and to a great extent still is) the way to go.

No, I'm not going to tell you that the Rails community has abandoned Mongrel in favor of something else. But something even more revolutionary did come along in 2008. Before briefly discussing what changed in '08, it's important to understand that Apache2 + Mongrel or Nginx + Mongrel work perfectly fine today and are, in fact, a good way to scale applications.

If you need to serve more requests, you can simply add extra mongrels and, assuming that you added extra nodes to the network, you can have them run Mongrel processes and use Apache2 (or Nginx, or any other load balancer) to load balance them when the requests come in.

Actually, you can even use a load balancer like Pen, which won't serve static content, and causes Mongrel to serve the whole request (even though this is not as fast as it would be with Apache2 or Nginx).

The only criticism that we are able to afford against this type of deployment is that it's not very straight-forward compared to something like mod_php. It's not as hard as proving or disproving that P = NP, but it can still be intimidating to newcomers.

I have a truly marvelous proof of the P = NP proposition, which this margin is too narrow to contain.

Furthermore, though it's a very good solution to scale up and out Rails applications, it requires a sizeable amount of resources, and each Mongrel process (which is mostly Ruby code) has a non-negligible memory footprint.

These are not huge tradeoffs as long as you have the resources and know what you are doing. It is, however, a solution that works best for those people who are deploying at least on a VPS (Virtual Private Server) or, even better, on a dedicated server.

Naturally, cloud services that are available through elastic computing a la Amazon Web Services are fine too.

It's not ideal, you might even think it's downright problematic, for people who want to deploy Rails on cheap shared hosting. Meanwhile, PHP and Apache2 are easily deployed pretty much everywhere.

In 2008, this last obstacle to the deployment of Rails was shattered by something called Phusion Passenger (aka mod_rails). This is a module for Apache2 to serve Rails applications. As you can imagine, it's roughly the Rails equivalent of what PHP has always had (only smarter and more optimized). Passenger is stable, very fast, and, especially when combined with Ruby Enterprise Edition, a free edition of Ruby 1.8 created by the same company (`http://phusion.nl`), it tends to have a relatively small memory footprint. Shared hosting companies love Passenger and it's extremely easy to set up thanks to an installer that takes care of everything and informs you about a simple manual step. Hongli Lai and Ninh Bui, the authors of Passenger, really saved the day.

37signals (the company that created Rails) and several other companies are now moving to Apache2 + Passenger and it is considered by many, including David (Rails' creator), to currently be the recommended way of deploying Rails applications in most circumstances.

The story of Rails' deployment pretty much ends here. There may be changes to it in the future. For example, it is likely that an Nginx version of Passenger will appear soon, even though it hasn't been announced yet as of the time of writing. Likewise, it's not farfetched to assume that Passenger may release a premium, commercial version of its module. But between Mongrel and (in particular) Passenger, we have reached a point where having a solid deployment in production is no longer a dream, and thanks to Passenger, deploying Rails is finally easy.

At the beginning of 2008, Zed Shaw published a now somewhat famous rant entitled "Rails is a ghetto." In this "highly critical" (to use a euphemism) piece, he disassociated himself from the Ruby and Rails communities in a categorical manner, and delegated the leadership of his project to others. Ever since, many people have felt less than enthusiastic about adopting Mongrel in production. This, coupled with the rise of a great product like Passenger, made Mongrel less prominent in the Rails community, though it is still successfully being used by many.

Deploying on Windows

It is usually not recommended to deploy Rails on Windows. Let that news sink in for a moment. Sadly, despite the diligent efforts of some, Windows is currently considered to be a second class citizen when it comes to Ruby and Rails. Though it can be done, and you shouldn't be ashamed of deploying on Windows, a series of caveats and poor performances are associated with this choice.

In fact, according to my latest "Great Ruby Shootout," Ruby 1.8 on Windows would be twice as slow as Ruby 1.8 compiled from source on GNU/Linux, against a set of synthetic benchmarks (using the Ruby Benchmark Suite, a project I created). These results are also confirmed by a great deal of anecdotal evidence, and Rails applications are reported to be (and are in my experience) much slower and less responsive on Windows.

> *You can find the December 2008 version of the shootout online at* `http://antoniocangiano` `.com/2008/12/09/the-great-ruby-shootout-december-2008`.

This is a sad state of affairs, I know, at least for Windows developers. It is possible that things may change in the future, but for the time being, my best recommendation is this: if you can, deploy on Linux, but if you need to deploy on Windows, read on.

Phusion Passenger takes advantage of *nix-specific features and as such is not available for Windows, nor are there plans to change this anytime soon. With this excellent option out of the picture, you are really only left with one solid alternative, and that's using Mongrel with Apache2 (or an equivalent server).

IronRuby Deployment

Deploying Rails with IIS 7.0 is currently far from being an established practice. There are initiatives like `http://www.codeplex.com/RORIIS`, but it's something that usually doesn't work out of the box and that I wouldn't recommend for now. The book *Deploying Rails Applications: A Step-by-Step Guide* (Pragmatic Bookshelf, 2008) proposes an approach that works, by hiding Apache behind IIS. This is a possibility whenever IIS is a must.

Things will change drastically once IronRuby becomes ready for primetime. With IronRuby, developing and deploying Ruby and RoR applications will be no different from deploying your typical ASP.NET application written in C# or Visual Basic. As a "Microsoft developer" you should definitely be excited about this perspective and pay close attention to the news surrounding this Ruby implementation. If you are a skilled C# programmer, you may also want to consider contributing to John Lam's IronRuby project.

For step-by-step instructions on how to install and configure Mongrel and Apache 2.2, I urge you to follow Paolo Corti's instructions, which are published on his blog at `http://www.paolocorti` `.net/2007/11/15/ruby-on-rails-applications-with-mongrel-cluster-and-apache-url-` `rewriting-on-windows`.

Deploying on GNU/Linux

As mentioned before, the recommended way to deploy your Rails application on Linux is to use Phusion Passenger. The process is very straightforward:

1. Ensure that you have Apache 2.2 installed. The name of the package will depend on the distro you are using.

2. Open a shell and install the Passenger gem by running `sudo gem install passenger`.

3. From the shell run `sudo passenger-install-apache2-module`.

This third step will provide you with step-by-step instructions on how to proceed with enabling the module as well as configuring a virtual host for your site in Apache's configuration files.

> *Passenger is now also known as mod_rack, thanks to its support for the Rack Web Server interface. As such, installing Apache2 + Passenger will be able to serve more than just Rails applications. Most Rack-enabled Ruby frameworks, including popular choices like Sinatra, Ramaze, and Merb, are supported by this deployment configuration.*

A virtual host entry will resemble the following:

```
<VirtualHost *:80>
    ServerName www.example.com
    DocumentRoot /apps/example/public
</VirtualHost>
```

Please note that the `DocumentRoot` needs to point to the `public` directory of your Rails application.

> *In any deployment, only the `public` directory should be readable to your visitors. For this reason, it is not uncommon to store the application on the disk and create symbolic links (for example, with `ln -s`) from the `public` folder of the application.*

Restarting an application through Passenger is as easy as touching a `restart.txt` file:

```
touch /apps/example/tmp/restart.txt
```

The extensive guide available at `http://www.modrails.com/documentation/Users%20guide.html` provides you with all the details you'll need to configure and fine tune your Phusion Passenger deployment.

> *To monitor your processes on Linux, you can use either Monit (`http://mmonit.com/monit`) or god, which is written in Ruby and available online at `http://god.rubyforge.org`.*

It's also worth pointing out that when developing on Windows and deploying on Linux, it's important to use an editor that's able to work with, and convert, code that has the Unix-style line end character. If you don't, you'll encounter problems on Linux due to the extra character placed at the end of each line by many Windows editors (for example, CR + LF). This is also important when committing code to a repository that may have commits from both Windows and *nix clients.

Tools of the Trade

SVN and Git are two popular source and revision control systems. Lately the Rails community has embraced the latter and there's been an explosion of code that's been released on GitHub (`http://github.com`).

Git happens to be a very powerful distributed revision (or version) control system that's used by countless popular projects, including Rails itself. On Windows you can use them both, even though SVN's support is the best among the two.

When developing Rails applications, it is highly recommended that you use revision control software like Git or SVN (but remember not to commit your `database.yml` file, adding it to the ignore list) in order to collaborate with other developers, and still be able to have full control over all the code that was committed at any given time.

Technically you could use Microsoft SourceSafe or Visual Studio Team System but those are often overkills when it comes to Rails applications, and if you intend to actively participate within the Rails community, it's a good idea to get acquainted with the basics of Git and SVN. If possible at all, consider using either one of them (preferably Git) for your own projects. If you've never used revision control software before, you'll be blown away by how useful it is.

And if you are looking for project management and bug tracking software as well, Redmine is a pretty good option (and as a bonus it's an open source Rails application that you can study and modify). It's available online at: `http://www.redmine.org`.

Finally, another tool of the trade is software for Continuous Integration (CI), which is aimed at monitoring commits to the repository by running the test suite at each commit, thereby notifying the users about commits that break the application. Popular options in the Rails world are CruiseControl.rb (`http://cruisecontrolrb.thoughtworks.com/`), Cerberus (`http://cerberus.rubyforge.org/`), and ContinuousBuilder (`http://agilewebdevelopment.com/plugins/continuous_builder`).

If you happen to be deploying and developing on Linux, you may want to consider Capistrano, which is an excellent system for uploading applications that are located in a repository or a local folder, to a remote, production machine. Once you define a Capistrano recipe, you will be able to redeploy your application, upon changes, in an entirely automatic manner. You can read more about it online at `http://www.capify.org`.

Unfortunately, support for Capistrano on Windows has recently been discontinued.

A Few Enterprise Pointers

Before letting you go and wrapping up this chapter, I'd like to provide you with a few pointers about "enterprise-y" topics that may interest you.

❏ Because you can use the method `establish_connection` on a per model basis, it is possible to let Rails applications communicate with multiple databases. A starting point is the wiki article: `http://wiki.rubyonrails.org/rails/pages/HowtoUseMultipleDatabases`.

> ### Freeze Your Application
>
> One common deployment issue is having different Rails versions on your development machine and your production server. An easy way to guarantee that your code will work in production, no matter what version of Rails is installed, is to "freeze your application" by copying your local Rails version within the `vendor\rails` directory. This process is entirely automated by running `rake rails:freeze:gems`. The reverse action is `rake rails:unfreeze`, which will remove the local copy.
>
> Likewise, it is possible to freeze the non-Rails gems required by your application by running `rake gems:unpack` (or `gems:unpack:dependencies` to include the dependencies as well). These gems will be placed in the `vendor\gems` directory of your project.
>
> Once Rails and the required gems are frozen, you can deploy your application without worrying about mismatching versions.

❑ To work with Legacy schemas you may have to overwrite some conventions via configuration. A good starting point is the previously mentioned wiki article: `http://wiki.rubyonrails.org/rails/pages/howtouselegacyschemas`.

❑ Composite primary keys are not supported by ActiveRecord. If you want to use them nevertheless, take advantage of Dr. Nic's plugin, which extends `ActiveRecord::Base`. It's available online at `http://compositekeys.rubyforge.org`.

❑ If you'd like to create your own plugins, you can get started with the Creating Plugins guide, available at `http://guides.rubyonrails.org/creating_plugins.html`.

❑ To use SQL Server as your database system, you can follow the steps outlined by this guide: `http://www.sapphiresteel.com/Using-SQL-Server-With-A-Rails`.

❑ If you intend to use Rails with DB2, you can get started by reading the InfoCenter documentation (at `http://tinyurl.com/rails-db2`) and by following the `http://db2onrails.com` blog (which I'm one of the authors of). Thanks to its pureXML technology, DB2 offers the ability to natively store XML documents and retrieve them through XQuery and SQL/XML. By using `find_by_sql` you'll have access to these features even though ActiveRecord doesn't support them directly. DB2 9.5.2 also includes a Text Search engine and its production-ready DB2 Express-C version is available free of charge.

❑ Oracle has published a nice article about getting started with Rails. You can find it at `http://www.oracle.com/technology/pub/articles/haefel-oracle-ruby.html`. If you decide to use Oracle as your main database, I recommend you check out the Oracle Enhanced Adapter as well, whose RubyForge project is available online at the URL `http://rubyforge.org/projects/oracle-enhanced`.

❑ Should you need to interface your Rails application with LDAP or Active Directory, consider using the ActiveLDAP gem available at `http://rubyforge.org/projects/ruby-activeldap`.

Upgrading to Rails 2.3

By the time you read this final section, Rails 2.3 is likely to have already been released. To fully understand the differences between Rails 2.2 and Rails 2.3, it is fundamental that you review the Rails 2.3 Release Notes available online at `http://guides.rubyonrails.org/2_3_release_notes.html`.

If you'd like to upgrade existing projects to the latest version of Rails, you can use `rake rails:update`, which will take care of updating configuration, script, and JavaScript files. This will often not be sufficient enough to upgrade from one version to another, because there could be other incompatibilities among the two (for example, formatted helpers are no longer available in Rails 2.3), but it's a good starting point for you to take over and manually upgrade the application from.

Developers who'd like to work with the latest development version of Rails (known as *edge*) can run the following task to download and freeze edge Rails in the `vendor` directory:

```
C:\projects\test> rake rails:freeze:edge
(in C:/projects/test)
cd vendor
Downloading Rails from http://dev.rubyonrails.org/archives/rails_edge.zip
Unpacking Rails
rm -rf rails
rm -f rails.zip
rm -f rails/Rakefile
rm -f rails/cleanlogs.sh
rm -f rails/pushgems.rb
rm -f rails/release.rb
touch rails/REVISION_922c528d428b5ab08611976dfe0037875a4bf387
cd -
Updating current scripts, javascripts, and configuration settings
```

As you can see this downloads the latest version, unpacks its code in the vendor folder, and then automatically performs `rake rails:update` for you.

Normally you wouldn't need to work with edge Rails, but if you were in an experimental mood, at least you'll know how it's done.

Summary

Looks like you made it, congratulations! As you reach the end of this final chapter, and therefore of this book, my sincere hope is that you'll have a much clearer picture of what Ruby on Rails development is like, as well as being able to start porting or creating your own Rails Web applications.

The aim of this book was to provide you with the fundamentals of the Rails framework and its philosophy, from start to finish, so that you can immediately begin working with Rails and progress in your journey of mastering both Ruby and RoR.

I wish you nothing but heartfelt good luck with this worthy endeavor.

LIMERICK
COUNTY LIBRARY

Additional Resources

In this appendix you will find a list of links and pointers to additional resources that can help you as you continue to study Ruby on Rails and attempt to bring your skills to the next level.

HTML and JavaScript

This book assumes that you are somewhat familiar with HTML and JavaScript. To follow along, you can probably get away with not knowing the latter, but a basic understanding of HTML is a must, and acquiring some knowledge of JavaScript is very beneficial as well.

HTML Links

- ❏ W3Schools' HTML Tutorial: `http://www.w3schools.com/html/DEFAULT.asp`
- ❏ HTML Primer: `http://www.htmlgoodies.com/primers/html/`
- ❏ HTML Code Tutorial: `http://www.htmlcodetutorial.com`
- ❏ HTML on Wikipedia: `http://en.wikipedia.org/wiki/HTML`
- ❏ XHTML on Wikipedia: `http://en.wikipedia.org/wiki/XHTML`
- ❏ HTML 4.01 Specification: `http://www.w3.org/TR/REC-html40/`
- ❏ XHTML 1.0 Specification: `http://www.w3.org/TR/xhtml1/`
- ❏ W3C's Markup Validator: `http://validator.w3.org`
- ❏ W3Schools' CSS Tutorial: `http://www.w3schools.com/css/`

JavaScript Links

- ❏ Mozilla's JavaScript guides: `https://developer.mozilla.org/en/JavaScript`
- ❏ W3Schools' JavaScript Tutorial: `http://www.w3schools.com/JS/default.asp`

- ❑ JavaScript on Wikipedia: http://en.wikipedia.org/wiki/JavaScript
- ❑ The JavaScript Programming Language (four parts): http://video.yahoo.com/watch/111593/1710507
- ❑ JavaScript — The Good Parts: http://video.yahoo.com/watch/630959/2974197
- ❑ The Theory of DOM (three parts): http://video.yahoo.com/watch/111582/992708
- ❑ Welcome to Firebug 1.0: http://video.yahoo.com/watch/111597/1755924

Common Ajax Libraries and Frameworks

- ❑ Prototype: http://www.prototypejs.org
- ❑ script.aculo.us: http://script.aculo.us
- ❑ jQuery: http://jquery.com
- ❑ dojo: http://dojotoolkit.org
- ❑ Ext JS: http://extjs.com
- ❑ MooTools: http://mootools.net
- ❑ YUI: http://developer.yahoo.com/yui/

Ruby and Rails

The Ruby and Rails communities are some of the most active in the development world. Because of this, you'll find an incredible wealth of information available for free online.

This section points out only some must-see links to tutorials and other useful resources in general as you start to explore the community and what it has to offer.

Useful Links

- ❑ Ruby on Rails homepage: http://rubyonrails.org
- ❑ Ruby homepage: http://ruby-lang.org
- ❑ Official Rails blog: http://weblog.rubyonrails.org
- ❑ Rails source code: http://github.com/rails/rails
- ❑ Rails bug tracker: http://rails.lighthouseapp.com
- ❑ List of Rails plugins (and more): http://www.railslodge.com
- ❑ Rails screencasts: http://railscasts.com (free) and http://peepcode.com (commercial)
- ❑ Weekly Rails podcasts: http://www.railsenvy.com/podcast
- ❑ Ruby and Rails documentation: http://ruby-doc.org and http://apidock.com
- ❑ Working with Rails: http://www.workingwithrails.com
- ❑ Ruby/Rails Open Source code hosting: http://rubyforge.org and http://github.com

- ❏ Try Ruby in your browser: `http://tryruby.hobix.com`

- ❏ Why's (Poignant) Guide to Ruby: http://poignantguide.net/ruby/

- ❏ An absolute beginner guide to programming in Ruby: `http://pine.fm/LearnToProgram/`

- ❏ The Book of Ruby (a highly recommended, comprehensive guide): `http://www.sapphiresteel.com/The-Book-Of-Ruby`

Hosting Services

Over the years a large number of hosting companies have added support for Rails. There are virtually countless such companies at this point and listing all of them here would be unfeasible. The following companies specialize in Rails hosting. They are not the only good hosting providers, but rather companies I feel I can recommend.

- ❏ Engine Yard (managed hosting): `http://www.engineyard.com`

- ❏ Joyent (managed hosting): `http://www.joyent.com`

- ❏ Rails Machine (VPS and dedicated): `http://railsmachine.com`

- ❏ Planet Argon's Rails Boxcar (VPS): `http://railsboxcar.com`

- ❏ BrightBox (VPS): `http://www.brightbox.co.uk`

- ❏ Slicehost (VPS): `http://www.slicehost.com`

- ❏ Linode (VPS): `http://www.linode.com`

- ❏ Rimu Hosting (VPS): `http://rimuhosting.com/rails-hosting`

- ❏ Morph Labs (cloud hosting): `http://www.mor.ph`

- ❏ Heroku (cloud hosting): `http://heroku.com`

- ❏ Web Faction (shared hosting): `http://www.webfaction.com`

- ❏ Hosting Rails (shared hosting): `http://www.hostingrails.com`

Keep in mind that Rails tends to work best when more resources are available than those that are usually provided by shared hosting companies. It is recommended that you deploy Rails on beefier configurations, like those offered by the rest of the aforementioned companies. On the plus side, shared hosting is very inexpensive and the hosting company usually manages the operating system for you. Yet this type of entry-level hosting is not ideal over all, and definitely not well suited for resource-intensive applications or sites that expect to receive a fairly large amount of traffic.

Getting Help

One of the greatest aspects of the Ruby on Rails community is the amount of support you can get entirely for free online. Here you'll find a few places where you can direct your questions and exchange ideas with fellow rubyists:

- ❏ You can get virtually instantaneous Rails support within the `#rubyonrails` channel on `irc.freenode.net`. Likewise, on the same server you can visit the `#ruby-lang` channel for Ruby. The `#rails-contrib` channel is more advanced and aimed at those who are trying to contribute to Rails' core.

❑ Ruby on Rails Talk is a mailing list where you can post your questions and clarify any doubts you may encounter. You'll find a Web interface at `http://groups.google.com/group/rubyonrails-talk`. There's also Ruby on Rails Core (for Rails' core developers) at `http://groups.google.com/group/rubyonrails-core` and Ruby on Rails Security if you want to read announcements about security issues: `http://groups.google.com/group/rubyonrails-security`.

❑ For Ruby, you can check out Ruby Talk (`http://blade.nagaokaut.ac.jp/ruby/ruby-talk/index.shtml`), which is mirrored for convenience on Google Groups: `http://groups.google.com/group/ruby-talk-google`. Alternatively, you can read all the mailing lists mentioned here in forum format at `http://www.ruby-forum.com`. Of course, other forums exist, and they are just a Google search away.

Recommended Books

Over the past few years there has been a surge of Ruby and Rails books being published. After reading this book, you may be wondering what you could read next to further your knowledge. There seems to be two possible directions: getting to know more about Ruby or gathering a greater level of insight into Rails. My recommendation is that you do both, and you are probably better off doing them at the same time.

For Ruby, if you are a novice programmer, I would suggest you read either of the following two books:

❑ *Ruby for Rails* by David A. Black, ISBN: 1932394699

❑ *Beginning Ruby: From Novice to Professional* by Peter Cooper, ISBN: 1590597664

They are both excellent at bringing you from "zero" to a solid knowledge of the language.

Should you already be an intermediate or experienced object-oriented programmer, you should probably be able to study either of the following two instead:

❑ *The Ruby Programming Language* by David Flanagan and Yukihiro Matsumoto, ISBN: 0596516177

❑ *Programming Ruby: The Pragmatic Programmers' Guide, Second Edition* by Dave Thomas, Chad Fowler, and Andy Hunt, ISBN: 0974514055

Flanagan and Matz's book is simply amazing. It covers — with a lawyer-like rigor — the core aspects of the language (both 1.8 and 1.9), like no other book I've read on the topic so far. Even experienced Ruby programmers can learn from it. Dave Thomas' book, on the other hand, is a bit broader in scope and more tutorial-like. Being the first English book on the subject, it's also worth pointing out that most of us (relatively) early adopters first learned Ruby thanks to this title.

For Rails, having already read the book you are holding, the next logical step is to read an excellent book that's published by Wrox as well:

❑ *Professional Ruby on Rails* by Noel Rappin, ISBN: 047022388X

Rappin does a great job of highlighting the best practices and providing practical advice for developing Rails projects with a test-driven approach. This is not a book for beginners and assumes that you know Rails already, but it will work well as your second book on the subject.

A third book, that will really help you move from an intermediate to an expert level, is:

❏   *The Art of Rails* by Edward Benson, ISBN: 0470189487

An enjoyable, thoroughly researched, and well-written book, *The Art of Rails* is guaranteed to make you a better Rails developer. The only caveat is that its target audience is intermediate Rails developers, so you shouldn't approach it until you have some experience under your belt.

Finally, to learn more about Prototype, script.aculo.us, and AJAX in general, consider the following two books:

❏   *Practical Prototype and script.aculo.us* by Andrew Dupont, ISBN: 1590599195

❏   *Professional Ajax, 2nd Edition* by Nicholas C. Zakas, Jeremy McPeak, and Joe Fawcett, ISBN: 0470109491

Also keep in mind that all of these books can help you become very familiar with the technologies at hand, but only through coding and practical experience will you be able to become a pro.

Index

updates, callback methods and, **290**
upgrading to Rail 2.3, 415–416
uploading files, 371
upto **iterator, numeric class, 95**
URIs (Uniform Resource Identifiers), 152
UrlHelper**, 375**
URLs
  default format in Rails, 151–152
  mapping to actions, 153
  Rails and, 37
  security of, 399
user interface. See ActionView
UTC
  migration timestamps, 144
  setting default time zone, 182–184
utility classes, ActiveSupport, 120

V

valid_password **method, 344**
validate **method, 281–282**
validate_on_create **method, 281–282**
validate_on_update **method, 281–282**
validates_format_of**, 205**
validation
  ActiveRecord, 281–283
  adding to blog application example,
    174–176
  callback methods and, 290
  of Comment model, 204–205
  helpers, 283–284
  testing, 297–298
value types, Ruby types contrasted with, 63
variables, 64–66
  class variables, 123
  declaring local, 330
  instance variables, 114
  not switching types, 64–65
  options for creating, 252
  sigils for defining scope of, 65–66
  snake_case convention, 64
VB (Visual Basic), 107

VB.NET, 76
vendor folder, in directory structure, 230
verbs. See HTTP methods
verify **method, filtering with, 342**
version control. See SVN (Subversion)
versions, Ruby, 133–134
Vi text editor, 24
views. See also MVC
    (Model-View-Controller) pattern
  adapting, 211–214
  analyzing blog application view, 163
  designing in MVC approach, 41–42
  interaction with models, 356
  pagination menu added to, 200
  templates. See templates, view
  view layer communicating with other layers,
    356–357
ViewState, issues with ASP.NET, 50
Virtual Private Server (VPS), 35, 411
visibility, of methods, 116–117
Visual Studio, 27–28
Visual Studio Team System, 414
VPS (Virtual Private Server), 35, 411
vulnerabilities
  ids and, 399
  XSS (cross-site scripting) attacks, 393, 394

W

warn **level, logger, 225**
Watir (Web Application Testing), 380
WCF (Windows Communication
    Foundation), 390
Web 2.0, 2, 10
Web Application Testing (Watir), 380
Web applications, shift from desktop
    applications to, 2
Web Developer toolbar, adds-on for Web
    developers, 374
Web developers, 374
Web development, challenges of, 2–3
Web forms, issues with ASP.NET, 50

powered by
books 24x7

Programmer to Programmer™

WITHDRAWN FROM STOCK

Take your library wherever you go.

Now you can access more than 200 complete Wrox books online, wherever you happen to be! Every diagram, description, screen capture, and code sample is available with your subscription to the **Wrox Reference Library**. For answers when and where you need them, go to wrox.books24x7.com and subscribe today!

Find books on

- ASP.NET
- C#/C++
- Database
- General
- Java
- Mac
- Microsoft Office

- .NET
- Open Source
- PHP/MySQL
- SQL Server
- Visual Basic
- Web
- XML